W0043989

SOLID MODELING
BY COMPUTERS
From Theory to Applications

PUBLISHED SYMPOSIA
Held at the
General Motors Research Laboratories
Warren, Michigan

1983   M. S. Pickett, J. W. Boyse, eds., *Solid modeling by computers: From theory to applications*, Plenum Press, New York, 1984.

1981   R. Hickling, M. M. Kamal, eds., *Engine noise: Excitation, vibration and radiation*, Plenum Press, New York, 1982.

1980   G. T. Wolff, R. L. Klimisch, eds., *Particulate carbon: Atmospheric life cycle*, Plenum Press, New York, 1982.

1980   D. C. Siegla, G. W. Smith, eds., *Particulate carbon: Formation during combustion*, Plenum Press, New York, 1981.

1979   R. C. Schwing, W. A. Albers, Jr., eds., *Societal risk assessment: How safe is safe enough?* Plenum Press, New York, 1980.

1978   J. N. Mattavi, C. A. Amann, eds., *Combustion modeling in reciprocating engines*, Plenum Press, New York, 1980.

1978   G. G. Dodd, L. Rossol, eds., *Computer vision and sensor-based robots*, Plenum Press, New York, 1979.

1977   D. P. Koistinen, N.-M. Wang, eds., *Mechanics of sheet metal forming: Material behavior and deformation analysis*, Plenum Press, New York, 1978.

1976   G. Sovran, T. A. Morel, W. T. Mason, eds., *Aerodynamic drag mechanisms of bluff bodies and road vehicles*, Plenum Press, New York, 1978.

1975   J. M. Colucci, N. E. Gallopoulos, eds., *Future automotive fuels: Prospects, performance, perspective*, Plenum Press, New York, 1977.

1974   R. L. Klimisch, J. G. Larson, eds., *The catalytic chemistry of nitrogen oxides*, Plenum Press, New York, 1975.

1973   D. F. Hays, A. L. Browne, eds., *The physics of tire traction*, Plenum Press, New York, 1974.

1972   W. F. King, H. J. Mertz, eds., *Human impact response*, Plenum Press, New York, 1973.

1971   W. Cornelius, W. G. Agnew, eds., *Emissions from continuous combustion systems*, Plenum Press, New York, 1972.

1970   W. A. Albers, ed., *The physics of opto-electronic materials*, Plenum Press, New York, 1971.

1969   C. S. Tuesday, ed., *Chemical reactions in urban atmospheres*, American Elsevier, New York, 1971.

1968   E. L. Jacks, ed., *Associative information techniques*, American Elsevier, New York, 1971.

1967   P. Weiss, G. D. Cheever, eds., *Interface conversion for polymer coatings*, American Elsevier, New York, 1968.

1966   E. F. Weller, ed., *Ferroelectricity*, Elsevier, New York, 1967.

1965   G. Sovran, ed., *Fluid mechanics of internal flow*, Elsevier, New York, 1967.

1964   H. L. Garabedian, ed., *Approximation of functions*, Elsevier, New York, 1965.

1963   T. J. Hughel, ed., *Liquids: Structure, properties, solid interactions*, Elsevier, New York, 1965.

1962   R. Davies, ed., *Cavitation in real liquids*, Elsevier, New York, 1964.

1961   P. Weiss, ed., *Adhesion and cohesion*, Elsevier, New York, 1962.

1960   J. B. Bidwell, ed., *Rolling contact phenomena*, Elsevier, New York, 1962.

1959   R. C. Herman, ed., *Theory of traffic flow*, Elsevier, New York, 1961.

1958   G. M. Rassweiler, W. L. Grube, eds., *Internal stresses and fatigue in metal*, Elsevier, New York, 1959.

1957   R. Davies, ed., *Friction and wear*, Elsevier, New York, 1959.

SOLID MODELING BY COMPUTERS
From Theory to Applications

Edited by
MARY S. PICKETT and JOHN W. BOYSE

General Motors Research Laboratories

PLENUM PRESS • NEW YORK — LONDON • 1984

Library of Congress Cataloging in Publication Data

Main entry under title:

Solid modeling by computers.

Proceedings of a symposium held Sept. 25–27, 1983, at the General Motors Research Laboratories, Warren, Mich.
Includes bibliographies and indexes.
1. Computer simulation—Congresses. 2. Engineering models—Data processing—Congresses. I. Pickett, Mary S. II. Boyse, John W. III. General Motors Corporation. Research Laboratories.

QA76.9.C65S65   1985   001.4′34   85-3581

ISBN-13: 978-1-4612-9730-7   e-ISBN-13: 978-1-4613-2811-7
DOI: 10.1007/978-1-4613-2811-7

Proceedings of a symposium on Solid Modeling by Computers, held September 25–27, 1983, at the General Motors Research Laboratories, Warren, Michigan

PREFACE

This book contains the papers presented at the international research symposium "Solid Modeling by Computers: From Theory to Applications," held at the General Motors Research Laboratories on September 25–27, 1983. This was the 28th syposium in a series which the Research Laboratories began sponsoring in 1957. Each symposium has focused on a topic that is both under active study at the Research Laboratories and is also of interest to the larger technical community.

Solid modeling is still a very young research area, young even when compared with other computer-related research fields. Ten years ago, few people recognized the importance of being able to create complete and unambiguous computer models of mechanical parts. Today there is wide recognition that computer representations of solids are a prerequisite for the automation of many engineering analyses and manufacturing applications.

In September 1983, the time was ripe for a symposium on this subject. Research had already demonstrated the efficacy of solid modeling as a tool in computer automated design and manufacturing, and there were significant results which could be presented at the symposium. Yet the field was still young enough that we could bring together theorists in solid modeling and practitioners applying solid modeling to other research areas in a group small enough to allow a stimulating exchange of ideas.

The purpose of this symposium was to stimulate interaction among members of the international research community working in diverse areas related to solid modeling and to discuss future research directions for the field. To accomplish this purpose, invitations to attend the symposium were extended to academic, industrial, and governmental researchers in nine countries.

The symposium was divided into four sessions: representation and analysis of solid models, the use of solid models in production technology, issues in integrating general surfaces into solid modelers, and the relation of artificial intelligence research to solid modeling. Following the formal presentation of each paper, there was a discussion period which was recorded and which has been included in this book. At the end of the fourth session, Prof. Herbert Voelcker and Dr. Michael Wesley presented a summary of not only the topics covered in the symposium but also important topics where little or no research is currently underway. Their summary is also included in this book.

M. S. Pickett J. W. Boyse

Many people played an important part in the planning and implementation of this symposium. Prof. Voelcker and Dr. Wesley contributed significantly to establishing the overall organization of the symposium and selecting the speakers and other participants. Prof. Alan de Pennington, Prof. Michel Melkanoff, John Hinds, and Pat Ambler served admirably as session chairmen. The local arrangements were ably provided by Shirley Worth Wyzner. We owe a deep debt to JoAnn Brock, the symposium secretary, who took over many administrative duties as well the secretarial tasks.

Publication of this book also required the assistance of many people. The discussion periods were edited by:

Vadim Shapiro—Session I
Dr. Robert Haar—Session II
Michael Lucius—Session III
Dr. Brian Schunck—Session IV
Dr. Ramon Sarraga—Summary

Nancy Balash and Joan Kmenta undertook the important job of editing the manuscripts for the papers. Dave Havelock and his group at the Research Laboratories were responsible for the artwork and the overall coordination of the publication. We deeply appreciate the assistance of all these people in publishing this book.

Mary S. Pickett
John W. Boyse

CONTENTS

SESSION I
REPRESENTATION AND ANALYSIS
OF SOLID MODELS

Session Chairman
ALAN DE PENNINGTON

*The University of Leeds
Leeds, England*

REPRESENTATION OF TOLERANCES IN SOLID MODELING: ISSUES AND ALTERNATIVE APPROACHES

ARISTIDES A. G. REQUICHA

University of Rochester
Rochester, New York

ABSTRACT

The lack of facilities for representing tolerances and related information is a major deficiency of contemporary solid modelers. This paper discusses the semantics of tolerancing for mechanical parts, with particular emphasis on the problems that arise when the features of physical objects cannot be assumed to have perfect form (*e.g.*, when a machined hole is not perfectly cylindrical). Alternative theoretical approaches are proposed, and the representational implications of each approach are explored.

INTRODUCTION

Tolerancing and surface-finish information is an integral part of the specification of mechanical components and assemblies. Tolerances are specified by designers and reflect functional and assemblability constraints. They do not prescribe unique inspection or manufacturing procedures, and should not be confused with accuracies attainable by specific machines or manufacturing processes. A tolerance specification defines a class of acceptable objects, and therefore it is simply a statement of a goal, which can be achieved by a variety of manufacturing methods.

Current generation solid modelers contain complete, that is, unambiguous representations of *nominal* or ideal parts, but lack tolerancing facilities. This is a serious deficiency. It implies that such modelers cannot support many design and production activities that require tolerancing information, such as fully automatic manufacturing and assembly planning. Today's industrial users of solid modelers must download nominal geometric data from the modelers into their older wire frame systems, and add tolerancing information manually to produce standard engineering drawings (perhaps in digital form). These drawings are then used for manual or computer aided process planning, programming of numerically controlled machine tools, and so forth.

Incorporating tolerancing information in solid modelers raises a host of questions which can be roughly reduced to three main issues.

- *Representation of tolerances.* How are tolerances to be represented in modelers? What is the semantics, that is, the geometric meaning, of such representations? When are they valid?

- *Analysis and synthesis of tolerance specifications.* Given two toleranced parts, are there instances of parts "in spec" that will interfere with each other and therefore will fail to assemble? Can knowledge about the mechanical function of a part be used to generate, that is, synthesize tolerance specifications for the part?

- *Applications of tolerancing information.* How are tolerancing data to be used for planning automatically the manufacture, inspection, and assembly of mechanical components?

This paper addresses representation of tolerances as the most pressing issue, because questions of representation, semantics and validity must be answered before any questions relating to the other two main issues can be resolved.

In the sections of this paper that follow, I first present an abstract view of tolerancing and construct some of the theoretical foundations of a modeling theory for toleranced objects, which is analogous to the nominal object theory discussed in my earlier papers [Requicha 1977b, 1980a, 1980b]. Next, I discuss object paramaterization; and then I propose several alternative approaches for defining the semantics of tolerance specifications. Finally the computational implications of these proposed approaches are analyzed.

AN ABSTRACT VIEW OF TOLERANCING

Mathematical Models—Tolerances serve to define a class of objects that are "similar" to a nominal object and that are interchangeable in assembly and functionally equivalent. Any such class is called a *variational class* [Requicha 1977a]. Mathematically, a variational class is modeled by a set of models of solids, which in turn are sets of points in E^3 (3-D Euclidean space).*

A physical solid and a mathematical point set that models the solid are quite different entities. However, for simplicity of language, I shall refer to both as a "solid" or "object," and use qualifiers such as "physical" or "abstract" when the distinction must be emphasized. Similar remarks apply to variational classes and their models.

Figure 1 illustrates the notions. Single solids, which are subsets of E^3, can be viewed as the elements of a modeling space M_s for solids. Variational classes are subsets of M_s, and can be viewed as the elements of a modeling space M_v for variational classes. (Spaces such as M_v, whose elements are sets of sets, are often called hyperspaces [Nadler 1978].)

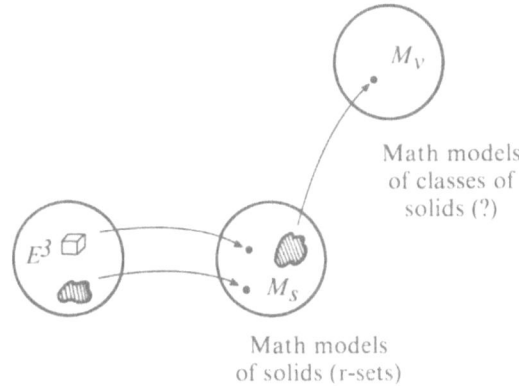

Figure 1. *Mathematical models for solids and variational classes.*

Not all subsets of E^3 are acceptable models for physical solids, and one should not expect all subsets of M_s to be acceptable models for variational classes. A sharp characterization is available for solid models—they are the so-called r-sets [Requicha 1977b, 1980a]—but not for variational classes. R-sets were selected as models for solids because they have the right properties (rigidity, boundedness, and so on) [Requicha 1977b, 1980a]. Unfortunately, an analogous list of desirable properties for variational classes is unknown. Presently only two properties can be listed.

- **Property 1.** A variational class should contain the nominal object.

- **Property 2.** A tolerance specification should not force any portion of an object's boundary to be perfect or in exact position.

My current conjecture is that a variational class is a bounded, closed, regular subset of M_s (in the topology induced by the usual Hausdorff metric [Nadler 1978]), because I suspect that regularity suffices to ensure that each element in the class has nearby solids which are also in the class and implies Property 2 above.

In summary, variational classes may be modeled by collections of r-sets, but the precise nature of such collections is largely unknown.

Representations—Tolerance specifications are *representations* of variational classes. Traditionally, tolerance specifications are a mixture of textual and

References pp. 18-19

graphical data that appear on blueprints. One must seek a roughly equivalent computational counterpart to such specifications, in a form compatible with solid modeling technology.

The most promising approach is to postulate that a variational class is to be represented as a nominal object in some arbitrary but unambiguous scheme [Requicha 1980a], together with a collection of assertions about the object's features. These assertions define geometric constraints that specify the allowable variations from the nominal object's shape. This is hardly a new or controversial approach, but it hides many ill-understood issues. For example:

- What is a feature?
- What assertions are allowable, and what do they mean geometrically?
- Is any collection of assertions satisfiable, or can contradictions arise? If there are contradictions, can one detect them algorithmically?

Much of the remainder of this paper is devoted to such semantic issues, because the precise meaning of tolerance specifications places strong constraints on their syntax, that is, on the data (or symbol structures) that must be added to nominal representations to define variational classes.

Variational classes essentially are families of similar objects. A standard method to define object families is *parameterization*, and therefore it is not surprising that object parameterization plays an important role in some of the approaches to tolerancing discussed below. Thus, before embarking on a discussion of tolerancing semantics, I shall summarize the relevant concepts from the theory of object parameterization, which has not received wide attention in the geometric modeling literature.

PARAMETERIZED OBJECTS

Object parameterization seems intrinsically connected with representation of individual objects. Let us work initially with a simple example, and study means to define a family of L-shaped objects, with parameters a, b, c, d, as shown in Figure 2.

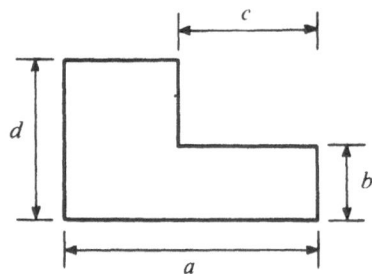

Figure 2. *A simple parameterized object.*

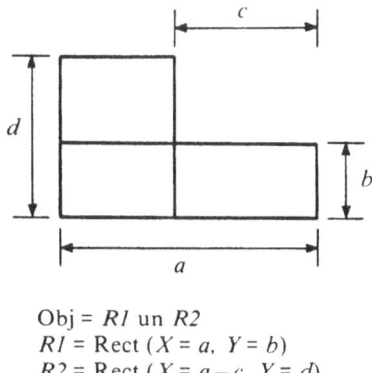

Obj = *R1* un *R2*
R1 = Rect ($X = a$, $Y = b$)
R2 = Rect ($X = a - c$, $Y = d$)

Figure 3. *A parameterization based on CSG.*

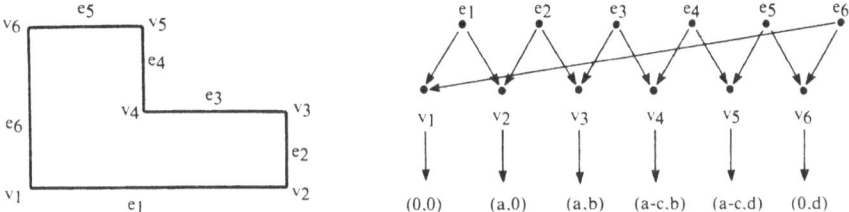

Figure 4. *A parameterization based on boundary representation.*

Direct Parameterization—The L-shaped object can be represented in 2-D constructive solid geometry (CSG) as a union of two rectangles, as shown in Figure 3. The figure also shows a possible definition for the object in PADL-like syntax [Brown 1982]. (The syntax should be clear; for example, Rect ($X = a$, $Y = b$) is a primitive rectangle, located at the origin of an XY coordinate system, and with length a and height b.) Assigning numeric values to the parameters a, b, c, d yields a specific L-shaped object, while assigning *ranges* of values ($a_0 - \Delta a \le a \le a_0 + \Delta a$, and so on) yields a *family* of L-shaped objects.

Object parameterizations can also be constructed in other representation schemes. Figure 4 shows an example: a parameterized L-shaped object in a 2-D boundary representation scheme based on an edge/vertex graph.*

For positive values of the primitive sizes the CSG-based parameterization always yields valid objects, although it may produce some which are rectangular

---

Exercise for the reader: For a given range of values of a, b, c, d, *do the two parameterizations above (CSG- or boundary-based) correspond to the same class of objects?*

References pp. 18-19

rather than L-shaped. On the other hand, the boundary-based parameterization may produce invalid objects, with self-intersecting edges. This is not surprising, and simply means that parameterizations inherit the characteristics of the representation schemes on which they are based.

Let us look again at the two exemplary parameterizations just described and attempt to generalize them. The user-specified parameters a, b, c, d control the particular object instance within the family; they will be called in the sequel *control parameters*, and aggregated into a vector $C = (a, b, c, d)$, called the *control vector*. The control parameters, however, are *not* the natural parameters of the base representations. For CSG, the natural parameters are the primitive sizes, while for the boundary representation the natural parameters are the vertex coordinates. To parameterize an object (or family) one expresses the *natural parameter vector N* in terms of the control vector C through a functional relationship $N = F(C)$. For the CSG example the natural parameters are related to the control parameters as follows:

$$n_1 = a,$$

$$n_2 = b,$$

$$n_3 = a-c,$$

$$n_4 = d,$$

where n_1, n_2 are the X and Y dimensions of the first primitive rectangle, and n_3, n_4 the dimensions of the second. (Similar equations can be written for the twelve vertex coordinates of the boundary representation example.) An object family is associated with a range of values for C, or, more generally, with some region K_c in the vector space where C lies. If we denote by $Obj(C)$ the particular instance of the object that corresponds to a specific set of control parameters C, then the object family is simply the set

$$ObjFamily = \{Obj(C) : C \in K_c\}.$$

Observe that one can always find the natural parameters N that correspond to any given C because the explicit equations $N = F(C)$ are available. The vector N defines unambiguously a solid (because the base representation scheme is unambiguous) provided that the corresponding representation is valid.

Direct parameterization is the basic method used in the PADL-2 system to support *generic* objects, that is, part family facilities.

Indirect Parameterization—Users often prefer to control objects through parameters such as distances and angles, which have obvious geometric meanings. For example, a vertex/edge graph might be defined by the distances between pairs of vertices rather than by vertex coordinates. Distances and angles can be expressed easily in terms of the vertex coordinates, and therefore one can set up equations of the form $C = G(N)$. This is precisely the converse of the situation described in the preceding section, and therefore will be called an *indirect* or *inverse* parameterization.

For a direct parameterization any control vector C in K_c has a corresponding N and defines unambiguously a solid in the family. (For simplicity, ignore here the validity problems associated with the base representation schemes.) For indirect parameterizations, however, it is easy to construct examples in which the geometric constraints implied by the selection of parameters are either insufficient or unsatisfiable. In other words, for some C in K_c one may find several corresponding N's or perhaps none. Validity and lack of ambiguity can be ensured through *invertible* parameterizations, for which the equations $C = G(N)$ are solvable and therefore the inverse function G^{-1} exists.

Interesting inverse parameterizations usually involve nonlinear functions G. For example, distances and angles are expressible in terms of coordinates through square-root and trigonometric functions. Nonlinearity, unfortunately, complicates the invertibility problem significantly. The most general mathematical result applicable to this problem is the inverse function theorem, which tells us that when the Jacobian determinant $J = |\partial C / \partial N|$ evaluated for $N = N_0$ and $C = C_0 = G(N_0)$ is not null, there is a neighborhood of (C_0, N_0) in which G is invertible. The theorem does not tell us, however, how big the neighborhood is or how to find a N_0 that corresponds to a given C_0. For invertibility throughout a whole region K_c the Jacobian must not vanish throughout the region, not just at a point, and it is usually very difficult to ensure that $J \neq 0$ throughout K_c because J is not constant (unless G is linear).

It is also important to realize that the inverse function theorem is not a global result. Thus one may find that $J(N_0, C_0) \neq 0$ and therefore G is invertible in a neighborhood of (N_0, C_0) and yet there is another pair of values (N_1, C_0) that satisfies the equations, that is, $C_0 = G(N_1)$. (Of course, N_1 cannot be too close to N_0; it must be outside the neighborhood where invertibility is guaranteed.) The global invertibility of G is determined by the behavior (especially the dimensionality) of the sets of roots of the equation $C = G(N)$. If G is linear the behavior of its roots is simple and well understood; for algebraic G's there are results from algebraic geometry (but useful G's in geometric modeling need not be algebraic); for nonalgebraic G's few general results are known.

A particular instance of the general invertibility problem has been studied extensively. It is the so-called graph rigidity problem, which may be stated as follows. Given an edge/vertex graph, as in Figure 4, and the lengths of the straight edges, can one find unambiguously (modulo rigid motions) the coordinates of the vertices? (Edge length specification can also be viewed as an indirect parameterization of a 2-D boundary representation in terms of vertex distances.) It is known that certain edge length specifications are unsatisfiable, while others have a continuum of solutions (nonrigid, continuously deformable graphs), while still others have several discrete solutions, that is, several corresponding

References pp. 18-19

graphs that cannot be deformed continuously into one another. It is also known that deciding whether a set of edge lengths has at least one corresponding graph is an NP-complete problem (see [Yemeni 1979], which contains further references on graph rigidity).

Inverse parameterizations have been studied by several authors in a geometric modeling context. Bellevaux and Crestin used optimization techniques to solve algebraic systems corresponding to geometric constraints, but did not address issues of validity and ambiguity [Bellevaux and Crestin 1980]. Robin Hillyard, in a 1978 Cambridge Ph.D. thesis on tolerancing [Hillyard 1978, Hillyard and Braid 1978a, 1978b] derived the Jacobian criterion from physical principles by using analogies from structural engineering. More recently, David Gossard and his students at MIT have been investigating inverse parameterizations as a design paradigm, in which the parameters are the handles that designers use to modify objects [Lin *et al.* 1981]. They have devised improved methods to compute the Jacobian and to identify the constraints that force a Jacobian to vanish. The Jacobian criterion had also been used implicitly in earlier work [Requicha 1977a, Gopin and Gossard 1979, Fitzgerald 1981] on *dimension graphs,* which are data structures that represent the relative positions of the various surfaces of an object. The dimensions are independent when the corresponding graph is acyclic. It turns out that relative positioning may be viewed as an inverse parameterization (through a change of origin), and that the corresponding Jacobian is the incidence matrix of the dimension graph; it follows that the graph is acyclic when the Jacobian is not null.

In summary, inverse parameterizations are attractive because they control objects through geometrically meaningful parameters, but they raise delicate problems. Because of the difficulty of determining whether a set of indirect parameters defines a valid object unambiguously, such parameterizations are best used only as an input technique: a user enters a set of inverse parameters, which are converted by a system's algorithms into a primary representation, for example, a boundary or CSG representation, and it is this latter that is stored. If the algorithms find only one of several solutions, or fail to find any solutions, no harm is done because only the unambiguous resulting representation may be stored, not the possibly ambiguous or unsatisfiable set of input parameters.

SEMANTICS OF TOLERANCING

Perfect-Form Semantics—A variational class is a family of objects, and therefore one may seek to represent variational classes through parameterizations, either direct or inverse. Suppose, then, that one parameterizes the L-shaped object shown in Figure 3, and specifies an allowable range for each control parameter, for example, $a_0 - \Delta a \leq a \leq a_0 + \Delta a$ and similarly for b, c, and d. This range specification defines a hyper-rectangle K_c in the vector space of control parameters. A model of a physical part P will be acceptable, that is, "in spec" if

$$P \in \{ Obj(C) : C \in K_c \}.$$

This semantics implies that only perfectly shaped objects are in spec, and clearly violates the condition expressed as Property 2 earlier. Nevertheless, it may be reasonable for applications in which one expects manufacturing processes to produce surfaces (*e.g.*, planes or cylinders) whose deviations from perfect form are much smaller than the tolerances specified for the parameters. It also seems to be in the spirit of traditional limit tolerancing and of some of the geometric modeling work on tolerancing (*e.g.*, Hillyard's), in which departures from perfect form are never mentioned.

In my view, perfect-form semantics does not provide a suitable basis for representing tolerances in solid modelers, because it ignores the *raison d'être* of many of the so-called geometric tolerancing methods which are being used increasingly in industry [ANSI 1973]. For example, ordered systems of datums or form tolerances (roundness, flatness, etc.) are unnecessary if form is assumed perfect. Assertions that specify allowable limits for parameters also are insufficient for expressing certain complex constraints used often in geometric tolerancing (*e.g.*, position tolerance at maximum material condition [ANSI 1973]).

Imperfect-Form Semantics—A simple approach for dealing with imperfect form is to use a surface-fitting technique in conjunction with perfect-form semantics. For example, a noncircular hole can be approximated by a perfect circle, perhaps by least-squares techniques or by using the largest inscribed circle, and the parameters of the approximation can be tested for compliance with the specified limits. The parameters of the fitted surface, however, provide no information on the goodness of fit. For example, the diameter of the fitted hole in Figure 5 may well be within prescribed limits but the hole itself may be quite unacceptable. Surface fitting is useful for establishing datums [ANSI 1973] but seems unsuitable for other requirements of modern tolerancing.

Tolerance zones—An alternative approach, which seems to capture the spirit of modern tolerancing practices, is to use *tolerance zones* and say that a part is in spec if the appropriate portions of its boundary lie within such zones. An outline for a theory of tolerancing based on tolerance zone concepts follows.

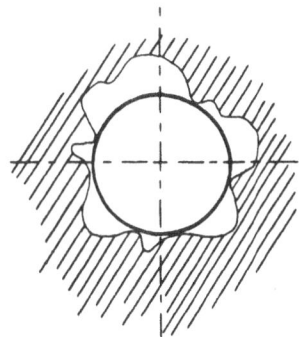

Figure 5. *Fitting an irregular hole with the largest inscribed circle.*

References pp. 18-19

First define a tolerance specification as a triple:

- A representation for the nominal solid S, in some arbitrary but unambiguous scheme.

- A decomposition of ∂S (the boundary of S) into *nominal surface features* F_i, which are homogeneously 2-D [Requicha 1977b] and whose union is ∂S.

- A set of assertions A_{ij} about the F_i.

Let us work with the simple example of Figure 6 and generalize later. The figure depicts a circular hole, which is the surface feature being toleranced, and three assertions that constrain its size, form and position to the indicated limits.* The geometric meaning of these constraints is illustrated in Figures 7 through 9.

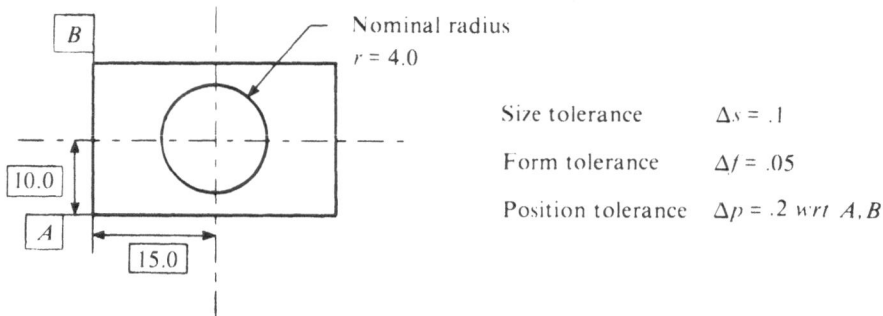

Figure 6. *A tolerance specification for a circular hole. (Drawing not to scale.)*

An actual hole satisfies the specified size constraint if the hole surface (or curve in the 2-D example) lies entirely within a tolerance zone which is the annulus shown in Figure 7. The position of this tolerance zone is arbitrary and can be selected to best advantage. Thus one can imagine sliding the annulus of Figure 7 over the actual part to determine if there is a position of the annulus for which the actual hole boundary is entirely in the tolerance zone. If so, the constraint is satisfied; if no such position can be found the constraint is not satisfied and the part is to be rejected.

The form constraint has a similar meaning (see Figure 8). The tolerance zone must have a specified thickness, but need not be centered about the nominal value.

To check the position constraint one can imagine pushing the object until the face A is against a perfect plane (the datum associated with A) and then pushing it tangentially with respect to A until face B touches a vertical datum. (The

---

For a complete specification for the object in Figure 6 one should add, for example, a size constraint on the rectangular outer boundary.

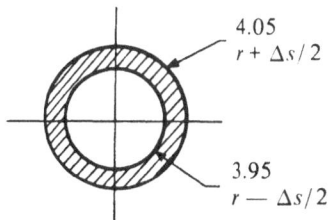

Tolerance zone position is arbitrary

Figure 7. Tolerance zone for size.

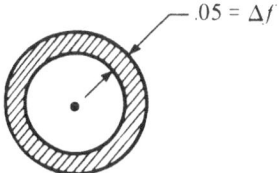

Inner and outer radii arbitrary $(r_2 - r_1 = \Delta f)$

Tolerance zone position arbitrary

Figure 8. Tolerance zone for form.

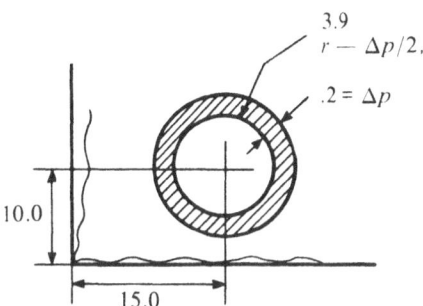

Figure 9. Tolerance zone for position.

order is important, because neither A nor B are perfect planes! As noted earlier, the association of datums with actual features can be viewed as surface fitting.) Once the position of the object with respect to the datum system has been established, the hole boundary is tested against the tolerance zone shown in Figure 9. The position of the tolerance zone with respect to the datum system is *fixed*; it cannot float as in the size and form tolerance zones. (This particular type of position tolerance is not widely used in practice, but it is easier to ex-

References pp. 18-19

plain than the more common types such as maximum material condition tolerancing.)

The three tolerances are to be tested independently. A hole is deemed acceptable only if it satisfies all the applicable constraints. Observe that a hole that satisfies a position constraint with value Δp also satisfies a size constraint with $\Delta s = \Delta p$, and, *a fortiori*, a form constraint with $\Delta f = \Delta s$. Therefore, constraints sometimes may be redundant, but in our particular example there is no redundancy because $\Delta p > \Delta s > \Delta f$.

This simple example conveys the general flavor of the tolerance zone approach but leaves many questions unanswered. For example:

- How are 3-D zones to be constructed? A tolerance zone for a vertical cylindrical hole should be a cylindrical annulus, but how high should it be? Should the nominal height be used? Should the zone be bounded at all?

- How does one identify surface features in an actual object, that is, how is the actual object's boundary to be decomposed into features to be tested for compliance with the tolerance specifications? (Note that an object of imperfect shape does not have neat sharp edges to delimit the relevant surface features.)

- How are tolerance zones to be defined for complex features, for example, for slots and pockets?

Specific answers to these questions have been given in [Requicha 1983], but other approaches may be worth exploring. In the remainder of this paper I shall focus on the last issue, defining tolerance zones for complex features, because it strongly influences the representational facilities that must be provided by solid modelers. I shall propose two basic approaches for constructing tolerance zones.

Parametrically defined zones—Consider the elongated boss shown in Figure 10. The corresponding CSG definition provides a direct parameterization of the boss in terms of a length b and width a, and enforces several symmetry and tangency constraints. The parameterization is used to construct a perfect-form tolerance zone, within which the imperfect-form features of the actual object must lie. Specifically, the tolerance zone is the set difference between a largest and a smallest acceptable instance, called a *maximal material condition* (MMC) object and a *least material condition* (LMC) object (see Figure 11).

The technique used to define tolerance zones in this example can be generalized to more complex features and can be used with base representations other than CSG (*e.g.*, boundary representations) and also with indirect parameterizations. The example, however, is deceptively simple because it hides a delicate problem. It is clear that the MMC and the LMC bosses correspond, respectively, to maximal and minimal values for the length and width. But how can one determine in more complex situations what are the "right" parameter values for the MMC and LMC objects? Are these objects unambiguously defined? (The general answer to this last question seems to be negative.)

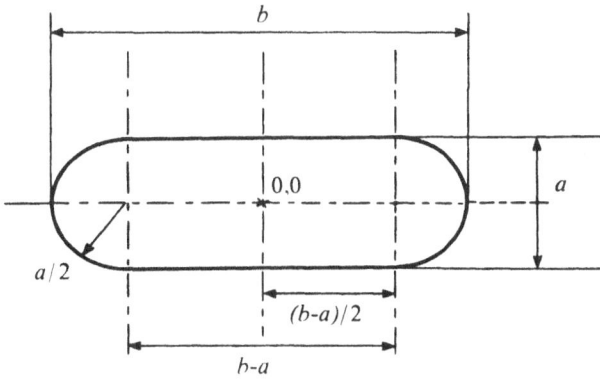

$Boss = R1$ un $C1$ un $C2$

$R1 = Rect(X = b\text{-}a, Y = a)$ at
$\qquad (X = -(b\text{-}a)/2, Y = -a/2)$

$C1 = Disk(R = a/2)$ at $(X = -(b\text{-}a)/2, Y = 0)$

$C2 = Disk(R = a/2)$ at $(X = (b\text{-}a)/2, Y = 0)$

Figure 10. *A parameterized boss.*

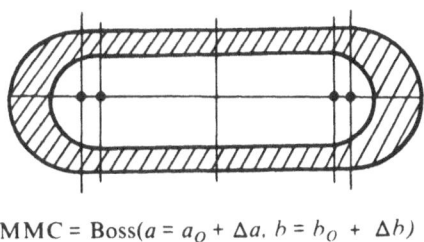

$MMC = Boss(a = a_O + \Delta a, b = b_O + \Delta b)$

$LMC = Boss(a = a_O - \Delta a, b = b_O - \Delta b)$

$Zone = MMC$ dif LMC

Figure 11. *A parametric tolerance zone for the boss.*

Nonparametric zones—The tolerance zones just discussed depend not only on the nominal geometry of features but also on how these are parameterized and represented. The alternative approach outlined in this section depends only on the features themselves and not on how they are represented. (A detailed exposition of this approach is contained in [Requicha 1983].)

Nonparametric tolerance zones are defined as the sets of points that are within a given distance of the nominal features. More precisely, a tolerance zone is the regularized set difference between two *offset* objects with specified

References pp. 18-19

offset values. The offset object that corresponds to a solid S and offset Δ is defined as follows:

$$O(\Delta; S) = \begin{cases} \{p : d(p,S) \le \Delta\} & \text{if} \quad \Delta \ge 0, \\ S{-}*O(-\Delta; c*S) & \text{if} \quad \Delta \le 0, \end{cases}$$

where $-*$ and $c*$ denote regularized difference and complement, and $d(p,S)$ is the distance between a point p and the set S, that is, the minimal distance between p and any point of S [Nadler 1978]. Again, one can think of a tolerance zone as the difference between MMC and LMC objects, but these are now defined by offsetting.

This definition leads to the natural tolerance zones for simple features (*e.g.*, an annulus for a circular hole), but does not produce the same zones as the parametric definition for more complex features (see Figure 12 for two examples).

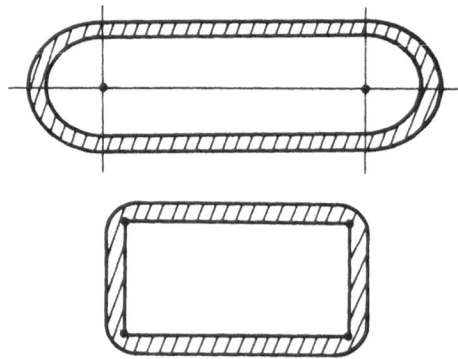

Figure 12. *Two examples of nonparametric tolerance zones.*

Nonparametric zones tend to have rounded corners even when the nominal features have sharp edges, while the parametric zones may have sharp edges. (The distinction does not seem to have practical importance.)

The definition of nonparametric tolerance zones is applicable to any feature, no matter how complex, and yields zones that depend only on the numeric values of the offsets and the point set which constitutes the nominal feature.

COMPUTATIONAL IMPLICATIONS

The two main approaches to imperfect-form tolerancing semantics proposed above have both representational and algorithmic implications.

Representational Implications—Both the parametric and nonparametric approaches require that one define, that is, name surface features, and then associate datums and attributes (tolerancing constraints and numeric values) with such features. However, parametric zones also require parameterized representations for surface features, means to define (or infer) MMC and LMC objects, and the association of numeric ranges of values to parameters. Representing parameterized features is a nontrivial matter, especially for indirect parameterizations, which have all the delicate validity and invertibility problems discussed earlier.

In the parametric approach, parameterizations must be specified by the user because they have tolerancing implications, and it seems difficult to separate the definition of nominal shape from the specification of tolerances. Such a tight coupling may be undesirable because users seem to prefer to deal first with nominal shape and then devise appropriate tolerancing schemes.*

The nonparametric approach is simpler, since it bypasses all the problems associated with parameterization, and permits a clean separation between nominal shape definition and tolerancing. Attribute representation is straightforward, and therefore the main problem in the nonparametric approach is the definition of surface features. Often a surface feature coincides with a face in an object's boundary representation, but sometimes it is either a subset of a face (*e.g.*, for so-called local tolerances [ANSI 1973]) or an aggregate of faces. Therefore, a boundary-based representation of features requires facilities for defining and naming subsets and aggregates of faces. But surface feature definition can also be based on CSG representations. Since an object's boundary is contained in the union of the faces of the primitives in the object's CSG representation, one can use primitive face names to refer to the corresponding portions of the object's boundary.

Algorithmic Implications—At this writing the algorithmic implications of the various approaches discussed above are not understood, mainly because nobody has yet, to my knowledge, implemented tolerancing facilities and tried to use them for tolerance analysis, process planning, and so forth. (As far as I know the only implemented tolerancing facilities in a solid modeler are those of PADL-1, and they have been used only to produce dimensioned drawings.) A parametric approach leads to tolerance zones that can easily be represented as objects in the modeler, and this may facilitate certain computations, for example, worst-case interference analysis. Nonparametric zones may lead to surfaces not present in the nominal-object representation scheme, but I suspect that all modelers eventually must be closed under offsetting if they are to support N/C code generation and the representation of rounds and fillets.

The PADL-1 system [Voelcker et al. 1978] provides an example of tightly coupled nominal and tolerancing specifications. Although I was the main designer of PADL-1's tolerancing facilities I always found them inconvenient because they force a user to choose a particular tolerancing strategy too early. Changing one's mind about what to tolerance in PADL-1 requires modifying the nominal definition.

References pp. 18-19

SUMMARY

Theories of mechanical tolerancing must deal with the geometric meaning of tolerance specifications and must take into account the imperfect shape of physical objects. This paper outlines a theory based on the notion of tolerance zones, and proposes two main approaches for constructing such zones.

The nonparametric approach may have less expressive power than the parametric one, but it is easier to implement and is independent of how features are represented. At Rochester we are investigating the nonparametric approach [Requicha 1983] and implementing nonparametric tolerancing facilities based on CSG in the PADL-2 system, but the parametric approach also seems worth exploring.

Many theoretical questions are still open, perhaps the most important one being the validity of tolerance specifications. However, the most pressing practical problems probably are whether these approaches are sufficiently powerful to express the tolerancing constraints needed in practice, and whether one can use them for automatic tolerance analysis, process planning, and other applications.

ACKNOWLEDGEMENT

The work described in this document was supported primarily by the National Science Foundation under Grants ECS-8104646 and MEA-8211424, and by companies in the Production Automation Project's Industrial Associates Program. Any opinions, findings, conclusions or recommendations expressed in this publication are those of the author and do not necessarily reflect the views of the National Science Foundation or the Industrial Associates of the P.A.P.

REFERENCES

[ANSI 1973]
"Dimensioning and Tolerancing," ANSI Standard Y14.5–1973, American Society of Mechanical Engineers, New York, New York, 1973.

[Bellevaux and Crestin 1980]
C. Bellevaux and J. P. Crestin, "About Geometrical Computations for CAD in Mechanical Engineering," in *Advanced Manufacturing Technology* (Proceedings of PROLOMAT '79), P. I. Blake, ed., North-Holland Publishing Company, Amsterdam, Netherlands, 1980, pp. 87–100.

[Brown 1982]
C. M. Brown, "PADL-2: A Technical Summary," *IEEE Computer Graphics and Applications*, Vol. 2, No. 2, March 1982, pp. 69–84.

[Fitzgerald 1981]
W. J. Fitzgerald, "Using Axial Dimensions to Determine the Proportions of Line Drawings in Computer Graphics," *Computer Aided Design*, Vol. 13, No. 6, November 1981, pp. 377–382.

[Gopin and Gossard 1979]
A. M. Gopin and D. C. Gossard, "Symbolic Dimensioning," *Proceedings of the First Annual Conference on Computer Graphics in CAD/CAM Systems*, Massachusetts Institute of Technology, Cambridge, Massachusetts, April 9-11, 1979, pp. 268-281.

[Hillyard 1978]
R. C. Hillyard, "Dimensions and Tolerances in Shape Design," Ph.D. Dissertation, Computer Laboratory, University of Cambridge, Cambridge, England, 1978.

[Hillyard and Braid 1978a]
R. C. Hillyard and I. C. Braid, "Analysis of Dimensions and Tolerances in Computer-Aided Mechanical Design," *Computer Aided Design*, Vol. 10, No. 3, May 1978, pp. 161-166.

[Hillyard and Braid 1978b]
R. C. Hillyard and I. C. Braid, "Characterizing Non-Ideal Shapes in Terms of Dimensions and Tolerances," *ACM Computer Graphics*, Vol. 12, No. 3, (SIGGRAPH '78 Conference Proceedings. Atlanta, Georgia, August 23-25, 1978) pp. 234-238.

[Lin *et al.* 1981]
V. C. Lin, D. C. Gossard and R. A. Light, "Variational Geometry in Computer Aided Design," *ACM Computer Graphics*, Vol. 15, No. 3, (SIGGRAPH/81 Conference Proceedings, Dallas, Texas, August 3-7, 1981) pp. 171-177.

[Nadler 1978]
S. B. Nadler, Jr., *Hyperspaces of Sets*, Marcel Dekker, New York, New York, 1978.

[Requicha 1977a]
A. A. G. Requicha, "Part and Assembly Description Languages I: Dimensioning and Tolerancing," Technical Memo No. 19, Production Automation Project, University of Rochester, Rochester, New York, May 1977.

[Requicha 1977b]
A. A. G. Requicha, "Mathematical Models of Rigid Solid Objects," Technical Memo No. 28, Production Automation Project, University of Rochester, Rochester, New York, November 1977.

[Requicha 1980a]
A. A. G. Requicha, "Representations for Rigid Solids: Theory, Methods, and Systems," *ACM Computing Surveys*, Vol. 12, No. 4, December 1980, pp. 437-464.

[Requicha 1980b]
A. A. G. Requicha, "Representations of Rigid Solid Objects," *Computer Aided Design*, J. Encarnação, ed., Lecture Notes in Computer Science No. 89, Springer-Verlag, New York, New York, 1980, pp. 2-78.

[Requicha 1983]
A. A. G. Requicha, "Toward a Theory of Geometric Tolerancing," *International Journal of Robotics Research*, Vol. 2, No. 4, Winter 1983, pp. 45-60.

[Voelcker *et al.* 1978]
H. B. Voelcker *et al.*, "The PADL-1.0/2 System for Defining and Displaying Solid Objects," *ACM Computer Graphics*, Vol. 12, No. 3 (SIGGRAPH '78 Conference Proceedings, Atlanta, Georgia, August 23-25, 1978) pp. 257-263.

[Yemeni 1979]
Y. Yemeni, "Some Theoretical Aspects of Position-Location Problems," *Proceedings of the 20th IEEE Symposium on Foundations of Computer Science*, San Juan, Puerto Rico, October 29-31, 1979, pp. 1-8.

DISCUSSION

Michel Melkanoff *(University of California–Los Angeles)*

I'm not quite sure whether I understood all of the ramifications about how to prevent certain undesirable conditions. How can your model prevent a weird kind of shape of the surface within a tolerance zone (for example, a surface that goes in and out like this)?

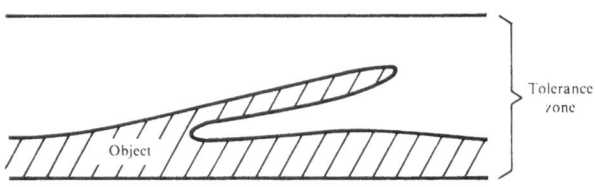

Requicha

Nothing in this theory prevents an object from doing that. If you have a theory based on tolerance zones, you must make an assumption that such things do not happen. And you will find that in one of the reports I wrote I said that you have to assume some type of slow variation. This assumption means that the surface of an object can have high frequency variations (they always do, that's what surface finish is about), but it cannot have low frequency large variations.

A. A. G. Requicha

Donald Vickers *(Lawrence Livermore Laboratory)*

Perhaps using single valued functions would take care of your slivers.

Requicha

It's a little difficult to find out what the domain of the function is. I would have to find a function over a face and check if its various values are abnormal. It gets very complicated.

David Gossard *(Massachusetts Institute of Technology)*

Could you comment on the role of function in the tolerance state, that is, on permissible variations that still maintain the functionality of the features of the component in the assembly for which it is destined.

Requicha

Mechanical function has a lot to do with this. Tolerances exist largely to ensure that parts will assemble and function correctly.

T. C. Woo *(University of Michigan)*

Suppose the tolerance zone is computed in extreme conditions. Are you assuming some kind of distribution within the zone or is it homogenous?

Requicha

Let me restate the theoretical inspection procedure. To find out if the boundary of an object is within a tolerance zone that has particular dimensions and shape, we first have to decide what tolerance we are talking about. Suppose it is size. If we can find a position for the tolerance zone such that the boundary of the object lies inside the tolerance zone, then the object is OK. If there is no position for the tolerance zone for which the boundary is inside, then the object does not satisfy the tolerance specifications. It is very hard to prove that something is not satisfactory. These specifications are mathematical; you cannot just implement them computationally, since there are an infinite number of measurements.

Sam Geisberg *(Applicon)*

Are you also going to address the problem of deriving the usual standard tolerances for engineering drawings from these tolerance specifications?

Requicha

Probably not. Whatever we do is pretty much equivalent to standard tolerancing practices, or at least it is not far from it. It's not easy to find out what really is the meaning of tolerancing practice in its usual way, since some of it is pretty loose. It is defined for specific cases and in special situations, but there are no general definitions that I am aware of.

Nils Muench *(General Motors Research Laboratories)*

Instead of looking at what the current practice in tolerancing is, it seems to me we should look at what it ought to be. In particular, there is the need to do a better job of analyzing the statistical stackup of tolerancing. We have some procedures (a Monte Carlo-like stackup of tolerances for assemblies) that we use on occasion, but it's not really the general practice in our industry. It seems to me that solid modeling research might do well to look at what actually goes into doing a proper job on front-end suspension or other complex parts. We should look at how we can build into the solid modeling system the proper statistical characteristics that are needed for the Monte Carlo stackup of tolerancing to verify that the part functions the way it should. It is really a change from what may be a standard industry practice.

Requicha

One may separate the issues into tolerance specification and the analysis of tolerances. You are really trying to determine what is the cumulative effect of having several things that are inaccurate, when something is known about the statistical distribution of these inaccuracies.

GENERATION OF SOLID MODELS FROM TWO-DIMENSIONAL AND THREE-DIMENSIONAL DATA

MICHAEL A. WESLEY and GEORGE MARKOWSKY*

*IBM Thomas J. Watson Research Center
Yorktown Heights, New York*

Now at Department of Computer Science, University of Maine, Orono, Maine

ABSTRACT

Many important CAD data bases exist only in wire frame (three-dimensional edge and vertex) or projection (two-dimensional planar view) form. In order to exploit the many advantages of computer-based solid modeling, the data descriptors of the objects in these data bases must be converted to solid form. This paper surveys methods for performing the transformation automatically, describes one polyhedral algorithm in some detail, and explores the degree of automation that is both possible and practicable.

INTRODUCTION

The early evolution of the mechanical design process has been characterized by a transition from *makers-of-things* (craftsmen) to *makers-of-drawings* (designers) [Jones 1980]. This transition allowed a change from the evolutionary build-it-and-see approach of the craftsman to the separation of trial-and-error from production provided by the mechanical drawing. The drawing made it possible to divide up production work, thereby increasing productivity, and made possible the design of things that are too big for a single craftsman.

The two-dimensional drawing as the medium for expressing a designer's concept of a three-dimensional mechanical design has evolved into the stylized art form of today's mechanical drawings with:

- Standardized multiple views of an object showing projections of the object's boundary,

- Auxiliary views showing details and allowing nonstandard viewing directions,
- Coded line types (*e.g.*, heavy, light, solid, dashed) to express concepts such as occultation,
- Symbolic representations of features (*e.g.*, a tapped hole, or the radius of a circle),
- Symbolic representation of machining requirements (*e.g.*, surface finish),
- Dimensions,
- Tolerances, and
- Textual annotations, including "not to scale" and "do not measure."

These stylized representations of objects could, in turn, be interpreted by skilled humans who could envisage, from the two-dimensional drawings, the three-dimensional nature of the object. This visualization, coupled with given dimensions, allowed some manual verification of the correctness of the design and its ability to meet its functional requirements. However, the production of drawings was expensive and itself error prone, particularly as the complexity of the design increased.

The first descriptions of computer aided design (CAD) systems appreciated the ability of a computer to interpret detailed functional semantics of a design. For example, SKETCHPAD [Sutherland 1963] allowed representation of relationships between objects (*e.g.*, a kinematic linkage) or geometric constraints (points to be evenly spaced on a circle). However, the first generation of CAD systems in production use did not exploit this potential and were essentially electronic draughting systems working still with only two-dimensional projections. These first generation systems greatly increased the productivity of designers and, through some additional functions, such as projection of lines between views and the ability to overlay drawings, helped to reduce errors.

A major extension to these electronic two-dimensional draughting systems introduced the third-dimension. Designs could now be described by their three-dimensional edge outlines known as their *wire frames*. Graphics systems offered real time rotation and scaling of images on the screen, and designer productivity was again increased.

The CAD system technologies described above are based on the representation of an object by its natural edges or, in the case of curved surfaces such as spherical or cylindrical, by their silhouette or other artificial edges and attendant vertices. These systems can give high performance visual feedback to the designer for his interpretation of the object. However, the object description data do not contain sufficient semantic information for immediate generation of volume properties of the object. The edge and vertex data do not indicate explicitly the location of surfaces and hence it is not known explicitly where a surface lies and where there is solid material. Thus we are dealing with computer assisted *draughting* systems which constitute the major fraction of installed CAD systems today.

A major increase in the semantic content of the design data base came from the explicit representation of objects as solids [Braid 1974, Baumgart 1974]. Surfaces are now defined explicitly and have associated inward and outward directions; edges have an associated direction to the interior of a face. Data now allow derivation of properties of objects as volumes. For a single object, properties such as volume moments can readily be found. For multiple objects, questions of interference, both static and dynamic, can be answered, and kinematics and dynamics of spatial mechanisms can be analyzed. In principle, the data can be used to generate tool paths for machining and fabrication operations and to generate programs for assembly robots. The combination of representation of objects as solids, and relationships between objects, can allow automatic investigation of all the properties of a product that depend on its volume geometry; this provides the basis for integrating computer-aided design with manufacturing.

A parallel extension to the CAD process is the concept of structured design. A complex object design may be expressed recursively in terms of subcomponents, forming a directed acyclic graph (often a tree) structure with the most primitive objects occurring at the terminal nodes. The combination of hierarchical design approach with primitive volume elements was proposed by Braid [Braid 1974]. Grossman showed the power of writing programs to express the tree structure [Grossman 1976], and Requicha has developed the theory of structured representation of objects [Requicha 1980].

The recognition of the advantages of solid modeling of objects, and the ability to represent them, leads to the problem of the user interface to a solid modeling system. Braid proposed a set of primitive volumes from which more complex objects could be synthesized using operations of volume addition and subtraction [Braid 1974]. Baumgart also proposed objects of translation or rotation of a planar shape [Baumgart 1974]. More recent work has led to solid modeling systems that have extended the class of representable objects by introducing surface patches. These surfaces are of particular interest to the aerospace and automobile industries and allow representation of complex curved surfaces that are at least C^2 continuous.

The discussion above has concentrated on the historical sequence of computer-based design from the viewpoint of mechanical engineering. In other domains different design symbolisms may be used. For example, in architecture, a design may be expressed in terms of elevations and floor plans, with symbolic descriptions of standard components such as doors and windows. Although similar advantages occur from the use of volume representations (*e.g.*, weight, load capacity, bill of materials), the same use of volume primitives may not be directly applicable as the means of design specification. For example, an architectural system may use an outline of the floor plans with symbolic descriptions of wall thicknesses, doors, windows, and so on, as input, and use extrusion op-

References pp. 46-48

erators to go from symbolic design to volume representation [Borkin *et al.* 1978]. Also, an architect may be more interested in the spaces than the solids.

In the domain of mechanical design, analysis, and manufacturing, the importance of solid modeling is firmly established [Wesley 1980]. New design systems are coming into production use that are based on design with, and representation of, solids. However, there remain many existing nonsolid design systems and also extensive data bases that could benefit from conversion to solid form. The existing nonsolid data bases may be in the form of:

- Paper based two-dimensional engineering drawings,
- Computer based two-dimensional engineering drawings, and
- Computer based three-dimensional wire frames.

Hybrid systems that mix nonsolid and solid forms, either as extensions to existing nonsolid systems or *vice versa*, also need to provide tools for conversion to solid form.

In this paper we will explore the problems of conversion of these nonsolid data to solid form. It should be recognized that, quite apart from any inherent algorithmic complexity in the conversion process, the original loss of semantic information incurred by the designer in mapping his solid design concept into a nonsolid data representation leads to problems in the reconstruction process. In particular, a two-dimensional or a wire frame representation does not necessarily correspond to a unique solid object, and reconstruction algorithms must be able to handle the case of multiple solutions.

In the sections that follow, we will first discuss the definition of solid objects, their boundaries and their projections. Then we will compare the existing approaches to solutions, discuss the problems remaining, and, finally, propose an approach to a complete solution.

DEFINITION AND REPRESENTATION OF SOLIDS

Although humans have a good intuitive grasp of the basic concepts of geometry, the algorithms used in computer-based geometry become surprisingly complex when full generality is sought. Formal definitions are needed more to provide a language for precise discussion than to allow detailed mathematical proofs.

The basic definitions of the point sets spanned by a solid polyhedral object and its faces may be taken from the wire frame algorithm given in [Markowsky and Wesley, 1980].

- **Definition 1.** A *face* is the closure of a nonempty, bounded, connected, coplanar, open (in the relative topology) subset of E^3 whose boundary is the union of a finite number of line segments.

- **Definition 2.** An *object* is the closure of a nonempty, bounded, open subset of E^3 whose boundary is the union of a finite number of faces.

These definitions may be extended to cover objects with "smooth" curved surfaces. These latter are the general class of objects allowed for the discussion below, but it will be seen that most of the work has been restricted to planar surfaced objects.

The aim of these definitions is, on the one hand, to avoid empty sets and dangling edges and faces, and on the other hand, to allow generality in the topological class of objects that can be represented. Notice that it is not assumed that an object is the closure of a connected set. This allows objects that consist of disjoint "solids" or even objects which intersect at edges, and so forth. One can argue that this last case, illustrated in polyhedral form in Figure 1, does not represent a "real" object, but in practice all sorts of strange objects can appear. In particular, in the process of synthesizing a manufacturable design from geometric primitives, the designer may wish to go through intermediate stages that are not manufacturable. Thus, rather than place constraints on the designer, these definitions are intended to handle the most general cases possible.

CSG Trees, Volume, and Boundary Representations—Definitions of objects in terms of point sets are clearly not suitable for direct computation, so other forms of representation are required. Requicha has formalized two approaches: the constructive solid geometry (CSG) tree and the boundary representation

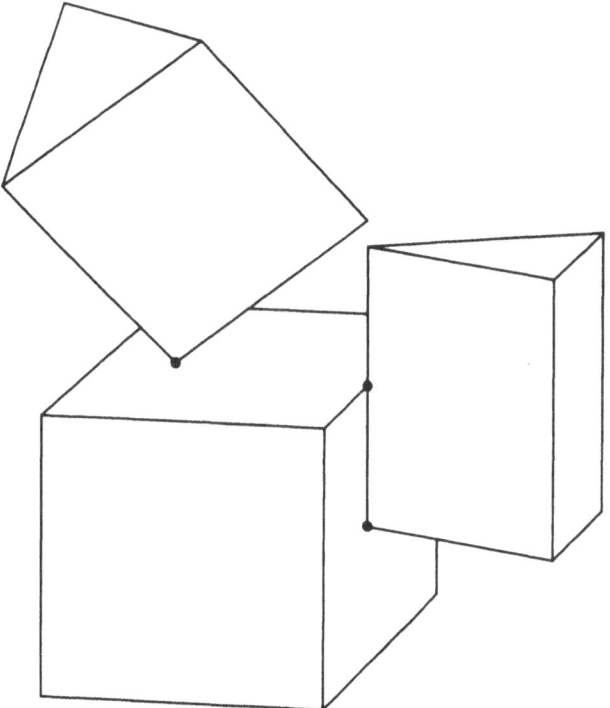

Figure 1. A typical polyhedral object.

References pp. 46-48

[Requicha 1980]. The two approaches will be used here for the classification of model representation. A *CSG tree* describes the recursive synthesis of composite objects from subobjects in terms of their relative positions (expressed as rigid body coordinate frame transformations), and primitive point set operations of union, intersection, and difference. A terminal subobject is an instance of a member of a small set of parameterized primitive volume objects. The set of primitive objects may include, for example, cuboid, cylinder, cone, and torus, and may be represented by the intersection of half spaces. The operations of union, intersection, and difference are defined by *regularized set operators* that guarantee that composite objects satisfy Definition 1 and Definition 2 above.

A special case of the CSG tree is volume filling, is generally recursive, and uses a single type of oriented volume primitive. One example, using a cube and binary subdivision, is the octree [Doctor and Torborg 1981]. These representations are approximations to objects with arbitrary surface orientations and are therefore orientation dependent. None of the work on volume reconstruction discussed below is based on volume filling.

The *boundary representation* of a solid object is an object description in terms of its boundary, that is, its faces, edges, and vertices and their connectivity. Clearly the boundary representation must satisfy certain rules in order to be able to represent the object shown in Figure 1 and to reject boundaries that do not enclose volumes, for example, the surface of a Klein bottle.

The basic ideas of boundary representation are that the boundary should be closed (*i.e.*, the boundary cannot have a boundary), orientable (*i.e.*, the object must have a consistent inside and outside), and should not self-intersect. Different authors have taken different approaches to the use of these ideas. For the wire frame algorithm, the concepts of closedness and orientability are embedded in cycles that have insides and outsides. A face is defined in terms of oriented cycles of edges (1-cycles) which, when nested in a tree hierarchy, express the concept that a face has an exterior and may have interior holes. An object is defined similarly in terms of oriented cycles of faces (2-cycles). From a computational point of view, there are local and global conditions to be satisfied. A local condition may be the connectivity in the edge sequence at a vertex in a face, or the face sequence in a solid at an edge. A global condition may be the closure and orientability of a cycle. The condition of no internal self-intersections of the boundary is expressed by tests for illegal (*i.e.*, internal) intersections between faces.

The quantities involved in the representation of geometric objects must be mapped into the data representations of the computer being used. Some quantities may be represented directly and exactly as integers, for example, the relationship that edge-*a* is bounded by face-*a* and face-*b*. These quantities have come to be known as the topological relationships of the object. Other, geometric, quantities that exist mathematically as real numbers cannot be expressed exactly by any finite length numeric data type. Thus we are faced with a choice between either inexact internal representation of the desired mathematical concept or exact (*e.g.*, integer) internal representation of a mathematical approximation. The problem is well known among workers in the field, but has received little attention so far in the literature [Sutherland *et al.* 1974]. The following discussion assumes that floating point approximations to real numbers are being used.

Designers of boundary representation based algorithms for generating solid objects have to deal with the need for global and local consistency and also with the consistency between the topology and geometry of objects. The *winged edge* representation [Baumgart 1974] has become widely used as a data structure for both the geometric and topological components of the boundary representation of solid objects.

Although both the CSG tree and boundary representation allow representation of any object that can be synthesized from the intersections of members of an allowable set of half spaces, there are fundamental differences between the approaches. An object described by a CSG tree is guaranteed to be a valid solid object, independent of the number representation of the machine used. The tree can be mapped into a character string and transmitted to another machine without loss of validity. On a given machine, the object may not be the required object, but at least it is guaranteed to be valid. Computation of the properties of a parent object must ultimately be performed in terms of the terminal nodes and is subject to numerical errors stemming from finite precision representation of any real numbers. The boundary representation of a parent object must be derived recursively from those of the subobjects. A boundary representation is a composite of real numbers (geometry) and integers (topology). Its recursive computation is subject to numerical errors. No system based on boundary representations known to the authors is able to guarantee the validity of an arbitrary object, let alone whether it is the correct object. The basic difficulty arises from the need, when computing the boundary of a composite object in terms of its subcomponents, to make local numerical decisions (*e.g.*, whether a vertex lies above, in, or below a surface) without being able to check the global consequences of the decision. Hence, although an object may satisfy local tests, it may not satisfy a global test. Numerical tests are generally performed with respect to a tolerance. Thus the validity of an object is also dependent on the tolerance used. These numerical issues play an important part in the practicability of converting two-dimensional and three-dimensional information to solid form.

CANDIDATE APPROACHES

Although there have been many partial solutions to the problem of automatic generation of solid object representations from two-dimensional or three-dimensional nonsolid inputs, there is no general and complete automatic conversion process known to the authors. In this section we discuss the various attempted solutions in terms of the approaches used. These approaches taken may be classified in terms of a number of parameters:

- Nature of the input data: single view, multiple views, or wire frame,
- Accuracy of solution: approximate or exact,
- Target volume object representation: CSG tree or boundary representation,
- Provision of clues to volume interpretation: use of labels or constraints on the manner of sequence of input,
- Constraints on class of surfaces handled: planar only or smooth curved, and
- Ability to handle all geometric configurations.

Fortunately, most of the approaches taken by the various authors can be typified by a dominant parameter and will be discussed in the parameter sequence given above. A sampling of the authors in the field and the parameter values associated with their work is shown in Figure 2.

Single View—Early workers in machine vision developed algorithms for deriving the three-dimensional visible surface structure of scenes containing polyhedral objects from camera images. The most successful methods [Huffman 1971, Clowes 1971] involved labelling the edges in the view as convex or concave. In the case of views of scenes with up to trihedral vertices and no cracks or shadows, the number of distinct vertex labelling classes is quite small (*e.g.*, eighteen) [Winston 1977]; relaxing constraints on the scene can expand the number of classes to many thousands. Waltz derived an effective algorithm for propagating local changes in an imperfectly labelled image to achieve global consistency [Waltz 1975].

This work in scene analysis has been used as the basis for construction of solids from single images. The Origami World of Kanade interprets a view in terms of folded paper objects, that is, objects constructed from planar material of zero thickness [Kanade 1978]. Sugihara has used a labelling approach in the formation of solid polyhedral objects from a hand-drawn sketch [Sugihara 1978, 1981]. The sketch is made up of straight lines, with hidden lines marked, and is input during an interactive sketching session with a tablet and display. A notable feature of this system is the ability to detect whether a given sketch can represent a valid polyhedral object and, for a sketch that meets this criterion, the ability to reposition vertices to make the sketch correct.

The Sugihara solid generation algorithm uses a linear programming technique to satisfy constraints on components of the boundary representation of the object (*e.g.*, that the vertices for a face be coplanar). The complexity of the largest sketch that can be handled is not stated, but application to highly complex scenes does not appear to be practicable. The author proposes this system for initial, rough input of the overall shape of a design.

Approximate Solutions—Many solid modeling systems have the basis for generating an approximate solution for the two-dimensional projection to vol-

	Sugihara	Kanade	Baumgart, Boyse	Aldefeld	Sutherland	Lafue	Idesawa	Preiss	Markowsky and Wesley	Sakurai and Gossard
Nature of the input data s — single view t — multiple perspective views l — multiple parallel views w — wire frame	s	s	l	l	t & l	l	l	l	l & w	l
Approximate or true solution a — approximate t — true	t	t	a	t	t	t	t	t	t	t
Output object representation b — boundary representation c — CSG tree w — wire frame	b	b	b	c	w	b	b	b	b	b
Clues to three-dimensional structures v — vertex e — edge f — face n — none	n	n	n	n	v & e	f	n	n	n	n
Surfaces p — planar c — curved n — none	p	p	p	c	n	p	p	p	p	c
All geometric configurations y — yes n — no	n	n	–	n	–	n	n	n	y	n

Figure 2. Sample of approaches to volume reconstruction.

ume problem, by using functions for forming a constant thickness lamina or extrusion from a planar shape. One of the earliest workers in solid modeling, Baumgart, used the intersection of polyhedral extrusions of each of a number of views to produce a volume object containing the true object [Baumgart 1974]. He showed a rearing horse figure reconstructed by this method from several views. A three orthogonal view example is shown in Figure 3. This approach has also been suggested by Boyse as a first step in an interactive two-dimensional to volume conversion [Boyse 1983].

Generation of CSG from Two-Dimensional Projections—Aldefeld has described ongoing work to construct a solid representation from two-dimensional projections based on identification of members of a set of primitive volumes

References pp. 46–48

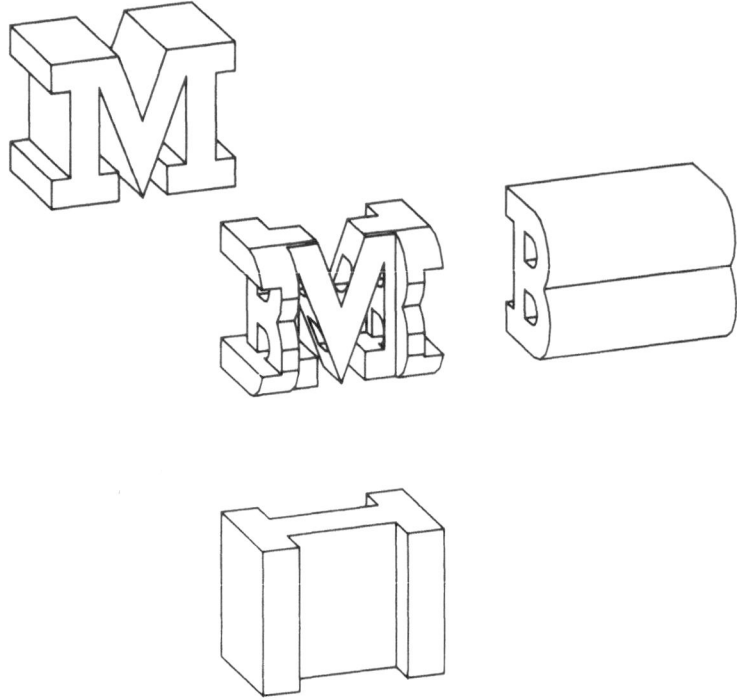

Figure 3. *A volume object as the intersection of extrusions of its views.*

whose combination (at present, only union is allowed) constitutes the object [Aldefeld 1983]. The motivation for the work is that it be incorporated into an existing two-dimensional draughting system.

In the description given, the system is limited to laminate primitive objects that are generated by planar shapes (composed of circular arcs and straight lines) that are parallel to one of the three orthogonal viewing planes. Thus, the class of primitive objects includes cuboids, cylinders, and so on. Note that both cylindrical and planar surfaces are handled but that the constraint on surface orientation is very restrictive. The system proceeds by segmenting the three views and then matches the segmented shapes to find instances of laminae. The relationship between volume object and the laminae may be described as a CSG tree.

The implementation is much simplified by the single class of oriented objects and exploits explicitly the semantics of extrusion to guide heuristic search techniques. Extension to cover negative objects (*i.e.*, difference operations) appears straightforward; extension to general object classes and orientations appears to be difficult, if not impracticable.

Provisions of Clues to Volume Interpretation—A problem arising in reconstructing a solid representation from two-dimensional and three-dimensional nonsolid data is the correlation of features between multiple views of the object. This process can lead to numerical errors, ambiguity, and computational complexity. Some workers have finessed the problem by requiring the user to give clues to the three-dimensional structures arising from a set of views. Other workers have addressed the full correlation problem and have not required the provision of clues.

Labels—Labelling corresponding edges and vertices in different views avoids multiview cross-correlation operations and leads directly to the construction of the three-dimensional wire frame of an object [Wesley and Markowsky 1981]. Appel and Stein show an early system for labelled input of polyhedra [Appel and Stein 1972]. The complete and automatic conversion of nondigital drawings is seen by the authors to be an impossible task. However, Sutherland described a multi-pen, large tablet based system for interactive digitization of existing engineering drawings; this system could also handle perspective projections as seen in photographs [Sutherland 1974]. Using two or more (up to seven!) pens, the user could indicate corresponding features (points and edges) in several views, both the basic orthogonal views and also auxiliary or detail views. Holders for pens simplified entry of constant values for a view, for example, all the features in a plane. Although not intended for generating solid representations, a three-dimensional straight line wire frame produced by this process could be converted to solid form by the wire frame algorithm [Markowsky and Wesley 1980].

Constraints on sequence of input—Lafue freed the user from some of the rigid and low-level data input requirements of having to identify corresponding points and edges in different views by adopting a *face-wise* approach. The user was required to input the nonnull area projection of each solid face in each view by a complete but unordered sequence of projected edges defining the face; a hole in a solid face was entered by defining a temporary bridging edge to link the exterior to the interior boundary. Thus the low level, multiview edge and vertex correlation problem has been constrained to the simpler, and less ambiguous, problem of cross correlation of faces, though the user now has the responsibility of entering the temporary edges consistently in all views. The three-dimensional wire frame generated in this manner was converted to solid form using a set of axioms expressing the local and global boundary representation rules and a theorem prover. Pathological cases were not covered [Lafue 1976].

Constraints on Classes of Surfaces Handled—In this section we describe the area that has received the most attention and has seen the most detailed implementations.

Planar surfaces—Idesawa elegantly described the general reconstruction problem in terms of projections and inverse projections, leading to an algorithm for the construction of a wire frame and thence a solid [Idesawa 1973, Idesawa *et al.* 1975]. He went on to present a polyhedron implementation with a partially successful heuristic approach to ghosts, that is, vertex and edge elements generated by the inverse projection process that are not part of the boundary repre-

References pp. 46-48

sentation of the target object. A rather complex example is shown. Preiss described a heuristic search approach based on satisfaction of geometric and topological rules, but gave few details and only simple examples [Preiss 1980].

Markowsky and Wesley have designed, implemented, and used two polyhedral algorithms. The first, the wire frame algorithm [Markowsky and Wesley 1980], finds all polyhedral solids with a given wire frame. The second, the projections algorithm [Wesley and Markowsky 1981], finds all polyhedral solids with a given set of orthogonal projections. The wire frame algorithm starts out with a given wire frame, all the components of which must exist in the final object. The projections algorithm uses the given views to generate a superset pseudo wire frame which contains ghost (that is, uncertain) components. An extended form of the basic wire frame algorithm must then handle both certain and uncertain components. Since the projections algorithm is an extension of the wire frame algorithm, the concepts of the wire frame algorithm and its terminology are reviewed first.

In the basic wire frame algorithm, the input data (a wire frame, Figure 4(a)) are processed to find all planar graphs containing more than two noncolinear edges. For each such graph, minimum enclosed areas (1-cycles of edges), using each edge twice with opposite sense, are found; these areas are nested in a tree hierarchy. From this hierarchy, candidate faces with an exterior boundary and possibly interior boundaries (*i.e.*, a face may have holes) are constructed; these are called *virtual faces* (Figure 4(b)). For each edge, a list of virtual faces is formed and ordered radially around the edge. Minimum enclosed volumes (2-cycles of faces) are found using each virtual face twice with opposite sense. These volumes are nested, again in a tree hierarchy. From this hierarchy, candidate volume regions called *virtual blocks* are found (Figure 4(c)). A final decision process assigns state *solid* or *hole* to each virtual block (Figure 4(d)), glues the solid blocks together, and finds all possible solid objects with the input wire frame. Note that there is always at least one virtual block that is an unbounded envelope block (*i.e.*, it is inside out) and that is always a hole.

The ability to handle all possible cases is embedded in the parts of the algorithm for finding enclosed regions (*e.g.*, bridges are ignored), for the handling of illegal intersections between virtual faces and in the final decision process. The correctness of objects is derived from the use of directed edges and faces, and from the rules governing the number of times and directions with which edges and faces are used.

The several stages of the projections algorithm are now described. Since many of these stages are quite similar to the corresponding stages of the wire frame algorithm, details are given only for those points which are different.

The early stages (1 through 3) of the projections algorithm are concerned with converting, by means of a back projection process, a set of projections of an object to a pseudoskeleton and thence to a pseudo wire frame for the object. This pseudo wire frame contains supersets of the vertices of all objects with the given projections. Furthermore, the edges of this pseudo wire frame partition the

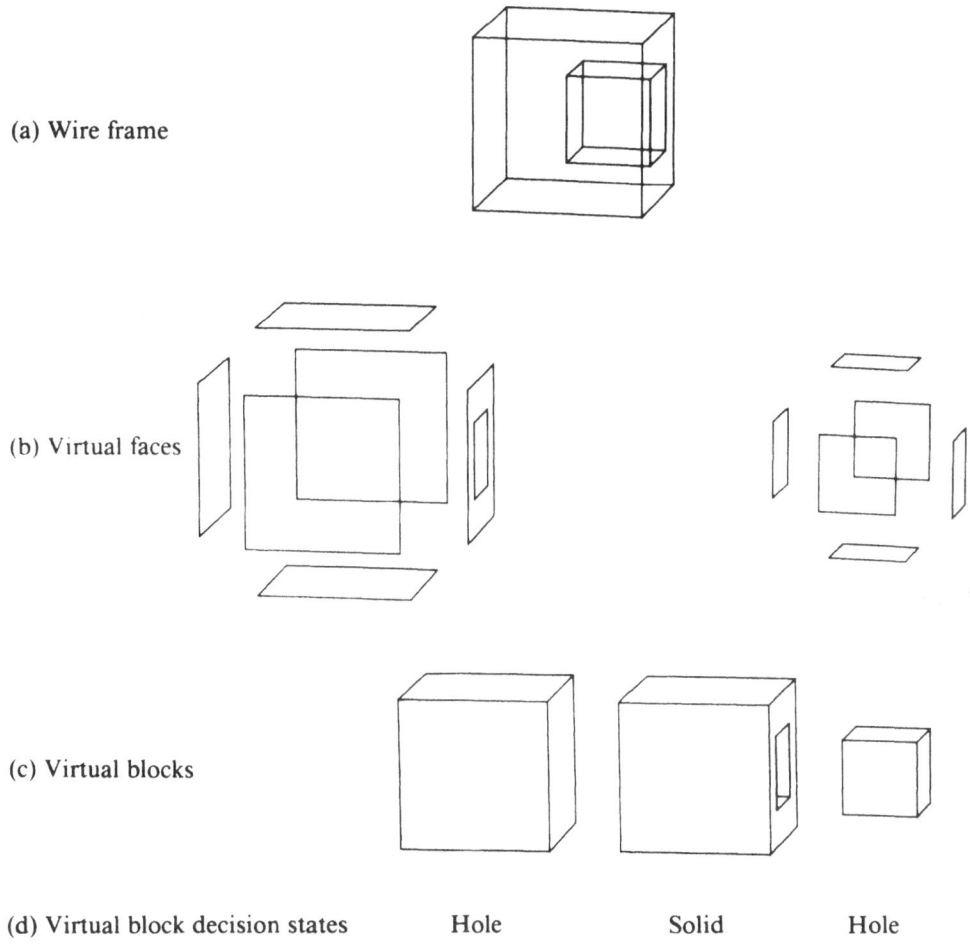

(a) Wire frame

(b) Virtual faces

(c) Virtual blocks

(d) Virtual block decision states   Hole   Solid   Hole

Figure 4. *The wire frame algorithm in action.*

edges of all objects with the given projections. The existence of various edges and vertices in objects may be known for certain or may be uncertain. All components of the pseudo wire frame are consistent with all the views.

The later stages (*i.e.*, 4 through 7) apply an extended form of the wire frame algorithm to a pseudo wire frame to find all polyhedral solid objects with the given projections.

The stages are now described briefly. They are illustrated by the reconstruction of the two wedges object shown with its projections in Figure 5.

Stage 1: Check Input Data—The input data to the basic algorithm are assumed to be a set of at least two distinct perpendicular projections of the wire frame of a polyhedral object. Extensions to handle more general forms of input data such as details, cross sections, and occultations are presented in the origi-

References pp. 46-48

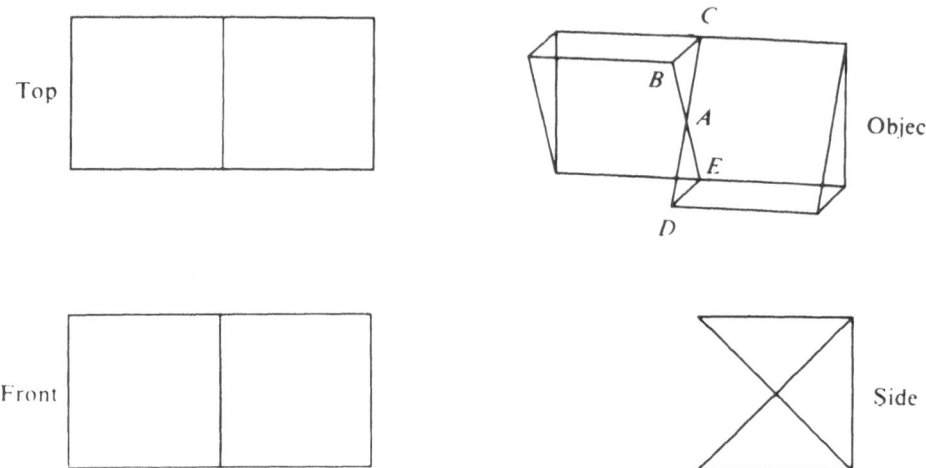

Figure 5. *The two wedges object and its projections.*

nal paper [Wesley and Markowsky 1981]. The data are checked for validity and reduced to canonical form with edges and vertices distinct and with edges intersecting only in vertices.

Stage 2: Construct Pseudo Vertex Skeleton—The vertices in each view are back projected to find all Class I vertices (*i.e.*, vertices formed by the intersection of noncoplanar edges) and some Class II vertices (*i.e.*, vertices formed by the intersection of only coplanar edges); at this point it is not possible to distinguish between vertex classes. While not all vertices may be recovered at this stage, enough are recovered to enable the recovery of all vertices after passing through the next stage. The Class I vertices of the two wedges problem are shown in Figure 6(a).

Stage 3: Construct Pseudo Wire Frame—The vertices constructed in Stage 2 form a skeleton for the pseudo wire frame. Edges are introduced based on the edges in the projections, as shown in Figure 6(b). These edges are checked for mutual internal intersections. Intersections may introduce additional vertices that are used to partition the edges. The remaining Class II vertices are constructed in this manner, as shown in Figure 6(c). The final set of vertices constructed here and in Stage 2 is the set of candidate vertices, and the final set of edges constructed in this stage is the set of candidate edges. Together the candidate edges and vertices form the pseudo wire frame. Note that candidate vertices (edges) might not be vertices (edges) or even points of the object. The candidate vertices are a superset of $V(Obj)$, that is, the set of all vertices of the object, and the candidate edges partition the elements of $E(Obj)$, that is, the set of all edges of the object. The edge connectivity of all vertices is examined and the candidate edge and vertex lists edited. The editing process may remove impossible items, simplify colinear edges, and update the classification of vertices

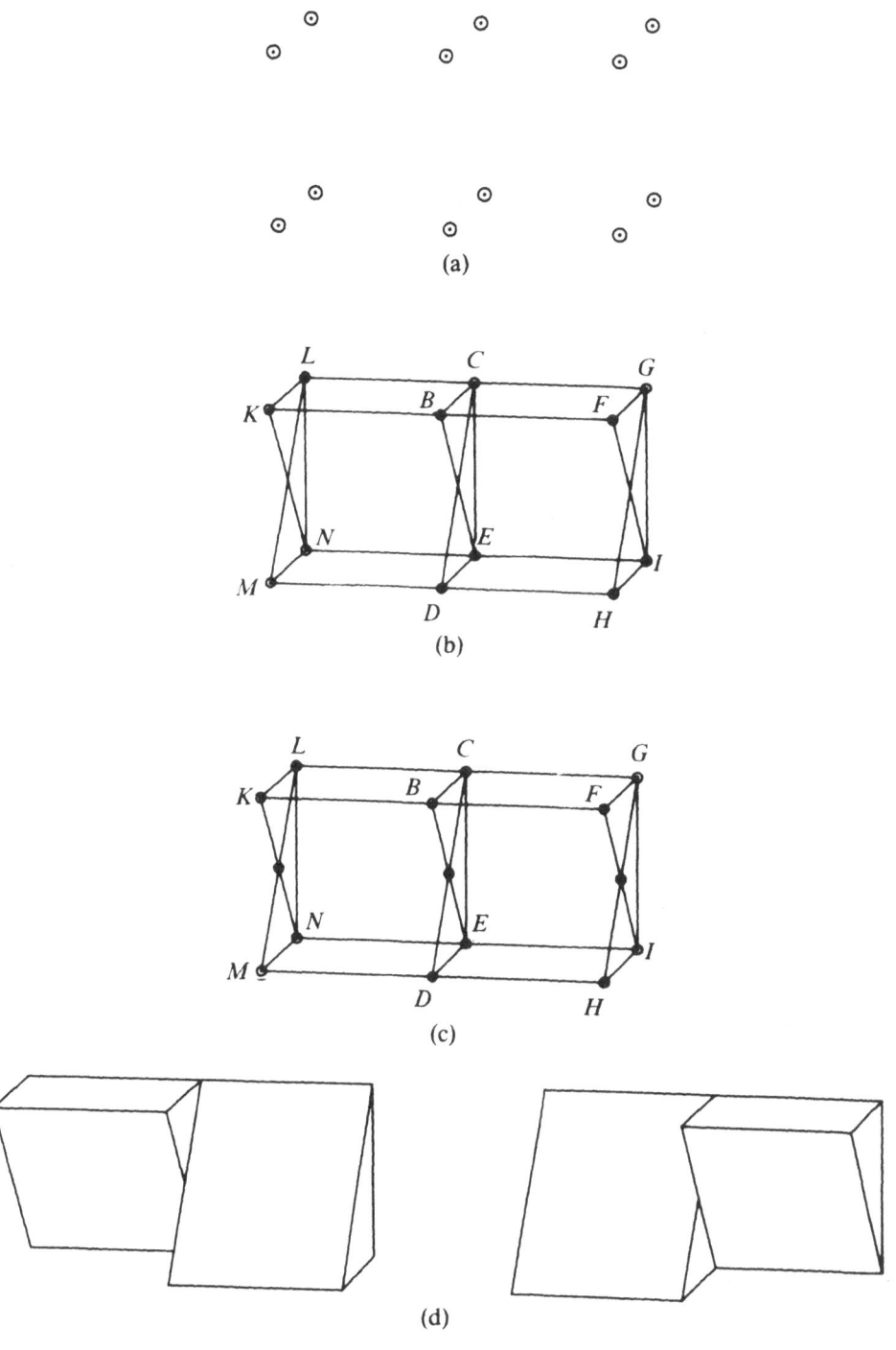

Figure 6. *Stages of the two wedges reconstruction.*

as Class I or II. Candidate edges and vertices which are the only possible candidates for some edges and vertices appearing in one of the projections are labeled as *certain* and must appear in a solution object; all others are labeled *uncertain* and may or may not appear in solution objects. In the two wedges problem, all the vertices and edges of the pseudo wire frame are uncertain.

Stage 4: Construct Virtual Faces—Beginning with the pseudo wire frame generated in Stage 3, all virtual faces are found in a manner analogous to that used in the wire frame algorithm. All uncertain edges are checked for containment in at least two noncoplanar virtual faces. Any edges not meeting this criterion are deleted and the virtual faces updated. Any impossible virtual faces (*e.g.*, any certain edges piercing the interior of a virtual face) are deleted. The consequences of deletions are propagated until a stable condition is reached. Note that coplanar loops such as *BEIF* and *CDHG* in Figure 6(c) will be found as virtual faces. The fact that these particular virtual faces intersect illegally will be recognized in the next stage.

Stage 5: Introduce Cutting Edges—Illegal intersections between two virtual faces such that both faces cannot exist in an object are handled by the introduction of a temporary *cutting edge* and attendant vertices along their line of intersection. The cutting edge partitions the virtual face into smaller independent virtual faces and will be removed in the final stages. In order to reduce later computational complexity, all the partitioning processes in the algorithm, be they of edges or faces, generate lists of siblings with common parent edge or face and also lists of correlations between edges or faces which cannot coexist in an object; these data structures are used in the final stages of the algorithm. Thus, cutting edges are introduced between the three Class II vertices in Figure 6(c).

Stage 6: Construct Virtual Blocks—Virtual faces are pieced together to form *virtual blocks* in exactly the same manner as in the wire frame algorithm. In the two wedges problem, six right-triangular prisms and an enveloping (*i.e.*, inside-out) cuboid are found.

Stage 7: Make Decisions—A depth-first decision process is used to assign the state *solid* or *hole* to each virtual block and hence to find all objects with the given projections. This process ensures that all cutting edges disappear in solution objects, that is, either they are totally surrounded by space or by material or they separate coplanar surfaces. Efficiency in the search process is obtained by careful pruning of the decision tree, for example, by recognizing that decisions involving partitioned edges and virtual faces may be propagated to the whole original edge or virtual face. The two possible polyhedral solutions found for the two wedges problem are shown in Figure 6(d). For each of the solutions, four prisms are assigned solid state and two are assigned hole state. The enveloping cuboid is always a hole.

A well known mechanical drawing problem is shown in Figure 7, and the stages of its reconstruction are given in Figure 8. The projections and reconstruction of an engineering object are shown in Figure 9.

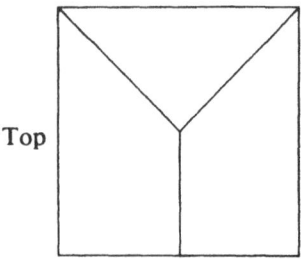

Top

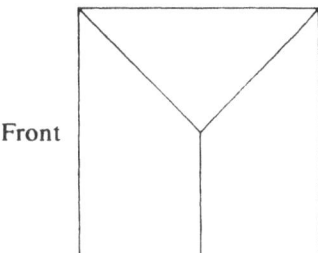

Front

Figure 7. *The two Y's problem.*

Curved and oriented surfaces—Sakurai and Gossard have extended the general polyhedron solution given above to handle certain cases of input data consisting of three orthogonal views made up from straight lines and circular arcs [Sakurai and Gossard 1983.] Thus, the solid may have certain planar, cylindrical, conical, spheroidal, and toroidal surfaces. The data representation used allows an object to have additional implicit nonvisible edges and vertices, such as *tangential* edges (*e.g.*, where a cylinder is tangent to a plane) and *silhouette* edges (*e.g.*, the projected outline of a sphere as seen in a view). The algorithm proceeds by inverse projection of the views and uses edge and vertex type rules to hypothesize the identity, in three-dimensions, of vertex and edge types. This is followed by identification of faces and the assembly of faces into solids to form all possible solids with the views. However, the requirement that the arcs in all views be circular constrains the surface orientations; a further constraint requires curved surfaces to intersect only with planar surfaces.

PROBLEMS

In the presence of so many partial solutions, the question of what remains to be done to achieve a full solution may be addressed in terms of several areas of unsolved problems.

Input Data Problems—When the input data are generated by humans, there is the probability of error arising from several sources. When the data are gener-

References pp. 46-48

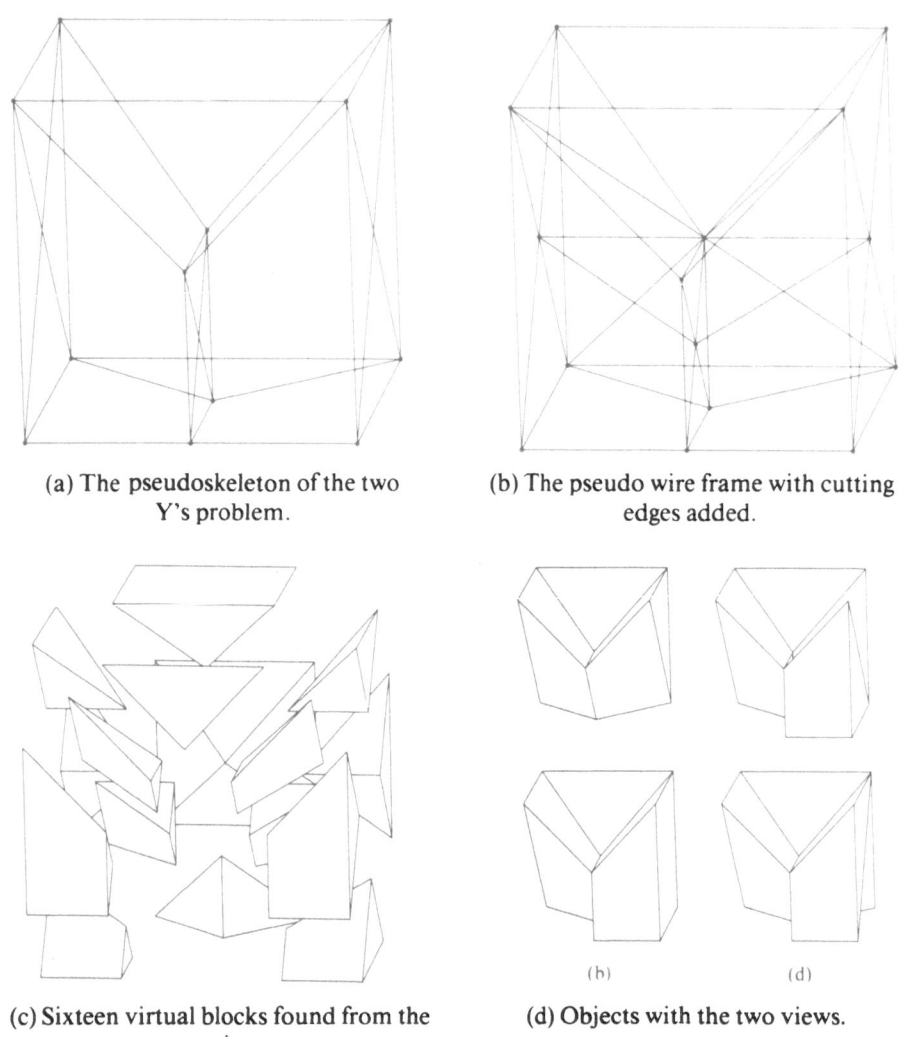

(a) The pseudoskeleton of the two Y's problem.

(b) The pseudo wire frame with cutting edges added.

(c) Sixteen virtual blocks found from the two views.

(d) Objects with the two views.

Figure 8. *Stages of the two Y's reconstruction.*

ated from manually produced engineering drawings, the caveats "do not measure" and "not to scale," frequently found in such drawings, become a major concern. It has been our experience in building solid models using dimensions taken from such drawings, and then generating drawings from the models and comparing with the originals, that positional errors are common. The drawings have the general appearance of the object but rely on the dimensions for the location of features. Further, the feature errors in several views may be inconsistent, so that direct generation of a solid is impossible. A preprocessing phase, using methods such as those of Fitzgerald, may be used to bring the given di-

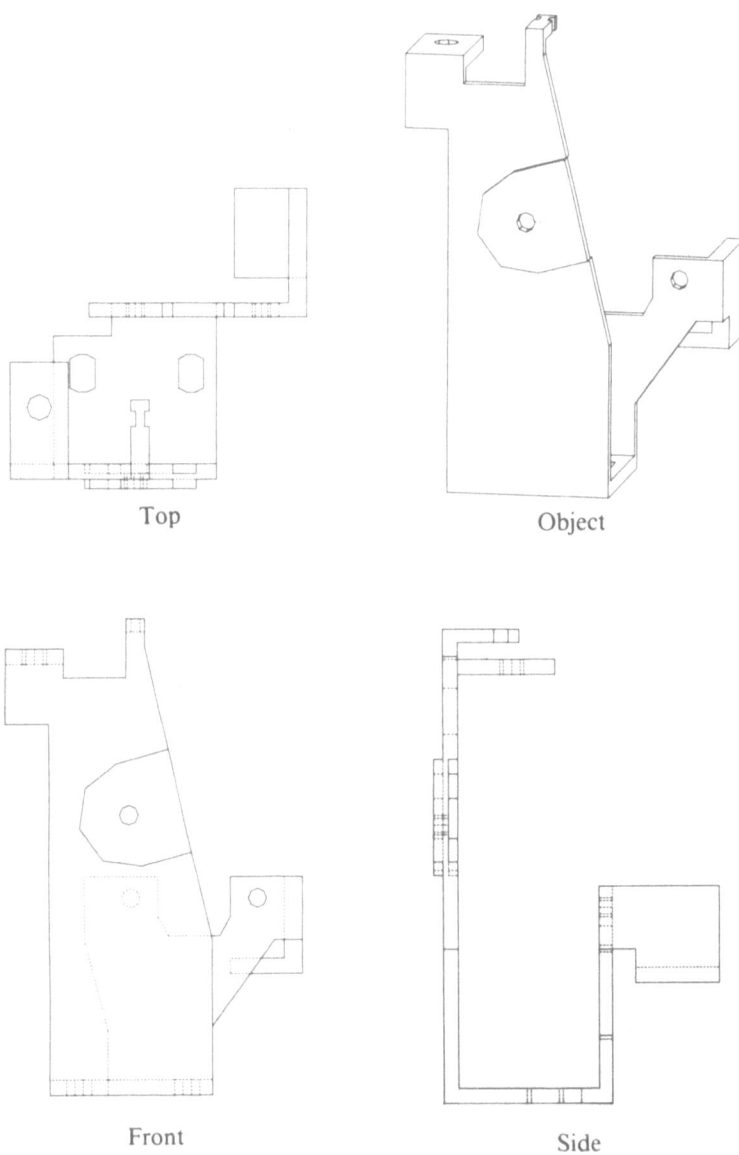

Top

Object

Front

Side

Figure 9. Projections and reconstruction of an engineering object.

mensions into accordance with the line and vertex positions [Fitzgerald 1981], at least in a single view. Human intervention will be needed to resolve topological discrepancies.

Electronic drafting systems modify the concept of measurement errors; the drawings *are* to scale to the resolution of the representation used. The human still has to decide where to put lines and where to omit them. In a complex object the probability of the human's being able to guarantee that the views are correct, complete, and consistent is still very low.

Numerical Problems—Numerical errors cause severe problems in any boundary representation modeling system when complex objects are involved. In the reconstruction problem, algorithms try to establish global properties from a sequence of local properties. For example, in the case when no three-dimensional clues are provided, the existence of a planar surface may be derived from the close numerical agreement of cross products (*i.e.*, normals) at adjacent nodes of an edge connectivity graph. In the presence of numerical error, this could lead to the entire upper surface of a finely divided geodesic dome being considered planar. Modeling systems generally have considerable difficulty with the numerical aspects of boundary representations even when there is higher level semantic information available (*i.e.*, parametric definition of a surface type with parameters to the precision of the system number representation). Numerical problems in reconstruction are not likely to be solved before the general numerical representation problems are contained. One CSG approach [Aldefeld 1983] may be more successful than the boundary representation approach for numerical reasons.

Computational Complexity—None of the published algorithms are accompanied by treatment of the computational complexity involved. In order to give a feel for some of the computational complexity issues, we give here a brief discussion of the stage-by-stage time complexity order of the projections algorithm for polyhedral objects. These measures are summarized in Figure 10.

Stages of the algorithm	Time complexity
1. Check input data V— number of vertices E — number of edges	maximum ($V \log V$, $E \log E$)
2. Construct pseudo vertex skeleton V — number of vertices N — number of views	less than V^N
3. Construct pseudo wire frame E — number of edges	less than E^2
4. Construct virtual faces D — vertex edge degree E — number of edges	maximum (D^2, E)
5. Introduce cutting edges F — number of virtual faces	less than F^2
6. Construct virtual blocks B — number of virtual blocks	B
7. Make decisions B — number of virtual blocks	less than 2^B

Figure 10. Complexity of stages of projections algorithm.

Stage 1: Check Input Data—The complexity of most of the tests in this stage is fairly low. The overall complexity of the stage depends on which tests are implemented. The following apply to input data with V vertices and E edges.

- Checking for duplicate vertices and edges in each view can be done in time V^2 and E^2 if a straightforward comparison is used, in time $V \log V$ and $E \log E$ if techniques based on sorting are used, or in time V and E if a hashing technique is used.

- Checking edges for nonvertex intersections requires time E^2 if done with brute force by looking at every pair of edges. The time complexity can be reduced significantly by partitioning space into zones and checking pairs of edges that are both in the same zone.

Stage 2: Construct Pseudo Vertex Skeleton—The time required for back projecting all the vertices depends on the number of vertices in each view. If done simply, this operation would involve taking all N-tuples of points, where N is the number of views, and seeing whether a point exists in 3-space that projects all the points in the N-tuple. A much better approach involves considering only points from each view that have a chance of intersecting in 3-space. For example, no point in 3-space could possibly project into (3,4,0) and (0,5,5) if projections are parallel to the Z and X axes. For projections parallel to the axes, it is easy to partition the vertices in each view into groups that have a chance of intersecting with vertices selected earlier in the N-tuple.

Stage 3: Construct Pseudo Wire Frame—It is hard to estimate the overall complexity of this stage because it is hard to say anything about how the edges in the different views will cooperate to create edges in the pseudo wire frame. For most objects this stage proceeds rapidly, because there are few sets of lines in the projections that are the images of the same line.

The intersection of pairs of edges can take E^2 time if all pairs are checked for intersection. If the pseudo wire frame is decomposed into geometrical zones this will proceed much faster.

Stage 4: Construct Virtual Faces—This stage proceeds rapidly. At each vertex of the pseudo wire frame, all pairs of edges are examined, and a face containing them is sought. The complexity of this step at each node is of order D^2 where D is the degree of the vertex. This is quite a bit better than working with all possible pairs of edges.

Once a pair of edges, E_1 and E_2, is selected, it is used to define a plane, P. The algorithm searches the edges of the pseudo wire frame that are contained in P for an oriented cycle beginning with E_2 and ending with E_2. If there are several edges in P at a vertex, the algorithm chooses the next left-most edge (relative to the orientation chosen at the starting vertex) and proceeds. Since the choices are forced, no trees are found and the algorithm quickly completes its search.

References pp. 46-48

Stage 5: Introduce Cutting Edges—The simplest way to introduce cutting edges is to check all pairs of virtual faces for intersection. This approach is time consuming because of the large number of faces involved. Once the edges are found, all the points of intersection among the cutting edges in each virtual face must be found. Clearly, the amount of time required depends on the number of edges and faces involved. Some refinements based on geometrical zones can be made to reduce the computation required. Cutting edges are a problem primarily with highly symmetrical objects, such as the ones that arise from posed problems. They occur less frequently in realistic objects.

Stage 6: Construct Virtual Blocks—The complexity of finding virtual blocks is linear in the number of virtual faces. If there are no contradictions in the objects, every virtual face will be in two virtual blocks. The algorithm finds the blocks by starting with a face and adding to it neighboring faces, trying to construct a two-dimensional polygonal surface such that crossing an edge always leads to another surface. Every virtual face belongs to at most two virtual blocks, and thus there is little searching to do since, at each edge, the choice of virtual face is forced. Virtual faces that belong to only one virtual block can be dropped, since they cannot be real faces of the object.

Stage 7: Make Decisions—Finding all solutions to the original problem is an exponential problem, since there can be exponentially many solutions even with three views of the object. With most real objects, the search proceeds very rapidly, especially in the cases where there is only one solution.

Our experience with the execution of this algorithm has been that the introduction of cutting edges in Stage 5 is itself computationally expensive and can also lead to a large number of artificially small potential edges and virtual faces. These in turn lead to a large number of virtual blocks. An exhaustive, depth-first search to assign the state *solid* or *hole* to virtual blocks is exponential in the number of blocks; the implementation relies on heavy pruning (*e.g.*, propagation of the decision properties of a partitioned edge to the whole parent edge) to reduce the computational complexity to manageable level. Observation of the block state assignment process in action has shown that once a state assignment decision is reached for a single block, the consequences generally propagate extremely rapidly. The provision of volume clues by the user (*e.g.*, the assertion that a spatial point is within material) should speed up the initial block decision process considerably.

Although the multipliers have not been discussed, the time (and, in fact, space) complexity of these algorithms is not a serious limitation on practicality. Even the exponential complexity of the final decision process has yielded to the pruning operation, and highly symmetric views generating about one hundred virtual blocks have been solved quickly.

Auxiliary and Symbolic Data—Apart from the Sutherland digitization procedure [Sutherland 1974] and the projection algorithm, none of the workers addresses the inclusion of data from auxiliary and detail views on two-dimensional projection inputs. This is not intrinsically difficult, but it is required for a full solution.

Treatment of symbolic data, such as description of a tapped hole or radius of a circle, is a much more difficult problem. It requires a knowledge-based approach with domains that include geometric relationships such as tangency [Light 1982], machining processes such as tapping, and mechanical drawing techniques and standards.

APPROACHES TO A USABLE SOLUTION

In view of all these problems, together with the need to resolve ambiguities, a near-term usable solution will have to be interactive. In this section we discuss a possible overall approach based on integration of the individual candidate approaches presented earlier in this paper.

Rather than risk absorbing all the data and either dying under the computational load or, after extensive computation, reporting that no solution is possible, a successive refinement approach is favoured with the system doing the detail work and expecting high-level guidance from the user. The first step will be to obtain an approximate volume shape into which details may be introduced later. The approximate solution approach of intersecting extrusions of the projections will bound the object space and give the user a feel for the overall shape. Alternatively, Sugihara's sketch input approach [Sugihara 1978] would also provide a volume starting point.

In order to reduce the computational load, the user will be able to guide the detail process. Onto the initial volume, the system will overlay additional three-dimensionally derived edge and vertex data. These data will already have been pruned to satisfy consistency tests (*e.g.*, a valid edge must separate an even, nonzero number of faces). Any further interactive pruning by the user can be expected to propagate and reduce the uncertain vertex, edge, and face sets. Assertion that points are in material will have a similar effect. Numerical errors can be reduced by user assertion of surface membership and even high level properties.

In principle, input data errors may be observed by the user and corrected. The localization of errors is a hard problem. An error may cause a global consistency test to fail at a point far from the originating error. In this case, the whole global net will have to be shown to the user for study and data error diagnosis.

The interactive approach also allows progressive handling of symbolic data. Initially, the conversion system will require the user to interpret the symbolic data; later, if the system acquires expert capabilities, the symbolic data can be processed more automatically. Invention is needed to handle a wider and less constrained class of surfaces. As a first step the work of Sakurai and Gossard

References pp. 46-48

must be extended to remove orientation and intersection constraints on curved surfaces [Sakurai and Gossard 1983].

SUMMARY AND CONCLUSIONS

In this paper we have examined the many partial solutions to the problem of constructing volume models from two-dimensional and three-dimensional non-solid data. Although none of these are in themselves complete, an evolutionary and interactive approach to a useable solution is proposed.

REFERENCES

[Aldefeld 1983]
B. Aldefeld, "On Automatic Recognition of 3D Structures from 2D Representations," *Computer-Aided Design*, Vol. 15, No. 2, March 1983, pp. 59–64.

[Appel and Stein 1972]
A. Appel and A. Stein, "A System for the Interactive Design of Polyhedra," *Proceedings of Online 72, International Conference on Online Interactive Computing*, Uxbridge, Middlesex, England, September 4-7, 1972, pp. 363–402.

[Baer *et al.* 1979]
A. Baer, C. Eastman, and M. Henrion, "Geometric Modeling: A Survey," *Computer Aided Design*, Vol. 11, No. 5, September 1979, pp. 253–272.

[Baumgart 1974]
B. G. Baumgart, "Geometric Modeling for Computer Vision," Ph.D Dissertation, Artificial Intelligence Laboratory Memo AIM-249, Stanford University, Stanford, California, October 1974.

[Borkin *et al.* 1978]
H. J. Borkin, J. F. McIntosh, and J. A. Turner, "Development of Three Dimensional Spatial Modeling Techniques for the Construction Planning of Nuclear Power Plants," *ACM Computer Graphics*, Vol. 12, No. 3 (SIGGRAPH '78 Conference Proceedings, Atlanta, Georgia, August 23-25, 1978) pp. 341–347.

[Boyse 1983]
J. Boyse, Private communication.

[Braid 1974]
I. C. Braid, *Designing with Volumes*, Cantab Press, Cambridge, England, 1974.

[Clowes 1971]
M. B. Clowes, "On Seeing Things," *Artificial Intelligence*, Vol. 2, 1971, pp. 79–116.

[Doctor and Torborg 1981]
L. J. Doctor and J. G. Torborg, "Display Techniques for Octree Encoded Objects," *IEEE Computer Graphics and Applications*, Vol. 1, No. 3, July 1981, pp. 29–38.

[Fitzgerald 1981]
W. J. Fitzgerald, "Using Axial Dimensions to Determine the Proportions of Line Drawings in Computer Graphics," *Computer Aided Design*, Vol. 13, No. 6, November 1981, pp. 377–382.

[Grossman 1976]
D. D. Grossman, "Procedural Representation of Three Dimensional Objects," *IBM Journal of Research and Development*, Vol. 20, No. 6, November 1976, pp. 582–589.

[Huffman 1971]
D. A. Huffman, "Impossible Objects as Nonsense Sentences," *Machine Intelligence 6*, B. Meltzer and D. Michie, eds., Edinburgh University Press, Edinburgh, Scotland, 1971, pp. 295–324.

[Idesawa 1973]
M. Idesawa, "A System to Generate a Solid Figure from a Three View," *Bulletin of the Japan Society of Mechanical Engineering*, Vol. 16, No. 92, February 1973, pp. 216–225.

[Idesawa *et al.* 1975]
M. Idesawa, T. Soma, E. Goto, and S. Shibata, "Automatic Input of Line Drawing and Generation of Solid Figure from Three-View Data," *Proceedings of the International Joint Computer Symposium*, 1975, pp. 304–311.

[Jones 1980]
J. C. Jones, *Design Methods: Seeds of Human Futures*, 2nd ed., John Wiley and Sons, Inc., New York, New York, 1980.

[Kanade 1978]
T. Kanade, "A Theory of Origami World," Report No. CMU-CS-78-144, Department of Computer Science, Carnegie-Mellon University, Pittsburgh, Pennsylvania, September 1978.

[Lafue 1976]
G. Lafue, "Recognition of Three-Dimensional Objects from Orthographic Views," *ACM Computer Graphics*, Vol. 10, No. 2 (SIGGRAPH '76 Conference Proceedings, Philadelphia, Pennsylvania, July 14-16, 1976) pp. 103-108.

[Light 1982]
R. A. Light, "Variational Geometry: Modification of Part Geometry by Changing Dimensional Values," *Proceedings of the Conference on CAD/CAM Technology in Mechanical Engineering*, Massachusetts Institute of Technology, Cambridge, Massachusetts, March 24-26, 1982, pp. 64–75.

[Markowsky and Wesley 1980]
G. Markowsky and M. A. Wesley, "Fleshing Out Wire Frames," *IBM Journal of Research and Development*, Vol. 24, No. 5, September 1980, pp. 582–597.

[Preiss 1980]
K. Preiss, "Constructing the 3-D Representation of a Plane-Faced Object from a Digitized Engineering Drawing," *Proceedings of the Fourth International Conference and Exhibition on Computers in Design Engineering*, Brighton, England, March 1980, pp. 257–265.

[Requicha 1980]
A. A. G. Requicha, "Representations for Rigid Solids: Theory, Methods, and Systems," *ACM Computing Surveys*, Vol. 12, No. 4, December 1980, pp. 437–464.

[Sakurai and Gossard 1983]
H. Sakurai and D. C. Gossard, "Solid Model Input through Orthographic Views," *ACM Computer Graphics*, Vol. 17, No. 3 (SIGGRAPH '83 Proceedings, Detroit, Michigan, July 25-29, 1983) pp. 243-247.

[Sugihara 1978]
K. Sugihara, "A Step Toward Man-Machine Communication by Means of Line Drawings of Polyhedra," *Bulletin of the Electrotechnical Laboratory*, Vol. 42, Nos. 11 & 12, 1978, pp. 848–871.

[Sugihara 1981]
K. Sugihara, "Mathematical Structures of Line Drawings of Polyhedra — Towards Man-Machine Communication by Means of Line Drawings," Third Laboratory of the Department of Information Science, Faculty of Engineering, Nagoya University, Nagoya, Japan, May 1981.

[Sutherland 1963]
I. E. Sutherland, "SKETCHPAD: A Man-Machine Graphical Communication System," *Proceedings SJCC*, Vol. 23, 1963, p. 329.

[Sutherland 1974]
I. E. Sutherland, "Three Dimensional Data Input by Tablet," *Proceedings of the IEEE*, Vol. 62, No. 4, April 1974, pp. 453–461.

[Sutherland *et al.* 1974]
Ivan E. Sutherland, Robert F. Sproull, and Robert A. Schumacker, "A Characterization of Ten Hidden-Surface Algorithms," *Computing Surveys*, Vol. 6, No. 1, March 1974, pp. 1–55.

[Waltz 1975]
D. Waltz, "Understanding Line Drawings of Scenes with Shadows," *The Psychology of Computer Vision*, P. H. Winston, ed., McGraw-Hill, New York, New York, 1975, pp. 19–91.

[Wesley 1980]
M. A. Wesley, "Construction and Use of Geometric Models," Chapter 2 in *Computer Aided Design*, J. Encarnação, ed., Lecture Notes in Computer Science No. 89, Springer-Verlag, New York, New York, 1980, pp. 79–136.

[Wesley and Markowsky 1981]
M. A. Wesley and G. Markowsky, "Fleshing Out Projections," *IBM Journal of Research and Development*, Vol. 25, No. 6, November 1981, pp. 934–954.

[Winston 1977]
P. H. Winston, *Artificial Intelligence*, Addison-Wesley Publishing Co., Inc., Reading, Massachusetts, 1977.

DISCUSSION

Wesley

I must say I feel nervous speaking to an audience that has so many people in it whose work I'm talking about. I see Chuck Eastman there and I see David Gossard is about to put up his hand, so I know I've got trouble coming.

Robert Johnson *(R.H. Johnson & Associates)*

As far as user iteraction is concerned, do any of the systems have the ability to make use of the coherence of the object as developed? In other words, if information is input in a number of steps, a different model would result at every step. It might be possible to use different algorithms at each subsequent stage rather than make a total appraisal of all of the environment. It could be a way of constructing a solid object.

Wesley

Forcing the user to work in a step-by-step consistent mode is a big constraint on how the user works and he may not want to do that. I think you are thinking very much of building a CSG representation. But to answer your question, no, I do not think that any of these systems do that.

M. A. Wesley

John Hinds *(General Electric)*

In one of the examples, you successfully reconstructed the objects from 1250 edges. Was that from three projections or four projections?

Wesley

No, that was just a wire frame. So the input data contained the three-dimensional vertices and the linking edges.

Hinds

Does that take a long time?

Wesley

Well, the code was written very much in the mode of "let's get it written," and so it's mostly n^2 code with occasional ventures into something a little more efficient if it seems necessary. That particular algorithm was run in a System IBM 370/168 and I think took rather less than a minute of CPU time. But that was a nonoptimized implementation. The potential customers who looked at the algorithm to convert a wire frame of that complexity to a solid model felt that it was a very acceptable price to pay.

David Gossard *(Massachusetts Institute of Technology)*

I was raising my hand to cheer you on. Your statement that most approaches are unable to handle wrong or incomplete data is absolutely right. I was curious to know of any work which has dealt with problems of either inconsistencies or incompleteness in various views of a geometric entity.

Wesley

I don't know of any such work. One can think of a lot of things one could do, but I haven't seen any explicit work to address that.

Michel Melkanoff *(University of California–Los Angeles)*

We are working on that area. We are trying to develop an algorithm for a simple, smart CAD system which can discover certain problems; in particular, one of the hardest problems is the inconsistency of multiple views.

Kalman Brauner *(Boeing Commercial Airplane Company)*

It is my understanding that you have done some work on being able to characterize conditions under which solutions are unique, *i.e.*, exactly one object is reconstructed given certain projections. Could you comment on that?

Wesley

One would very much like to be able to look at the input data and come up with a statement about the number of solutions. The only way we have of doing it is to find them all and count them. We haven't found any cheaper way of doing that. Every time you try to think about measures for what might be clues towards ambiguities, it really seems that you might as well do the whole job and see what comes out.

Brauner

So, for example convexity or a lack of holes is not adequate?

Wesley

Right.

Fumihiko Kimura *(University of Tokyo)*

I feel that your comment on a graphic approach to the user interface is very interesting. Have you done any work in this area?

Wesley

I think that you, Professor Kimura, are well qualified to make that comment because you in fact have worked extensively on the interactive design of objects. I didn't mention your work because I felt it came outside this little classification I was using, but I think your design with tablet input describing geometric components of an object is very interesting. We have not done any work on that.

FINITE ELEMENT MESH GENERATION FOR USE WITH SOLID MODELING AND ADAPTIVE ANALYSIS

MARK S. SHEPHARD and MARK A. YERRY

Rensselaer Polytechnic Institute
Troy, New York

ABSTRACT

The automatic generation of finite element models from solid models is discussed. A fully automatic finite element mesh generator based on a modified octree approach is presented. Its possible integration with self-adaptive analysis procedures to form an automated finite element processor is also discussed.

INTRODUCTION

The use of solid modeling techniques allows for the automation of many time-consuming engineering calculations that are carried out as part of the design process [Requicha and Voelcker 1982, Boyse and Gilchrist 1982]. Algorithms have been developed to automate the calculation of the various mass properties used in engineering calculations. However, the more advanced engineering analysis calculation of quantities, including stresses, displacement, temperature distributions and flow properties, have yet to be automated. Today, it is common to calculate these quantities using the finite element analysis technique. Therefore, if algorithms can be developed that automatically define finite element models yielding an acceptable degree of accuracy, a majority of the advanced engineering calculations can also be automated.

To automate the finite element modeling process a number of capabilities must be available. The first is the ability to subdivide the geometry of interest into a set of simple shapes that constitute a valid finite element mesh. Then the analysis attributes of loads, material properties and boundary conditions must be associated with the finite element mesh so that the analysis can be carried out. The analysis of a valid finite element mesh generated by an automatic meshing algorithm will ensure that the results obtained are reasonable and convergent; however, there is no assurance that the results obtained will yield the required level of accuracy. Thus, there is also the need for the analysis model to be automatically improved until the required level of accuracy is obtained. Finite element analysis codes that selectively improve the finite element model to control the discretization errors are referred to as adaptive analysis programs.

The purpose of this paper is to discuss those capabilities needed to automate the finite element modeling process and to describe some specific procedures currently being developed in those areas. In particular, the next section outlines the steps of an automated finite element modeling process with emphasis on the role of adaptive finite element analysis. The following section gives a description of the modified octree mesh generator for the automatic meshing of solid models. The last section discusses how the modified octree mesh generator may be combined with adaptive analysis techniques to form an automated finite element modeling processor for solids.

AUTOMATED FINITE ELEMENT MODELING AND ADAPTIVE ANALYSIS

The use of solid modeling techniques in conjunction with automatic finite element model generation and adaptive analysis techniques will allow for the automation of the finite element modeling process. The obvious key needed to start this process is the complete and unique geometry employed by solid modelers [Requicha and Voelcker 1982]. Without such a description it is not possible to automate the discretization of the geometry into a finite element mesh.

In this paper, an automatic mesh generator is one that is capable of generating graded meshes for any geometry with no input from the user past an indication of those areas where the mesh is to be finer. A number of two-dimensional algorithms have been developed that can automatically generate planar meshes [Cavendish 1974, Tracy 1977, Bykat 1976, Yerry and Shephard 1983]. However, none of these procedures is in common use in the commercial finite element preprocessors. This is because these mesh generators are often implemented in such a manner that they require as much user-defined input as the more popular techniques, such as blending function mesh generators [Haber *et al.* 1981], while producing poorer meshes. The meshes produced by the triangulation algorithms are often limited to triangular elements which are not as commonly used as quadrilateral elements in practice. Blending function mesh generators are well suited to produce quadrilateral elements. In addition, the elements produced by the blending function mesh generators are less distorted than those produced by other procedures. (The more distorted an element, the less accurate it is.) Since the blending function mesh generators are fairly simple to use in two dimensions, there has not been a great need to move to more fully automated procedures.

This situation is not as true for the meshing of three-dimensional solids, where any technique requiring the user to specify mesh information following rules as required by a mesh generator is difficult to use. Therefore, there are currently a number of investigators attempting to develop fully automatic mesh generators for use with solid modelers [Wördenweber 1980, Van-Phai 1982, Sluiter and Hansen 1982, Yerry and Shephard 1984]. There are a variety of approaches being taken to the development of automatic mesh generators for solids. Several are extensions of the two-dimensional triangulation algorithms which first triangulate the solid's surface. The interior of the solid is then meshed, based on the surface triangulation, by cutting off elements one at a time, creating elements by a domain subdivision approach or some other similar technique. Other algorithms directly define solid elements by a type of slice-and-dice procedure. The next section describes an automatic three-dimensional meshing algorithm that directly defines solid elements using an encoding technique.

In addition to the finite element mesh, a finite element analysis requires the input of problem attribute information including the loads, material properties and boundary conditions along with analysis control information. Currently this attribute information is defined in terms of the finite element mesh. In an automated finite element process, this attribute information must be specified in terms of the problem geometry, not a finite element mesh. Such an approach has the obvious advantage of allowing for more general and efficient attribute specification. In addition, attribute specification in terms of the original geometry fits into a general design environment employing an integrated database with the attributes being associated directly to a part and its geometry.

In principle, it would seem a straightforward process to generalize specification of the various attributes required for a finite element analysis, and for many classes of problems it actually is. For example, it is not difficult to specify all required attribute information in terms of the geometry of a solid part if that part is going to be analyzed as a solid. However, the specification of all the required analysis attribute information for a structure such as an aircraft fuselage is difficult to do directly in terms of the detailed geometry. The reason for this is that such structures are not analyzed as solid parts but as a series of one- and two-dimensional members in space that represent parts that are in fact three-dimensional. For example, the various frame members in a fuselage are normally represented to the analysis program as beams or truss elements that are represented as a line between two points. Even more difficult to handle in a general manner is the case in which such members are represented as the combination of truss and shear panel members to ensure the proper type of response is obtained by the analysis model. In these cases, not only must the software be rich enough to reduce the three-dimensional frames to proper one-dimensional members, but it must be able to determine how the analysis model should be defined for those parts or allow the user to conveniently specify the analysis model as additional attribute information associated with the geomet-

References pp. 74-77

ric model. An additional complication in this process is that the assumptions about the type of analysis modeling to be used are dependent on the particular analysis to be carried out. For example, the skin of an aircraft fuselage is considered fully effective for the free vibration analysis and is represented as shell elements, while in the static analysis under ultimate load, the skin is assumed to be buckled and is therefore represented as a series of shear panels. Thus the general specification of analysis attribute information is a complex problem that not only raises difficult database problems, but will require the careful use of engineering judgement and the extensive use of artificial intelligence.

The objective of the remaining portions of an automated finite element modeling process is to produce results that yield the required degree of accuracy. This portion of the process is carried out by an adaptive analysis program [Babuska and Rheinboldt 1978, Peano and Riccioni 1978, Zare and Rheinboldt 1979, Rheinboldt and Mesztenyi 1980, Carey and Humphrey 1981, Shephard 1981, Gago et al. 1983] which must:

- Perform the required finite element analysis,

- Estimate the discretization errors to determine those portions of the analysis model that are not yielding the required degree of accuracy, and

- Improve the model portions of the mesh that are not satisfactory in the next analysis circle.

By definition this process is an iterative one in which the steps of analysis, error estimation and mesh improvement are carried out for the required number of steps. Thus, an additional important aspect of an adaptive finite element code is the computational efficiency of the process.

The single most important feature of an adaptive finite element code that will determine if the finite element process can be automated is the prediction of errors present in the current analysis model. The procedures used to predict the discretization errors are called *a posteriori* error estimators because they employ the results of the current analysis. It should be pointed out that the accurate prediction of the errors present in a particular finite element model, knowing the results for that model, is not a simple task since the exact results are not known.

A simple but instructive manner of viewing the process of *a posteriori* error estimation is to consider the example of the finite element analysis for stresses and displacements by the standard stiffness method. In such an analysis, the finite element model will always meet the required displacement boundary and continuity conditions. Thus, the only source of errors in the solution will arise from the dissatisfaction of equilibrium conditions which result in the mismatch of traction boundary conditions, jumps in tractions between elements, and the dissatisfaction of the differential equations of equilibrium within the element. Given these known conditions and the solution for a given finite element mesh, one approach to *a posteriori* error estimation is accomplished in three stages.

- *Stage 1.* The residual loads associated with the sources of equilibrium dissatisfaction are determined. The current finite element results are the exact solution to the original problem subject to the applied loads minus the residual loads. Thus the exact solution to the original problem is equal to the current results plus the solution of the same object subjected to the residual loads only. The remaining difficult step is to obtain an accurate solution for the problem subjected to the residual loads. The current finite element mesh will yield no results when the residual loads are applied. (It was unable to represent that portion of the load to begin with.)

- *Stage 2.* Assuming that most of the error will be picked up by the introduction of the next set of approximating functions, these functions are introduced for use in error estimation. (For example, it is commonly assumed that most of the error in a series expansion is associated with the first term that was neglected.)

- *Stage 3.* The residual loads are applied to the finite element model with the next set of modes introduced and solved in at least an approximate manner.

The results obtained for the residual loads acting through the improved modes are considered the error in the current solution.

Approaches based on the type of procedure just outlined have been found to accurately predict the errors in global quantities such as total strain energy. However, techniques for predicting the errors in more important design parameters, such as peak displacements, peak stresses and crack tip intensity factors, require additional consideration, with procedures for their estimation currently under investigation [Babuska and Miller 1984].

If the error estimators indicate that the current finite element mesh does not yield the required accuracy, the finite element model must be improved. In most cases, the accuracy of portions of the model is adequate, so it is only necessary to selectively improve those portions of the model that will increase the accuracy where needed. Error indicators are typically calculated on an element-by-element basis so they can be used to indicate those portions of the mesh that must be improved in order to obtain the desired accuracy. It must be pointed out that although elemental error estimators can be used for indicating the elements that should be improved to reduce the error, they are often not the optimal indicators for this purpose [Dunavant 1980].

Once the elements requiring improvement are determined, the finite element mesh in that area must be improved. There are two basic approaches to carrying out this improvement. The first is to subdivide each of the selected elements into a number of smaller elements, thus reducing the maximum element size. (This approach is referred to as the *h-method* because the element size, *h*, is being reduced.) The second approach is to increase the polynomial order of the elements selected. (This approach is referred to as *p-method* since the polynomial order of the element, *p*, is increased each time.) Although most finite element users would consider h-convergence as the normal method of mesh improvement, the p-convergence approach tends to be more accurate and much more efficient from the standpoint of total solution time [Babuska and Szabo 1982, Szabo and Babuska 1982].

The computational efficiency of an adaptive analysis program is an important consideration because the process requires the solution to several finite element meshes. Since the meshes analyzed in the process of an adaptive analysis are obtained by the selective improvement of the mesh of the previous step, it is possible to reduce the solution cost of the new mesh by accounting for the results of the previous mesh. As an example of how this may be done, the solution of the previous mesh could be used as the starting point for the improved mesh and its iterative solution process. The section on combining the modified octree technique with self-adaptive analysis will give a more complete indication of how the computational efficiency of the process can be improved.

THE MODIFIED OCTREE MESH GENERATOR

Overview of the Modified Octree Technique—The generation of a finite element mesh with the modified octree mesh generator can be thought of as a two-step process. The first step in the process is to form an initial discretization of the object in terms of a modified octree representation. The second step is to modify that representation to yield a valid finite element mesh.

Before discussing the modified octree representation, a brief description of the octree representation [Meagher 1980, Jackins and Tanimoto 1980, Doctor and Torborg 1981] is in order. The octree representation of a three-dimensional object is a valid discretization which, in itself, cannot be effectively used as a finite element mesh. The octree for a three-dimensional object is constructed by first placing the object in an encompassing cube in an integer domain. The cube is then subdivided into eight smaller cubes representing the octants of the original. Each octant is then tested to see if it is inside the object (full), outside the object (empty), or partially inside the object (partial). The homogeneous octants are then flagged to show whether they are full or empty, and the partial octants are subdivided into eight new octants which are also tested in the above manner. The process is continued until the object is resolved to a satisfactory degree.

Although the octree does represent a valid discretization that could be considered a finite element mesh, it suffers from the following drawbacks [Yerry and Shephard 1984]:

- The interior is represented by a small number of large elements.
- Neighboring octants may be at different levels, thus requiring special consideration in a finite element analysis.
- All nonvertical and nonhorizontal boundaries are represented as a series of re-entrant corners (90° inside corners).

- A much larger number of elements than required for finite element solution accuracy are required to yield an acceptable geometric representation of the model boundary in that analysis.

The first two drawbacks are minor but the last two are not acceptable from the standpoint of computer cost and solution accuracy. (The re-entrant corners introduce artificial singularities into the problem that can strongly degrade the solution accuracy in some problem types even for a very fine octree.)

The modified octree is a discretization of a volume that does not have the drawbacks of the octree representation. These drawbacks are eliminated by introducing an additional terminal node of the tree, the cut octant. This modified octree serves as a base to construct a finite element mesh. The basic steps in the modified-octree mesh generating process are:

- *Step 1.* Set up an integer coordinate system that contains the object to be meshed.

- *Step 2.* Generate the modified octree representation of the object accounting for the mesh gradation information specified with respect to the geometric model.

- *Step 3.* Break the modified octree up into a valid finite element mesh.

- *Step 4.* Pull the nodes on the boundary of the modified octree to the appropriate vertices, edges and faces of the original geometry.

- *Step 5.* Smooth the locations of the node points to create a better conditioned finite element mesh.

Once the modified octree is available, it is broken into a set of valid finite elements. Currently the 3-simplex (tetrahedron) is being used as the element shape. However, other element shapes should be possible. For example, each tetrahedron can be subdivided into four bricks, or, in the specific case of the modified-octree mesh generator, it would be straightforward to use a combination of bricks, pyramids and tetrahedra. After this integer finite element mesh is available, the final steps include pulling nodes to the boundary and smoothing the nodal locations to insure the best possible element shapes for the given element topology. The resulting mesh is output in a form usable by standard finite element analysis codes. The following subsections indicate the major considerations of the procedure. A more detailed description of the early stages of the process is available elsewhere [Yerry and Shephard 1984].

The process outlined above is carried out with limited communications with the geometric model. The modified octree and the mesh topology are constructed in the integer coordinate system using an *in/out* test. The *in/out* test asks the geometric modeler if a given point is inside or outside the object, an operation that can be quickly carried out on any solid model representation. For use in the modified octree mesh generator, information on mesh density in the neighborhood of the point is also returned. The mesh density information is the level of the tree that should be used when representing that point. Changing the level by one roughly corresponds to changing the element size by a factor of two. This level information is attribute information associated with the solid model itself. The pulling of boundary points to the appropriate vertices, edges and faces takes the mesh from the integer coordinate system to the real coordinate system of the object. This operation, called a *pull* operation, will take a point known to be on the boundary of the object and ask the geometric model to return the coordinates of that point on the appropriate vertex, edge or face. This operation is more difficult than the *in/out* test, but it is one that can be addressed by a solid geometric representation.

Cut octants—To improve the geometric representation of the octree it is necessary to include another possibility for a terminal node or leaf of the tree. The cut octant is the additional terminal node that is necessary to improve the geometric representation. The term *cut octant* is used to represent a cube with an arbitrarily shaped portion removed. There are several requirements that the particular method for cutting octants will have to meet in order to be used efficiently:

- The integer tree should be retained.
- There should be a small amount of information needed to determine the shape of the cut octant.
- The cutting information should be easily generated using an *in/out* test.
- The *in/out* test results should be represented in the same manner between neighboring octants.
- The cut octant should be easily broken up into finite elements.

In order for a cutting method to work well with the *in/out* test, it must utilize a finite number of points on the octant. The cutting methods addressed here only consider points that lie on the edges of the octant. With this restriction the intersection of the cutting surface and the face of the octant will be a straight line. Currently, only the eight corner points and twelve mid-edge points are considered.

The algorithm developed for the determination of the cutting points does not require an *in/out* test for each of the twenty mid-edge and corner points. This method uses the *in/out* test information about the corner nodes to determine which mid-edge nodes must be examined. Only the mid-edge nodes that lie between a corner that is in and one that is out must be checked. The cutting surface points for any cut octant are obtained using the *in/out* test information for eleven to fourteen points. With this information, the shape of faces of the octant that are cut by the surface are defined. At this point, the cut octant definition will be completed with the determination of the shape cutting surface.

One approach to defining the cutting surface is to allow only single planar cuts. However, for many objects there will be situations when the cutting surface points generated by the algorithm outlined above are not coplanar. In these situations, the fourth requirement listed above can be violated. Therefore, it is necessary to include a more extensive set of octant cutting surfaces that will properly represent the *in/out* test.

This information can be represented with the addition of a set of two planar cut octants and a limited number of three planar cuts. The additional cuts require the storage of the information that defines the planar sections of the cut. To specify this information it is only necessary to store an ordered list of the cutting surface points and the endpoints of the line segments that form the intersections of the planar facets. An efficient scheme that employs specific relationships in the integer coordinate systems of the cut octant and the global octree is used to determine the specific cut octant from the limited amount of stored data.

Generation of the modified octree—The modified octree is identical to that of the octree except for the additional terminal node, the cut octant, and the information needed to specify it properly. Before discussing the generation of the modified octree, it is necessary to introduce two basic concepts that pertain to the tree structure. The first is the integer coordinate systems used, while the second is the tree itself along with the tree traversal routines used. To a major extent, the computational efficiency of the mesh generator is directly related to the number and manner of tree traversals required. Computational efficiency is also maintained by reducing the number of *in/out* tests required to generate the model. With these basic structures in hand the modified octree for an object can be generated.

The procedures used to define, store and manipulate the modified octree are directly tied to the integer coordinate system in which it is defined. The modified octree's coordinate system is referred to as an integer coordinate system because all points used are identified by a set of integer values. Given the edge length of a cube that entirely surrounds an object and given the center of that cube, the integer coordinate system can be generated. This system is defined within the cube, with an integer edge length of two raised to the maximum number of levels of the tree.

When the trees are examined for manipulation or drawing, there is a procedure, referred to as *traversing the tree*, for obtaining the information from the storage arrays. This traversal can be accomplished in several ways. The method used here is referred to as sequential allocation, because a specific order is used for the tree traversal when examining an octant (parent) or those it can be subdivided into (children), in which there is no need to maintain a set of pointers to determine where to look next or to determine the position in the integer coordinate system. With this method, the tree is stored in a one-dimensional status array. The status of an octant is a flag which determines its type: 0—empty, 1—partial, 2—complete, or 3—cut octant. A queue is used during octant subdivision to maintain the sequential ordering for traversing the tree.

The status of the octants is determined by the *in/out* information for the corners of the octant. Checking each corner of every octant encountered while traversing the tree will result in a repeated examination of some points. For a large

References pp. 74-77

model with a fine resolution, this redundant checking would take a considerable amount of time. In an extreme case, some points may be checked as many as fifty times. This redundant checking could be avoided by keeping a list of each point that has been examined. As more entries are added to the list, the time required to search for a particular point increases. Eventually, it will take longer to search the list than to perform the multiple *in/out* tests, thus making it an unacceptable method.

Proper utilization of the sequential allocation scheme allows for a drastic reduction in the number of redundant checks without requiring any searching to determine if a point has been checked before. Some points will still be checked as many as four times. However, this is a substantial reduction from the fifty possible checks and it is much more efficient than an algorithm that would require searching.

The generation of the modified octree begins by obtaining the coordinate system data and a maximum level for empty octants from the solid model definition.

The status of an octant is determined by the *in/out* information about the corner points. This information consists of a flag indicating when a point is inside or outside of the solid model, a number associated with the primitive that the point is within, a boundary level and a maximum interior level. The level for boundary representation is a value assigned to the solid model to control the boundary resolution of the tree. The maximum interior level is a value assigned to the solid model to regulate the size of the interior octants.

The first status to be examined is that of the empty octant. All of the corner node points must be out to be considered empty. If this were the only criterion, a large number of solid models would not be represented properly or at all. This is because large portions of the solid models can lie within octants that have no corner points within the solid model. This difficulty is overcome by not considering an octant to be empty until it is at a minimum level as dictated by the corner point boundary and interior levels.

All of the corner points must be within the solid model before an octant would be considered complete. If this were the only criterion to be met, it would be possible to have a complete octant with corner points in two nonintersecting primitives, a circumstance which is not acceptable. An octant is considered complete if all of the corner points are inside the solid model, its level is equal to or below the maximum interior level, and its level is below or equal to the boundary levels of the corner points when the points lie in different primitives.

The only terminal status left to discuss is that of the cut octant. For a cut octant, between one and seven corner points must be outside the solid model. In addition to this, its level must be equal to or below the lowest boundary level associated with the corner points. Even after meeting these criteria it is still possible for this octant to be considered empty. This occurs when the cutting surface lies on a face of the octant and the cut octant has no volume.

Any octant that does not meet any of the above criteria is considered partial, which will be further examined as the tree construction is continued.

Once the status of an octant is determined, only the cut octants must be processed further to determine the cutting surface points. The octants can be grouped according to how many points are outside the model. The cutting surface points are found for each of the groups individually. In order to obtain these points in the proper order, a locally based coordinate system is used extensively [Yerry and Shephard 1984]. The method requires a minimum number of additional *in/out* tests to identify the surface points.

The modified octree is generated with a tree traversal that determines the status of the octants and the cutting surface points. The tree obtained in this manner can have some branches that have only empty terminal nodes. These are removed with an algorithm that searches the status array for these situations. When one is found, the terminal nodes are removed from the status array and the parent is assigned the empty status. This algorithm must be repeated until there are no branches with only empty terminal nodes.

To make it easier to obtain a finite element mesh from the modified octree, a second modification to the tree is necessary. This second modification limits the difference in level between neighboring cut and complete octants. An octant can have three types of neighbors: face neighbors, edge neighbors and corner neighbors. The neighbors are characterized by the geometric feature that they share with the octant. Thus, a face neighbor has a face in common with the octant. The octant has a total of twenty-six neighbors consisting of six face neighbors, twelve edge neighbors and eight corner neighbors. These neighbors can be identified by the local coordinate of one of the points that are shared.

The limits on the difference in level depends on the neighbor under consideration. The second modification allows the face and edge neighbors to have a difference in level of one. There is no direct limitation placed on the difference in level of corner neighbors. However, the limits on the face and edge neighbor will automatically restrict this difference to two levels. The task of the second modification is to check the difference in level between the complete or cut octant and its neighbors, and to refine the octant when this difference exceeds the given limits.

Mesh generation—The method used for generating a mesh, consisting of tetrahedron elements, constructs several lists that are required to completely describe the mesh. These lists contain the nodal point coordinates, boundary node flags, element connectivities, nodal connectivities and boundary triangle connectivities. The information in these lists is obtained from the modified octree during tree traversals.

Before the mesh is generated it is necessary to obtain information that will be required by that algorithm. Information is needed for recognition of mid-edge nodes and for nodal point numbering. To classify the complete octants for transition meshes, it is necessary to recognize what mid-edge nodes are to be included on the octants. Flags indicating which mid-edge nodes are to be included

References pp. 74-77

are set during the second modification. There are twelve edge flags required for each complete octant. To reduce the amount of storage required, bit flags are used. This method requires the use of one integer word for each complete octant.

The modified octree is basically a set of nonconnected volumes. For this reason the only way to introduce nodes is by looking at the individual volumes. The problem here is that there is no way to determine when a node already has a number. Searching a list of nodal point coordinates for points already numbered would be a time-consuming process. To avoid this, a method was created that uses the modified octree to number nodes. This algorithm uses the results of the sequential allocation method to determine an octant's neighbors that were encountered previously during the traversal. The nodes on the octant that are shared with these neighbors have already been numbered.

In addition to properly numbering the nodes, it is necessary to obtain the node numbers used on the neighboring octants. This is made possible by creating a list of octant connectivities. The octant connectivities contain all of the nodes that are contained on each of the complete and cut octants. The local coordinate system and local node numbering are used to help order this list. A word containing twenty-seven bit flags is used to indicate which nodes are included on the octant and the order in which they are stored in the octant connectivity. Using this information one can obtain the node number for any position on any octant.

The nodal numbers and octant connectivities are obtained from two traversals of the tree. The first traversal locates all of the neighbors that are encountered before the complete and cut octants. The second traversal, which numbers the nodes and defines the octant connectivities, is performed simultaneously with the traversal to construct the mesh.

The procedures used to construct the finite element mesh operate by meshing octants one at a time, with specific considerations given to insure properly matched meshes on the faces of neighboring octants. Two approaches have been investigated for carrying out the process. One employs a surface triangulation followed by a volume tetrahedronization. This is similar to the approach used by [Wördenweber 1980]. The process begins by triangulating the surface of an octant into the minimum number of triangles, utilizing the octant's node points. This triangulation is then used to divide the interior into tetrahedra. Proper mesh matching is insured by checking the position in the integer coordinate system.

The second procedure employed requires less computational effort in that all complete octants are automatically meshed while cut octants are meshed using a set of mesh templates.

The automatic method used for generating the meshes for the complete octants is depicted in Figure 1. It uses the twelve mid-edge node flags to automatically determine which configuration to use. If there are no edge flags set, the

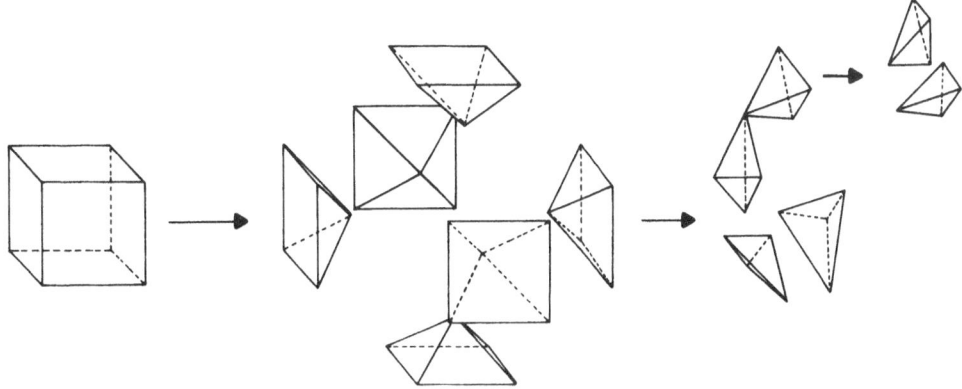

Figure 1. *Complete octant subdivision when edge flags are set.*

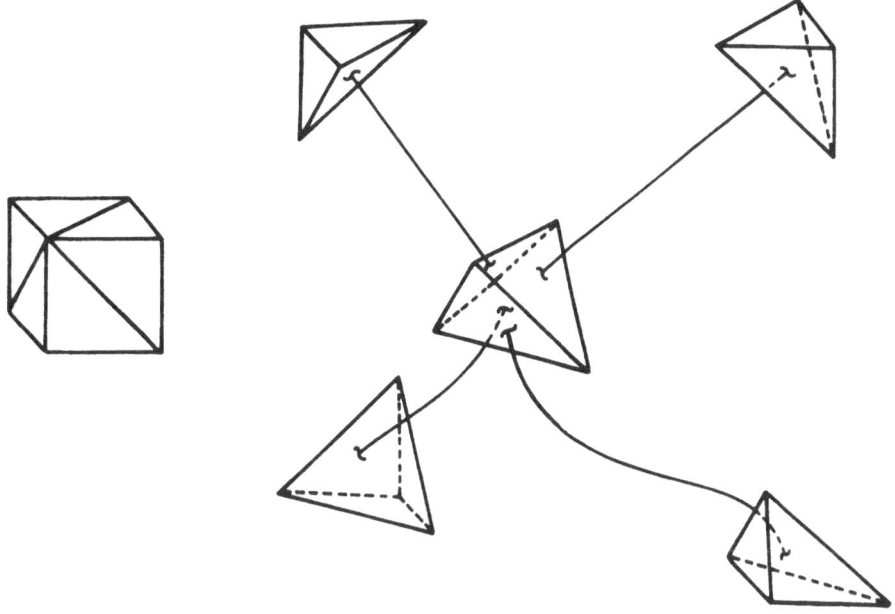

Figure 2. *Complete octant subdivision when all neighbors are at same level.*

octant is subdivided into five tetrahedra (Figure 2). When at least one edge flag is set, the octant is divided into six pyramids (Figure 1). Each pyramid contains a face of the octant, and the top of the pyramid is the centroid of the octant. These pyramids can be meshed individually by examining the edge flags for the octant face contained on the pyramid. If there are no mid-edge flags set on the face, the pyramid is divided into two tetrahedra. If at least one mid-edge flag is set on the face, the pyramid is divided into four tetrahedra. The corners of each of these tetrahedra are defined by the endpoints of an edge of the octant, the centroid of the octant and the center of the face. Any of these tetrahedra that contain a mid-edge node will be further subdivided into two more tetrahedra.

The pattern of the diagonals used in the process of subdividing an octant dictate the diagonals to be used on the neighboring faces. This consideration is handled automatically by simply flipping between two possible matching diagonal patterns based on the coordinates of a corner of that octant.

The cut octants have to be meshed using a different procedure than the one for the complete octants. Here, each of the cut octants is handled more or less individually. This procedure begins by recognizing which cut octant has to be meshed. The cut octants can be identified by the list of cutting surface points, the number of corner points out and the two planar facet dividing lines [Yerry and Shephard 1984]. Once a cut octant is recognized, a predetermined set of elements and local nodal connectivities is obtained directly from data arrays developed from a set of mesh templates. Figure 3 indicates two of the cut octants with meshes. The global element connectivities can now be obtained by referencing the octant connectivities.

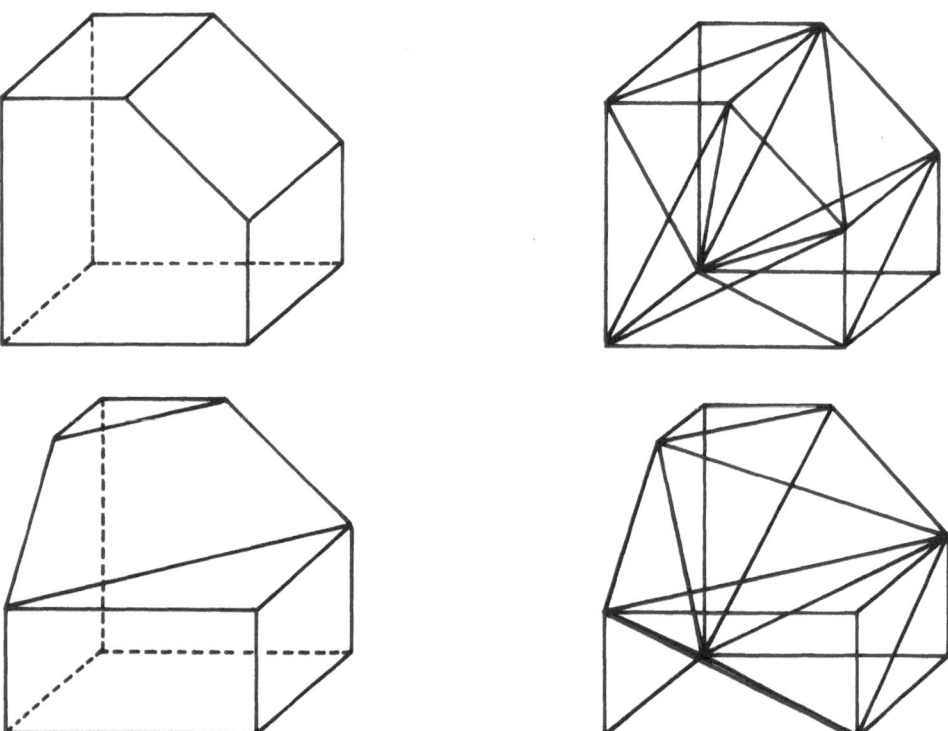

Figure 3. *Cut octant meshes.*

The mesh is constructed during a tree traversal. This tree traversal is used to number the nodes, set up the octant connectivities and set up the element connectivities. It is important to note that various steps in this process are to be carried out more or less simultaneously during the required tree traversal.

At this point, a complete finite element mesh in the integer coordinate system can be generated. Since the meshing algorithms for the individual octants use well-shaped elements, the entire integer mesh consists of well-shaped elements. The only major deficiency of the resulting meshes is that the boundary nodes are in the integer coordinate system and not on the actual object boundary. Figure 4 shows the integer mesh for the crankshaft of a single cylinder motor. The solid model for this crankshaft is constructed from five cylindrically shaped superquadric primitives. Finer tolerances were assigned to the primitives representing the bearing surfaces to produce this slightly graded mesh.

The two steps required to arrive at the final mesh include pulling of the boundary nodes to the boundary of the solid model and smoothing of the internal nodes of the mesh. These boundary nodes have to be determined by examining the modified octree representation. The boundary nodes for the cutting surface are easily found for the cut octants. These nodes are flagged during a tree traversal. The boundary nodes on the other faces of the cut octants and the boundary nodes on the complete octants are more difficult to identify. These nodes are identified by locating the empty neighbors of the complete and cut

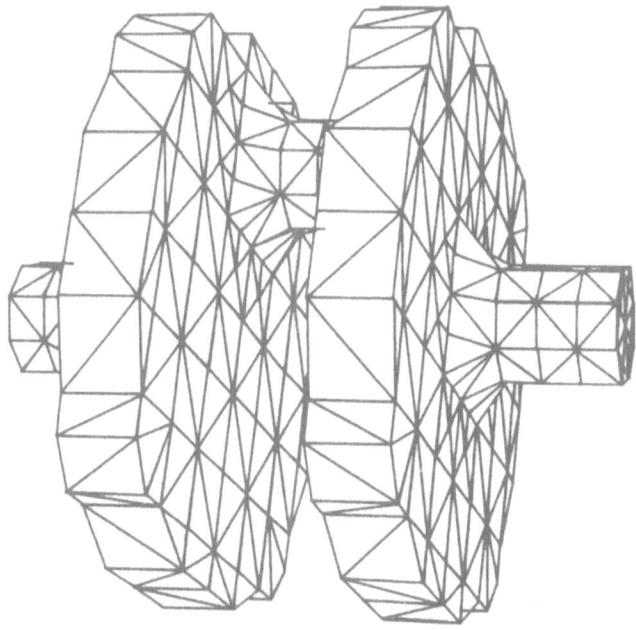

Figure 4. Integer mesh for crankshaft.

octants. When a neighbor is empty, the nodes that are in common are the boundary nodes. In order to locate these nodes, the algorithm's emphasis is placed on the identification of the empty neighbors.

Ideally, placing the boundary nodes on the surface of the actual object consists of indicating to the solid modeler that a particular node is a surface node, then having the modeler return the appropriate location of a surface point. In practice, this is a nontrivial operation that must address some of the particular aspects of the solid model representation. To indicate these operations the Rensselaer Polytechnic Institute modeler based on superquadrics [Barr 1981] will be considered.

The superquadric solid modeler uses primitives that are described by the quadric surface [Barr 1981] given by:

$$F(X, Y, Z) = \left[\left(\frac{X}{a_1}\right)^{2/\varepsilon_2} + \left(\frac{Y}{a_2}\right)^{2/\varepsilon_2} \right]^{\varepsilon_2/\varepsilon_1} + \left(\frac{Z}{a_3}\right)^{2/\varepsilon_1} \tag{1}$$

$$X = \frac{X_1}{F(X_1, Y_1, Z_1)}$$

$$Y = \frac{Y_1}{F(X_1, Y_1, Z_1)}$$

$$Z = \frac{Z_1}{F(X_1, Y_1, Z_1)}$$

where (X, Y, Z) are the coordinates of the surface point and (X_1, Y_1, Z_1) are the coordinates of the given point.

This equation is used by the *pull* operation to determine possible surface representations for the given point. The point returned by the *pull* operation is the surface point that is closest to the given point. These calculations have to be made only for primitives that contain the given point. The pulling process requires these operations to be performed for every boundary node.

Now that the boundary points have been pulled, it is possible to perform the element smoothing. This smoothing is done by looping over the nodal connectivities and placing all interior nodes at the centroids of the nodes to which they are connected. This nodal smoothing is a nonlinear process that converges within a few iterations over the interior nodes. Three iterations are performed for the work presented here.

The final mesh for the crankshaft is shown in Figure 5. This figure demonstrates the improvement in the boundary representation that results from the pulling operation. Figure 6 shows the final mesh of a cube with an off-center spherical cavity. Mesh gradation is controlled by the finer tolerance that is applied to the spherical primitive. Figure 7 shows three views of the final mesh for a drive shaft yoke. The mesh is constructed from a solid model consisting of eleven primitives with tolerance levels applied to create mesh gradations.

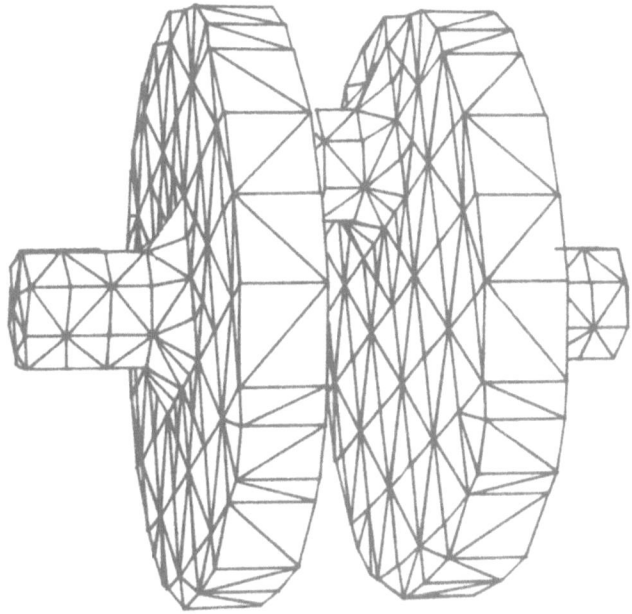

Figure 5. *Final mesh for crankshaft.*

MODIFIED OCTREE MESHES AND ADAPTIVE ANALYSIS

The modified octree mesh generator can be used to generate user-graded meshes for standard finite element analysis programs. It can also be used in conjunction with an adaptive finite element analysis capability to create an automated finite element processor for solid objects. The input to this processor would consist of a valid solid representation, the problem attributes of loads, material properties and boundary conditions defined in terms of that geometry, and information on the required accuracy. In addition, mesh gradation information, also tied to the geometry, may be input to reduce computational cost. The output of the processor would be the analysis results related to the original geometry. With this capability the user would not need to see any finite element meshes.

The internal data structures of this processor would be radically different from that of a standard finite element analysis program. First, the program must be able to accept a geometric definition of a problem instead of a finite element mesh with the attribute information specified in terms of the mesh. Although this could be accomplished by adding the geometric information to standard finite element data structures, it is an undesirable approach because the static storage structures of current finite element codes are not well suited for an adaptive environment where the finite element model is changing. On the other hand, the tree structures used for the modified octree mesh generator can be effectively used to track any mesh modifications.

References pp. 74-77

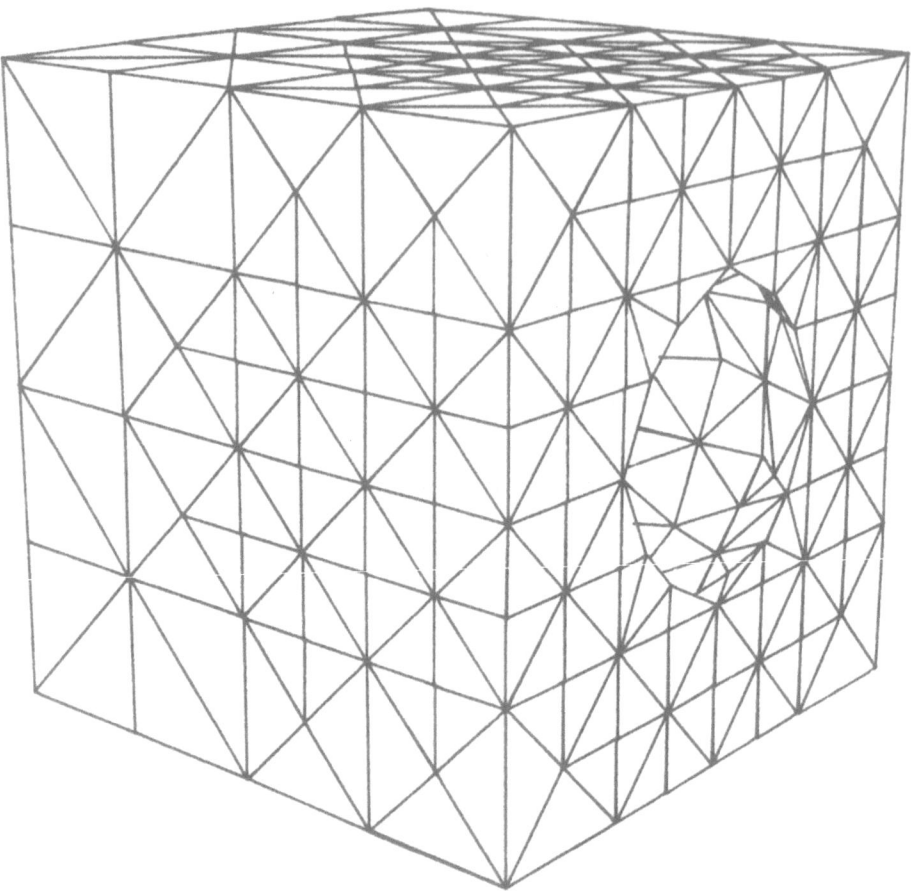

Figure 6. *Mesh for cube with off-center spherical cavity.*

The modified octree mesh generator and its tree storage structures also have the advantage of representing a two-way bridge between the problem geometry and the analysis model. This bridge can be effectively employed in any mesh refinement process to automatically improve the analysis model's representation of the geometry as the mesh is adaptively improved. The importance of this feature can be indicated by considering a specific example. Consider a problem with a rounded re-entrant corner that is initially idealized in the course starting finite element mesh as a sharp corner. The high stress gradients caused by the corner singularity are likely to cause the adaptive analysis program to improve the finite element discretization in that area. If the representation of the geometry in that area is not also improved to more accurately represent the rounded corner, artificially high stress gradients will be determined.

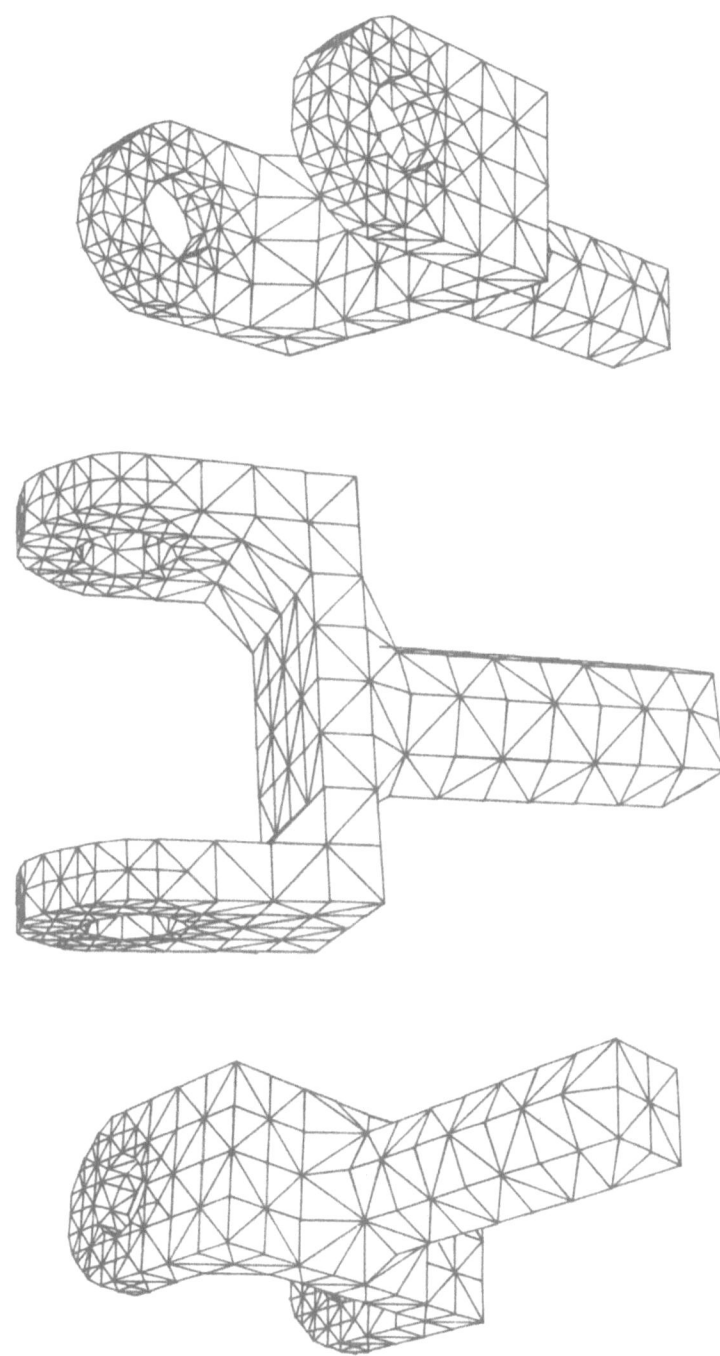

Figure 7. *Three views of final mesh for driveshaft yoke.*

The information generated during the mesh generation process and the tree storage structures used by the modified octree mesh generator can be used effectively to improve the computational efficiency of the adaptive analysis process. An important aspect of minimizing solution cost is the appropriate ordering of unknowns to deal effectively with the sparseness of the global stiffness matrix. Specific ordering algorithms have been developed to carry out this process. These algorithms can be effectively interfaced to the data structures of the modified octree mesh generator since the connectivity graphs required for reordering already exist as part of the meshing process. This is true for both the ordering of the original finite element discretization and proper placing of the new degrees of freedom introduced during the adaptive analysis.

The adaptive analysis process requires several analyses of continually improving finite element discretizations. Since the mesh at step $i+1$ is obtained by making selective improvements to the mesh at step i, it is possible to make use of the efforts expended during step i in the solution of step $i+1$. One approach to this is to employ an iterative solution technique that is sensitive to the initial starting vector, such as Gauss-Seidel iteration, and use the solution for the mesh of step i as the starting vector for step $i+1$. Such a technique is attractive for single load cases or non-linear problems, but it has a drawback for multiple load case problems since the solution must be carried out for each load case. Another approach is to employ direct solution techniques and to gain solution efficiency through the use of reanalysis techniques [Kleiber and Lutoborski 1978, Yang 1977, Row et al. 1977, Law and Fenves 1981]. The objective of a reanalysis technique is to update the factorized stiffness equations from step i to account for the discretization improvements made in going to step $i+1$. For a banded symmetric system modified by a rank one matrix, the number of operations required to update the system using reanalysis techniques is proportional to n times m [Law and Fenves 1981], where n is the number of unknowns and m is the semibandwidth. This represents a substantial savings over the number of operations required to triangulate the entire system, which is proportional to n times m squared.

The efficient application of reanalysis techniques during adaptive analysis requires special consideration since the modifications in going from step i to $i+1$ will add new degrees of freedom and, depending on how the mesh improvements are carried out, will change existing stiffness terms at various locations in the system. Such general system modifications make it more difficult to update the factorized stiffness equations in an efficient manner. One method to attack this problem is to view the matrix factorization and updating process through graph representations and operations [Law and Fenves 1981]. Again the tree-storage and various connectivity information generated during the modified octree meshing process can play an important role in using these procedures.

An area that must be addressed in using adaptive analysis for solids is the dependable prediction of the discretization errors present, which means the development of error estimators for solid elements. At some point in the process of developing an error estimator the norm in which the error will be measured must be addressed. However, it is more convenient to begin with a consideration of the discretization error without reference to a specific norm. As indicated earlier, the only direct measure of solution error available is the measurable dissatisfactions which, for a displacement-based stiffness solution with conforming elements, are equilibrium dissatisfactions. For three-dimensional elements the residuals associated with equilibrium dissatisfactions are represented by jumps in surface tractions between elements, a residual associated with the dissatisfaction of the equilibrium within the element, and the mismatch of various traction boundary conditions.

One possible way to estimate the errors caused by these residuals is to introduce improved modes into the finite element model; for example, increasing the polynomial order of the elements, one would load the mesh with the residual loads and solve. The results obtained can be used as an estimate of the error present in the mesh. This approach has the disadvantage that the error analysis requires the solution to a large system of equations.

To be useful, the determination of the error estimators must take a small fraction of the computation time required to solve the finite element equations. Several approaches to estimating the discretization error associated with these residual loads have been derived; these approaches yield accurate estimates of the error in the total strain energy. A recent procedure [Shephard and Yunus 1983] introduces the improved modes to individual elements, applies the residual loads on an element-by-element basis, holding the previous elemental degrees of freedom fixed and not accounting for continuity between elements. Although approximate, the error in total strain energy estimated by this procedure for the problems tested has been quite accurate. Additional new procedures are being developed to estimate errors in more meaningful norms such as peak displacements and crack tip intensity factors [Babuska and Miller 1984].

CONCLUDING REMARKS

This paper addressed the requirements of an automated finite element modeling processor for use in an integrated design system where the geometry of parts is defined by a solid modeler. Although current capabilities are far short of those outlined here, there is a tendency in industry today to use the finite element analysis technique as if such procedures were available. In particular, an ever-increasing percentage of the finite element models being analyzed today are being defined by users that know little or nothing about the finite element method and the approximations associated with it. Since the manner in which the finite element mesh is laid out is one of the approximations being made and it has a substantial effect on the results obtained, this is a dangerous situation. Thus, there is a need not only to develop improved mesh generating algorithms so that meshes can be defined automatically, but also to develop automated procedures to control the accuracy of the resulting model.

References pp. 74-77

Substantial progress is being made in developing the various procedures required for an automated finite element processor. Automatic mesh generators such as the modified octree mesh generator presented in this paper will soon allow valid finite element meshes to be generated automatically. Procedures and the required mathematical foundations for effective *a posteriori* error estimation are becoming available. These procedures, coupled with efficient adaptive analysis capabilities, will represent a capability for the automatic finite element modeling of solid objects.

ACKNOWLEDGEMENT

The authors would like to express their appreciation to the Engineering Mechanics Department of the General Motors Research Laboratories for supporting the development of the modified octree technique. In addition the authors would like to acknowledge the support of the National Science Foundation under grant ISP-20240, the Center for Interactive Computer Graphics Industrial Associates and the Alcoa Foundation for their general support in automated finite element modeling.

REFERENCES

[Babuska and Miller 1984]
I. Babuska and A. Miller, "The Post-Processing Approach in the Finite Element Method, Part I: Calculation of Displacements, Stresses and Other Higher Derivatives of Displacements," to appear in *International Journal for Numerical Methods in Engineering*, 1984.

[Babuska and Rheinboldt 1978]
I. Babuska and W. C. Rheinboldt, "*A Posteriori* Error Estimates for the Finite Element Method," *International Journal for Numerical Methods in Engineering*, Vol. 12, No. 10, 1978, pp. 1597–1615.

[Babuska and Szabo 1982]
I. Babuska and B. A. Szabo, "On the Rates of Convergence in the Finite Element Method," *International Journal for Numerical Methods in Engineering*, Vol. 18, No. 3, 1982, pp. 323–341.

[Barr 1981]
A. H. Barr, "Superquadrics and Angle-Preserving Transformations," *IEEE Computer Graphics and Applications*, Vol. 1, No. 1, January 1981, pp. 11–23.

[Boyse and Gilchrist 1982]
J. W. Boyse and J. E. Gilchrist, "GMSolid: Interactive Modeling for Design and Analysis of Solids," *IEEE Computer Graphics and Applications*, Vol. 2, No. 2, March 1982, pp. 27–40.

[Bykat 1976]
A. Bykat, "Automatic Generation of Triangular Grid: I—Subdivision of a General Polygon into Convex Subregions. II—Triangulation of Convex Polygons," *International Journal for Numerical Methods in Engineering*, Vol. 10, No. 6, 1976, pp. 1329–1342.

[Carey and Humphrey 1981]
G. F. Carey and D. L. Humphrey, "Mesh Refinement and Iterative Solution Methods for Finite Element Computations," *International Journal for Numerical Methods in Engineering*, Vol. 17, No. 11, 1981, pp. 1717–1734.

[Cavendish 1974]
J. C. Cavendish, "Automatic Triangulation of Arbitrary Planar Domains for the Finite Element Method," *International Journal for Numerical Methods in Engineering*, Vol. 8, No. 4, 1974, pp. 679–696.

[Doctor and Torborg 1981]
L. J. Doctor and J. G. Torborg, "Display Techniques for Octree Encoded Objects," *IEEE Computer Graphics and Applications*, Vol. 1, No. 3, July 1981, pp. 29–38.

[Dunavant 1980]
D. A. Dunavant, "Local *A Posteriori* Indicators of Error for the p-Version of the Finite Element Method," Doctor of Science Thesis, Sever Institute, Washington University, St. Louis, Missouri, 1980.

[Gago *et al.* 1983]
J. Gago, D. W. Kelly, O. C. Zienkiewicz, and I. Babuska, "*A Posteriori* Error Analysis and Adaptive Process in the Finite Element Method: Part II — Adaptive Mesh Refinement," *International Journal of Numerical Methods in Engineering*, Vol. 19, No. 11, 1983, pp. 1621–1656.

[Haber *et al.* 1981]
R. B. Haber, M. S. Shephard, J. F. Abel, R. H. Gallagher and D. P. Greenberg, "A General Two-Dimensional, Graphical Finite Element Preprocessor Utilizing Discrete Transfinite Mappings," *International Journal for Numerical Methods in Engineering*, Vol. 17, No. 7, 1981, pp. 1015–1044.

[Jackins and Tanimoto 1980]
C. L. Jackins and S. L. Tanimoto, "Octrees and Their Use in the Representation of Three-Dimensional Objects," Internal Report, Department of Computer Science, University of Washington, Seattle Washington, August 1980.

[Kleiber and Lutoborski 1978]
M. Kleiber and A. Lutoborski, "Modified Triangular Factors in the Incremental Finite Element Analysis and Nonsymmetric Stiffness Changes," *Computers & Structures*, Vol. 9, 1978, pp. 599–602.

[Law and Fenves 1981]
K. H. Law and S. J. Fenves, "Sparse Matrices, Graph Theory and Reanalysis," *Proceedings of the First International Conference on Computation in Civil Engineering*, ASCE, New York, New York, 1981, pp. 234–249.

[Meagher 1980]
D. J. Meagher, "Octree Encoding: A New Technique for the Representation, Manipulation, and Display of Arbitrary Three-Dimensional Objects by Computer," Technical Report IPL-TR-80-111, Image Processing Laboratory, Rensselaer Polytechnic Institute, Troy, New York, October 1980.

[Peano and Riccioni 1978]
A. Peano and R. Riccioni, "Automated Discretization of the Error Control in Finite Element Analysis Methods," *Proceedings of the Second World Congress on Finite Elements*, October 1978.

[Requicha and Voelcker 1982]
A. A. G. Requicha and H. B. Voelcker, "Solid Modeling: A Historical Summary and

Contemporary Assessment," *IEEE Computer Graphics and Applications*, Vol. 2, No. 2, March 1982, pp. 9–24.

[Rheinboldt and Mesztenyi 1980]
W. C. Rheinboldt and C. K. Mesztenyi, "On a Data Structure for Adaptive Finite Element Mesh Refinements," *ACM Transactions on Mathematical Software*, Vol. 6, No. 2, June 1980, pp. 166–187.

[Row *et al.* 1977]
D. G. Row, G. H. Powell and D. P. Mondkar, "Solution of Progressively Changing Equilibrium Equations for Nonlinear Structures," *Computers & Structures*, Vol. 7, 1977, pp. 654–665.

[Shephard 1981]
M. S. Shephard, "The Finite Element Modeling Process — Will It Be Automated?" *New and Future Development in Commercial Finite Element Methods*, J. Robinson, ed., Pitman Press, Bath, England, 1981, pp. 451–468.

[Shephard and Yunus 1983]
M. S. Shephard and S. Yunus, "*A Posteriori* Error Estimates for Linear Triangles Using h- and p-Hierarchic Modes," Department of Civil Engineering, Rensselaer Polytechnic Institute, Troy, New York, 1983.

[Sluiter and Hansen 1982]
M. L. C. Sluiter and D. C. Hansen, "A General Purpose Automatic Mesh Generator for Shell and Solid Finite Elements," *Computers in Engineering*, L. E. Hulbert, ed., Vol 3, Book No. G00217, ASME, August 1982, pp. 29–34.

[Szabo and Babuska 1982]
B. A. Szabo and I. Babuska, "Stress Approximations by the h-and p-Version of the Finite Element Method," Report WU/CMM-82/1, Center for Computational Mechanics, Washington University, St. Louis, Missouri, March 1982.

[Tracy 1977]
F. T. Tracy, "Graphics Pre- and Post-Processor for Two-Dimensional Finite Element Programs" *ACM Computer Graphics*, Vol. 11, No. 2 (SIGGRAPH '77 Conference Proceedings) pp. 8–12.

[Van-Phai 1982]
Nguyen Van-Phai, "Automatic Mesh Generation with Tetrahedron Elements," *International Journal for Numerical Methods in Engineering*, Vol. 18, No. 2, 1982, pp. 273–289.

[Wördenweber 1980]
B. Wördenweber, "Volume-Triangulation," CAD Group Document No. 110, Computer Laboratory, University of Cambridge, Cambridge, England, 1980.

[Yang 1977]
W. H. Yang, "A Method for Updating Cholesky Factorization of a Banded Matrix," *Computer Methods in Applied Mechanics and Engineering*, Vol. 12, 1977, pp. 281–288.

[Yerry and Shephard 1983]
M. A. Yerry and M. S. Shephard, "A Modified-Quadtree Approach to Finite Element Mesh Generation," *IEEE Computer Graphics and Applications*, Vol. 3, No. 1, February 1983, pp. 39–46.

[Yerry and Shephard 1984]
M. A. Yerry and M. S. Shephard, "Automatic Three-Dimensional Mesh Generation by the Modified-Octree Technique," to appear in *International Journal for Numerical Methods in Engineering*.

[Zave and Rheinboldt 1979]
P. Zave and W. C. Rheinboldt, "Design of an Adaptive, Parallel Finite-Element System," *ACM Transactions on Mathematical Software*, Vol. 5, No. 1, March 1979, pp. 1–17.

DISCUSSION

Michel Melkanoff *(University of California–Los Angeles)*

Is it possible in your system to interactively point to the places where you want a finer gradation of mesh?

Shephard

The way we can have a finer gradation currently is to assign tolerance information to the surfaces and to the volumes of the primitives. That will control mesh gradation in three dimensions. We haven't looked at interactive procedures that would allow the user to specify finer gradation in some areas in three dimensions; we are doing that in two dimensions. The mesh generation is fully automatic, but the user is allowed to specify his tolerance information. If the mesh is displayed and the user does not like it, it is possible simply to change tolerances wherever desired.

Tolerance information can be associated with volumes, areas and boundaries. We've looked at some methods to allow various combinations in two dimensions, but three-dimensional modeling is a little bit harder because it is hard to specify predictable tolerance information and visualize the final results. There are some simple radial techniques that could be used interactively. It definitely can be done. It involves going down the tree another level at the desired locations to remesh it.

M. S. Shephard

Melkanoff

This approach of automatically remeshing in selected areas seems to improve the speed, then.

Shephard

Yes, it is fairly quick. I say "fairly quick" because we don't really have enough experience with the three-dimensional approach to say that it is going to be very fast. We know the two-dimensional one is extremely fast in comparison with many triangulation algorithms that must perform many checks. We have been very careful to reduce checking to a minimum. For example, in three dimensions with reduction of the in/out test we could invoke the in/out test for a point only once, but then we would have to ask subsequently, "Has this point been tested previously?" We didn't want to do that. We don't want to do any searching, so we have come up with a specific algorithm that knows what is in the tree. Thus for some points we will ask the in/out information as many as four times, but that's much faster than any type of searching. We avoid all the searching we can for speed purposes.

John Woodwark *(University of Bath)*

Could you say a little bit more about the mesh point smoothing process.

Shephard

To obtain better shaped elements, we are using a fairly simple procedure that I've always found adequate. I call it a "local Laplacian." It's not a true Laplacian; this terminology came from looking at a set of finite difference relationships that you would get on a rectangular grid for Laplacian equations. The procedure I am calling local Laplacian involves taking each point and looking at all the nodes it's connected to (either by lines or by all the nodes of any element it's connected to), then recomputing the nodal coordinates as the centroid of all those points. Obviously, when you do that for one point, the point changes; so the procedure has to be done iteratively. It converges very rapidly; we typically do about three cycles.

There are other procedures for doing smoothing but, in my opinion, the most important aspect of obtaining good element shapes is not the details of smoothing but the element topology. It's not even the details of the element topology; it's the number of elements coming to a single point which really controls the shape of the mesh you can finally get. It is more important than any smoothing algorithm you can think of.

Burkhard Wördenweber *(University of Cambridge)*

You started off with quadrilateral zones. Why do you convert to triangles or tetrahedra?

Shephard

The basic problem is the diagonals of a tetrahedron. The only way to isolate diagonals of a tetrahedron is with a pyramid, with a base that is square. We can do that, but we wanted to get something complete working first, and tetrahedra are quite satisfactory. Mixed meshes are one type of refinement we can look at.

The standard analyst would probably have walked out of the room by now because he doesn't want to see anything if it's not all bricks. You can get all bricks; it's easy enough to do. We've done it in two-dimensions. The triangles are subdivided into quadrilaterals, and the complete quads based on their neighbors can be subdivided directly into the quadrilaterals. The SDRC software takes tetrahedra and makes them into bricks.

I have a real concern for bricks that are not parallelepipeds. They tend not to be very accurate. I believe (and it's only a belief, I don't really have the results to confirm it) that in solid meshes generated with any automatic mesh generator, you're probably going to be better off with tetrahedra than with badly shaped bricks formed from coarse tetrahedra. Badly shaped bricks are worse than tetrahedra for analysis. There is one paper by Stricklen and co-workers in the 1977 *International Journal for Numerical Methods in Engineering* which gives a comparison of two-dimensional rectangular elements with triangular elements and what happens when you start distorting those elements. The results presented in that paper tend to support my previous comments.

James Cavendish *(General Motors Research Laboratories)*

Suppose I have a solid with an edge that is a general space curve. How are you going to stack up nodes along that edge?

Shephard

I wish I had the complete answer for that. We wanted to do that without *a priori* edge information. The reason we wanted to do that is because it keeps the mesh generator quite general. We ask in/out information to get the basic mesh topology, and then all the points are just put where they're supposed to be. It does not appear that it is going to be fully satisfactory. The way we will have to do it is with some *a priori* information to make sure that the mesh generator knows it's going to have to pull things to that edge so it will put enough points in there. With our mesh generating technique we can force the octree to have that happen. We haven't implemented that yet and the details on how to implement it are somewhat uncertain. One possibility is that it may be necessary to get a little bit away from the mesh templates we use and to use a tetrahedronizing algorithm, not on a model level, but on individual cut octants.

Cavendish

The problem is that you're basically breaking the solid octants into a rectangular decomposition. It is okay as long as the solid looks like that. But if the solid doesn't have that kind of a shape, it seems as if the method just isn't designed to cope with it. For that simple yoke it was obvious, since it looked like a union of bricks. How about something more complicated?

Shephard

We've done a bracket with an angle hole through it and a cube with an off-center sphere inside and had no trouble. Because of the cutting methods we can get these other shapes. But what you do point out is that there will always be a biasing based on your coordinate system. It is unavoidable. A mesh generator such as this does not follow the geometry as nicely as does a mapping mesh generator that starts from the surface and works in. It's one of the disadvantages you have to live with. For solution accuracy, I'm not convinced what the best shaped mesh is supposed to be and I don't really care, as long as I can guarantee that the mesh is good enough. I don't mind if I have ten extra elements in it, as long as I didn't have to put them in there by hand. Certainly, octrees have been demonstrated to be able to do any topology if you go far enough in a tree. The problem is to do it at a high enough level in the tree so you don't have more elements than you really want.

FINITE-ELEMENT ANALYSIS FOR THE NAIVE USER

BURKARD WÖRDENWEBER

University of Cambridge
Cambridge, England

ABSTRACT

The paper describes the role of mesh generation mediating between computer aided design and finite-element analysis. It illustrates one particular approach to mesh generation which reduces the need for mesh visualization and interaction. The method relies on engineering expertise to derive an appropriate test object for analysis from the geometric model. It then proceeds to generate an initial coarse mesh which may subsequently be refined to suit object geometry, material properties and load case specification. The method avoids the sensitive calculations necessary for adaptive methods and permits analysis at different levels of complexity and cost.

The paper introduces the recent developments within the BUILD geometric modeler, a product of the University of Cambridge Computer and Engineering Departments. In particular, the application program for finite-element mesh generation, together with its underlying algorithms, is described in detail.

COMPUTER AIDED DESIGN

Computer aided design helps the user to conceive and outline a sketch or plan. In communication with the computer, the user first produces a sketch to determine spatial layout and then adds detail, thus realizing more and more of the plan. When the plan is fully modeled, the user may simulate its performance and consider specific aspects such as aesthetics, practicality or cost.

At first glance, a system for computer aided design looks like a graphics program whose task it is to display a complex object or scene. The capability of drawing and rendering assists visualization and first verification of the design.

References pp. 98-100

Secondly, the system permits the user to create and modify the design which gives rise to the picture. With this drafting capability it is possible to realize the design.

Thirdly, the system knows about the domain of designs. For example, a geometric modeler for three-dimensional solid objects will not permit the creation of the infamous devil's fork or Klein bottle which fails to have an interior distinct from an exterior. The knowledge about a domain implies that the set of possible objects is consistent with its natural environment and compatible with the designer's intentions. Also, the model may be simulated in its environment within some hypothetical constraints, and useful experience may be gained from its performance.

Systems for computer aided design are available for geometric modeling of architecture or engineering components, electronic circuits and layout for VLSI. They communicate plans within a team of designers and between designer and management. Such systems increase the speed of the design process by providing critical feedback to the user. This paper deals specifically with computer aided design of three-dimensional solid objects.

ENGINEERING ANALYSIS

Engineering analysis is concerned with the consistency of plans and their compatibility with the environment. Analysis may justify a finished design or, alternatively, may lead to alterations of the plans.

In geometric modeling, analysis is currently implemented on three distinct levels. First, with graphics the user can visualize his design and gain insight into geometric configuration and spatial layout. Secondly, evaluation of properties such as surface area, mass and centre of gravity provide a preliminary assessment of the object's performance. Finally, the model may be simulated, that is, analysed either statically or dynamically with respect to stresses and strains, vibrations, temperatures, electric or magnetic potential or flow.

Analysis according to the above methods requires hypothetical assumptions about the physical realization of a design, its environmental constraints and the particular test case under consideration. Few assumptions are necessary for a simple analysis, whereas a more elaborate analysis may demand many. The accuracy of the results is proportional to the validity and relevance of the assumptions. Consequently, the visualization, with the fewest assumptions, is used most frequently, whereas a costly simulation, whether numerical or within a test rig, is applied only to determine very specific aspects of the design.

This paper describes a system for finite-element mesh generation from geometric models. It illustrates model simulation of stresses and strains and demonstrates the system's potential and the general need for less complex analysis than is presently provided by three-dimensional finite-element analysis.

BUILD

During the 1960s, work on graphics at the Computer Laboratory of the University of Cambridge led to the establishment of the Computer Aided Design Group. Research focused on sculptured surfaces [Forrest 1969]. Early developments resulted in a modeler for shell structures, Multipatch [Armit 1970], for which a first finite-element analysis program was written [Gill 1972]. In the early 1970s research in volume modeling, BUILD-1 [Braid 1975], paved the road for a new generation of geometric modelers. BUILD-3 is the result of years of experience in volume modeling [Braid 1979b].

The BUILD modeler stores an object in terms of its boundary, which in turn is defined by the connected graph of vertices, edges, and faces using the winged-edge pointer structure [Baumgart 1972]. The graph expresses what shall here be referred to as the topology of the object. Topological entities such as vertices, edges and faces are associated with geometric entities, that is, points, curves and surfaces, which specify location and shape.

An object may be altered by changes in either topology or geometry. Euler operations [Braid 1979a] are transitions in the topology of an object which are valid with respect to the Euler-Poincaré formula. The complete, that is, sufficient and necessary set of operations is fairly small and contains operations such as *make-vertex-face* and *make-edge-vertex*. The Euler operations maintain a closed and orientable boundary and, hence, guarantee that the object remains a manifold, or well-formed polyhedron. The geometric entities may be changed independently of the topology. For example, the surface equations for a face may be changed without altering its topology. All operations for the creation and manipulation of objects are based on the above indivisible transitions.

Higher-level operations include the so-called set and local operations. *Set operations* are applied to primitive objects, such as cubes, cylinders and spheres, as well as to composite objects. The operations, *add, subtract* and *negate*, correspond respectively to the regularized Boolean operations on point sets, U^* (union), $-^*$ (difference), and c^* (complement) [Requicha and Voelcker 1977].

Local operations are applied to single objects. The operator *sweep* extends an object along a translation; similarly, *swing* integrates an object over the path of a rotation (Figure 1). A suite of local operations affects only a small subset of the overall object. For example, *tweak* (Figure 2) alters the geometry attached to topological entities, *chamfer* (Figure 3) inserts local topological detail and *set-surf* alters the surface equations for individual faces. The user is invited to create further operations to suit particular requirements.

The BUILD modeler can represent and manipulate a number of curve and surface types. Curves are either arcs, quadrics or B-spline approximations. Quadric, B-spline [Solomon 1983] and double-quadratic surfaces [Varady 1982] are incorporated, and procedures are provided for their evaluation and intersection. There is a general operator for the interrogation of geometric data which is

References pp. 98-100

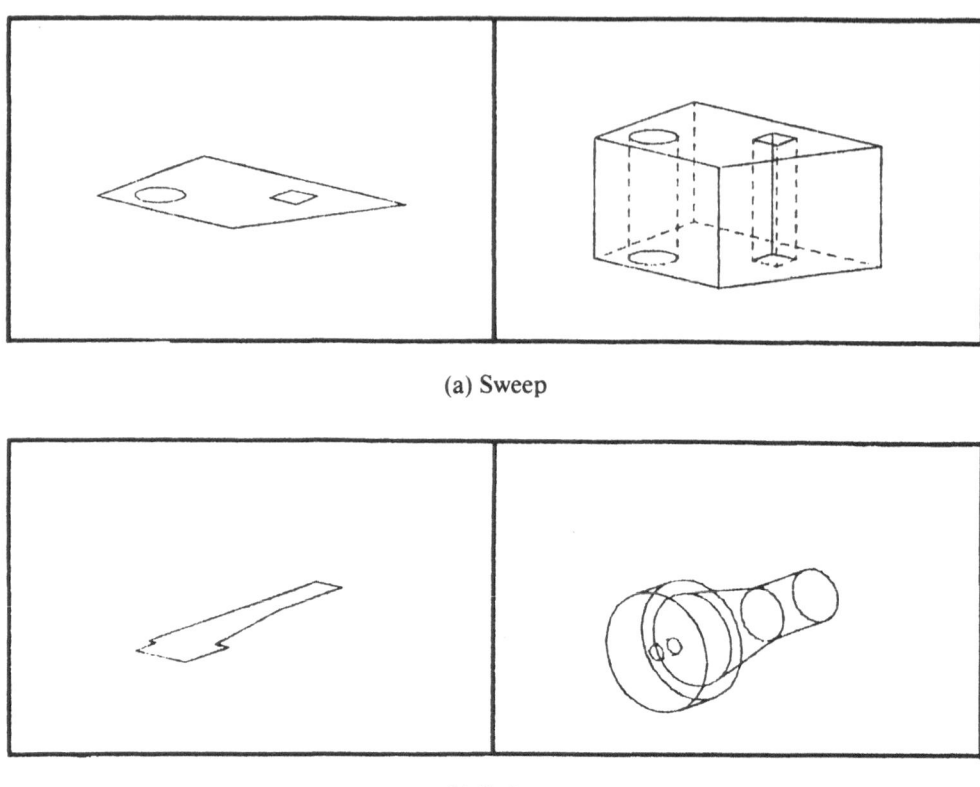

(a) Sweep

(b) Swing

Figure 1. *The local operations, sweep and swing.*

used internally to the program. This operator, together with routines for the traversal of the topological structure, simplifies protocols to support application programs.

The BUILD-3 modeler is written in Algol 68C and makes extensive use of abstract data types, operators and the facility of separate compilation [Braid and Hillyard 1977]. The setup as a workbench has encouraged the development of programs for dimensioning and tolerancing [Hillyard 1978], part classification [Kyprianou 1980] and finite-element mesh generation [Wördenweber 1981]. The following section describes in detail the algorithms for mesh generation and analysis used by the Omega program.

OMEGA

Topological Algorithms—The Omega program consists of two main algorithmic components: triangulation and refinement. *Triangulation* subdivides a two-dimensional polygon into triangles or a three-dimensional polyhedron into

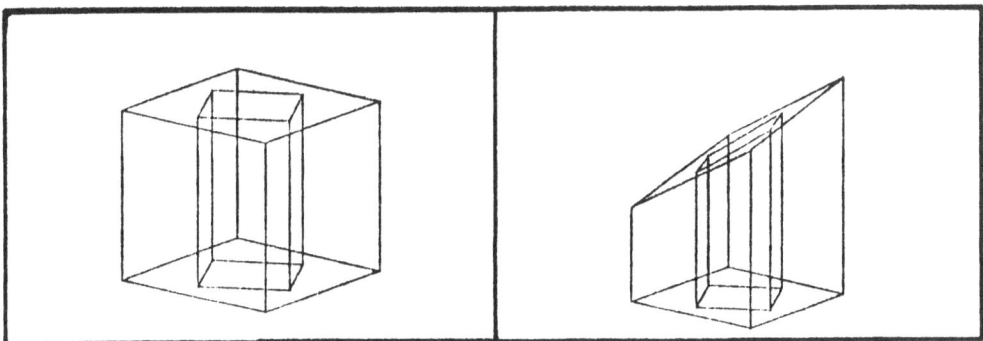

Figure 2. An example of tweaking to alter an object's geometry.

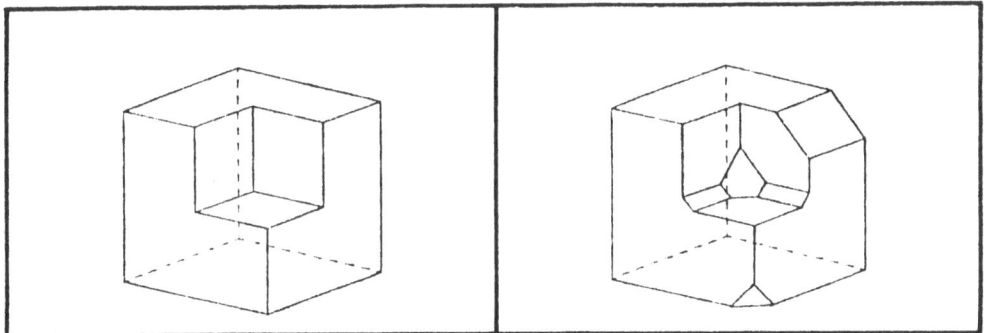

Figure 3. An example of chamfering to insert local detail.

tetrahedra. *Refinement* increases the number of edges, triangles or tetrahedra, or it may be used to convert all triangles in a mesh to quadrilaterals and all tetrahedra to hexahedra.

Consider a two-dimensional, planar face with V vertices, E straight edges and H holes. With at least one hole, the face is said to be multiply-connected and a special operation, OPj, is applied, which reduces the number of holes. The operation joins one hole loop to the perimeter loop by inserting two edges which are geometrically identical but topologically distinct. The edges are chosen such that they do not interfere with any other edge of the face, that is, they intersect with other edges in, at most, a common vertex. The resulting simple face can then be triangulated by iterative application of operation $OP1$, which replaces an edge-vertex-edge triplet with a new edge and creates a triangle between them. Again, the triplet has to be chosen such that the resulting triangle does not interfere with any vertex of the remaining face. There will, most certainly, be a choice of triplets, and preference criteria have to be chosen which will select the most suitable positions [Wördenweber 1981]. When the face is reduced to three vertices and edges, operation $OP0$ replaces all edges and vertices by one trian-

References pp. 98-100

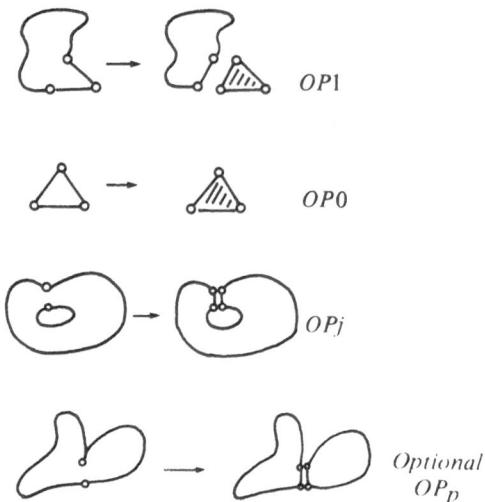

Figure 4. Operations for triangulation of two-dimensional polygons.

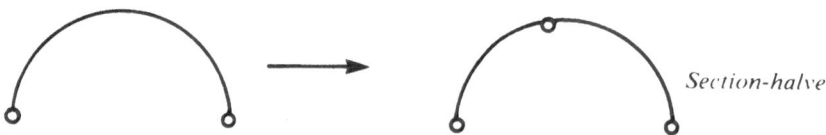

Figure 5. The one-dimensional refinement operation, section-halve.

gle. The operation OPp is optional for the triangulation of two-dimensional polygons and may be used to speed up the subdivision (Figure 4). All interference tests are based on intersection routines for planar triangles, straight edges and vertices and can be carried out in linear time after preprocessing for spatial ordering.

A refinement operation is a transition within a so-called shape grammar [Stiny 1975] and replaces a connected subset of a mesh by another set of elements. Refinement operations have in the past been used for pattern generation [Stiny 1977] and mesh refinement [Leyvraz 1976]. Special operations may now serve surface rendering [Wördenweber 1983b] and conversion of element type in a finite-element mesh [Wördenweber 1984]. Refinement operations are also used within triangulation in order to handle curvilinear geometry.

If the edges of a two-dimensional face are curved or the face is embedded in a curved surface, then edges may have to be divided before triangulation. For any curvilinear face a so-called *planar equivalent* can be computed, the triangulation of which is valid both for the planar and curvilinear face. The planar equivalent is constructed from the curvilinear face by the substitution of planar for curvilinear geometry and by the application of the one-dimensional refinement op-

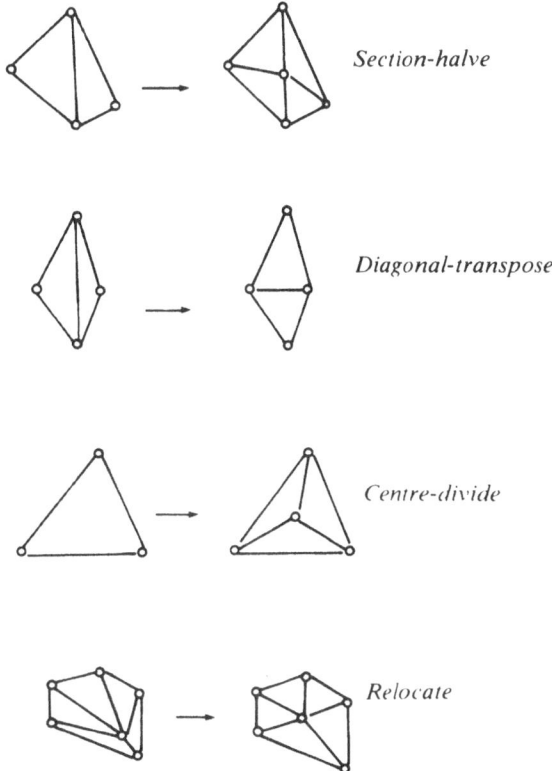

Section-halve

Diagonal-transpose

Centre-divide

Relocate

Figure 6. *Two-dimensional refinement operations.*

eration, *section-halve* (Figure 5), if necessary for the consistency of the resulting face. With the planar equivalent, all computations for the triangulation can be carried out in planar space. No curvilinear intersections have to be computed.

For three-dimensional mesh generation, the two-dimensional triangulation is applied to all faces of the three-dimensional object and the planar equivalent constructed for the resulting surface triangulation using the two-dimensional *section-halve* and *diagonal-transpose* operations (Figure 6). Interior cavities of a multiply-connected object are joined to the perimeter by application of the three-dimensional operation OPj. Operations OPi, $i=0,1,2,3$, subtract tetrahedra from the object along i triangles; and operation OPi is carried out in preference to $OP(i+1)$. Operation OPp cuts a toroid at a triangular cross section and thus reduces the genus of an object. The set of operations is closed over the set of manifolds (Figure 7). According to the Euler-Poincaré formula, the triangulation of a two-dimensional polygon contains the smallest possible number of triangles. It is coarse for three-dimensional polyhedra for which no formula can determine the minimum number of tetrahedra.

References pp. 98-100

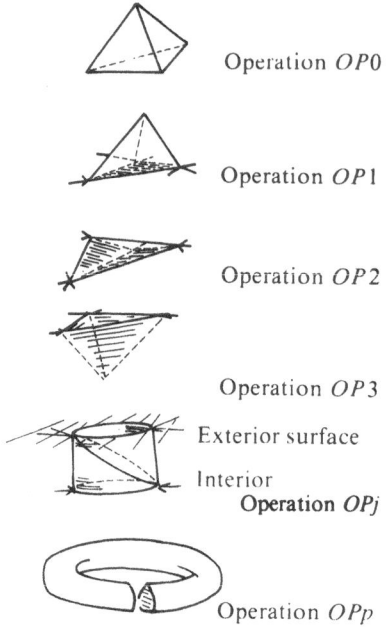

Operation $OP0$

Operation $OP1$

Operation $OP2$

Operation $OP3$

Exterior surface

Interior

Operation OPj

Operation OPp

Figure 7. Three-dimensional triangulation operations.

Implementation of Topological Algorithms—The mesh, whether surface or volume, is a faceted representation of the geometric model. Its topology reproduces exactly the topology of the initial object, but it is presented in a simple format compared with the complexity of the winged-edge pointer structure.

The geometry of the mesh is implicit and references the data within the geometric modeler. An approximate geometry may be associated and maintained within the mesh. Every triangle can keep account of three, six, or ten points and their respective surface normals. From this extra information, point position and normal may be computed over the parametric triangular patch using linear, quadratic or cubic shape functions respectively.

Because of the exact topology, the mesh may be updated incrementally to keep in step with changes made to the model. The affected subset has to be cut out of the mesh and a new graft computed to fit to the new part of the surface in the model.

A face with V vertices is triangulated in $O(V \log V)$ time. It takes $O(F)$ time to compute the surface triangulation for F faces and between $O(V \log V)$ and $O(V^2)$ for the subsequent volume triangulation. For a typical object (Figure 8) of 47 faces, 132 edges and 87 vertices, it takes 4 seconds of CPU time on an IBM/370 to compute the surface triangulation of 172 triangles, and 30 seconds of CPU time for the volume triangulation of 257 tetrahedra.

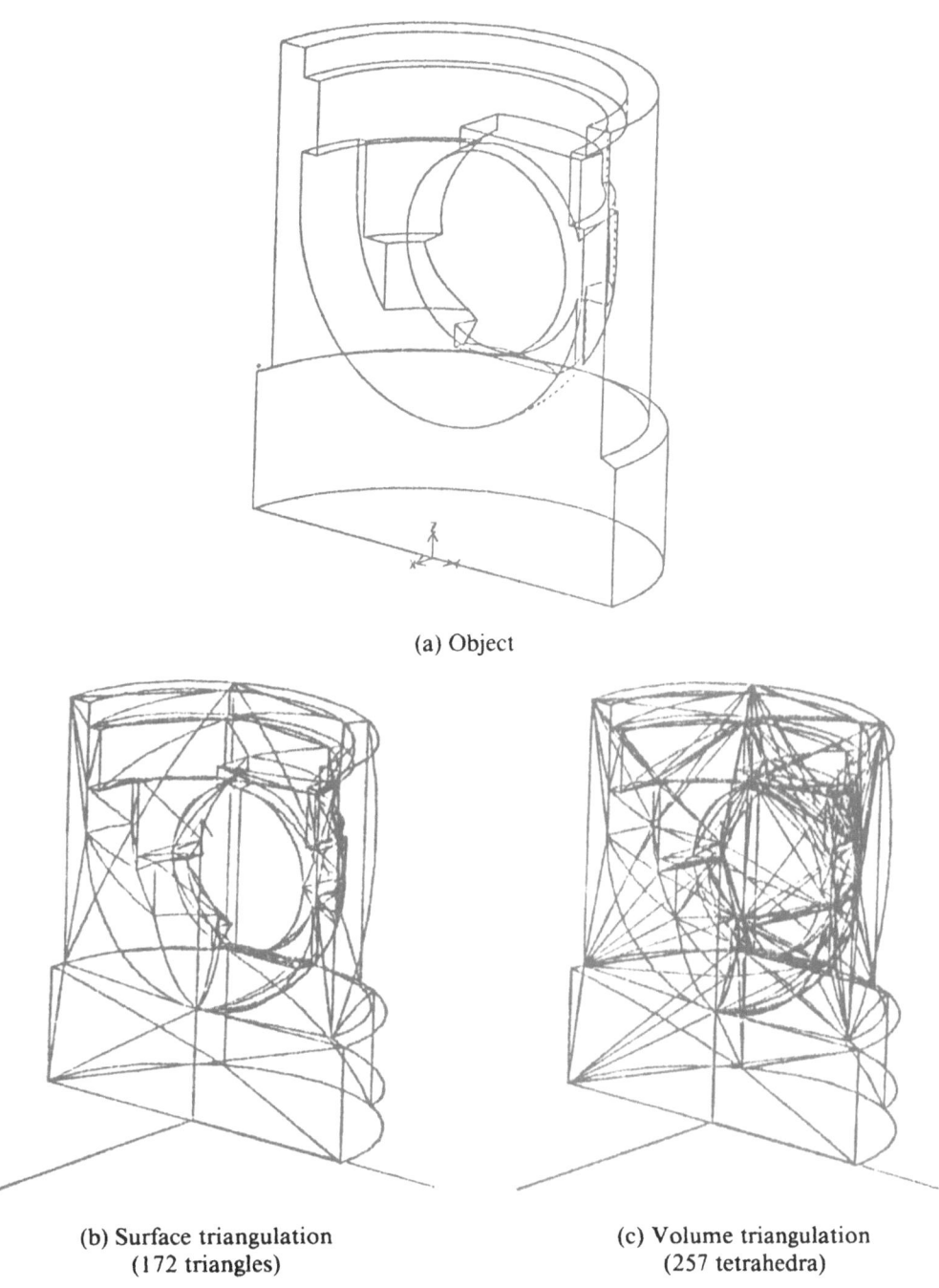

(a) Object

(b) Surface triangulation
(172 triangles)

(c) Volume triangulation
(257 tetrahedra)

Figure 8. *Surface and volume triangulation of a piston.*

References pp. 98-100

Numerical Algorithms—The meshes resulting from the triangulation are coarse and may require further processing to become suitable for finite-element analysis. For instance, skew or distorted elements should be avoided and the elements should be distributed more densely in areas of higher stress concentrations and less densely in unimportant parts of the object. The refinement operations can be used to affect mesh densities, geometric resolution of the approximate geometry, shapes and patterns of elements within the mesh as well as element types. Meshes of triangles or tetrahedra can be improved by a series of refinement operations, such as *section-halve, diagonal-transpose, centre-divide* or *relocate*, all of which affect only a small set of elements at a time and also maintain compatibility between elements. The refinement operations for conversion of element type (Figure 9) have a global effect unless transition elements are employed to ensure compatibility with the surrounding mesh. There is sufficient scope in refinement to enable generation of conventional finite-element meshes and still to welcome new research and development in analysis.

An experimental analysis program has been implemented in conjunction with the mesh generator to analyse two-dimensional parts with respect to stresses and strains. It handles meshes with triangular or quadrilateral, linear or quadratic isoparametric elements and was written to test estimators for discretization error and clusters for mesh subdivision as described below.

A comparison of refined and unrefined meshes and the corresponding change in the results of the analysis provide an indication of the error and inform about convergence. The computation of residual forces does not require a comparison with a previous analysis run and is a valuable measure of absolute error. At present, a good estimator of the discretization error can be computed *a posteriori* from the residuals along element boundaries [Biederman and Babuska 1982]. The estimates are reliable in a suitably dense and convergent mesh but require the absence of singularities. With knowledge about the discretization er-

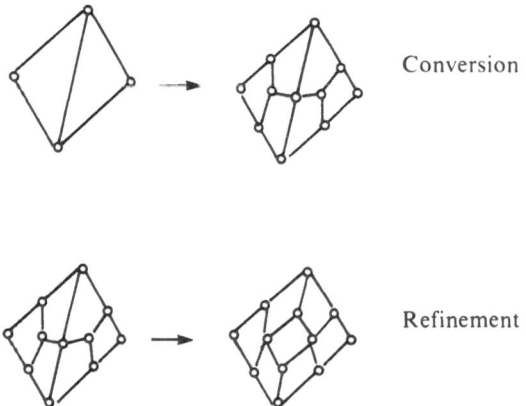

Conversion

Refinement

Figure 9. *Change of element type and refinement of a mesh.*

ror, the accuracy of a subsequent analysis run can be improved by use of higher-order elements (p-conversion) or by increasing their number (h-conversion) [Szabo and Babuska 1982].

The triangulation and refinement algorithms create nodes and elements in a fairly random order. To reduce the size of the stiffness matrix, an algorithm for renumbering could be employed at a cost of $O(N \log N)$ [Akyus and Utku 1968]. Alternatively, the mesh may be treated as a collection of what shall here be referred to as clusters [Wördenweber 1983a]. Each *cluster* contains a connected set of elements or clusters. A cluster is formed, at present, by seeding a mesh at a number of elements and growing the clusters outwards from the seed points until they touch. During Gaussian elimination, the degrees of freedom internal to a cluster are eliminated, and the stiffness system is solved for the degrees of freedom on the boundary and back-substituted into individual clusters. A simple, linear order algorithm is adequate to number elements and nodes within clusters. The cluster subdivision can be used with some of the commercially available analysis programs [Egeland and Araldsen 1974]. It will be indispensable with the new generation of adaptive mesh generators and analysis systems.

Implementation of Numerical Algorithms—Both h- and p-conversion have been used successfully for *adaptive mesh generation*, that is, mesh refinement according to error estimates of successive analysis runs. A program such as Fears [Babuska and Rheinboldt 1982] starts with a coarse mesh. It inserts more elements where discretization errors are large and thus refines the mesh until it meets cost or error bounds. Currently the complete analysis has to be repeated after every refinement step. If more were known about the propagation of the perturbation introduced by refinement itself, relaxation could continue within clusters and over a number of iterations.

The Omega System—Most operations for mesh generation and refinement are local to Omega and work on an internal data structure. The data structure for surface triangulation contains topological and geometrical entities. In addition it keeps a record of corresponding topological entities in the database of the geometric modeler. Every topological entity points to a set of topological or geometric entities:

polyhedron	$o = (m_i, ->w)$	$i=1,...,k$
mesh	$m = (t_i)$	$i=1,...,l$
triangle	$t = (e_i, v_i, s, ->x)$	$i=1,2,3$
edge	$e = (v_i, t_i, ->y)$	$i=1,2$
vertex	$v = (p, ->z)$	
shape function	$s = $ (coefficients of N_{ij})	
point	$p = $ (vector)	

For example, the polyhedron (o) contains a set of meshes (m_i) and indirectly references the original model ($->w$). Here w,x,y,z refer to object, face, edge and

References pp. 98-100

vertex entities of the geometric model, respectively. N is the shape function for the parametric patch, which varies according to the spatial coordinates of the parametric patch. The database may be implemented using, for example, the relational model.

Only a small interface has to be provided by the geometric modeler in order for the application program to access and traverse the topology of the model and interpret its geometry. The algorithm for surface triangulation expects the model for a three-dimensional object to consist of a set of connected faces. It is not a strict requirement, although it does assist the algorithm for triangulation if no curve of any edge and no surface of any face subtends an angle greater than $180°$.

A number of simple functions should be provided by the modeler for retrieval of topological and geometric entities and for determination of simple intersections. The following protocol suffices.

$$\text{Topological: object() } -> w$$
$$\text{faces}(w) -> x_i$$
$$\text{edges}(x) -> y_i$$
$$\text{vertices}(y) -> z_i$$

$$\text{Geometrical: intersection of straight line with face } (str,x) -> p$$
$$\text{intersection of plane with edge } (pl,y) -> p$$
$$\text{location } (z) -> p$$
$$\text{face normal } (p,x) -> \text{vector}$$
$$\text{edge direction } (p,y) -> \text{vector}$$

With the above data structure and protocol, surface triangulation and refinement become processes independent of the geometric modeler.

NAIVE USE

So far, analysis has been treated solely as an application of geometric modeling, where the part to be analysed happened to be the object modeled in the CAD system. It is apparent to any analyst that test objects are rarely identical with the model for design and that they have to be derived from the model under consideration for particular load cases. Also, the test objects require additional data, called attributes, which define material properties, loads and restraints. This last section of the paper illustrates the benefits that may be gained from a closer liaison between geometric modeling and finite-element analysis and demonstrates the need for further research and development in CAD.

Immediate Application—In many cases, the amount of detail in the model exceeds that required for analysis. The analyst may choose a cross section through a three-dimensional object and use plane strain analysis on the result-

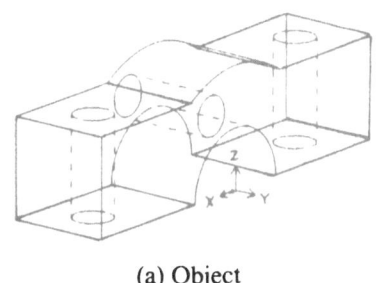

(a) Object

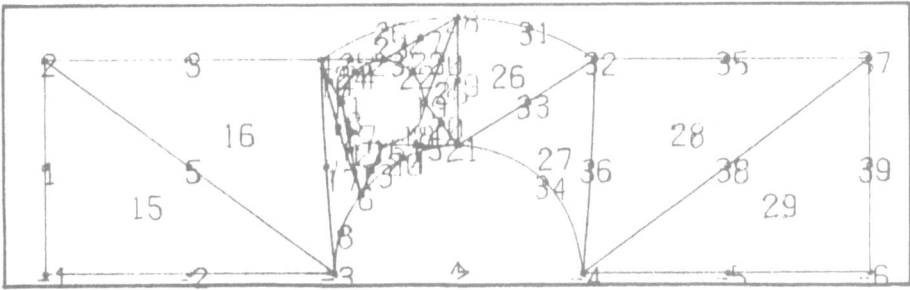

(b) Two-dimensional mesh

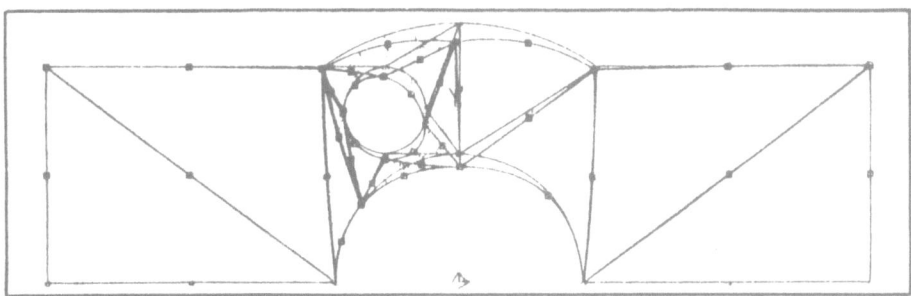

(c) Plane strain analysis (see color plates following p. 158).

Figure 10. *Analysis of a cross section of a test object.*

ing two-dimensional mesh (Figure 10). Many rotational parts are represented adequately by an axisymmetric section (Figure 11). The surface triangulation (Figure 12) of a three-dimensional model may lead to an analysis using shell elements for plane stress. Alternatively, and with the same surface mesh, the boundary-integral method can be used for analysis of the interior, provided that there are no changes of material properties or body forces under the surface. For the same analysis, but using the finite-element method, a three-dimensional mesh of the volume is necessary (Figure 13). A simple volume triangulation is sufficient for homogeneous material. Inhomogeneous materials may be mod-

References pp. 98-100

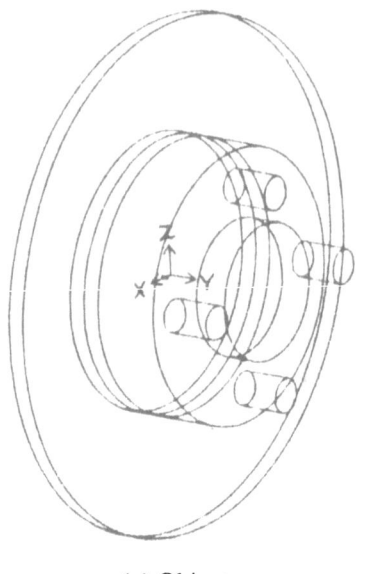

(a) Object

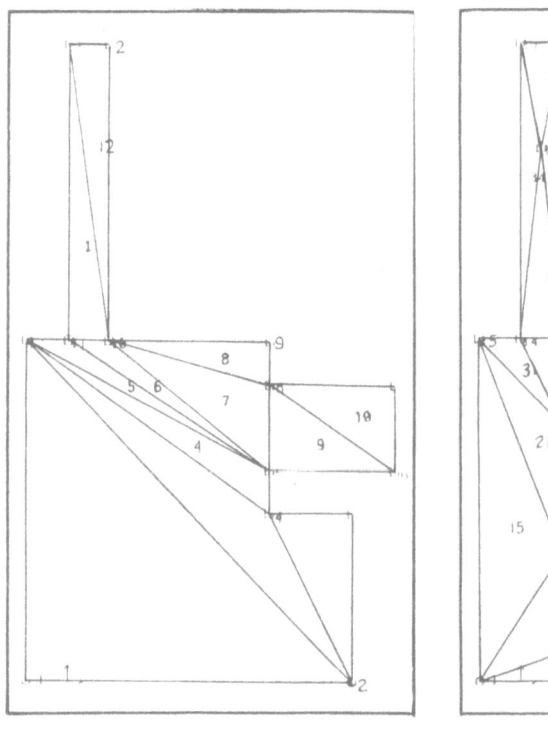

(b) Simple mesh   (c) Refined mesh

Figure 11. *Axisymmetric section of an object.*

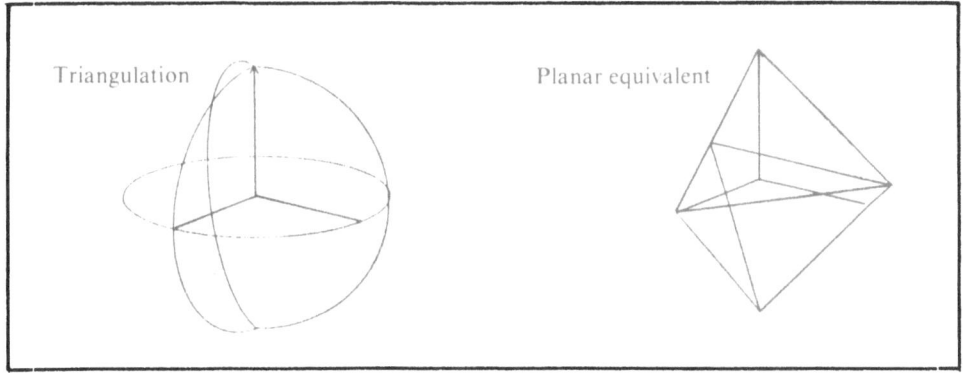

(a) Triangulation of a sphere

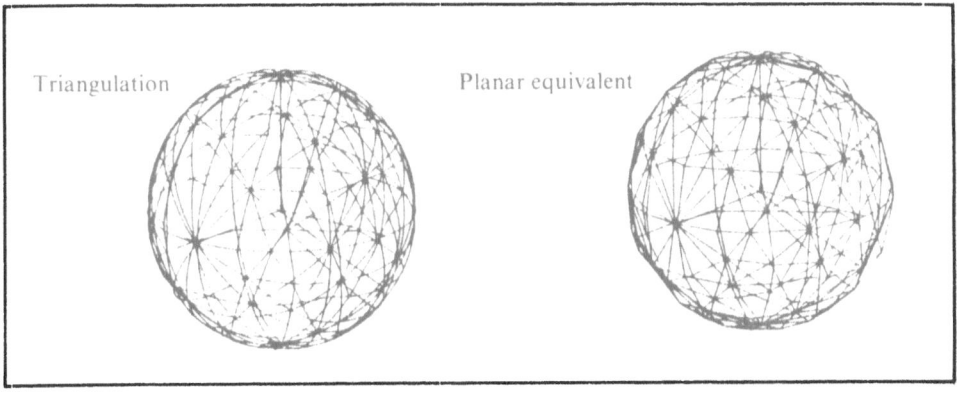

(b) Refined triangulation

Figure 12. *Surface triangulation of a sphere.*

eled by separate surfaces around regions of distinct material properties. In this case, the mesh can be constructed by volume triangulation between the different layers. The same technique may be employed to mesh infinite regions surrounding a test object.

Topological Features—It is one of the properties of the triangulation that a mesh, whether surface or volume, is isomorphic, that is, topologically identical with the model. Unlike other faceting algorithms, which are not based on the topological framework of the model, triangulation is consistent in that it does not accidentally miss small detail. If this detail is insignificant with respect to an analysis, it must be removed explicitly.

The geometric modeler may offer a set of routines for further interpretation of topology and geometry. For example, it may have procedures to determine whether a curve or surface is convex or concave at a point or throughout its

References pp. 98-100

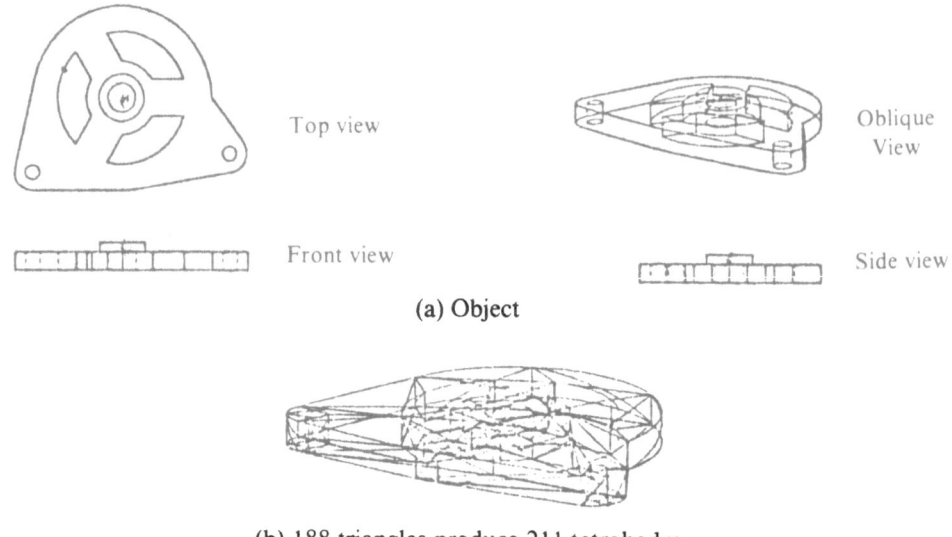

Top view

Oblique View

Front view

Side view

(a) Object

(b) 188 triangles produce 211 tetrahedra

Figure 13. *Volume triangulation of an object.*

scope along edge or face respectively. It may be able to distinguish between translational and rotational parts or determine whether a set of faces is either a hole or a boss. Knowledge about features such as these is valuable not only for the purpose of part classification, but also assists object modification prior to analysis. The remainder of this section lists four possible examples of the term *feature*, all of which are very relevant to geometric modeling and its application.

Error estimates become unreliable in the presence of weak singularities, such as sharp, concave edges. They may mislead in the proximity of strong singularities, such as cracks, point loads and restraints. For example, an adaptive mesh generator would concentrate refinement around a point force and the process

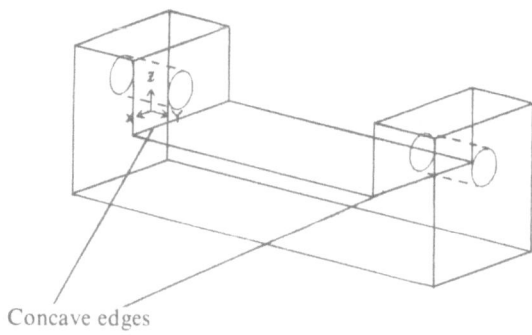

Concave edges

Figure 14. *Marking of simple features on an object prior to mesh generation.*

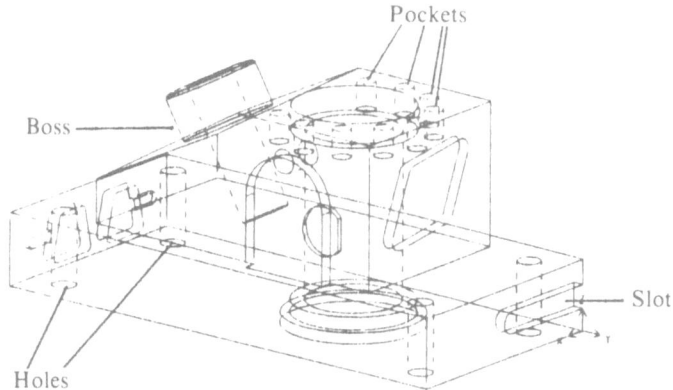

Figure 15. *Complex features of an object.*

would start to diverge, unless the force were distributed along the edge or face of the object. Concave edges and point loads represent *simple features* of the object [Allan 1978]. Their presence could be determined prior to mesh generation and marked on the model (Figure 14).

A combination of simple features indicates a *complex feature* [Kyprianou 1980], such as a hole, pocket, slot, groove or boss. The complex feature need not be relevant to the analysis. For example, a row of holes in a connecting rod may be of particular concern to the analyst or could easily be substituted with an ordinary rod of different material properties. In either case, when the user has to specify a load case, he or she should also have the option of selectively including or disregarding complex features (Figure 15).

The connecting rod of the above example may be of little concern except for its function as a connection element. Then a simple beam could take the place of the rod. It is important that the user be able to idealize the object for analysis and even reduce the dimension of the components. The *faceset* or the *skeleton*, that is, the representation by centre lines, is the third type of feature and provides the relevant information to assist the user with the idealisation of the object (Figure 16).

Finally, features may be used solely within the geometric modeler or, at other times, the information should be carried over into the mesh generator. In a set of gears, for example, parts of the object are repeated. In this case only a prototype of the repeated part, or *factor*, has to be meshed and its stiffness matrix computed. Subsequently, subelements or superelements may be used to analyse the object.

CONCLUSION

Full utilization of the potential in geometric modeling enhances the flexibility of the mesh generator and analysis program. More importantly, the geometric

References pp. 98-100

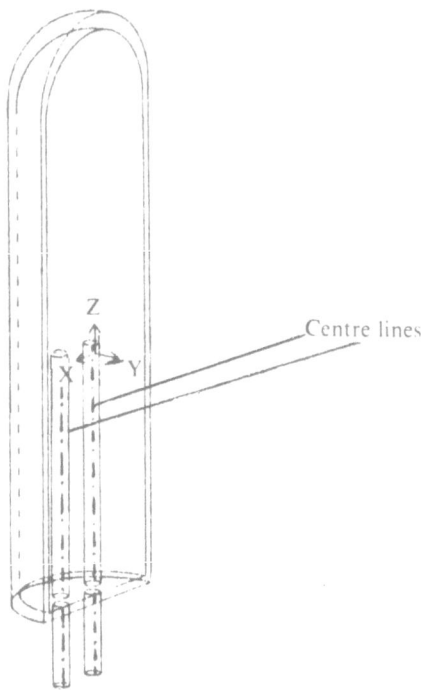

Figure 16. The skeleton, a representation of centre lines used for idealisation of the object.

modeler and the mesh generator together enable the user to analyse his design on more than one level. The modeler offers aids for visualization, provides measurements, such as sizes and angles, and can compute mass properties and moments. Simple features identify likely trouble spots or flaws in the design. An inexpensive finite-element analysis can be carried out on a cross section or axisymmetric view. Triangulation of the surface allows finite-element analysis of the shell and boundary-integral analysis of the volume. A full-fledged finite-element analysis of the volume can be graded according to the amount of geometric and topological detail included in the actual test object. Throughout, error estimates provide the user with the necessary insight into the relevance and validity of results obtained. Thus, the analysis is available simply as a design tool for experienced and inexperienced users.

REFERENCES

[Akyus and Utku 1968]
F. A. Akyus and S. Utku, "An Automatic Node-Relabeling Scheme for Band-Width Minimization of Stiffness Matrices," *AIAA Journal*, Vol. 6, No. 4, April 1968, pp. 728–730.

[Allan 1978]
D. K. Allan, "Classification and Coding," Monograph No. 2, Brigham Young University, Provo Utah, 1978.

[Armit 1970]
A. P. Armit, "Computer Systems for Interactive Design of Three-Dimensional Shapes," Ph.D. Dissertation, Computer Laboratory, University of Cambridge, Cambridge, England, 1970.

[Babuska and Rheinboldt 1982]
I. Babuska and W. C. Rheinboldt, "A Survey of *A Posteriori* Error Estimates and Adaptive Approaches in the Finite Element Method," Technical Note BN-981, University of Maryland, College Park, Maryland, 1982.

[Baumgart 1972]
B. G. Baumgart, "Winged Edge Polyhedron Representation," Computer Science Department Report No. STAN-CS-320, Stanford University, Stanford, California, 1972.

[Biederman and Babuska 1982]
M. Biederman and I. Babuska, "The Finite Element Method for Parabolic Equations, *A Posteriori* Error Estimators and Adaptive Approaches," Technical Note BN-983/4, University of Maryland, College Park, Maryland, 1982.

[Braid 1975]
I. C. Braid, "The Synthesis of Solids Bounded by Many Faces," *Communications of the ACM*, Vol. 18, No. 4, April 1975, pp. 209–216.

[Braid 1979a]
I. C. Braid, "Notes on a Geometric Modeler," CAD Group Document 101, Computer Laboratory, University of Cambridge, Cambridge, England, 1979.

[Braid 1979b]
I. C. Braid, "Geometric Modeling — Ten Years On," CAD Group Document 103, Computer Laboratory, University of Cambridge, Cambridge, England, 1979.

[Braid and Hillyard 1977]
I. C. Braid and R. C. Hillyard, "Geometric Modeling in Algol 68," CAD Group Document 92, Computer Laboratory, University of Cambridge, Cambridge, England, 1977.

[Egeland and Araldsen 1974]
O. Egeland and P. O. Araldsen, "Sesam-69—A General Purpose Finite Element Method Program," *Computers & Structures*, Vol. 4, January 1974, pp. 41–68.

[Forrest 1969]
A. R. Forrest, "Curves and Surfaces for Computer-Aided Design," Ph.D. Dissertation, Computer Laboratory, University of Cambridge, Cambridge, England, 1969.

[Gill 1972]
J. I. Gill, "Computer-Aided Design of Shell Structures Using the Finite Element Method," Ph.D. Dissertation. Computer Laboratory, University of Cambridge, Cambridge, England, 1972.

[Hillyard 1978]
R. Hillyard, "Dimensions and Tolerances in Shape Design," Ph.D. Dissertation, Computer Laboratory, University of Cambridge, Cambridge, England, 1978.

[Kyprianou 1980]
L. K. Kyprianou, "Shape Classification in Computer-Aided Design," Ph.D. Dissertation, Computer Laboratory, University of Cambridge, Cambridge, England, 1980.

[Leyvraz 1976]
R. Leyvraz, "Iterative Generation of Optimal Triangular Grids for the Solution of 2-Dimensional Field Problems," Proceedings of COMPUMAG (Oxford, England, March 31-April 2, 1976), Rutherford Laboratories, SRC, Chilton, Didcot, Oxon., England, 1976.

[Requicha and Voelcker 1977]
A. A. G. Requicha and H. B. Voelcker, "Constructive Solid Geometry," Technical Memo No. 25, Production Automation Project, University of Rochester, Rochester, New York, 1977.

[Solomon 1983]
B. J. Solomon, "Surface Intersections for Solid Modeling," Ph.D. Dissertation, Computer Laboratory, University of Cambridge, Cambridge, England, 1983.

[Stiny 1975]
G. Stiny, *Pictorial and Formal Aspects of Shape and Shape Grammars*, Birkhauser Verlag, Basel, Switzerland, 1975.

[Stiny 1977]
G. Stiny, "Ice Ray: A Note on the Generation of Chinese Lattice Designs," *Environment and Planning B*, Vol. 4, No. 1, June 1977, pp. 89–99.

[Szabo and Babuska 1982]
B. J. Szabo and I. Babuska, "Stress Approximation by the h- and p-Version of the Finite Element Method," Report WV/CCM-82/1, Center for Computational Mathematics, Washington University, St. Louis, Missouri, 1982.

[Varady 1982]
T. Varady, "An Experimental System for Interactive Design and Manufacture of Sculptured Surfaces," *Computers in Industry*, Vol. 3, Nos. 1 and 2, March and June 1982, pp. 125–135.

[Wördenweber 1981]
B. Wördenweber, "Automatic Mesh Generation of 2- and 3-Dimensional Curvilinear Manifolds," Ph.D. Dissertation (available as Computer Laboratory Technical Report No. 18), University of Cambridge, Cambridge, England, 1981.

[Wördenweber 1983a]
B. Wördenweber, "Finite-Element Mesh Generation from Geometric Models," *COMPEL, International Journal for Computation and Mathematics in Electrical and Electronic Engineering*, Vol. 1, No. 4, 1983, pp. 23–33.

[Wördenweber 1983b]
B. Wördenweber, "Surface Triangulation for Picture Production," *IEEE Computer Graphics and Applications*, Vol. 3, No. 8, November 1983, pp. 45–51.

[Wördenweber 1984]
B. Wördenweber, "Finite Element Mesh Generation," accepted for publication, *Computer Aided Design Journal*, 1984.

DISCUSSION

Christopher Brown *(University of Rochester)*

This is a general question to all finite element meshers. If your general computer resource were relatively parallel (I mean you had a hundred powerful computing engines with shared memories), how would it change your perception of the problems?

Wördenweber

Can we really make use of parallel processing with benefit in mesh generation? The answer to that is most certainly yes. You can readily see that with something like clusters. It would be an ideal test situation for a powerful engine to see whether you could do the meshing operations within the clusters, then further in to the boundaries of clusters or higher clusters and back. You can do that independently through even adjacent clusters. Yes, it most certainly would be useful.

B. Wördenweber

John Woodwark *(University of Bath)*

Could you say a little bit more about your clustering element? In particular, how do you choose the seed tetrahedron for the clustering processing?

Wördenweber

At the moment I don't really choose; I just seed and see what happens. If somehow two small clusters start running into each other I just merge them. If I have one cluster getting too big, I seed it again.

Woodwark

But you must have some way of choosing the seeds to start with.

Wördenweber

Statistics tells me that if I just do a random sample I get away with murder. Perhaps you can come up with a better method and tell me afterwards.

SESSION II
USE OF SOLID MODELS
IN PRODUCTION TECHNOLOGY

Session Chairman
MICHEL A. MELKANOFF

*University of California
Los Angeles, California*

THE APPLICATION OF GEOMETRIC MODELING TO METAL CASTING TECHNOLOGY

JOHN T. BERRY and J. A. M. BOULET

Georgia Institute of Technology
Atlanta, Georgia

ABSTRACT

In the course of a large scale cooperative research effort between two major universities, The Georgia Institute of Technology and The University of Michigan, several geometric modeling packages have been examined and utilized in the building of various casting/rigging configurations. Modelers scrutinized include TIPS-1, PADL-1, ROMULUS and CAT-1. The test castings involved have included simple laboratory shapes as well as industrial product parts.

In general, we have found that acceptable model forms can be built without major difficulty. In some cases, depending for example upon the availability of primitives, certain approximations are necessary; in other instances the limited number of allowable statements has dictated such approximations. Furthermore, we have learned that work remains to be done on the questions of blending and the representation of other patternmaking needs such as parting line determination, an area in which one surface-type modeler, DUCT, has already made extensive progress.

The most pressing needs of metal casting engineers working in this area, however, are applications packages to provide geometric modelers with the general purpose physical simulation schemes now available and the special purpose casting-oriented simulators under development.

This paper will describe the CADCAST team's experience with the present generation of modelers, as well as its work in developing various applications packages which are intended for integration into package suites designed to fill the needs of the industry in the near future.

INTRODUCTION

There are many potential roles for geometric modeling in the solidification processing area. These roles encompass both the larger aspects of foundry engineering, such as the evolution of the layout of plant and equipment assemblies, and the more detailed aspects of the casting design and its relation to the rigging associated with the filling and feeding of the mold cavity.

The modeling of the casting/rigging system itself represents an important initial task for the practicing foundry engineer. At present, the foundry engineer is most often presented with a drawing or set of drawings which describes the geometry and topology of a casting on which to make a quotation. Sometimes, however, he receives a pattern or set of patterns. In the future, these forms of communication are likely to be replaced by sets of tapes or discs, or by the direct linking of computer systems used by the foundry and the engineer.

Having received the basic casting design information, the foundry engineer will add the rigging, that is, the gating and risering systems.* To undertake this, it appears most likely that a first approximation will be obtained by using one of the currently available commercial rigging design software packages, such as AFSoftware, Novacast, or CRUSADER [see References] as well as those methods presented in recent articles [Kotschi 1983, Ruddle and Suschill 1983].

One of the tasks generally required here is the provision of risers or feeder heads, which will provide a reservoir of molten metal sufficient to feed the shrinkage occurring during the cooling and freezing of the liquid metal in the casting proper. A further important task is integration of the total rigging system, which promotes the quiescent entry of molten metal through a system of runners and gates into the mold cavity as well as the feeding action through the feeders. The presently available first-level software library for rigging design already referred to is not generally based on a geometric modeler, but provides useful working data for the foundry engineer by using some simple, scientifically based axioms and certain well-established items of codified empirical information. Such systems are normally run on personal computers or

---

* *Gating System: That part of a casting which conducts the molten metal from the entrance into the mold through to the mold cavity associated with the shape of the cast. In turn, the elements consist of the pouring basin, the down sprue, the various runner bar elements, and finally the ingates which admit the molten metal to the actual mold cavity for the shape to be cast. Specialized elements that might be incorporated into such a system are a sprue well and slag traps which are designed to promote cleanness of the metal stream and in some cases a reaction chamber for* in situ *treatment of the molten metal, as in the Inmold™ process. See Figure 5.*

Risering System: The part of a casting rigging composed of risers, often described as riser heads or feeder heads. They are essentially meant to act as reservoirs of molten metal which will feed the liquid metal within the mold cavity for the part to be cast as it cools and subsequently solidifies. They are generally located adjacent to or in very close proximity to the mold cavity.

microcomputers. The riser design of such programs is based upon Chvorinov's modulus approach [Chvorinov 1940] as modified by others, while the gating system portion follows the Bernoulli-based approach described in the literature (see, for example, [Flinn 1963]). Typical tasks that such software can accomplish are dimensioning and positioning of risers, placement of chills (*i.e.*, localized heat sinks), padding or modification of casting design features, and design of a gating system.

The total rigging system so designed would be the starting point for the geometric model building which would then take place. Here the foundry methods engineer would create, on the computer, the three-dimensional model of the object to be cast, together with its feeding and gating system.

In the course of the Georgia Institute of Technology/University of Michigan CADCAST program, various castings have been modeled at the Georgia Institute employing a variety of modelers: TIPS-1, PADL-1, ROMULUS, CAT-1 and DUCT [see References]. Though none of these programs is capable of modeling all casting geometries, the range of shapes that each of these programs can model is remarkable. The cost of licensing one of these modelers varies from about $250 to $100,000. The size of computer necessary to achieve reasonable response times with one of these modelers ranges from one with a 128 kilobyte memory and a 16-bit processor to one with a 512 kilobyte memory and a 32-bit processsor. Sample shapes modeled by some of these programs are illustrated in Figures 1 through 4. On the average, the number of commands entered by the user in modeling one of these shapes is between twenty and forty.

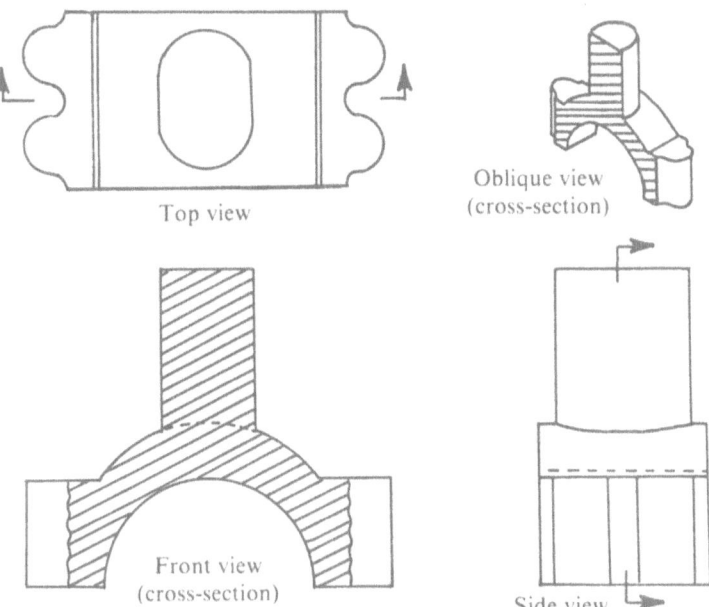

Figure 1. *Bearing cap modeled with PADL-1.*

References pp. 115-116

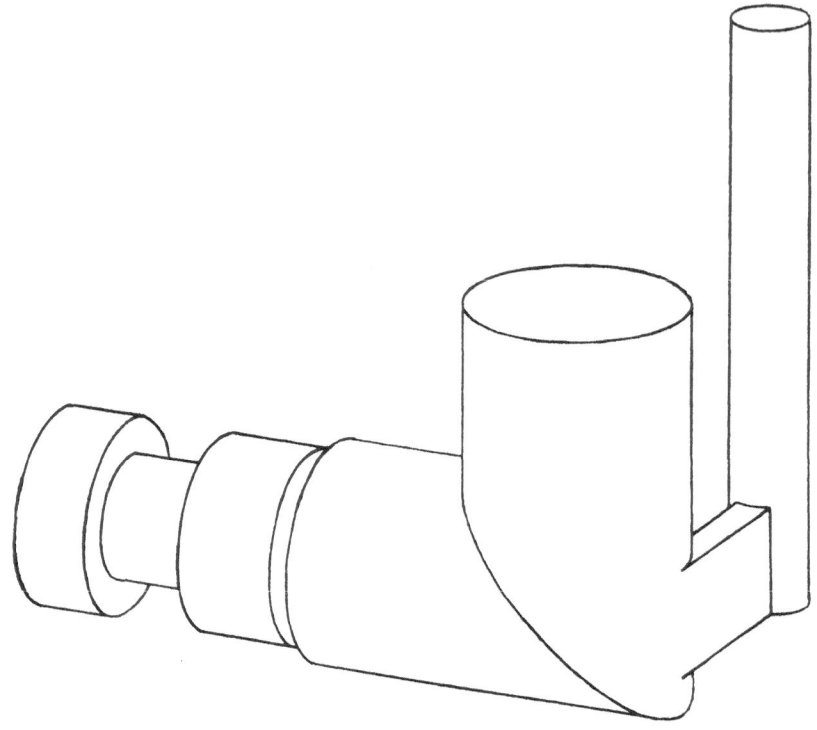

Figure 2. *Test casting modeled with ROMULUS.*

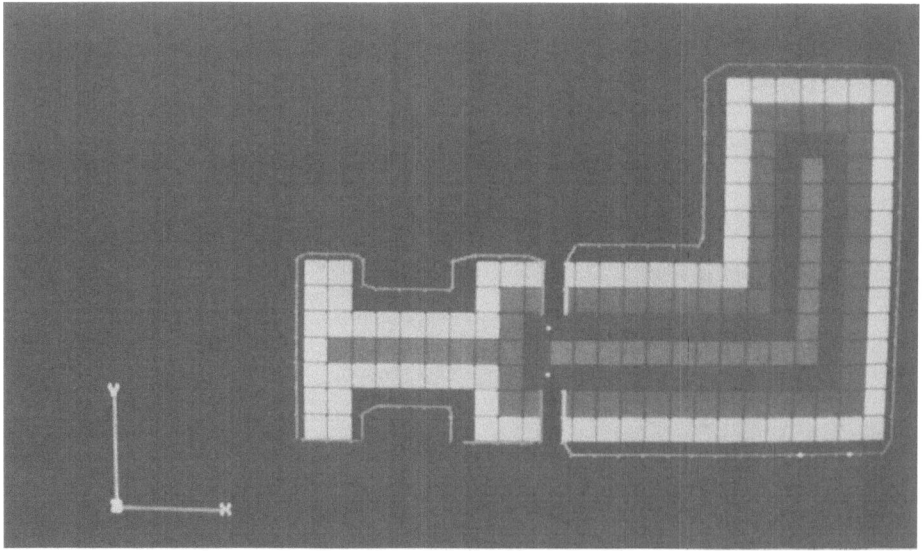

Figure 3. *Cross section of a casting/rigging system modeled with CAT-1,*
showing simulated temperature variation (see color plates following p. 158).

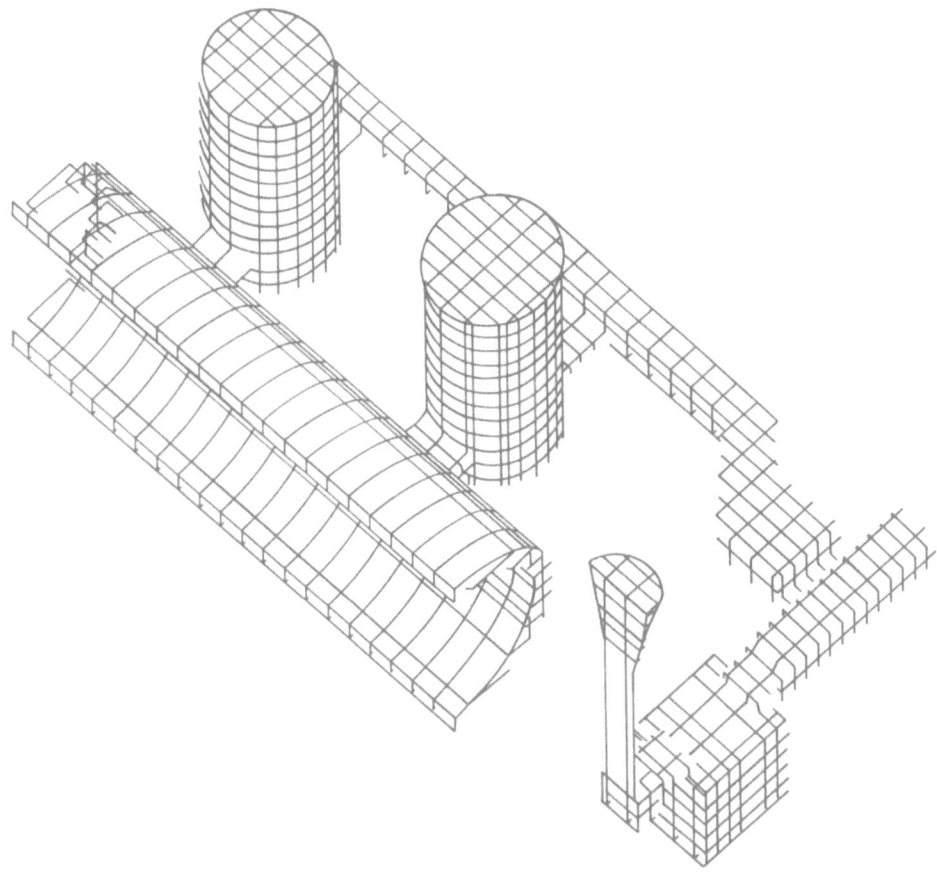

Figure 4. *Machinability test piece with commercial foundry rigging, modeled using TIPS-1.*

Clearly many highly complex industrial castings will need an extremely large number of command statements. Consequently, modelers constrained to a small number of statements are of only limited use in describing commercial castings. In addition, only some modelers are capable of blending surfaces; fewer still are capable of locating a parting line.* DUCT, however, has this latter feature [Welbourn 1982]. Regarding complex surfaces showing double curvature, some modelers, such as TIPS-1, do permit insertion of user-defined

---

*Parting Line: *In order to separate the sand mold from the pattern in a convenient manner, the patternmaker designates a parting line (or split line) which will separate the upper part of the mold (the cope) from the lower part (the drag). Although in simple cases the line concerned will remain on one plane (the parting plane), in more complex shapes a series of planes and even portions of curved surfaces may be involved. Location of this plane is currently regarded as one of the important aspects of the art of patternmaking.*

elements. Such capabilities are extremely desirable in any modeler to be used in connection with castings applications.

MODELING REAL CASTING ASSEMBLIES

One of the castings modeled, depicted in Figure 4, was in fact poured in a commercial foundry [Berry *et al.* 1984]. Although the casting itself is simple in configuration, being essentially a thick-walled hollow cylinder, the rigging is of special interest because of its complex design.

The casting, a machinability test log, is poured and fed through a complicated series of shapes, each having its own particular role. The system concerned contains three major features:

- A gating system which conducts clean molten metal into the casting cavity in an even manner,

- A reaction chamber which permits the treatment and inoculation of the molten metal, and

- A feeding sytem which acts as a reservoir of molten metal capable of transmitting liquid to the cooling casting proper.

Figure 4 shows the assembly split along a vertical plane which passes through the down sprue to which liquid metal is supplied from the pouring ladle. On either side of the down sprue are the reaction chambers. It is in these chambers, the dimensions of which are strictly governed by practice, that the desulfurization and inoculation* of the molten metal (cast iron in this instance) takes place. Figure 5 shows a partial model of this portion of the rigging.

The horizontal passages leading out of each chamber contain slag traps, so that any ingested slag (nonmetalic impurities) or undesirable reaction products are captured before they can flow into the casting. The portion of the rigging which runs parallel to the axis of the cylindrical casting promotes the trapping motion because it will not begin to fill until the molten metal has passed over the slag trap. The runner bar, which is parallel to the axis of the cylindrical casting and through which the molten metal flows, is also designed in such a way as to promote the even entry of the metal into the ingates. These design constraints require controlling both the runner bar and the ingate.

Clearly the possession of a geometric modeling facility would permit the foundry engineer to check out in detail many aspects of such a system. Simple commands would allow a cross section to be cut on the horizontal parting plane (Figure 6), in the vertical plane passing through the sprue and the reaction

---

Inoculation: A term used to describe a treatment given to molten gray or ductile cast irons to refine the eutectic graphite flake size. This is accomplished by adding a powdered material to either the pouring ladle or the metal stream as it enters the mold. Alternatively, the powdered inoculant may be placed within a reaction chamber within the gating system. Such chambers may also contain nodularizing agents to change the morphology of the graphite from a flake to a spheroidal variety.

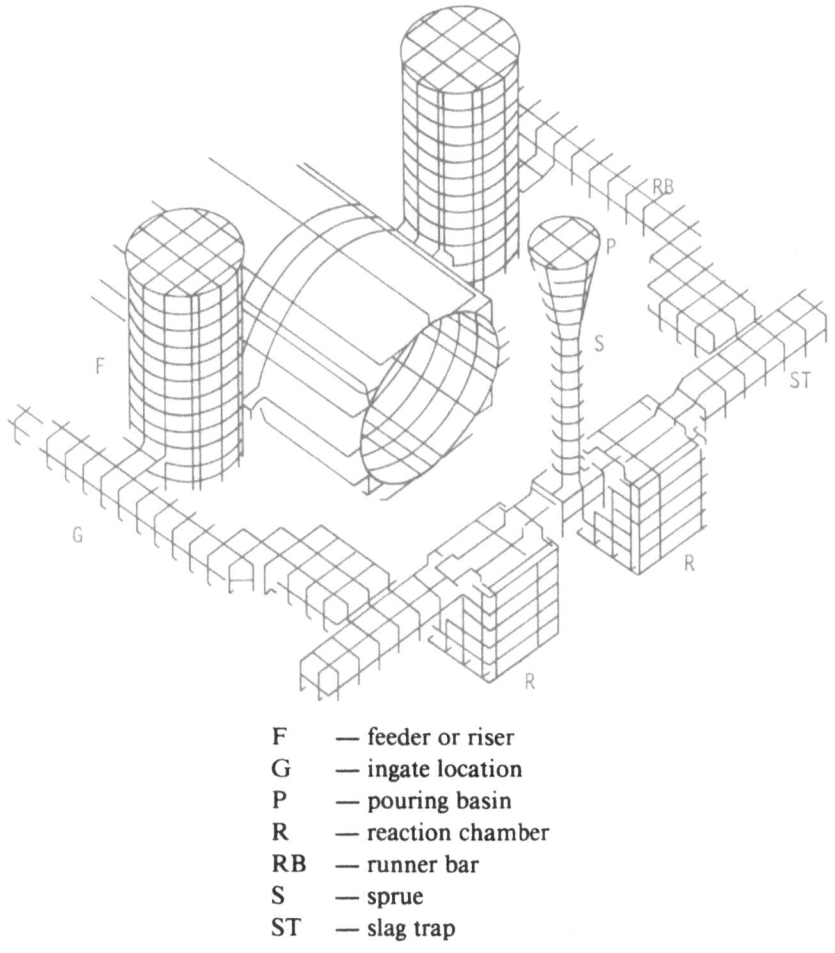

F   — feeder or riser
G   — ingate location
P   — pouring basin
R   — reaction chamber
RB   — runner bar
S   — sprue
ST   — slag trap

Figure 5. *Portion of the rigging system from the TIPS-1 model of Figure 4, showing reaction chambers and slag traps.*

chamber (Figure 7), or in a parallel vertical plane which passes through the ingate-riser-casting region (Figure 8).

Having checked out intrinsic features of such components of the rigging, the engineer can determine whether there are design aspects of the casting which might be adjusted to improve its castability. It is at this point that the exciting possibility emerges of the foundry engineer conversing with the casting designer while both are viewing the model. Such rapid and obviously effective means of communication would clearly promote better understanding between the designer and the supplier.

A second important commercial aspect of the potential of the geometric modeling of castings hinges upon casting yield. This quantity essentially measures

References pp. 115-116

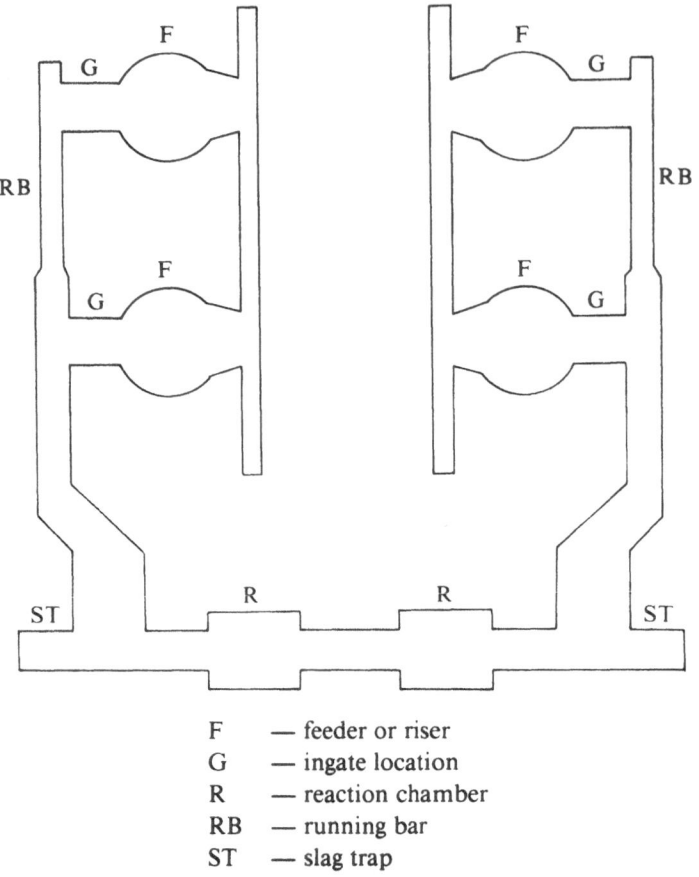

F   — feeder or riser
G   — ingate location
R   — reaction chamber
RB   — running bar
ST   — slag trap

Figure 6. *Cross section of TIPS-1 model of Figure 4 made on plane of the parting line.*

the efficiency of a particular rigging system. Indeed, it may well constitute one of the first points of contact between the foundry and the designer. To determine the selling price of a casting, the foundry methods engineer must know how much metal has to be melted and poured to produce one sound and properly dimensioned casting. Use of the modeler permits a tremendous saving here. The procedure adopted might be:

- Input the command statements to model casting only.

- Use preprocessor and volume calculation routines to determine casting volume.

- Input the command statements to model the rigging only.

- Use preprocessor and volume calculation routines to determine rigging volume.

- Utilize the computed casting and rigging volumes.

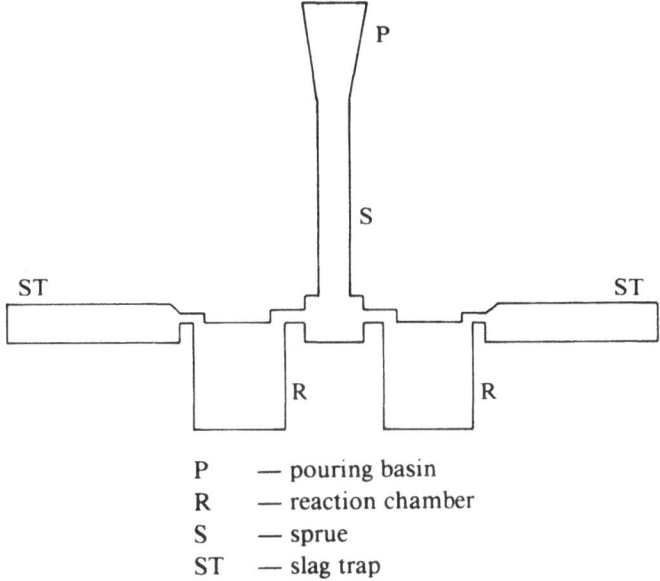

P — pouring basin
R — reaction chamber
S — sprue
ST — slag trap

Figure 7. *Cross section of TIPS-1 model of Figure 4 made through sprue, reaction chambers and slag traps.*

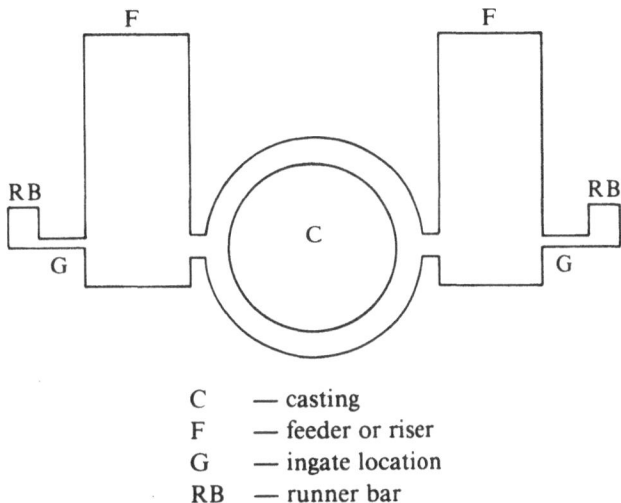

C — casting
F — feeder or riser
G — ingate location
RB — runner bar

Figure 8. *Cross section of TIPS-1 model of Figure 4 made through risers, ingates and casting.*

References pp. 115-116

As a final check of the suitability of a given rigging design, the foundry methods engineer would link the geometric modeler with a physical simulation system. This link would permit the engineer to pour and freeze the model on the computer. With a more complex casting design, the engineer might wish to check out only certain features of the system. The linking together of the modeler and the simulator is one of the present areas of concern for the Georgia Institute of Technology/University of Michigan team and, although this falls outside the scope of the present paper, it has been discussed elsewhere [Boulet and Dalton 1983]. At present this is an area where concentration of research effort is critically needed.*

CONCLUSIONS

Basic concerns of the casting engineer include the yield, soundness and material properties of his product. The ability to predict these qualities is a prerequisite for effective design of castings and riggings. With the advent of relatively inexpensive graphic display devices, interactive programming techniques, and advanced numerical methods for the solution of nonlinear partial differential equations, it is now possible to increase significantly the foundry methods engineer's ability to predict all aspects of a casting before pouring. The potential increase in productivity associated with implementation of computer aided design techniques based on a geometric modeler will not be fully realized for some time to come, but the day when one can "pour it on the computer" is approaching.

Although the present generation of geometric modelers does not contain all of the routines that are of interest to the patternmaker or the foundry methods engineer, and much work needs to be done on linking geometric modelers and casting simulators, good approximations of many real castings can be readily built. The potential for increased productivity of the methods engineer, the enhancement of communication between the methods engineer and the casting designer and, finally, the more accurate estimation of casting costs are all highly encouraging.

ACKNOWLEDGEMENTS

The work described in this paper forms part of the CADCAST program underway at the Georgia Institute of Technology and the University of Michigan. The Program Director at the University of Michigan is Prof. Robert D. Pehlke. The program is supported by the National Science Foundation (Dr. William

*For a more extended discussion of this important topic, the reader is referred to the progress reports of the CADCAST project underway at the Georgia Institute of Technology and the University of Michigan.

Spurgeon, Program Manager) and by industry. At the Georgia Institute of Technology further support from the State of Georgia is gratefully acknowledged.

The team acknowledges the contributions in the area of model building of Mr. F. Balboni, formerly of the Georgia Institute of Technology and now with IBM Corporation. The team also acknowledges help received from the organizations supplying the TIPS-1, PADL-1 and ROMULUS models illustrated in the paper.

REFERENCES

[AFSoftware]
D. C. Schmidt, *RISER User's Manual, 1984*, available from American Foundrymen's Society, Golf and Wolf Roads, Des Plaines, Illinois 60016.

[Berry *et al.* 1984]
J. T. Berry, F. Salamé, E. E. Underwood, and C. W. Meyers, "Final Report: An Investigation of Factors Affecting the Machinability of Ductile Cast Irons," prepared for the Ductile Iron Society, P. O. Box 1105, Mountainside, New Jersey 07092, April 1984.

[Boulet and Dalton 1983]
J. A. M. Boulet and B. B. Dalton, "A CAD System for Solidification Simulation," presented at the American Foundrymen's Society Casting Congress, 1983.

[CAT-1]
Cat Guide, The User's Manual, Cat Soft 1.1, 1982, Catronix Corporation, 120 Ralph McGill Boulevard, N.E., Suite 800, Atlanta, Georgia 30308, Attn: Dr. Jo Ellen Bradham.

[Chvorinov 1940]
N. Chvorinov, "Theory of Casting Solidification," *Giesserei*, Vol. 27, No. 11, 1940, pp. 201–208; Vol. 27, No. 12, 1940, pp. 222–225.

[CRUSADER]
J. E. Pickin and A. Beattie, *CRUSADER Method Design System User's Manual, 1984*, available from Steel Castings Research and Trade Association, Astbank Road, Sheffield, S23TT, England (Telephone 0742-28647).

[DUCT]
T. H. Gossling, "The DUCT System of Design for Practical Objects," *Proceedings of the World Congress on the Theory of Machines and Mechanisms*, Milan, Italy, 1976.

[Flinn 1963]
R. A. Flinn, *Fundamentals of Metal Casting*, Addison-Wesley, Reading, Massachusetts, 1963.

[Kotschi 1983]
R. Kotschi, "Computer Methods in the Foundry," presented at the 1983 Engineering Foundation Conference on the Modeling of Casting and Welding Processes, New England College, Henniker, New Hampshire, July 31–August 5, 1983.

[Novacast]
Novacast software available through Novacast, Ronnebyvag 1, Box 2034, S-372 02 Ronneby, Sweden.

[PADL-1]
H. B. Voelcker, A. A. G. Requicha, E. E. Hartquist, W. B. Fisher, J. E. Shopiro, and N. K. Birrell, "An Introduction to PADL: Characteristics, Status, and Rationale," Techni-

cal Memo No. 22, Production Automation Project, University of Rochester, Rochester, New York, December 1974.

[ROMULUS]
P. Veenman, *ROMULUS: User's and Programmer's Guide*, Shape Data Ltd., Cambridge, England, 1979.

[Ruddle and Suschill 1983]
R. W. Ruddle and A. L. Suschill, "Riser Sizing by Microcomputer," presented at the 1983 Engineering Foundation on the Modeling of Casting and Welding Processes, New England College, Henniker, New Hampshire, July 31–August 5, 1983.

[Sillen 1983]
R. Sillen, "Microcomputers and Programs for Foundry Calculations," *Modern Casting*, Vol. 73, No. 8, August 1983, pp. 35–37.

[TIPS-1]
N. Okino and TIPS-1 Working Group, "TIPS-1," Institute of Precision Engineering, Hokkaido University, Sapporo, Japan, 1978.

[Welbourn 1982]
D. B. Welbourn, "Computer. Aided Engineering in the Foundry Industry," *Giesserei*, Vol. 69, No. 25, 1982, pp. 734–744.

DISCUSSION

Kalman Brauner *(Boeing Commercial Airplane Company)*

The first of your conclusions was that the modelers needed to be more powerful rather than more convenient. What do you find lacking, specifically?

Boulet

A modeler needs to combine the power of boundary representations for doing sculptured surfaces and the convenience of a CSG tree. That's the thing that would be, of course, wonderful to have.

J. A. M. Boulet

Robert de Monts *(Dassault Systems)*

One subject you've not touched on is the manufacture of the molds. You've discussed the design aspect of the mold, but you've also got to do the manufacturing of that mold. That's also an issue between boundary and constructive geometries.

Boulet

I believe I mentioned that a little bit at the beginning but I was referring primarily to sand molds that were created for one single casting and were not reusable. In that case, as I indicated, much of the manufacture of such molds is literally "man"u-facture. It's done in an artful way by people with many years of experience. However, your comment is a good one because there are a lot of castings that are made with permanent molds in another fashion wherein the molds could be designed more carefully. The geometry could be specified completely ahead of time. That sort of casting could benefit much more immediately from the use of geometric modeling.

David Racklyeft *(General Motors Advanced Product and Manufacturing Engineering Staff)*

I don't understand the advantage of the CSG modelers. Are you saying that if you had a boundary representation modeler which could do Boolean operations, that that would satisfy your desire of mixing the two?

Boulet

No, I'm referring to the compactness of the database and the idea of using a primitive generic object that can be moved around as a separate entity in the system.

Racklyeft

I understand the compactness of the database. Could you expand on the idea of a generic object that can be moved around.

Boulet

The boundary representation modelers that we've used don't conveniently allow for creation of something that you can really call a primitive in the sense that you can call it up and have a specified list of parameters, then change some parameter such as the radius and put another instance of it anywhere you want. I'm not saying that can't exist: it probably does exist in some modelers. But the ones that we've used don't have that function in as convenient a form as you find it in CSG modelers.

Michel Melkanoff *(University of California-Los Angeles)*

Could you possibly control the temperature of various parts of the mold and even keep that under computer control to fit in with requirements that you find are stringent?

Boulet

Yes, as a matter of fact another aspect of our project is some work that one of the faculty members at Georgia Tech is doing in the area of using heat pipes inserted into the mold as opposed to using passive chills, which is the common usage now. Active heating elements, specifically heat pipes, could be used either to put heat in or to take heat out, to control very precisely the variation of the temperature at the interface between the mold and the metal; then, in principle, you could design the mold very accurately and know you would get a sound casting with no shrinkage. You would not spend time pouring some trial runs to make sure that it would work.

Melkanoff

Would the same thing apply to forging?

Boulet

Yes. Ideally you'd like to be able to sit down and design everything and know that the product that's going to be produced not only was sound, but also had the desired microstructure and desired mechanical properties.

James Cavendish *(General Motors Research Laboratories)*

K. K. Wang has done some modeling of injection molding. Does he use the TIPS system?

Boulet

Yes, he does.

Cavendish

I imagine injection molding is a bit like casting.

Boulet

Great similarities, yes.

Cavendish

Does the TIPS system work pretty well for him or not?

Boulet

He's here, I'll let him answer the question.

K. K. Wang *(Cornell University)*

We use TIPS only for on-line distribution of the models.

James Korein *(University of Pennsylvania)*

You've touched on the idea of automatic design of the riggings for these molds. Did you have in mind a rule-based system approach?

Boulet

There are rule-based systems that exist now. As a matter of fact, in the paper there are some references to some systems that are in use now based on Chvorinov's rule, Bernoulli's equation, and so forth. I was talking about including those in the model and in the simulation.

Korein

Exactly how would you have your system go about designing the rigging? Would it use heuristics?

Boulet

I wasn't talking about that at all. I would be satisfied if I could simply include them in the model. I could do the heuristics and look at the results. I don't believe many people have begun to think even that far ahead. But some day.

Melkanoff

I suppose that it might be feasible to consider certain parametrization of the riggings and then define various rules for certain types of riggings. And then find out after it was poured whether it was more or less satisfactory. I could imagine that kind of expert approach.

Boulet

The algorithms that already exist for that sort of thing could be applied directly if you could do the simulation in the first place.

SHAPE FEATURES IN GEOMETRIC MODELING

GRAHAM E. M. JARED

University of Cambridge
Cambridge, England

ABSTRACT

This paper dicusses two aspects of shape features in geometric modeling. Firstly, it outlines research carried out at the University of Cambridge on the recognition of shape features from a geometric model for the purpose of part classification and coding. Secondly, some description is given of work currently in progress on the representation of shape features in the BUILD-4 geometric modeler.

INTRODUCTION

An often quoted measure of the quality of an artificial intelligence system is whether the user can tell if he is interacting with a computer program or a person. Perhaps a similar measure of the standard of a geometric modeling program would be if the user could tell whether he was using a computer model of an object or interacting with the actual physical object in his hand. This perhaps farfetched analogy serves to illustrate what should be one of the primary aims of solid modeling, that is, to provide a computer shape model as useful in design, analysis and manufacture as the physical prototype.

It is inevitable that the overall shape of a part will be strongly influenced by its various functions. However, it is rarely the case that one particular face fulfills a specific design purpose; it is usually sets of faces forming bosses or pockets that allow a part to play its appointed role. Further, it is not often that only one face of an object results from the application of a manufacturing process; sets of faces are formed by, for example, drilling a hole or milling out a pocket. Lastly, such questions as, "Which part of the geometric model relates to the boss that performs such and such a function?" are often difficult to answer with present geometric modelers, whether they are based on constructive solid geom-

References pp. 132-133

etry, boundary, or other representations. These three examples illustrate some of the contexts in which the availability of shape feature information from a geometric model would be particularly useful. At the design stage it would be desirable to be able to describe a part in terms of the shape features put in to perform particular functions. Decisions on the means of manufacturing a part may be facilitated by the availability of information on the shape features that can be produced by a particular process. Lastly, a task such as stress analysis is greatly facilitated by the presence of shape feature data.

This paper firstly describes a program recently developed by Kyprianou [Kyprianou 1980] for the automatic recognition of shape features from a boundary representation generated by the BUILD-4 geometric modeler [Braid 1979, Stroud 1980]. It then goes on to present work by Cary on the generation and modification of geometric models by the direct manipulation of simple or low-level shape features [Cary 1980]. Finally, it outlines a programme currently in progress that brings together these two streams of work to allow shape feature data input by the designer to be included in the geometric model of a part and thus to be available to downstream application programs such as finite-element mesh generation and process planning.

BACKGROUND

The need for an automatic feature recognition program arose as part of a Ph.D. project on automatic part classification and coding started in 1977. Virtually no academic work on the theoretical aspects of part classification pre-existed and such work as had been carried out on feature recognition from a geometric model had been done as an adjunct to the automatic generation of data for N/C machining. An algorithm for the decomposition of 2.5-D parts (those composed purely of horizontal and vertical faces and, roughly speaking, manufacturable by a 3-axis machine) had been described by Grayer in his work on the automatic generation of N/C tapes [Grayer 1975]. Here the part is decomposed into laminae representing its horizontal faces, each lamina having a z-height associated with it. This data structure efficiently represents the arrangement of hole contours in each lamina and relationships between laminae, but cannot be extended to general 3-D parts and is thus a poor starting point for a general feature recogniser.

In another work on the decomposition of 3-D objects [Woo 1975], an algorithm is given that works from the unevaluated description of an object, in this case the set of volume primitives and the operations to combine them into the final object. This data structure is examined recursively for primitives in a particular relation which can produce a feature, such as parallel faces separated by a distance which may produce a slot in the object, until all volumes have been inspected. This method was rejected because it was dependent on the designer's sequencing of volume operations and because it was thought to be slow as it required repeated examination of the object description.

A new approach to feature recognition was adopted based on the use of feature grammars which are similar to the shape grammars defined by Stiny [Stiny 1976, 1977, Stiny and Mitchell 1978] for the generation of architectural shapes.

FEATURE GRAMMARS

For the purposes of the feature recognition program, Kyprianou devised a feature language which may describe all possible shape features. He named the finite specification of such an infinite language a *feature grammar*. Such grammars are similar to phrase-structure or Chomsky grammars [Chomsky 1965]. A feature grammar is defined in terms of *feature primitives* as a 4-tuple (S,T,P,I) where S is a finite set of *structural primitives*, T is a finite set of *terminal primitives*, P is a set of *production rules* showing how a feature may be generated from other elements of the grammar, and I is a finite set of *initial primitives* or starting points from which features in the particular language are generated. All shape features in the language are made up of terminal primitives or parts of terminal primitives; initial primitives are made up of elements of S and T, but must contain a substructure that is an element of S. The three basic structural primitives used in constructing the feature grammar in the feature recogniser are shown in Figure 1; they are a convex edge, a concave edge and a so-called smooth edge, that is, one where there is no change in surface normal between the adjacent faces.

Shape features are divided into two general classes as far as the feature recogniser program is concerned: depressions and protrusions, the finer divisions of which are detailed in the following section. In general, *protrusions* determine the external shape of a part, and *depressions* the internal shape. For examples of how the feature grammar is used to parse geometric models, the reader is referred to Kyprianou's original text [Kyprianou 1980].

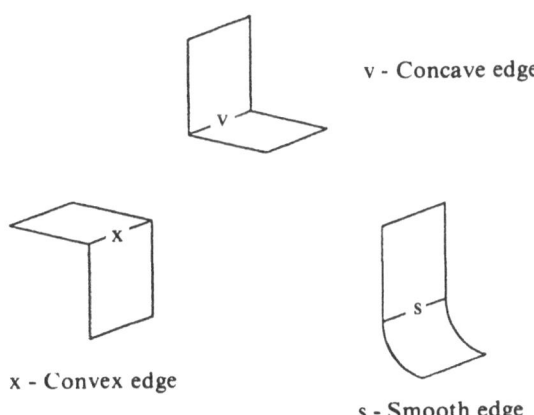

v - Concave edge

x - Convex edge

s - Smooth edge

Figure 1. *Structural primitives.*

References pp. 132-133

THE FEATURE RECOGNISER

As previously mentioned, the feature recogniser acts as the first phase of a two-stage program for automatic part classification and coding. The recogniser builds a *faceset* data structure which is then interpreted by the program's second phase to produce a part code in a particular classification scheme. This second phase interrogates the faceset structure via an interface program which has been previously generated by a translator from a metalanguage description of the classification scheme being used. The translator input consists of a series of *rule* statements that specify the shape features used to classify objects, and *class* statements that are used to allocate the digits of the part code to the features described in the rules. The output from the translator is an Algol68C program segment which may be compiled and linked into the second phase of the classification program. Thus the feature recogniser and part code generator may be used with any classification scheme that can be described by the metalanguage input to the translator.

The feature recogniser itself may be divided into several phases of scanning the geometric model and building up the faceset data structure. In the first phase all the edges, vertices and loops of the model are examined and initially classified as convex, concave or smooth edges (the structural feature primitives in Figure 1); loops are classified by their constituent edges as concave, convex or hybrid, that is, mixed, containing both concave and convex edges; vertices are classified as concave or convex according to the incident edges. Smooth edges are re-examined and classified as concave or convex according to the local curvatures of the adjoining surfaces. Vertices are marked as concave if two or more incident edges are concave; otherwise they are considered to be convex. This marking phase does not generate any new data structures; it just uses marker fields in the elements of the geometric model to retain its information.

In the next stage a list of faces of the object is created and divided into lists of primary and secondary faces. A *primary face* is defined as containing a concave edge, or enclosing inner loops, or being embedded in a concave curved surface (Figure 2). In order to increase the efficiency of subsequent phases the list of

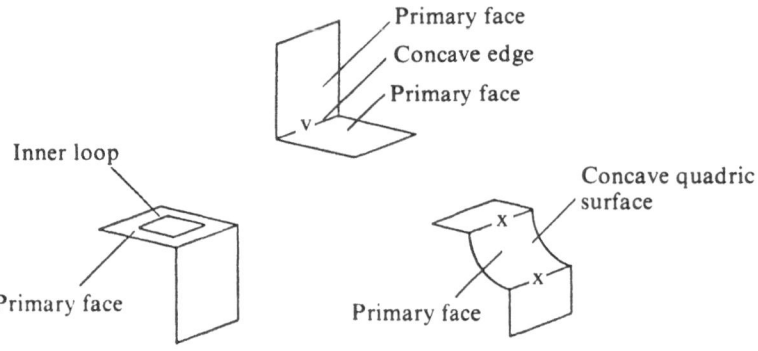

Figure 2. *Primary faces.*

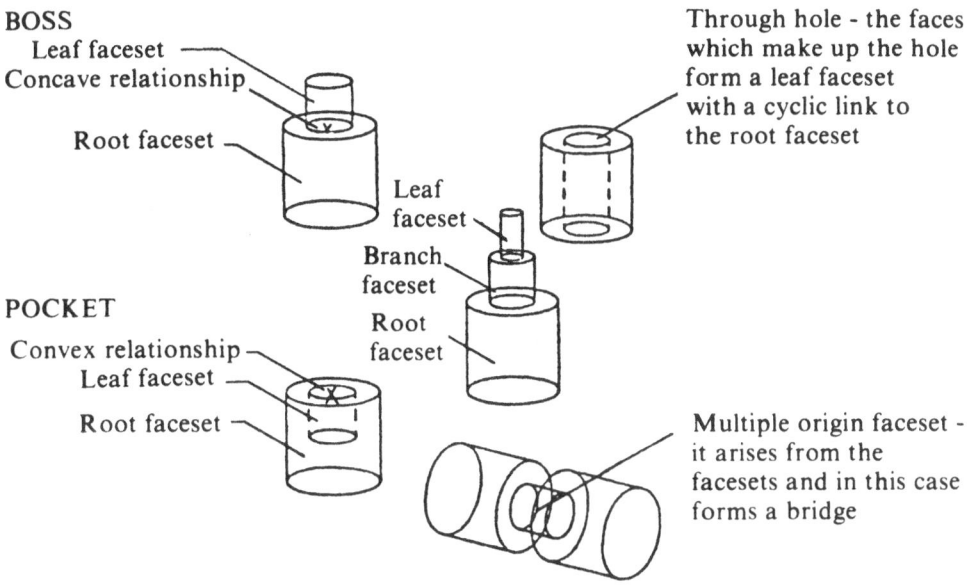

BOSS
    Leaf faceset
Concave relationship
    Root faceset
        Leaf faceset

Through hole - the faces which make up the hole form a leaf faceset with a cyclic link to the root faceset

Branch faceset

POCKET
    Convex relationship
    Leaf faceset
    Root faceset
Root faceset

Multiple origin faceset - it arises from the facesets and in this case forms a bridge

Figure 3. Faceset types.

primary faces is sorted according to their morphological content as measured by the number of inner loops they contain. Primary faces with an equal number of inner loops are differentiated by the following criteria in order of priority: the number of concave vertices contained, the number of sets of concave edges and, finally, the overall number of concave edges in the face.

The third phase builds the faceset data structure which is to be used both for the recognition of individual features and of the overall shape of the parts. Each faceset is built up by a recursive search which starts from the peripheral loop of a primary face and includes all faces traversed which are not already contained in another faceset. Finally, the primary face list is scanned for facesets originating from inner loops. Facesets are classified into root, branch, leaf and cyclic. Examples illustrating each type are shown in Figure 3. The root, branch and leaf classifications refer to the position of the facesets in the tree representing the hierarchy of facesets. Further, facesets may have multiple origins, that is, spring from two or more facesets as, for example, the bridging faceset in Figure 3. A cyclic faceset is a special case of a multiorigin faceset where one of the origin facesets occurs more than once. The sorting of the primary face list in the previous phase of the recogniser means that the initial faceset of the search should be a root faceset.

Having constructed the faceset structure, the recogniser scans it in the remaining phases using algorithms based on the feature grammars discussed earlier. The first recognition phase scans the facesets for simple depressions. As the faces of a potential depression are examined they are added to a *base list* or a

References pp. 132-133

B - Base faces

In this example each base face has
   2 concave vertices
   1 set of connected concave edges
   3 concave edges

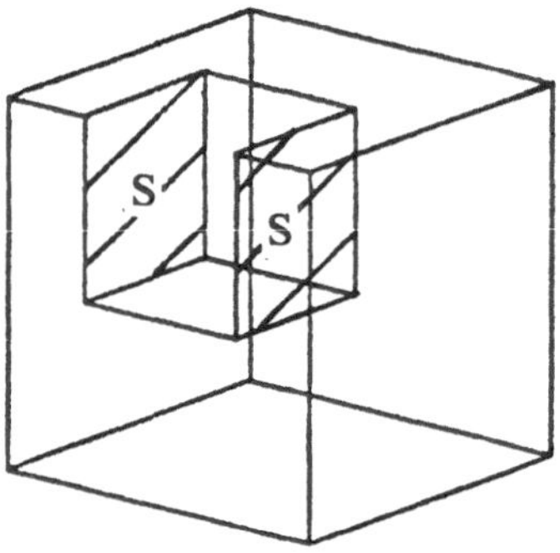

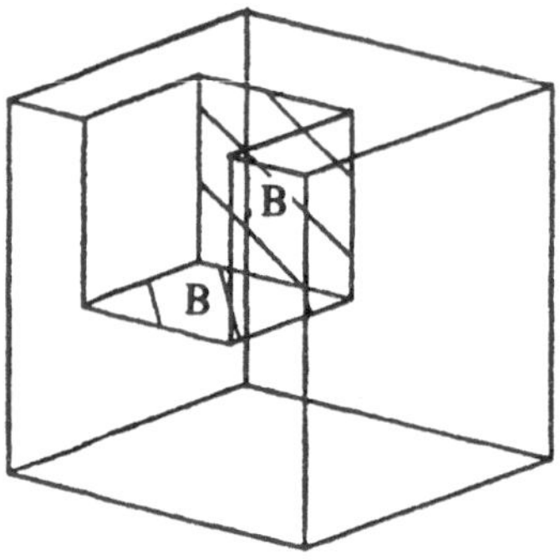

S - Side faces

In this example each side face has
   2 concave vertices
   1 set of connected concave vertices
   2 concave edges

Figure 4. *Vertex, edge, and loop classification.*

side list, according to their geometry, to facilitate later processing of the depression (Figure 4). Depressions are categorised into two types: *grooves,* which are formed where two faces meet at a concave edge, and *slots,* which covers all other depressions. *Pockets* are classed as a special case of slots in which a loop enclosing the depression consists entirely of convex edges. When a simple depression has been discovered, it is examined to find its convex boundaries,

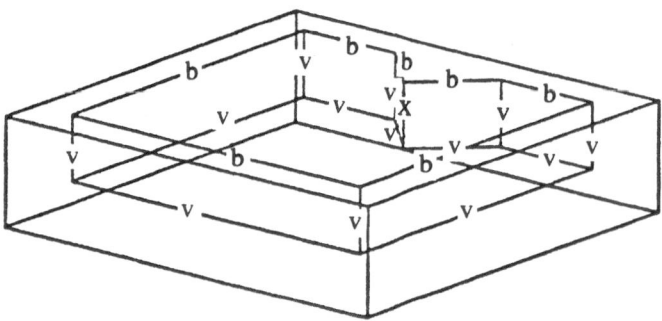

v   Concave edges in the depression
b   Edges forming the convex boundary
x   Convex edge shared by faces of the depression

Figure 5. *A depression.*

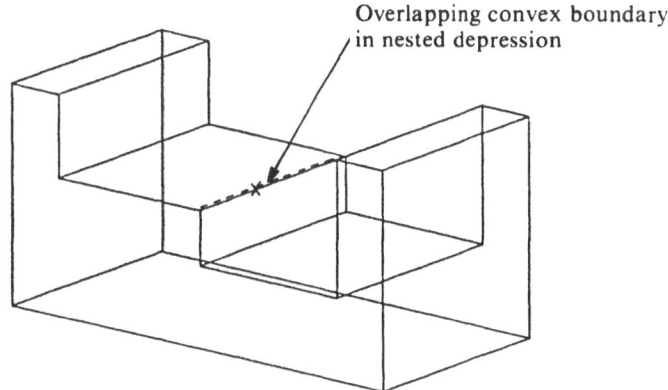

Figure 6. Nested depressions.

which are accumulated in a list. In forming depression boundaries, concave edges are rejected outright and convex edges are checked to avoid including those where side faces of the depression meet (Figure 5). Finally, the list of convex boundaries of all depressions is scanned to check for nested depressions where the convex boundaries overlap. Where nested depressions are detected they are coalesced into a single complex depression (Figure 6).

Protrusions are normally recognised from concave boundaries, so depressions with more than one convex boundary are examined for concave boundaries which have been included in their edge network. Each concave boundary detected gives rise to an *implicit protrusion*. Such a protrusion springs from a concave boundary that is contained in two or more facesets, for example, in two different faces as in Figure 7. Note that implicit protrusions do not arise from inner loops.

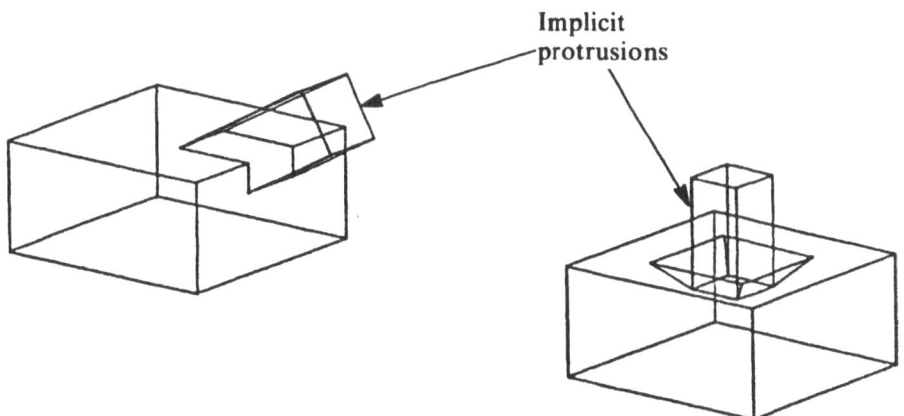

Figure 7. Examples of implicit protrusions.

References pp. 132-133

The final phase of the recogniser considers each faceset separately in turn, using local shape information from the faceset and its relation to adjoining ones to determine the overall shape of the part. The facesets are divided into two lists: first, those which determine the external shape of the part, that is, root facesets and those linked by concave relations; and second, those that give the internal shape of the part, that is, node and leaf facesets generated from convex relations. Local geometric information is used to classify each faceset into one of three types: planar, curved or indeterminate.

The edges of *planar facesets* are subdivided into groups of parallel edges and the largest group is chosen to indicate a major orientation in the faceset. A cross section of the faceset is formed by intersecting it with a plane perpendicular to this largest group of edges. This cross section and the length of the longest edge in the chosen bundle form the shape descriptor of the faceset.

Each surface of a *curved faceset* is analysed to discover such attributes as the axis of rotation of certain quadric surfaces, for example, cone and cylinder, and the direction of generators of other quadrics, such as parabolic cylinders. The faceset is then divided into subgroups which share a common surface, and those subgroups which share a common axis of rotation are placed adjacent in a list of subgroups within the faceset. The shape descriptor of a curved faceset consists of a list of its surfaces along with their type and attributes, and, additionally, a pointer to the highest and lowest vertices of each subgroup.

Indeterminate facesets may be divided into two categories. The first, those that are formed by cutting a curved faceset by a plane, may be processed as special cases of curved facesets. The second, those which can be formed by adding a planar shape to a curved faceset, cannot be processed since they need special purpose algorithms (see Figure 8).

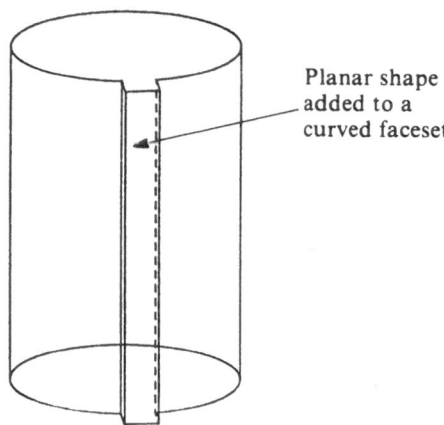

Planar shape added to a curved faceset

Figure 8. Example of an indeterminate faceset which requires a special purpose algorithm.

At this point, the shape descriptions generated by the recogniser may be printed out or passed to the second stage of the automatic part classification program. They cannot as yet be preserved and used by design or application programs to reference the features recognised in the geometric model. Before examining the work currently in progress to make this possible, a parallel piece of work on the use of simple shape features in referencing parts of a geometric model must be discussed.

SIMPLE SHAPE FEATURES IN THE USER INTERFACE TO THE BUILD-4 MODELER

During the construction or modification of the geometric model of an object, the user frequently wishes to refer to a particular part of its shape where, for example, a new piece is to be added or an existing bit deleted or modified. At least three distinct methods of reference may be distinguished:

- *Method 1.* Light pen or cursor pointing on a screen image of the object. This is often combined with other inputs such as textual commands to resolve ambiguities between several items surrounding the picture space coordinates indicated.

- *Method 2.* Naming all elements of the model, such as faces, edges and vertices, with, for example, integer or textual labels which may then be displayed on a picture of the object.

- *Method 3.* Specifying a "procedure" to be executed by the user-interface program in order to find the required feature.

Method 2 has several drawbacks: new names are needed for each new element of the geometric model as it is created; items referred to by existing names may disappear, leaving dangling references; and any procedure for automatic generation of new names is likely to produce names which depend on the designer's ordering of operations. Method 1 is fine for interactive sessions, but it leads to difficulties in storing and recalling records of the user's actions. These difficulties are often overcome by translating light pen or cursor hits into an intermediate code similar to the input languages for Method 2 or Method 3. The level of success achieved using Method 3 is entirely dependent on the quality of the language used to specify feature-finding procedures. The recogniser described previously was not immediately available for use as part of the program to implement decoding of feature-finding procedures, so an initial study using simple low-level features was carried out [Cary 1980]. A simple language was devised which could be used to refer to features of a part that could be easily detected, for example, "the top face" or "the leftmost edge of the bottom face." The code implementing this was deliberately kept simple and initially worked only in terms of the vertices of the object; thus it was prone to error when dealing with objects with curved surfaces. Directions such as top, left, or right were taken from the view of the object last displayed on the screen. The program has

References pp. 132-133

been successively upgraded, allowing more sophisticated procedures and using more complex geometric calculations [Anderson 1983], so that the current syntax of feature expressions may be written in a pseudoBNF form in which I indicates alternatives and [ ] enclose optional items:

```
<feature expression>  ::=  BODY I OBJECT
                            I <topon type> <integer>
                            I <name>
                            I <direction> [<qualifier>] <feature type>
                              [OF <feature expression>]

<topon type>  ::=  FACE I EDGE I VERTEX I LOOP I FACESET

<direction>  ::=  TOP I BOTTOM I LEFT I RIGHT I FRONT I BACK
                  I NEAREST I FURTHEST I THE
                  I A I AN I <vector>

<qualifier>  ::=  CURVED I PLANAR I STRAIGHT I HOLE I INNER
                  I QUADRIC I PATCH I SMOOTH I FEATURE

<feature type>  ::=  FACE I EDGE I VERTEX I LOOP I BOSS
                     I POCKET
```

so that expressions such as

LEFT BOSS OF TOP FACE

and

LEFT CURVED EDGE OF THE INNER LOOP OF BOTTOM FACE

can now be used. Note that *boss* and *pocket* feature types are now available. They match bosses and pockets created by explicit user commands as described in the next section. The immediate advantages that the availability of these higher-level feature types bring may be seen from the feature expression necessary to access the hatched face in Figure 9. Without boss and pocket types the expression is:

HATCH TOP FACE OF FRONT FACE OF THE INNER LOOP OF
BOTTOM FACE OF THE INNER LOOP OF TOP FACE

With the boss and pocket types, this may be replaced by:

HATCH TOP FACE OF BOSS [OF POCKET OF TOP FACE].

The part of the expression enclosed by brackets is redundant since the object contains only one boss.

SHAPE FEATURES IN USER INPUT TO BUILD-4

A project is currently in progress in the University of Cambridge Engineering Department CAE Group to allow high-level shape features to be explicitly formed in a part by user commands with their structure and relations, then retained as part of the geometric model. For example, the commands to BUILD-4 to make the model of the basic shape (without the blended edges) of the object in Figure 9 would be:

CUBE −80 80 −60 60 0 50

MAKE RECTANGULAR POCKET 140 BY 100 DEPTH 40 ON

  TOP FACE

MAKE RECTANGULAR BOSS 40 BY 60 HEIGHT 30 ON BOTTOM

  FACE OF POCKET

CYLINDER

MODIFY BY SXY 10 SZ 50

SUBTRACT

Several problems arise from this apparently trivial extension to the user interface of the modeler. The shape features of an object will be easily handled as long as only the commands for making bosses and pockets are used. However, it may be necessary to call the feature recogniser program after every other command,

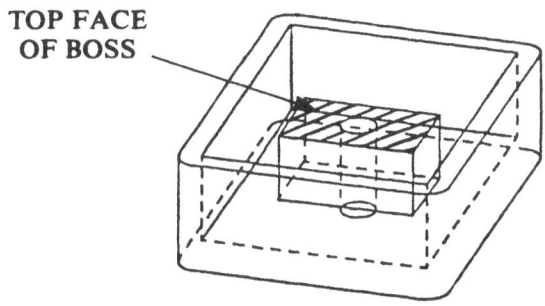

Figure 9. *Feature-finding example.*

References pp. 132-133

such as volume set operations, which may have added, destroyed or modified features. It should also be noted that the feature data built into the model relates only to the designer's view of the part. It may well be that with a suitably chosen set of basic shape features, the designer's structuring of a part will coincide with the perception of its features by downstream users of the geometric model. It is, however, likely that such users may need to scan the part again with the feature recogniser to generate a different organisation of the shape feature data which decomposes the part into a new set of features. Nevertheless, the production of shape feature data structures during the design process, their use as references in further modification, and their availability in later stages of analysis and manufacture amply justify the effort expended to include them in the geometric model.

ACKNOWLEDGEMENTS

The author wishes to acknowledge a substantial debt to past and present members of the CAE Group, especially Lyc Kyprianou, Anthony Parkinson and Charles Anderson.

REFERENCES

[Anderson 1983]
    C. Anderson, "The BUILD-4 User's Guide," CAE Group Document 116, Engineering Department, University of Cambridge, Cambridge, England, 1983.

[Braid 1979]
    I. C. Braid, "Geometric Modeling — Ten Years On," CAD Group Document 103, Computer Laboratory, University of Cambridge, Cambridge, England, 1979.

[Cary 1980]
    C. A. G. Cary, "The BUILD Feature-Finder," CAD Group Document 109, Computer Laboratory, University of Cambridge, Cambridge, England, 1980.

[Chomsky 1965]
    N. Chomsky, *Aspects of the Theory of Syntax*, The M.I.T. Press, Cambridge, Massachusetts, 1965.

[Grayer 1975]
    A. R. Grayer, "A Computer Link Between Design and Manufacture," Ph.D. Dissertation, University of Cambridge, Cambridge, England, 1975.

[Kyprianou 1980]
    L. K. Kyprianou, "Shape Classification in Computer-Aided Design," Ph.D. Dissertation, Computer Laboratory, University of Cambridge, Cambridge, England, July 1980.

[Stiny 1976]
    G. Stiny, "Two Exercises in Formal Composition," *Environment and Planning B,* Vol. 3, No. 2, December 1976, pp. 187–210.

[Stiny 1977]
    G. Stiny, "Ice Ray: A Note on the Generation of Chinese Lattice Designs," *Environment and Planning B*, Vol. 4, No. 1, June 1977, pp. 89–98.

[Stiny and Mitchell 1978]
G. Stiny and W. J. Mitchell, "The Palladian Grammar," *Environment and Planning B,* Vol. 5, No. 1, June 1978, pp. 5–18.

[Stroud 1980]
I. A. Stroud, "The BUILD Picture Book," CAD Group Document 104, Computer Laboratory, University of Cambridge, Cambridge, England, 1980.

[Woo 1975]
T. C. Woo, "Computer Understanding of Design," Ph.D. Dissertation, University of Illinois, Urbana, Illinois, 1975.

DISCUSSION

Sam Geisberg *(Applicon)*

You want to incorporate these features as elements of your data structures so that you will be able to use them in semantic description of the design of a manufacturing process. Is that right?

Jared

Yes. However, we feel that it's not satisfactory to describe a model purely in terms of its features. Most designers can think in terms of features, but they like to escape from it a little bit and have the ability to adjust the model slightly. If they could do just a few set operations it would be so much quicker to achieve their final result. What we see is a new range of operations which allow these features to be put in and also allow the local operations and set operations on the model. The feature recognizer would be used afterwards to tidy up the mess that's left and reimpose the feature structure on the model.

G. E. M. Jared

Christopher Brown *(University of Rochester)*

I missed the connection of shape grammars with the program that Dr. Kyprianou devised. Could you elaborate on that? And could you tell me if you do deal with three-dimensional shape grammars.

Jared

Basically shape grammars are the underlying mathematical structure which describes the algorithms that Kyprianou used in his recognizer. Three-dimensional shape grammars are a possibility but it would take a larger mind than I've encountered to be able to handle them. It's complicated enough to describe the feature grammars that Kyprianou uses, which contain curved items and more topological terms. The original Stiny paper worked with shapes defined by just points and lines, so you can see how the degree of complexity increases. However, a three-dimensional shape grammar would be very interesting.

Herbert Voelcker *(University of Rochester)*

Can you assure consistency between your feature builder and your feature recognizer? For example, suppose the user builds some pockets and bosses and such and then does some operations on them. If you then applied the feature recognizer, is it possible that what a user called a boss could become a pocket?

Jared

The answer is, not quite. I think that you can say that there is some common agreement between most people as to what features are. There is, of course, a fairly grey area of disagreement, though I think most people think that a hole is a hole and a boss is a boss! Of course one can prompt the recognizer by giving it sets of shapes which the user knows about so that it can recognize modified instances of these. This is all speculation, to some extent, because so far we just have the recognizer and the model; we've made some experiments with keeping these data structures and transferring them through to the drawing process to draw bosses and holes in different colors.

Michel Melkanoff *(University of California–Los Angeles)*

I think this question ties up with one I had about the fact that this somewhat resembles fuzzy languages and fuzzy sets. When you say "the" boss or something like that, that might well be described through a fuzzy set which is fairly unique.

Jared

Yes. Well, as you saw in the final example I gave, there are infinite possibilities for combinations of bosses and pockets and so forth, but even a relatively useful part has one boss, one pocket, and one through hole.

John Boyse *(General Motors Research Laboratories)*

Does the work that you described on parts classification cover, or distinguish, a wide enough class of parts so that you think it would be industrially useful or is there a lot more work to do before it would be useful?

Jared

The recognizer itself is fairly well understood, whereas the part coding aspect of this program still needs a fair amount of work before it could be industrially useful. It was tried out on one industry parts classification scheme for rotational parts. That was all Kyprianou had time for in the two and half years it took him to do his thesis.

James Korein *(University of Pennsylvania)*

You've mentioned ruled surfaces as a part of face description. How complete is your support of ruled surfaces; how are they input and what kind of operations can you perform on them?

Jared

In fact, they arise only where they come in as a subset of quadric surfaces, such as parabolic cylinders, elliptical cylinders and so forth. They are in our full implementation of general quadrics. There are fairly limited facilities for directly inputting these ruled surfaces. However, they do arise as natural consequences of the operations that we allow in the program, such as defining a plan view of a prismatic part which can contain parabolas, ellipses and so forth, and then sweeping that into the prismatic part. In the same way, we allow the specification of the profiles of rotational parts—there again we get ruled surfaces. These profiles can contain ellipses and in fact also B-splines. So we get "cylindrical" B-spline surfaces.

David Gossard *(Massachusetts Institute of Technology)*

I was a little confused about the rationale that motivated you to create the feature recognizer. It seemed that your remark about trying to recapture the intent of the designer leads to the obvious question, "Wouldn't it be more appropriate to provide the designer with input methods which allow him to specify manufacturing process information in the features?"

Jared

I would agree that in this business one really needs all the clues one can get; to retain the designer's perception of the structure of the part would be very useful. But I don't think it's the complete answer to the question. I have some examples of "interesting" parts where at least my naive conception of how a designer would construct it using features falls down completely. It's quite easy to see how my example part of the last figure which just has one boss and one pocket could be concocted. However, these other examples are very much open to question as to how you would make them by only using features. Then, after that, they are open to question as to what, in fact, are the features in the part (it would be easy to structure them in different ways).

Melkanoff

I would guess that often the designer doesn't quite realize what the manufacturer may need. So that to trust his judgement about what's needed later is somewhat dangerous in my opinion.

Jared

I feel that we haven't by any means solved all the problems. I think that I've pointed out the mechanism for retaining this information, and a recognizer that can reconstruct it. We now have some tools which we can use for some experiments. I think that's as far as we can claim to have gone.

Kalman Brauner *(Boeing Commercial Airplane Company)*

It would appear that there is not a unique classification for a particular part. If that is true, what is the effect on the inverse process, where you have a library of parts and you want to go backward? You have a certain desired part, such as a bracket, and you want to describe the classifications; so you go into your library and retrieve those things that already have been designed. It seems that the ambiguity would induce problems there.

Jared

There is a unique intermediate data structure coming out of the feature recognizer. There's by no means a unique classification from that feature structure. This was, in fact, one reason why the intermediate feature data structure was kept relatively low level. A lot of work goes into the second phase, where you read the metalanguage description and the part classification scheme and then attempt to parse the feature structure with that classification scheme. If you devised a suitably awkward classification scheme, it could quite easily come up with different classifications for the same part. But I think we've at least got a relatively good one-to-one mapping between the geometric model and the feature data structure in the first phase.

NUMERICAL CODE GENERATION FROM A GEOMETRIC MODELING SYSTEM

G. T. ARMSTRONG, GRAHAM C. CAREY and ALAN de PENNINGTON

University of Leeds
Leeds, England

ABSTRACT

A geometric modeling system (GMS) can, in principle, model the geometric aspects of a manufacturing environment from an entire manufacturing cell through to the tooling details. It offers the capability of an unambiguous model of the component workpiece at all stages of manufacture, thus giving a representation of the stock to be removed by the material removal process. The conversion from a representation suitable for graphics to one more applicable to manufacture can be made. Preliminary studies suggest that a GMS having multiple representations and dimension and tolerance information, together with machinability data, will facilitate the selection of appropriate manufacturing processes and tooling to produce the specified geometry and surface finish. With minimal human intervention, a prototype system would give process planned N/C code, making use of available production engineering data. A further advantage of using the geometric modeler is that the N/C code generated can be verified for all types of invasive machining.

INTRODUCTION

This paper reports further results of a study into the use of geometric modelling techniques in deriving numerically controlled cutter paths for side and end milling, as used in small to medium batch manufacturing [Armstrong *et al.* 1979]. Related requirements for experimental and prototype product manufacture are outlined.

An important aspect of factory automation is full CAD/CAM integration. This is a vast and complex subject. The way in which automation is achieved will depend on a company's corporate strategy which includes such aspects as

References pp. 153-154

product improvement, manufacturing efficiency, quality improvement, market development and the organization, and people.

The experience gained from the development of a prototype system for automatic N/C code generation is discussed.

AUTOMATIC N/C CODE GENERATION

The problem that was studied is as follows:

> "Given complete geometrical descriptions of a part to be produced, the stock from which it is to be machined, and the available tooling and fixtures, design appropriate algorithms and representations which will automatically yield an acceptable strategy (setups and toolpaths) to produce the part on a milling machine."

In the area of aids to N/C code generation there have been two parallel activities, one working with sculptured surfaces [Tan 1979] and the other on unsculptured components. Each has used an N/C vertical milling machine for the manufacture of the test pieces. The unsculptured work reported here has concentrated on prismatic parts describable by the PADL-1 system [Voelcker and Requicha 1977].

CHARACTERIZATION OF THE MILLING ENVIRONMENT

A summary of the milling characteristics identified by Armstrong is given here and shown in Figure 1 [Armstrong 1982]. Related work on N/C code verification has been carried out at the University of Rochester [Hunt and Voelcker 1982].

Figure 1 illustrates a typical milling operation setup. Material removal is concerned with the transformation of the initial workpiece W_0 to the final component P by using tooling T and fixtures F as necessary. In analysing the milling process there are two main classes of tooling objects to be considered:

- S, which is any part of the cutter, chuck and machine tool to be considered in collision detection but which must not be used to attempt to remove material, and

- C, which is the part of the cutter which is designed to remove material.

In order to analyse cutter paths the movement of the machine tool with respect to the workpiece must be considered. This will require a knowledge of the physical geometry of the cutter and the parameters that define its range of movement so that the regions swept out by the tool may be examined. Although technological conditions such as feeds, speeds and monitoring of coolant supply are recognised as being equally important, they are not dealt with fully here.

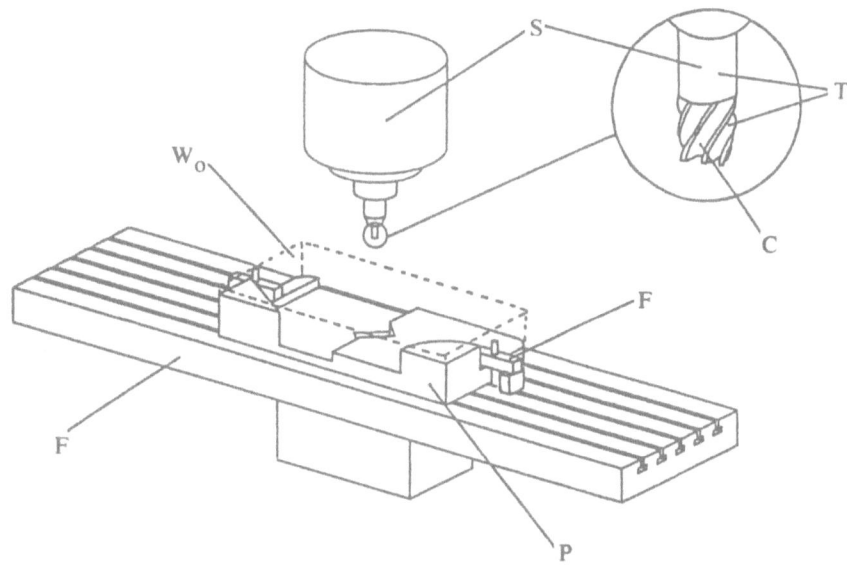

Figure 1. *Point sets relevant to analysis of the milling process.*

For the movement of the tool along each path i, the region swept out by the tool may be divided into two regions, CP_i and SP_i. (These are the regions swept out by C and S, respectively. CP_i is analogous to the operative swept region (OSR) described by [Hunt and Voelcker 1982]).

The transformation of W_0 may be achieved in a number of stages:

$$W_1 = W_0 \, -^*CP_1$$
$$W_2 = W_1 \, -^*CP_2$$
$$\cdots$$
$$W_n = W_{n-1} \, -^*CP_n$$

where the operator $-^*$ is the regularized set difference operator [Requicha and Voelcker 1977].

For satisfactory completion of machining, W_n, the final workpiece, will be congruent with P, the finished component.

Manufacturing Conditions—To ensure satisfactory, noninvasive machining strategies, various tests must be applied to the point sets W_0, P, CP_i and SP_i as follows:

- *Workpiece suitability.* The part P must be entirely contained within the initial workpiece W_0. Account should be taken of the different coordinate systems that may have been used in the definition of the part and the workpiece.

$$W_i \, \&^* P = P \quad 0 \le i \le n,$$

References pp. 153-154

where $\&^*$ is the regularized set intersection operator defined in [Requicha and Voelcker 1977].

- *Invasive machining.* This occurs when the tool moves either into the finished component P or any part of the clamps or fixtures F. These conditions may be stated formally as:

$$CP_i \&^* (F \, U^* \, P) = \emptyset \quad 0 < i \leqslant n,$$

$$SP_i \&^* (F \, U^* \, W_{i-1}) = \emptyset \quad 0 < i \leqslant n$$

where U^* is the regularized set union operator defined in [Requicha and Voelcker 1977].

- *Cutting strategy effectiveness.* The material removed by the cutter is defined by

$$CP_i \&^* W_{i-1} \quad 0 < i \leqslant n.$$

If the cutting strategies are to be effective, then

$$\sum CP_i \&^* W_{i-1} \neq \emptyset$$

- *Clamping conditions.* No tool movement is permitted to divide the workpiece into two or more disjoint solids unless the clamping is sufficient to hold each of these solids on the machine table. The distinction between swarf and large pieces of material must be made.

- *Technological conditions.* Deflections of the tool and the workpiece must remain within the limits prescribed by the surface finish and tolerance requirements. During the generation of cutter paths, attention must be given to the choice of factors such as spindle speed, feed rate, coolant supply, method of swarf removal and cutter type. The derivation of a formal relation between all these factors constitutes an extensive study in its own right [Yelloweley *et al.* 1978, Vogel 1979].

- *Stock concentrations.* Stock concentrations are regions of material to be removed that are large relative to the tool size. These, together with engineering data such as dimension and tolerance information, could be used as a guide to efficient tool selection, cutting strategies and setup selection.

Prototype System—The prototype software developed at the University of Leeds has, as input, descriptions of a part and the stock from which it is to be machined. From this it generates setup information and produces roughing and finishing strategies for the selected setups. This experimental machining module has been linked with the PADL-1 geometric modeling system.

Choice of Representation Scheme for Manufacture—Armstrong compares boundary, constructive solid geometry (CSG) and cell decomposition representation schemes and concludes that all could be used during the derivation of acceptable cutting strategies [Armstrong 1982]. Decisions in manufacturing planning often involve consideration of local geometries. If some spatial ordering is imposed upon the representations by deriving a decomposition of cells, each of which holds either a boundary or CSG representation of the material in the cell, then local regions of interest will be readily accessible. These cells may also hold local representations of fixtures and the final part which is to be produced.

Spatially Ordered Representation Scheme—This approach uses a decomposition imposed by a lattice work of planes parallel to the major axes. It is advantageous to keep the internal details of the resulting cells simple; the positioning of the lattice planes has been implemented to achieve this. The cells are derived from the boundary representation of the part. Infinite planes are then positioned coincident with each planar face and tangential to each cylindrical halfspace. This particular method is appropriate to the PADL-1 domain. In a larger geometric domain it is likely that each plane would be positioned to pass through each vertex and line of tangency of the component. The lattice planes for a simple part are illustrated in Figure 2. Slices through the resulting decomposition, normal to the vertical axis, are shown in Figure 3.

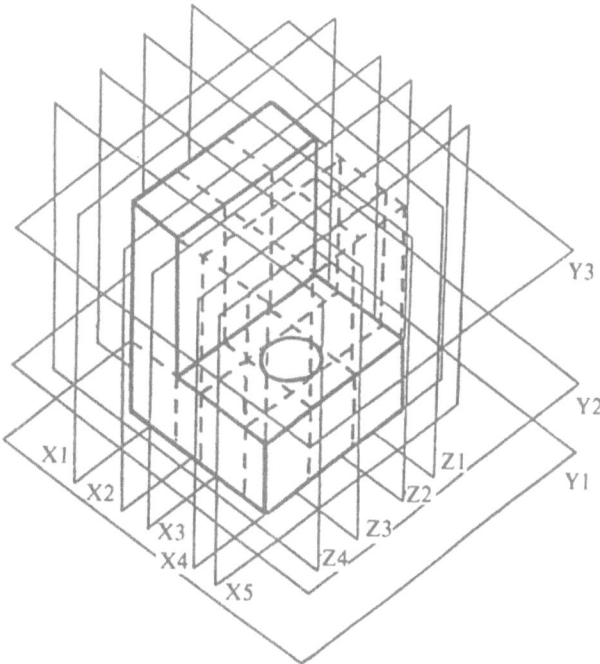

Figure 2. *Lattice planes for a simple part.*

References pp. 153-154

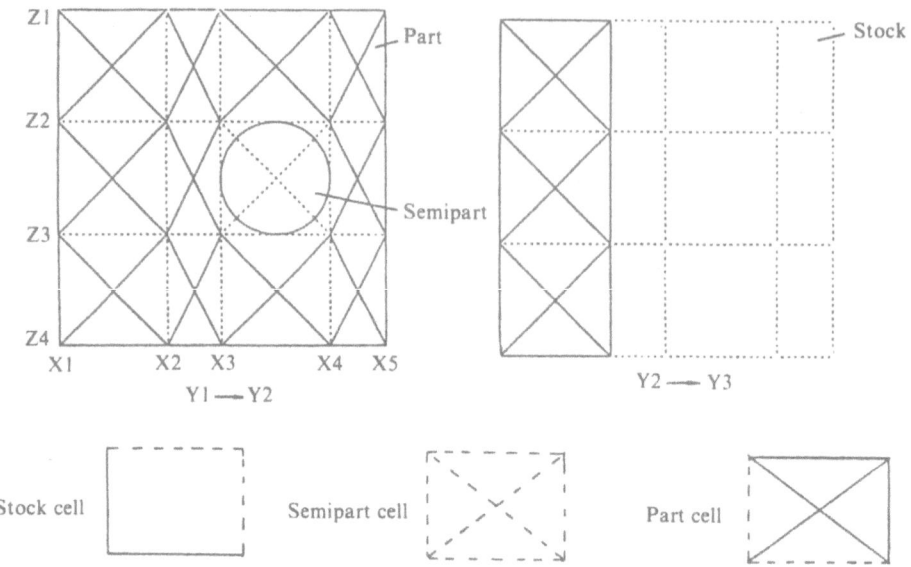

Figure 3. *Slices through decomposition.*

For the present implementation, the stock is assumed to be a rectilinear block, so each resulting cell is represented as one of the following:

- **Stock cell.** The cell contains only stock material, all of which must be removed. Any of the six cell boundary faces may be of type *stock* when it lies on the face of the stock, *part* when it lies on the face of the part and *internal* when it does not correspond to any real surface.

- **Part cell.** The cell contains only finished part material, none of which must be removed.

- **Semipart cell.** The cell contains both part material and stock material.

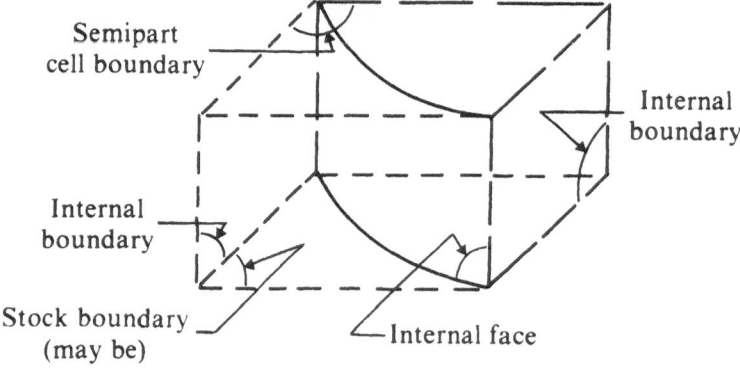

Figure 4. *Example of semipart cell.*

Fundamental Algorithms—Having obtained a cell decomposition, various low-level routines are provided which, given a cell and a tool path positioned relative to that cell, indicate whether that tool path is permissible within the cell, and, if not, what subset (if any) of the path is permissible. This is deduced by first identifying other cells through which the path passes, and then checking for a collision with internal cell faces within these cells.

Application Modules—The setup derivation, roughing, and finishing modules make use of the fundamental algorithms by testing required paths against cells in a given order. For example, where a path is not permissible within a cell, then all the cells below it in the search sequence can be marked as unmachinable in that setup.

As paths are tested and confirmed, the cell representations are modified by adding pointers so that future analysis will be based on up-to-date details of the workpiece.

Derivation of Setups—The method adopted here works from a list of setups to be tried. Initially this list contains all six of the setups assumed possible. These are with the tool axis aligned to the positive or negative X, Y, or Z axes of the PADL-1 system. Each setup on the list is examined to find the volume of material which can be removed. This is done by analysing the smallest tool possible passing along each face in each cell. Each tool is selected from a tool file which holds available tool diameters and their maximum cutting length. Once all the setups have been considered, the one in which the most stock can be machined away becomes the confirmed setup and is removed from the list. The cell representation is then updated to reflect the removal of material during the setup. This is repeated until all the stock material has been removed or no more setups remain on the list. This is shown in Figure 5.

Job Identification: MBB TEST PIECE

Total Stock Volume = 2869.6 Cubic Units

Setup +Z
Volume Removable = 2120.0
Percentage = 73.9

Setup −Z
Volume Removable = 745.4
Percentage = 26.0

Total Stock Removed = 2866.0

Percentage = 99.9

MINIMUM TOOL REQUIREMENTS

Number	Radius	Depth
1	0.600	5.10
2	0.600	6.50

Figure 5. *Setups derived for MBB test piece.*

References pp. 153-154

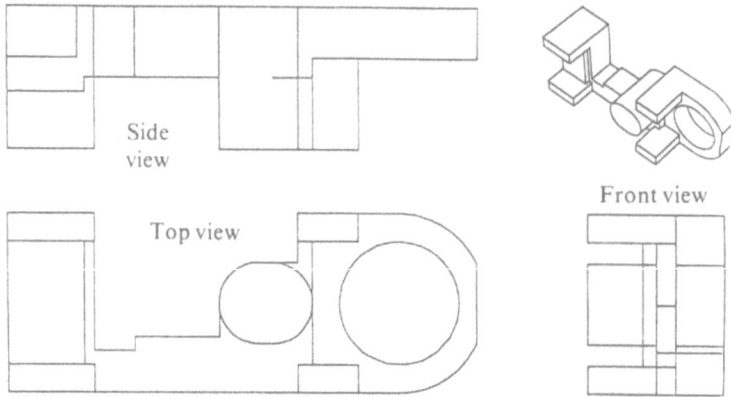

Figure 6. *PADL-1 drawing of MBB test piece.*

Derivation of Roughing Cuts—A simple strategy consisting of a number of parallel paths running along the length or width of the workpiece has been implemented. The user must choose to which axis the paths are to be parallel. He must also specify a single tool size since the algorithm has not been implemented for multiple tools.

Only those cells accessible by the tool are selected and as the cutter paths within a cell are derived they are concatenated to any previous path if no collision is detected. If a collision is detected, then paths are generated to lift the tool to a safe plane above the workpiece, to rapidly traverse to the next position directly above where material removal may continue, and then lower the tool into the workpiece. If a cell is marked as having had all material removed in a previous setup, the feed rate is changed to rapid within that cell (see Figures 6 and 7).

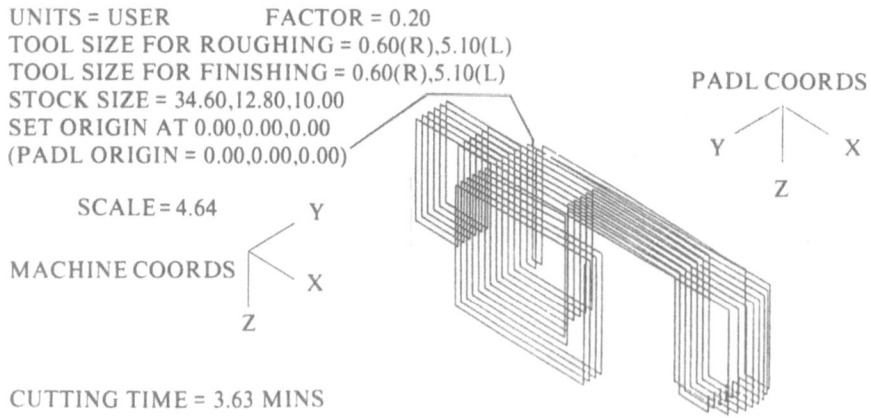

Figure 7. *Roughing cuts in −Z Setup of MBB test piece.*

Derivation of Finishing Cuts—The spatially ordered cells are scanned until a face is found that requires machining, then the continuation of the face in the neighbouring cell is found, in the direction that would cause climb milling.* The next linked face or boundary is found, and so on, until either the starting point is revisited or the workpiece boundary is encountered. At this stage, generation of the finishing path may proceed in the opposite direction, causing conventional milling. All faces are flagged once they have been machined, to prevent repeated machining later (see Figure 8).

At present, only a single finishing pass is taken, although provisions exist for generating a contouring cut to remove cusps, followed by a final finishing cut.

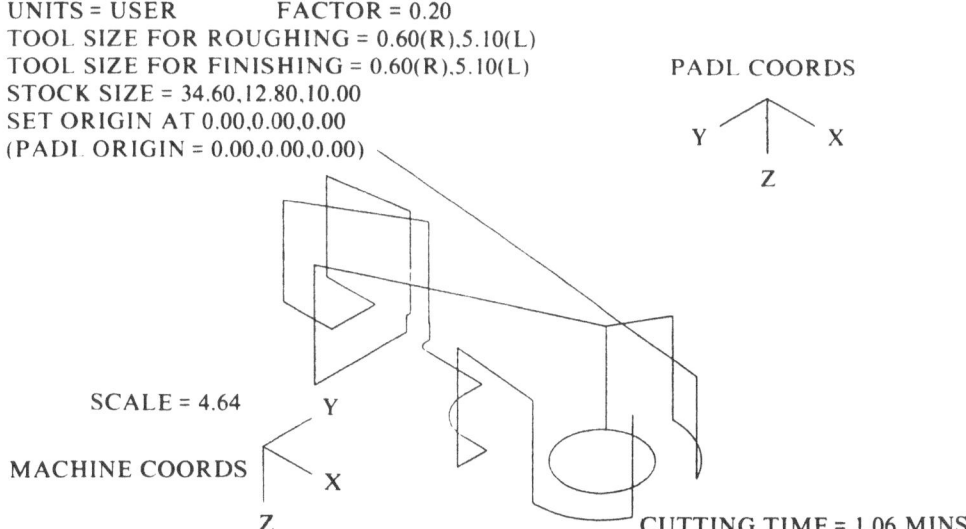

```
UNITS = USER          FACTOR = 0.20
TOOL SIZE FOR ROUGHING = 0.60(R),5.10(L)
TOOL SIZE FOR FINISHING = 0.60(R),5.10(L)      PADL COORDS
STOCK SIZE = 34.60,12.80,10.00
SET ORIGIN AT 0.00,0.00,0.00
(PADL ORIGIN = 0.00,0.00,0.00)
```

SCALE = 4.64

MACHINE COORDS

CUTTING TIME = 1.06 MINS

Figure 8. *Finishing cuts in −Z Setup of MBB test piece.*

Figures 9 and 10 show examples of the MBB component after rough and final machining respectively.

Prototype System Conclusions—Using the PADL-1 geometric modeling system, an experimental machining module has been implemented which takes a geometric definition of a nominal, that is, untoleranced component and auto-

---

*In **climb milling**, also called **down milling**, the work is fed in the same direction as the rotating milling cutter. The cutter in fact comes "down" onto the workpiece to begin its cut. In **conventional milling**, also called **up milling**, the work is fed against the direction of the rotating milling cutter. The cutter begins its cut into the workpiece so that it removes material in an "upwards" motion [Yankee 1979].*

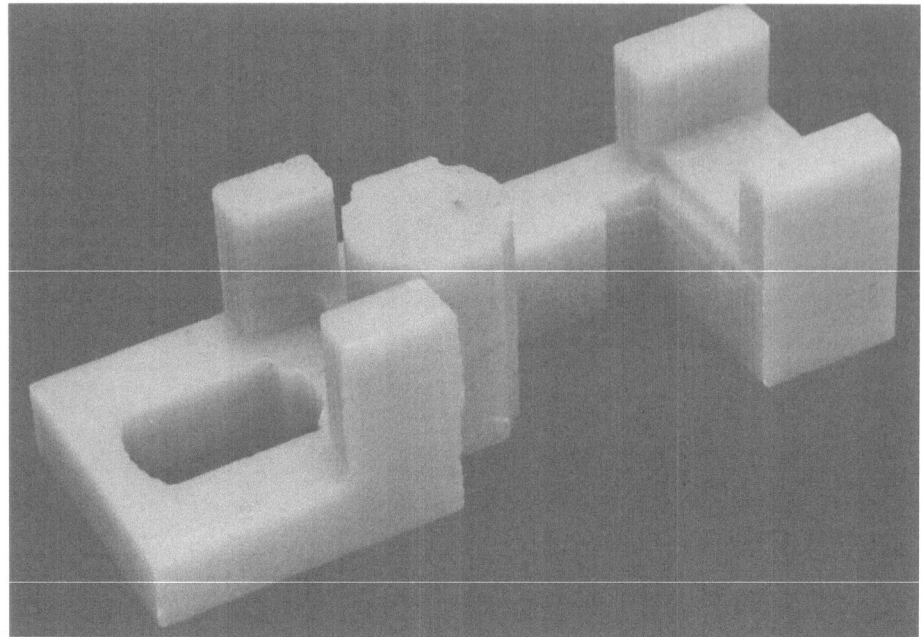

Figure 9. *MBB test piece after rough machining.*

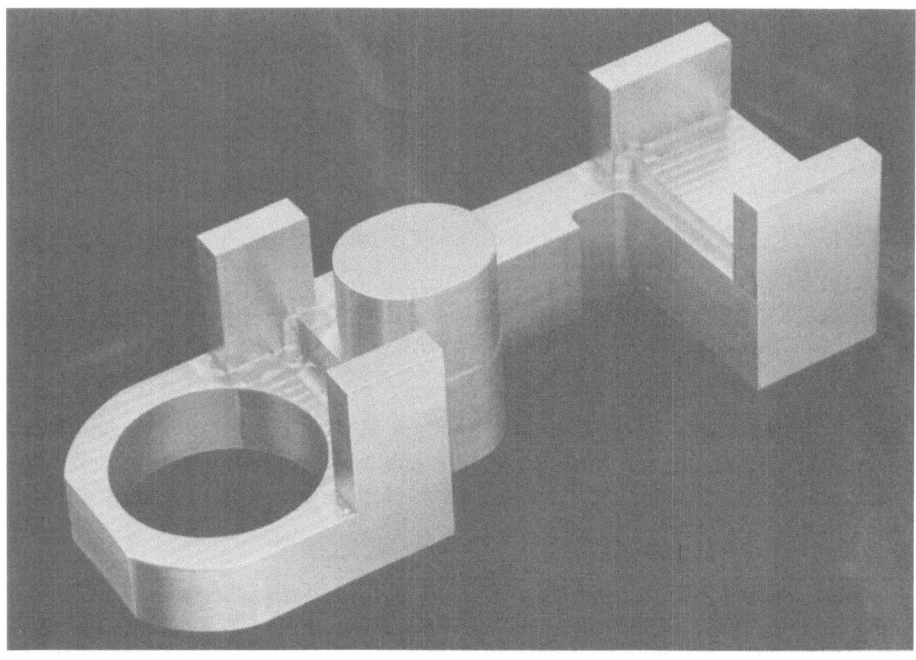

Figure 10. *MBB test piece after final machining.*

matically generates noninvasive roughing and finishing cutter paths to machine the component on a N/C machine using side and end mill cutters.

A series of setups may be derived based on the maximum material removed by the available tooling. However, these do not take account of methods by which the workpiece may be secured to the machine table, nor do they account for surface types and required surface finish.

This experimental work makes extensive use of a spatially ordered representation scheme which is derived from the boundary file of the PADL-1 modeler. The technique may be extended for use by other modeling systems since most hold a boundary representation. One advantage of a spatially ordered representation scheme as implemented here, other than the speed of data access, is that each cell contains only a few surface types.

In this implementation, minimal attention has been given to the technological considerations mentioned earlier, which are, however, recognized as playing a significant role in manufacture. The discussion of manufacturing conditions mentions that stock concentrations should be used as a guide to efficient tool selection, cutter strategies and setup selection. No work has been done in this prototype system to extract stock concentrations, and consequently a few undesirable effects have arisen.

As an example, during the rough machining the algorithms machine from one side of the component to the other. This will often result in thin walls of stock material remaining for the last path to clear. These walls are likely to fracture if machined incorrectly. Secondly, again during roughing, if the material to be removed is sparsely distributed, then the cutter will spend an unnecessarily large amount of time moving in air.

CURRENT RESEARCH WORK AND EMPHASIS

CAD/CAM Systems—There are functions of CAD that would benefit greatly from access to manufacturing data and, similarly, there are functions of CAM that require calculations of a geometric nature. Further automation will necessitate a true integration between CAD and CAM systems. An example of an integrated system, shown in Figure 11, would enable:

- Geometric calculations pertinent to the manufacturing environment to be made,

- Manufacturing details to be accessed and examined during design,

- Estimation of the cost of alternative designs and process plans,

- Simulation of manufacturing processes,

- Product changes to be implemented with minimal lead time, and

- Production to adapt rapidly to changes in the manufacturing environment. This is especially necessary in a flexible manufacturing system.

References pp. 153-154

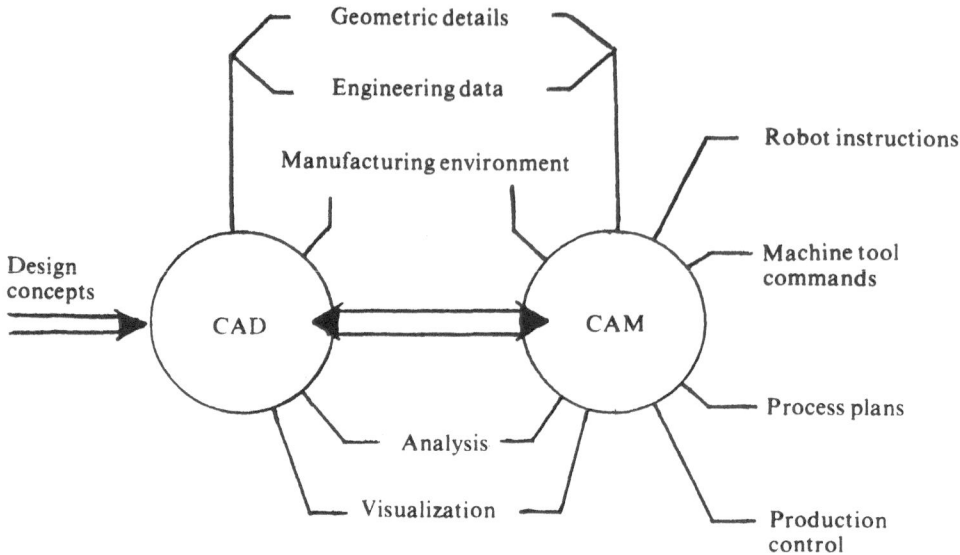

Figure 11. CAD/CAM integrated system.

If the integration of CAD and CAM is to be achieved, then a large amount of engineering data such as geometric and technological details of the component, the machine tool and the tooling must be held in the computer. In addition, some means must be derived for characterising the machining operations which individual machines are capable of undertaking.

Attention must be given to the relationship between the data to ensure that inconsistencies do not occur. Some engineering data are well defined and fall into the category of facts and figure. However, human manufacturing knowledge and experience are difficult to record.

Geometric and Engineering Data—At present, manufacturing information obtained from engineering drawings consists of the geometric details of the component and engineering data: dimensions and tolerances, surface finish requirements, datum faces, and often notes relating to methods of manufacture, types of fit, special finishing requirements and so on. Geometric modeling systems are able to represent unambiguously the geometric data relating to the starting workpiece, intermediate workpieces and the final component. Much effort is currently being applied to the problem of associating engineering data with the geometric data [Requicha 1977, Wickens 1982].

Manufacturing Environment—If an automatic choice of tooling, machine tools, clamps and fixtures, and machining strategies is to be made, then the technical, geometric and production control information must be available. This would include:

- Physical geometries of all aspects of the manufacturing environment from the manufacturing cell through to the tooling details, including the relative positional data,
- Technical data concerning permissible modes of operation, forces and power requirements, and accuracy of the operation,
- Scheduling control information giving data indicating the production state of the machine tools and also their running costs, and
- Manufacturing rules and company production practices.

Extension of the Prototype System—From the experimental work described earlier, it is possible to identify at least four areas in which further work should be conducted:

- The enhancement of representation schemes based on spatial ordering, to accommodate more complex geometries and machining processes,
- The investigation of other representation schemes for the derivation of acceptable cutting strategies,
- The further analysis of milling and other machining processes, and
- The inclusion of other manufacturing applications such as production control and planning systems.

This work and other associated studies related to application modules working from a geometric modeling system have indicated that there is a need for further work on representation conversion. In this prototype machining module a representation conversion has taken place from a boundary scheme to a spatially ordered scheme.

Machining can be viewed as a two-pass process: rough machining followed by finish machining. There is a need for representation schemes that accommodate the different machining requirements. The conversion to spatially ordered cells as described above is based on the geometry of the final object and therefore offers advantages for final machining.

For rough machining the largest tool consistent with the amount of material to be removed, the clamping arrangements, the power of the machine tool, the workpiece and the final component should be adopted. In many circumstances rough milling may be viewed as a collection of simple tool moves in the plane perpendicular to the tool axis.

There is a need for a representation scheme that will accommodate the different tool approach angles and the range of tools available on the machine tool. For each roughing tool the width and depth of cut and the feeds and speeds for different material types must be determined to give most efficient use of the power available.

One method presently under investigation is to impose a grid over the region to be removed. The grid size would be related to the width and depth of cut of

References pp. 153-154

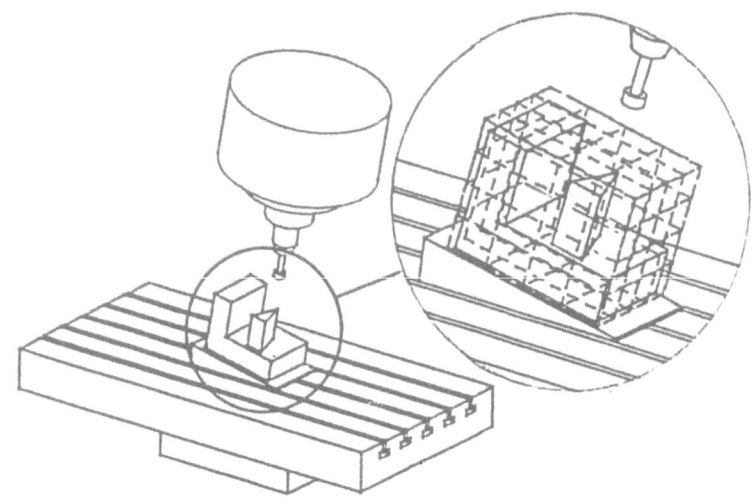

Figure 12. *Grid, workpiece and spindle.*

the tool being considered, and its orientation would be with respect to the cutter spindle (as shown in Figure 12).

By examining the grid with respect to the region of material to be removed, the suitability of the tool will be determined. Point membership classification (PMC) [Tilove 1980] with respect to the region of material to be removed can be performed on the grid points to find the regions of stock concentration. The

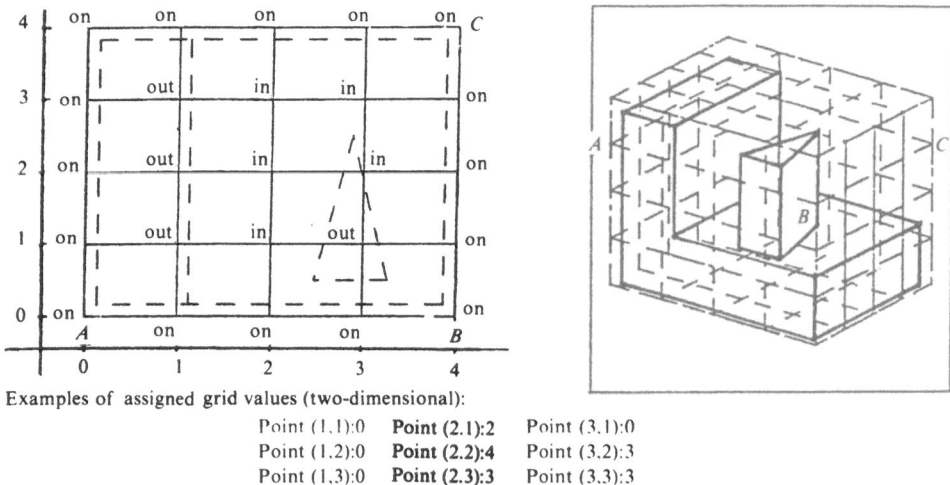

Examples of assigned grid values (two-dimensional):

Point (1,1):0	**Point (2,1):2**	Point (3,1):0
Point (1,2):0	**Point (2,2):4**	Point (3,2):3
Point (1,3):0	**Point (2,3):3**	Point (3,3):3

Figure 13. *A two-dimensional example of a grid.*

PMC function returns a value of *on, in* or *out* of the solid of interest. After completing the PMC, each *in* point will be considered in relation to the other points to find its depth into the material to be removed. A numerical value can be assigned to the *in* points to give an indication of the number of other *in* points surrounding it. A simple example is shown in Figure 13.

For a tool to be suitable for stock removal, the values returned must exceed a predetermined figure. This will depend on the manufacturing requirements, material specifications, and company-specific requirements and would be determined by experimental analysis.

Once a potential tool has been selected by the above method, the specific machining strategies can be determined. For each depth of cut, machining may be considered as a 2.5-dimensional process. This fact will be used together with machining rules and practices to ensure efficient strategies are produced. These will undoubtedly take a similar form to existing area clearance algorithms [CAM-I, Persson 1978, Sabin 1973].

ACKNOWLEDGEMENTS

The authors would like to express their thanks to Professor Cole, Head of the Department of Mechanical Engineering, for his support and encouragement of the CAD/CAM work. We have benefited from many discussions with Professor H. B. Voelcker, University of Rochester, and also with our colleagues in the Geometric Modeling Project.

The Science and Engineering Research Council is acknowledged for the provision of research studentships for G. T. Armstrong and G. C. Carey. Appreciation is also due to J. H. Fenner and Co. Ltd., for providing an invaluable opportunity to learn more about the manufacturing environment.

REFERENCES

[Armstrong 1982]
G. T. Armstrong, "A Study of Automatic Generation of Non-Invasive NC Machine Paths from Geometric Models," Ph.D. Dissertation, University of Leeds, Leeds, England, 1982.

[Armstrong *et al.* 1979]
G. T. Armstrong, M. Susan Bloor, A de Pennington and J. S. Swift, "Computer Representations of Parts in Mechanical Engineering," *Eurographics 79, International Conference and Exhibition*, Bologna, Italy, October 1979.

[CAM-I]
APT IV Computer System Manual, Vol. 2. Subroutine Library (A4V3), Computer Aided Manufacturing—International Inc., Arlington, Texas.

[Hunt and Voelcker 1982]
W. A. Hunt and H. B. Voelcker, "An Exploratory Study of Automatic Verification of Programs for Numerically Controlled Machine Tools," Technical Memo No. 34, Production Automation Project, University of Rochester, Rochester, New York, 1982.

[Persson 1978]
H. Persson, "NC Machining of Arbitrarily Shaped Pockets," *Computer Aided Design*, Vol. 10. No. 3. May 1978, pp. 169–174.

[Requicha 1977]
A. A. G. Requicha, "Part and Assembly Description Languages I: Dimensioning and Tolerancing," Technical Memo No. 19, Production Automation Project, University of Rochester, Rochester, New York, 1977.

[Requicha and Voelcker 1977]
A. A. G. Requicha and H. B. Voelcker, "Constructive Solid Geometry," Technical Memo No. 25, Production Automation Project, University of Rochester, Rochester, New York, 1977.

[Sabin 1973]
M. A. Sabin, "Computer Aided Part Program Generation," *Proceedings of the Second IFIP/IFAC International Conference on Programming Languages for Machine Tools*, PROLOMAT '73, Budapest, Hungary, 1973.

[Tan 1979]
S. T. Tan, "The Computer Aided Manufacture of Sculptured Surfaces — An Interactive Approach," Ph.D. Dissertation, University of Leeds, Leeds, England, 1979.

[Tilove 1980]
R. B. Tilove, "Set Membership Classification: A Unified Approach to Geometric Intersection Problems," *IEEE Transactions on Computers*, Vol. C-29, No. 10, October 1980, pp. 874–883.

[Voelcker and Requicha 1977]
H. B. Voelcker and A. A. G. Requicha, "Geometric Modeling of Mechanical Parts and Processes," *Computer*, Vol. 10, No. 12, December 1977, pp. 48–57.

[Vogel 1979]
S. A. Vogel, "Metcut Machinability Processor for NC," *Proceedings of the First Annual Conference on Computer Graphics in CAD/CAM Systems*, Massachusetts Institute of Technology, Cambridge, Massachusetts, April 9–11, 1979, pp. 5–12.

[Wickens 1982]
L. P. Wickens, "GMTR/3 Dimensions and Tolerances: A General Study," Geometric Modeling Project, Department of Mechanical Engineering, University of Leeds, Leeds, England, 1982.

[Yankee 1979]
H. W. Yankee, *Manufacturing Processes*, Prentice-Hall, Inc., Englewood Cliffs, New Jersey, 1979, p. 147.

[Yelloweley *et al.* 1978]
I. Yelloweley, A. Wong, and B. DeSmit, "The Economics of Peripheral Milling," *Proceedings of the SME Sixth North American Metalworking Conference*, Gainesville, Florida, 1978.

DISCUSSION

Kalman Brauner *(Boeing Commercial Airplane Company)*

Has all your work been predicated on PADL-1 paths or those sorts of motions? Have you considered cutters that follow more general curved paths?

Carey

The work that I have reported here has been done just on the PADL-1 modeling system. Some of the extensions that I was talking about in reference to trying to use the cutting capabilities are being done on a more general CSG modeler with more than just cylinders and blocks positioned orthogonally. This general modeler has all the sphere, cone, torus and other primitives.

G. C. Carey

Brauner

Are the algorithms going to be similar? Are they generalizable?

Carey

At the moment we are investigating how it can extend into the more complex geometries.

Herbert Voelcker *(University of Rochester)*

I should say I was an examiner on the thesis that was described. Graham has given some good reasons why this cell decomposition was used. There's another interesting reason to use that particular cell decomposition: within each cell you have only one type of boundary geometry, and thus you're never confronted with the transition from a planar to a cylindrical surface within a cell. That's a peculiarity of the decomposition that Leeds has used to advantage.

Michel Melkanoff *(University of California-Los Angeles)*

Have you made any efforts to optimize the cutting strategy by trying various orders and then picking from among the various possible orders the one which would provide the most cutting for the least time?

Carey

Not in this particular instance.

Melkanoff

It's not too difficult, it seems to me, because in most of these the order can be changed, and of course lots of combinations are possible.

Carey

Yes. In the case of the roughing structures, it was following a certain rule that it would go backwards and forward across the component. Obviously one could try to impose an order based on stock concentration or whatever. Then with a stock concentration there would be different machine instructions that you could adopt and compare different times and so forth. That will be considered in the next implementation.

John Hinds *(General Electric)*

There seem to be four cases in machining or moving the cutter: entry, slot cut, continuous cut, and exit. All I saw there were straight plunge cuts and retractions, which may not even be legitimate types. Have you thought about that kind of variety?

Carey

In this particular implementation we haven't distinguishd between those types of cuts. However, the system knows when it is plunging and so could alter the feed rates accordingly. And then when you're doing a circular interpolation as well, it could generate a continuous cutter path.

Hinds

Often what makes or breaks the system is whether you can do tangential exits and entries on command, rather than coming in directly. So there's a lot more variety.

K. K. Wang *(Cornell University)*

What is the current cutting strategy you're using and how do you carry out those strategies? Are you using machine commands or is it all built in?

Carey

For the roughing, it follows the rule that it will pass backwards and forwards across the component, and it will go down to the maximum depth of cut that it can, which in this particular case is the same as the length of the cutter surface. Obviously, this is not ideal when you're machining anything other than wax. But then one could alter that type of cut according to the material specifications and the power of the machine tool. For finishing, the algorithm works its way sequentially through the facial cells until it finds a face within a cell that it hasn't yet machined. Then it looks just at the extent of the face that it can machine. If an obstruction is found, it realizes it can't pass through so will lift the cutter to a safe plane and then drop down again when it can actually go back to machining the surface. So the algorithm takes account of the size of the cutter, examining each move to see if there's an obstruction or not.

Wang

And your rules are fixed?

Carey

Yes, the rules are fixed.

Wang

It seems fairly easy for your system to take the initial stock and pretend to follow the path and essentially build a model for the finished piece as cut by the system so that you could compare it with the original design. Do you plan to do that?

Carey

Yes, that's one of the things you can do. As you are cutting, you're modifying your work piece; obviously one test you can do is for complete machining, that is, to test whether the modified work piece is in fact the same as the designed component. For example, a right angle corner may have been designed in the component which is in fact too strict a design requirement. The machining rule would indicate incomplete machining, but in practice machining would be complete.

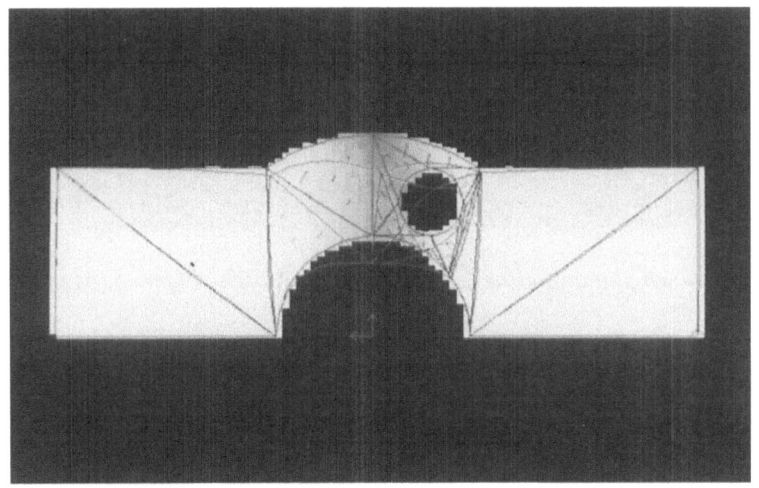

Plane strain analysis (see Wördenweber, Figure 10(c), page 93).

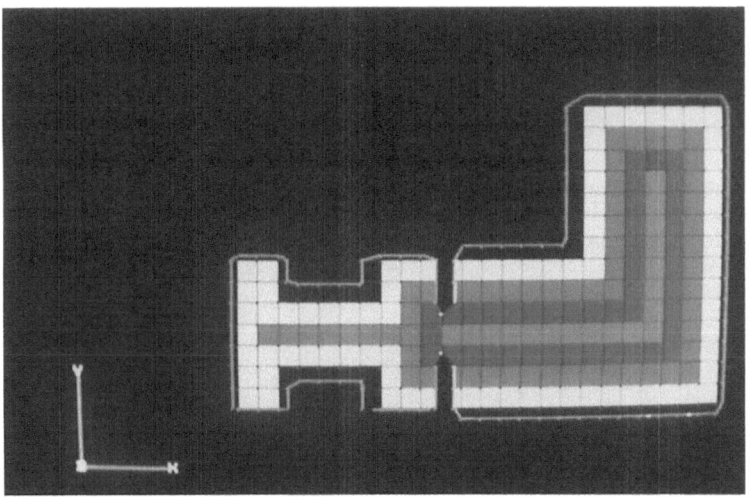

*Cross section of a casting/rigging system showing simulated temperature variation
(see Berry and Boulet, Figure 3, page 108).*

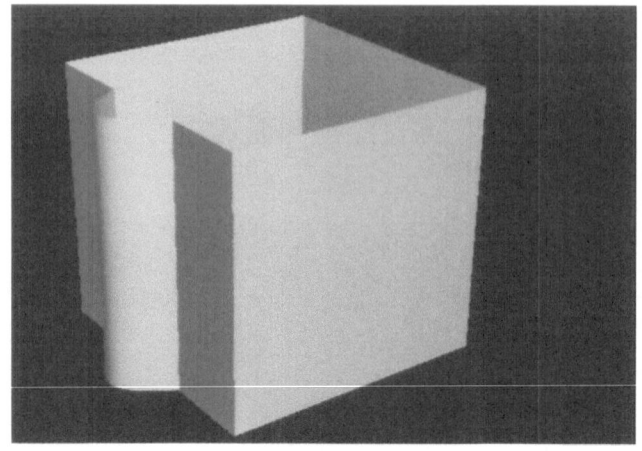

An extruded planar outline (see Sarraga and Waters, Figure 5, page 197).

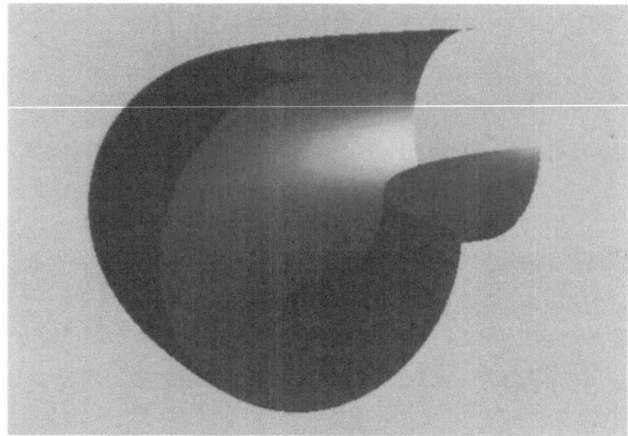

Three-sixteenths of a torus (see Sarraga and Waters, Figure 6, page 197).

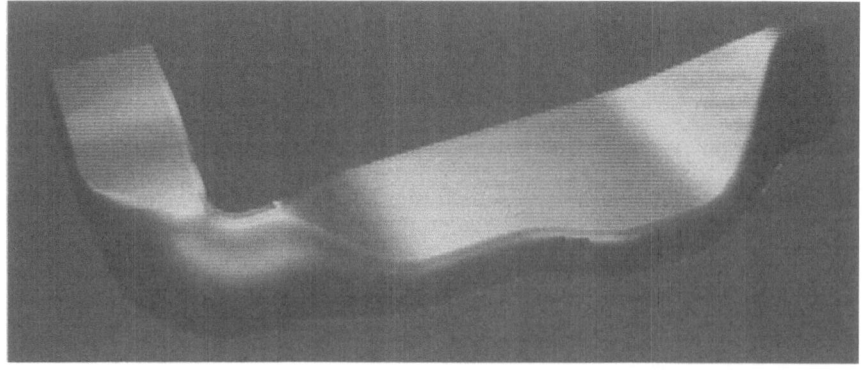

*A duct modeled with the GMSolid lofting facility
(see Sarraga and Waters, Figure 7, page 198).*

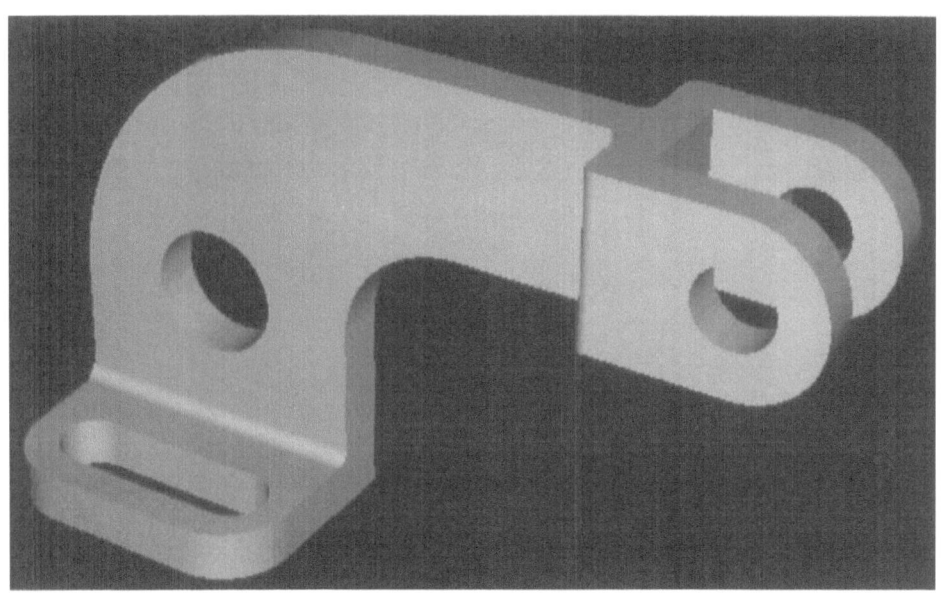

A bracket modeled in GEOMAP-III (see Kimura, Figure 3(a), page 215).

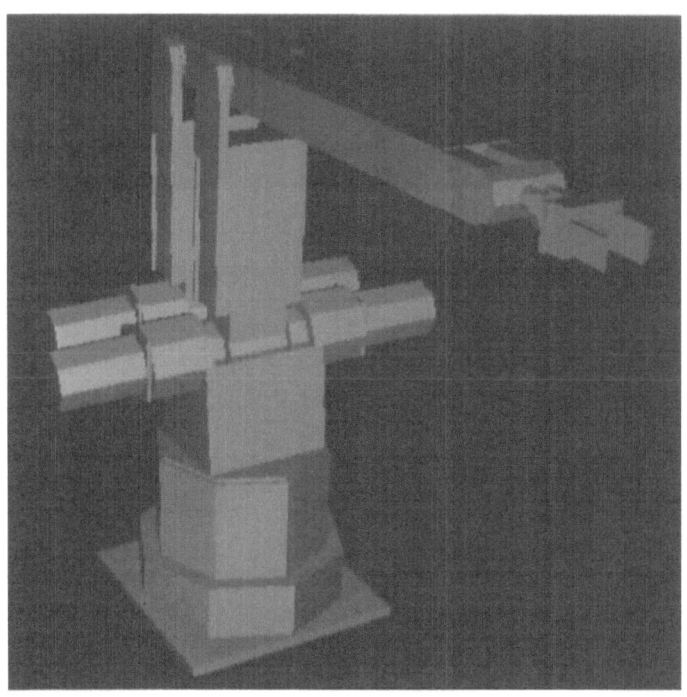

A robot modeled in GEOMAP-III (see Kimura, Figure 3(b), page 215).

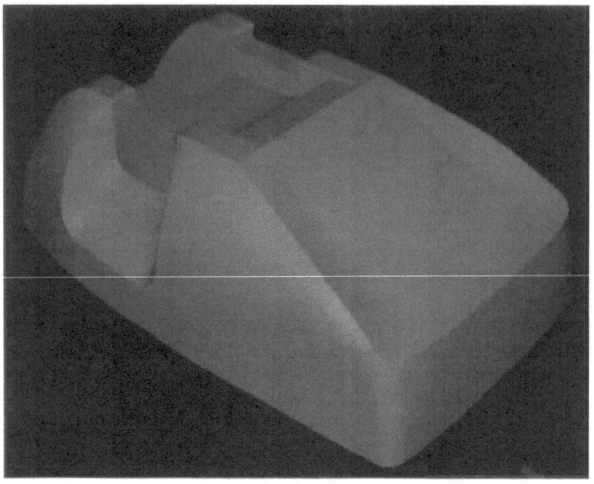

A telephone modeled in GEOMAP-III (see Kimura, Figure 22(b), page 231).

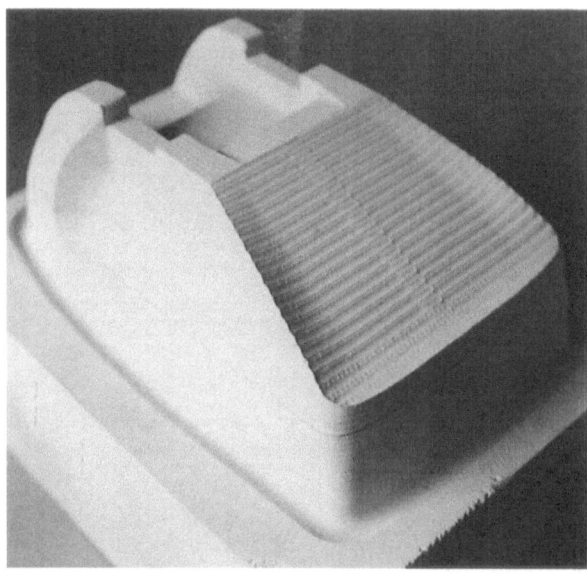

Three-dimensional model of the telephone (see Kimura, Figure 22(c), page 231).

ROBOTEACH: AN OFF-LINE ROBOT PROGRAMMING SYSTEM BASED ON GMSOLID

MARY S. PICKETT, ROBERT B. TILOVE and VADIM SHAPIRO

General Motors Research Laboratories
Warren, Michigan

ABSTRACT

The goal of the RoboTeach project is to provide a tool for programming industrial robots that does not require the use of physical robots, prototype parts, or other production facilities. Instead, the user of the system will program robots off-line utilizing GMSolid to model the geometrical aspects of a robot's workplace and interactive computer graphics techniques to develop, simulate, and debug robot programs.

RoboTeach consists of four complementary subsystems in various stages of investigation and development. These subsystems deal respectively with robot workcell layout, program generation and editing, program simulation, and program translation and down-line loading. The technical issues surrounding the design of RoboTeach are described, with particular emphasis on the merits of utilizing a solid modeling system to support advanced manufacturing applications.

INTRODUCTION

A major force motivating the emergence of solid modeling was the belief that sophisticated computer aided manufacturing systems would require informationally complete geometric models of objects, such as parts and tools, and also powerful computational capabilities to analyze and manipulate geometric information. General Motors Research Laboratories has been active in the area of solid modeling since 1977 [Boyse and Gilchrist 1982]. The RoboTeach off-line programming system is our first attempt to utilize GMSolid in an advanced manufacturing application. The bulk of this paper describes the application, the preliminary design of the RoboTeach system, and various research issues raised. Implications of this work, particularly as it relates to solid modeling technology, are discussed in the concluding section.

References pp. 177-180

Problem Description and Related Work—The vast majority of robot manipulators in production use today were taught by being led through a specific sequence of motions. This teach-by-showing method has served industry well in the past, primarily because the applications involved little or no program logic and were relatively few in number. The increased use of robots at General Motors (and elsewhere) has motivated us to seek alternative programming methods because teach-by-showing takes a great amount of time, often requires the use of prototype parts and other production facilities, and is cumbersome (at best) for use with applications involving conditional execution and external program inputs.

We use the term *off-line programming* to refer to any method for developing and debugging programs for industrial robots that does not require the use of physical robots, prototype parts, or other production facilities. Powerful geometric modeling tools are obviously required, and we were thus motivated to consider basing such a system on GMSolid.

There appear to be three major and largely independent streams of research relevant to off-line programming.

Development of high-level language—A number of high-level languages have evolved for robot programming. Several recent survey articles [Bonner and Shin 1982, Gruver *et al.* 1983, Soroka 1983] review some of these languages, discuss current trends, and contain extensive bibliographies for further reference. A major goal of that work is to identify the data types, control structures, and procedural capabilities needed for specifying complex tasks.

Robot programming languages do not qualify as off-line programming systems. While program logic can be developed without the use of prototype parts or production facilities, initial values of program variables related to geometric objects, such as points and coordinate systems, are typically specified by conventional teaching. Furthermore, there is no obvious way to debug a program written in a high-level language (to test that programmed points are reachable, that programmed motions are free of collisions, and so forth) without executing the program on a robot in a real or simulated production environment.

Graphic simulation—Partly in response to the need to debug robot programs before executing them, a second stream of research evolved aimed at simulating graphically the effect of executing a robot program. Geometrical aspects of the robot's workplace (*e.g.,* the robot, tool, parts, fixtures, and so forth) are described in a geometric modeling system. The simulator operates on the initial geometric model and the robot program; it updates the geometric model to reflect the execution of the program. Examples of this work are provided in [Soroka 1980, Meyer 1981, and Kretch 1982]. Various kinds of errors in a program can be detected and the program modified before it is actually executed on a robot. Estimates of the amount of time required to execute motion commands are usually available.

Simulation systems alone do not qualify as off-line programming systems, because they provide no assistance in generating or modifying the program.

Cell layout—A third stream of research is aimed at utilizing a geometric modeling (or other CAD) system to aid in the initial layout of the robot work-cell and to compute initial values for geometric parameters of the robot program. Cell layout involves the selection of a suitable robot, the design of the tool and holding fixtures, and the spatial arrangement of the robot, parts, and other objects in the robot environment. Examples of this approach are reported in the literature [Derby 1982, Kretch 1982, Soroka 1982, de Pennington *et al.* 1983, Dillmann 1983, Sjouland and Donath 1983].

Cell layout systems obviously provide some of the capabilities found in the simulation systems described above. A key difference is that simulation systems operate on executable robot programs, while user commands in cell layout systems can not generally be executed by any real robot.

Initial Feasibility Study—A project to study the feasibility of basing an off-line robot programming system on GMSolid was initiated late in 1981. The goal of the feasibility study was to carry the entire process through for a limited set of robot operations in a simple but realistic application. This study involved a spot welding application for a future car line [Pickett and Zarger 1983].

The feasibility study demonstrated the ability to:

- Model robots and tools in GMSolid,
- Access existing workpiece data from an industrial CAD database,
- Define the robot tool position and orientation from data in the database,
- Specify simple robot operations (weld points, approach and departure distances, configuration changes, speed changes),
- Perform simple error checks (such as joint constraint violations),
- Display the path of the robot arm for straight line or joint interpolated motion,
- Generate a robot program in VAL to perform the specified operations, and
- Execute the VAL program.

In this initial system, all of the user's interactions were in terms of existing models of the robot and part. At no time was the user required to specify such things as the coordinates or Euler angles for the robot tool.

RoboTeach Project—The long term goal of the RoboTeach project is to provide a single system combining the descriptive power of high-level programming languages with interactive workcell layout, program generation, and program simulation. General requirements for such a system have been spelled out [Guthrie *et al.* 1982].

The RoboTeach system is intended to provide a test-bed for research related to advanced manufacturing applications and also to provide useful intermediate

References pp. 177-180

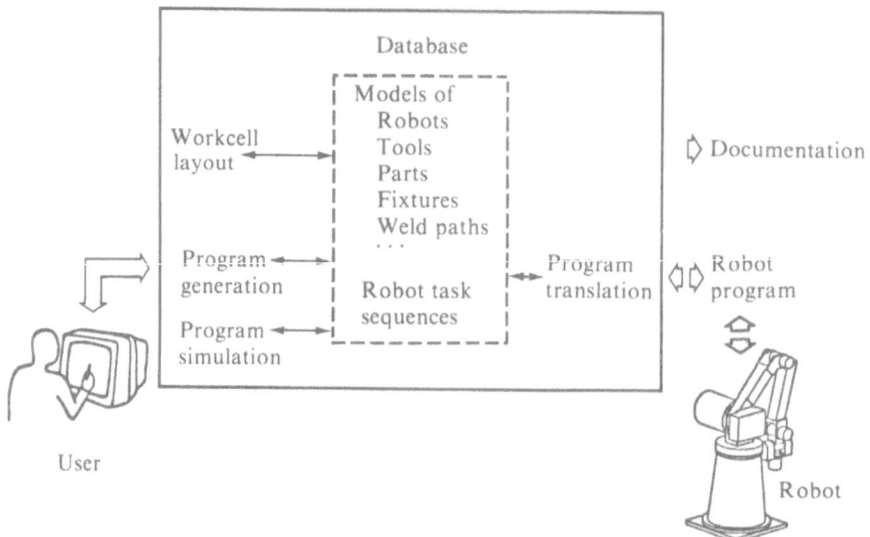

Figure 1. *Overview of the RoboTeach system.*

results in the form of prototype components for a production off-line programming facility. The major components of RoboTeach illustrated in Figure 1 are in various stages of investigation and development. The remainder of the report describes these components in greater detail and provides suggestions for future research and development.

WORLD MODELING

The heart of the RoboTeach system is the geometric database which contains representations of robots, robot tools, workpieces to be processed, and other objects in the environment of the robot workcell. A network database (like that described in [Warn 1975]) is used to represent the world model, permitting maximum flexibility in defining the appropriate links between components of the model.

The process of generating and simulating the robot program may well uncover modifications necessary in the design of tools, fixtures and the work environment; therefore, it is important to be able to move readily between the modeling system and the programming system.

Robots—The robots are modeled using the GMSolid mechanism facilities [Tilove 1983]. A model of the Cincinnati Milacron T^3 robot is shown in Figure 2. Each robot supported by the system is modeled once and placed in a standard library; copies are produced as required by the user. The use of geometrically complete models is necessary to support such facilities as hidden line removal and interference detection.

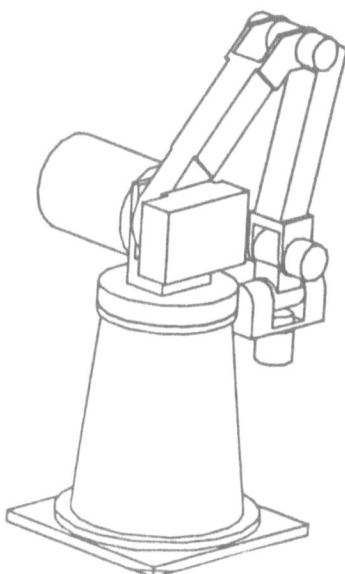

Figure 2. *Robot model selected for task.*

In addition to the coordinate systems used to define the joints of the mechanism, each robot contains two other coordinate systems: the base coordinate system and the mounting plate coordinate system. The base coordinate system determines how the robot is positioned at the time it is created. The mounting plate coordinate system determines how tools will be mounted on the face plate of the robot.

The robot models also include information on the joint position limits, the appropriate algorithm for solving the inverse kinematics problem, and parameters for the kinematics algorithm. As the capabilities of RoboTeach are expanded, other items such as joint velocity and acceleration limits will be added.

Tools—Robot tools are attached to robots using the rigid joint defined for mechanisms in GMSolid. A tool is defined by three entities: a solid model of the geometric shape of the tool, a mounting coordinate system, and a positioning coordinate system. These are shown in Figure 3 and discussed below.

When a tool is mounted on a robot, the mounting coordinate system is made to coincide with the mounting plate coordinate system of the robot. If the user wishes to experiment with different bracket sizes and shapes for extending the reach of the robot, the mounting coordinate system can be offset as shown in Figure 3. Once the correct size and angle for the bracket is determined, the bracket itself can be designed.

When the user commands a robot to move to a particular location, the positioning coordinate system is made to coincide with the selected target location.

References pp. 177-180

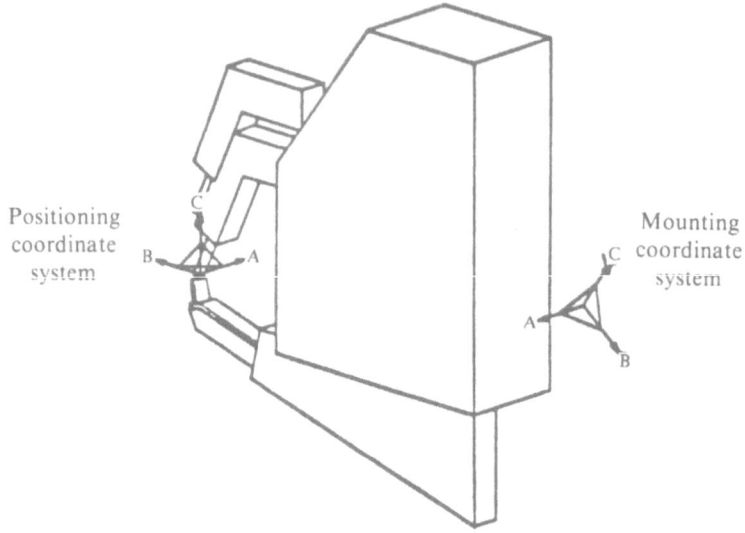

Figure 3. *Tool with its coordinate systems.*

The positioning coordinate system thus defines the position and orientation of the tool end effector. For instance, if the user wants to maintain a constant offset between the tool and the surface of a workpiece (as is necessary for painting applications), the positioning coordinate system of the tool can be offset from the physical tool.

It would be easy to allow the robot's tool to be modeled as a collection of lines, which would permit us to make use of existing wire frame tool models. However, we are reluctant to sacrifice geometric completeness of the robot and tool models since this would destroy one of the primary advantages of using an off-line system for simulation, namely, automatically checking for interference between the robot and its environment.

Other Objects in the Workcell—Many of the workpieces and fixtures in a robot's environment will be available from a wire frame or solid CAD database. If they are not available, crude models quickly generated in GMSolid, such as the rack and parts feeding line in Figure 4, will usually suffice.

The use of wire frame workpieces and fixtures decreases the ability of the system to perform automatic interference checking, although GMSolid does provide the ability to determine whether a line intersects a solid. Systems for automatic generation of solid models from wire frame models [Wesley and Markowsky 1984] generate a very large number of possible solids for a given wire frame and thus are not yet a practical solution to the conversion problem.

Locations—We use the term *location* to mean the position and orientation of the robot tool. One of the major features of an off-line programming system is the ability to extract locations from a CAD database.

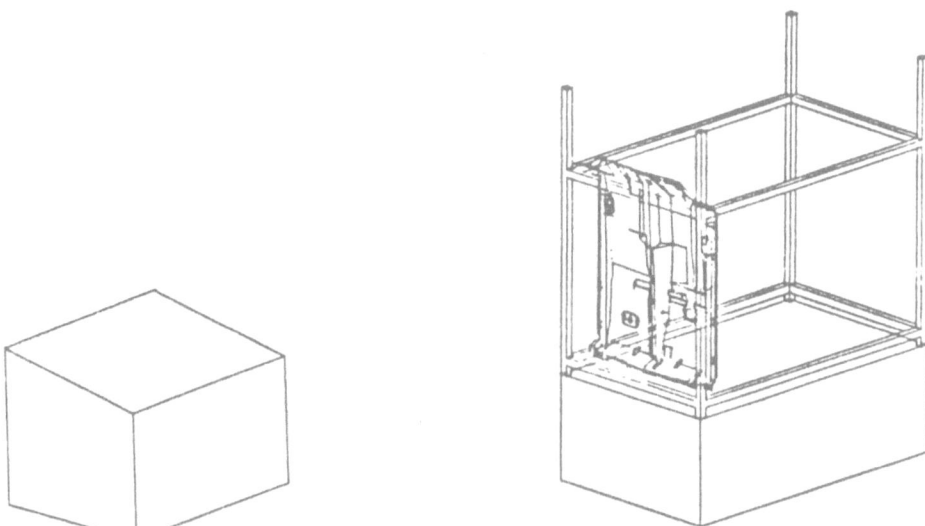

Figure 4. *World model for workcell layout example.*

RoboTeach currently uses coordinate systems to represent locations. There are many facilities provided to create and modify these coordinate systems; for instance, surface normals can be generated automatically and coordinate systems can be rotated to align given vectors with other vectors or points.

In some situations (tools with rotational symmetry, for instance), the user may not want to constrain the tool placement completely. RoboTeach does not currently support partially constrained locations. In addition, our users would like to specify a location as "the reachable coordinate system closest to the given coordinate system." However, there is no metric which our users have all agreed upon for determining the distance between locations. Instead, today the user generates a number of locations which satisfy a constraint (*e.g.,* a common sliding vector); the *test reach* facility described below provides a quick test for the reachability of these locations.

Future Modeling Enhancements—Among the modeling capabilities that must be added to RoboTeach is the ability to specify permanent attachments of locations to objects in the workcell (*e.g.,* weld points on a car body). Today, if the car body is repositioned to allow the weld points to be more easily reached, the weld points must be moved explicitly also. RoboTeach also requires a facility for specifying the movement of objects solely as a function of time (*e.g.,* the movement of workpieces on a moving conveyor).

Objects modeled in GMSolid do not currently include any tolerance information. It is clear that assembly and other applications will require such information. Much research remains to be done on representation and analysis of tolerances. Several approaches to this problem have already been outlined [Gugel 1974, Evans 1976, Requicha 1984].

References pp. 177-180

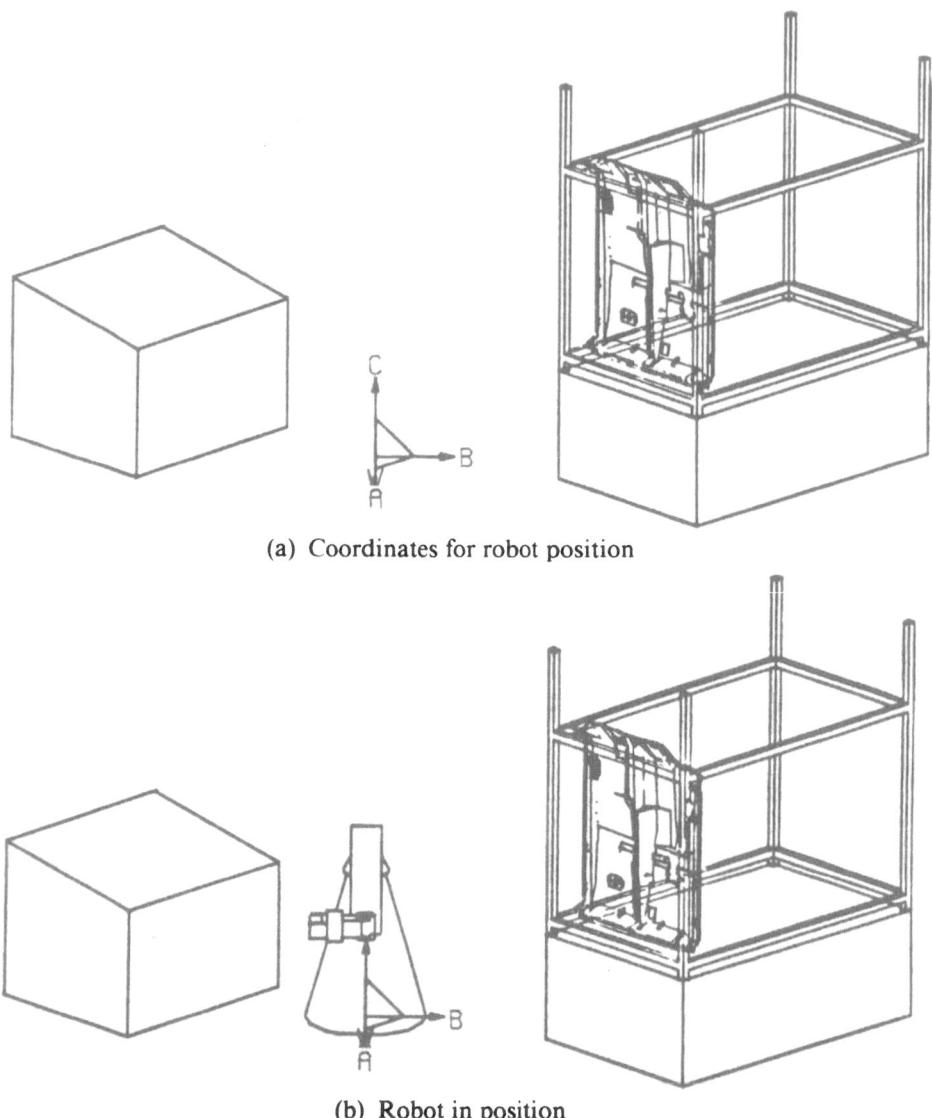

(a) Coordinates for robot position

(b) Robot in position

Figure 5. *Placement of robot in world model.*

WORKCELL LAYOUT

The primary function of the workcell layout subsystem is to enable the user to create and position robots and tools in an environment containing workpieces and other objects. Consider, for example, a workcell layout in which a robot is to be used to transfer parts, in this case automobile floor pans, from a shipping rack to the first stage of a parts feeding line. The elements of the world model for this task are shown in Figure 4; Figures 5 through 7 illustrate the functional capabilities of RoboTeach in creating such a layout.

Positioning the Robot—In order to create and position a robot for a specific task, the user must first select the desired robot and define a coordinate system specifying the desired initial position of the robot (Figure 5(a)). The system copies the selected robot from the models in the robot library, positioning it so that the robot base coordinate system coincides with the coordinate system defined earlier. It then selects and copies a standard tool from a tool library and attaches the tool to the robot (Figure 5(b)).

The user must now determine whether or not the motions required for the parts transfer operation are feasible. The mechanism modeling features of GMSolid may be used to modify the joints of the robot directly, but this procedure is very tedious and subject to error. The heart of the layout subsystem is an *exercise robot* function that enables the user to position the robot tool by specifying the desired position and orientation of the tool.

Verifying the Robot's Reach—To exercise a robot, the user defines a coordinate system as shown in Figure 6(a), using tools described in the section on modeling. The system computes all sets of robot joint angles that force the tool positioning coordinate system to coincide with the user-selected coordinate system and that are within the joint limits stored in the robot model. If no solutions exist, a "cannot reach" message is displayed; if one or more solutions exist (corresponding to multiple configurations that yield the same tool position and orientation), the world model is updated and each solution is displayed as shown in Figure 6(b).

It is not usually the case that the robot in its initial position will reach all required points. Various functions are available for moving the robot and/or the part. A *test reach* function is provided to enable the user to execute the robot solution program on any number of coordinate systems; the test reach function indicates which coordinate systems are reachable and which are not. (Thus, by creating a number of coordinate systems along a trajectory, the user can easily estimate how far in a particular direction the robot can reach.) New tools can be defined and attached to robots, tool mounting coordinate systems can be modified to simulate brackets, joint angles can be read and compared to joint limits, and so forth. Taken together, these functions enable process engineers to develop concept studies, as illustrated in Figure 7, in far less time than is possible using current, largely manual techniques.

Limitation of Scope—The layout system models kinematic properties of robot manipulators, but it possesses no understanding of programmable robot controllers. The *exercise robot* function analyzes the relationship between joint angles and end-effector position, but it does not produce a trajectory or estimate the time required to move. In RoboTeach, these functions are part of the simulation subsystem which is discussed later.

The existing prototype system supports only the robot shown (a geometrically simplified but kinematically accurate model of a Cincinnati Milacron T^3 robot). The addition of other robots and various other enhancements are currently underway.

References pp. 177-180

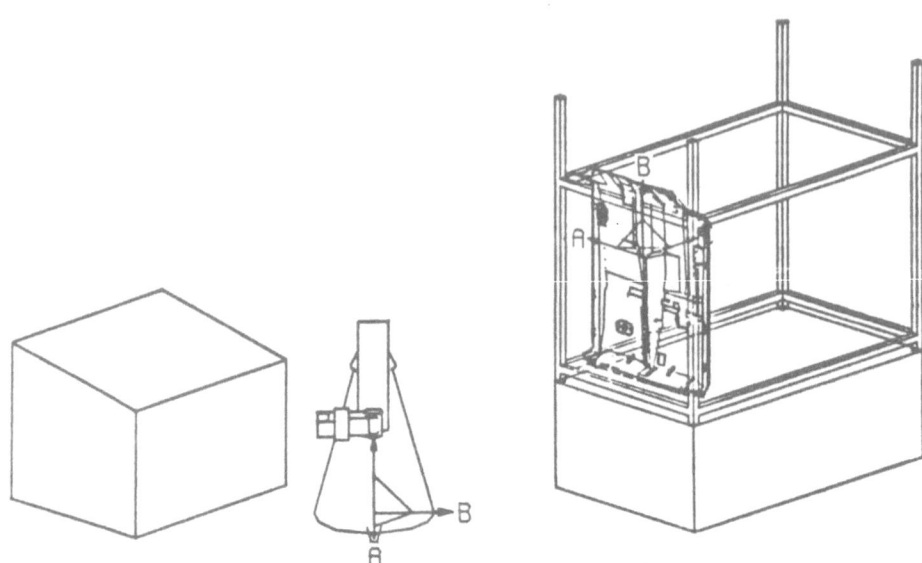

(a) Establishing coordinates for the *exercise robot* function.

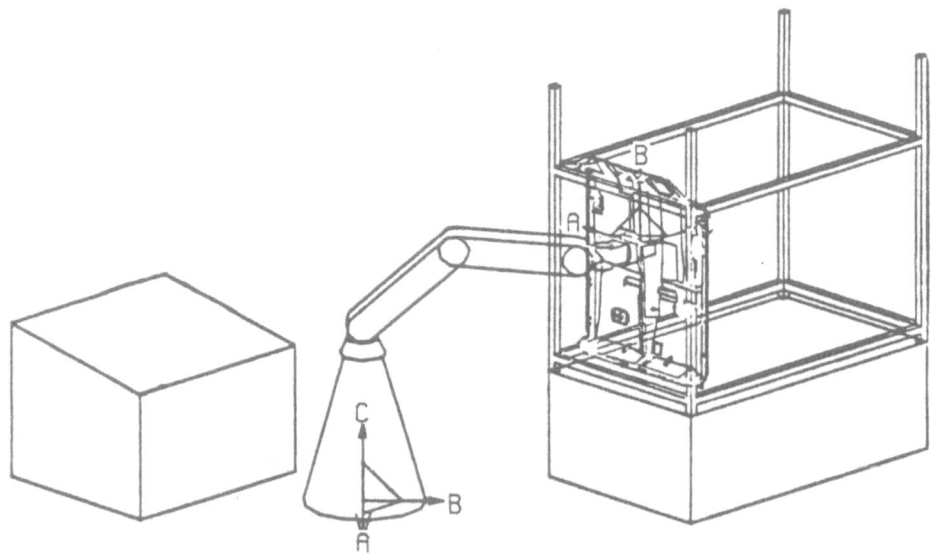

(b) One *exercise robot* solution.

Figure 6. *Exercising robot to test its ability to reach extreme positions.*

Research Implications—We pass now to a discussion of the major technical issues raised by workcell layout and our plans for future research in this area. The power of the workcell layout system arises from the facts that, first, it is

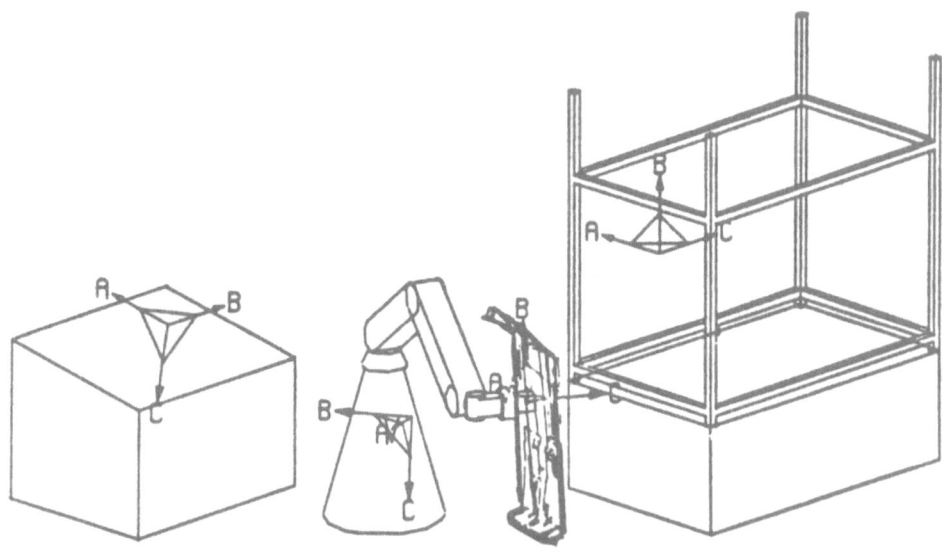

(a) Robot moving part along coordinate-defined path.

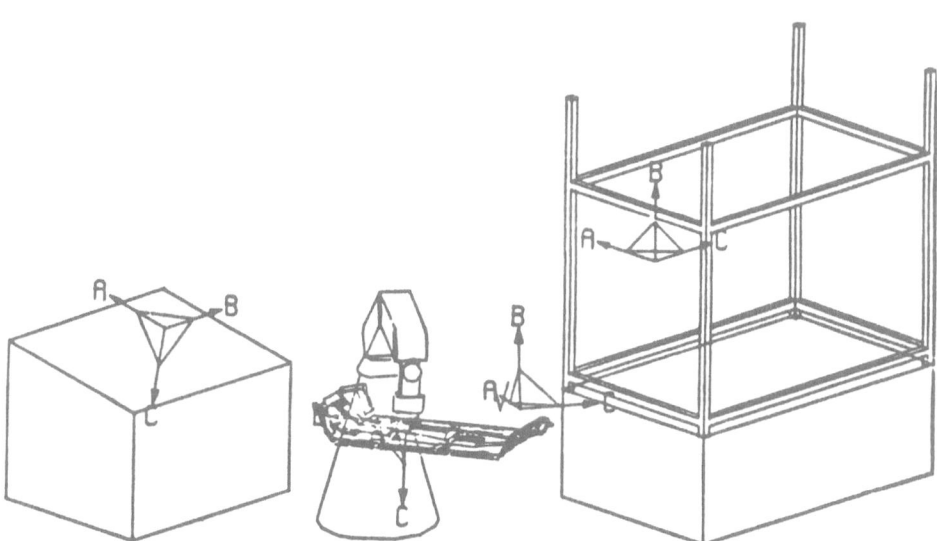

(b) Position of robot and part as movement along coordinate-defined path continues.

Figure 7. *Workcell layout concept study.*

embedded in a powerful system for modeling and manipulating geometric objects, and, second, it is capable of solving problems related to kinematic properties of robot manipulators. We shall focus on this second strength in the discussion below.

References pp. 177-180

As discussed earlier, the robot model contains the name of an appropriate robot solution (or inverse kinematics) procedure, as well as the parameters (such as link lengths and joint limits) that typically are input to such procedures. In the current implementation, the solution proposed by Paul was used, and we had originally planned to add a new solution program for each new robot [Paul 1982]. It soon became clear that the approach is unwieldy. General Motors uses a large variety of robots, and the design and implementation of solution programs require specialized expertise. To expedite the addition of new robots to the system, more general techniques are desirable. We are currently investigating a new numerical approach that will provide a general scheme for solving inverse kinematics problems for five- and six-degree-of-freedom robot manipulators [Tsai and Morgan 1984].

A second line of current research is aimed at providing automatic or semi-automatic robot placement capabilities. That is, we would like to enable the user to specify a plane (usually the floor) and a number of locations; the system would suggest where on the plane the robot can be placed to reach all locations. We are considering two approaches to the problem. The first is based on the use of mechanism analysis software to produce a single (in some sense optimal) placement. The second is based on the use of geometric models of the robot's workspace to produce a subset of the plane corresponding to admissible robot positions.

REPRESENTATION OF ROBOT TASK SEQUENCES

The workcell layout subsystem allows the user to position entities in the workcell, but it does not have a requirement for remembering sequences of locations or allowing specification of operations at each location; simulation in the workcell layout subsystem is limited to positioning the robot at each separate location when it is defined by the user. This section describes the representation of robot task sequences used by the program generation and simulation subsystems.

Questions and Assumptions—The following interrelated issues required resolution:

- How high level the task specification would be,
- How independent of the application it would be
- How independent of the robot type it would be, and
- Whether its form would be textual or a data structure.

We first distinguished between *task-level* programming systems (what to do) and *robot-level* programming systems (how to do it) [Lozano-Pérez 1982]. Due to the wide variety of applications of robots within General Motors, we decided to focus our attention initially on a robot-level system. We felt that application-oriented task descriptions could be compiled into the robot-level task specification later.

The decision to direct our efforts towards a robot-level system conflicted somewhat with our desire for robot independence, since the task sequence now had to specify how to accomplish a task using robots with a wide variety of functions. There is as yet no agreement on a fundamental repertoire of robot functions. Efforts are underway to define such a basic function set (see [D'Souza *et al.* 1983] and [CAM-I 1983] for examples). However, these efforts are complicated by the rapidly changing robot technology, particularly in the area of sensors and communications among components of integrated workcells.

Since strict robot independence is impossible in a robot-level system, we felt that our task representation had to be flexible. We thus decided to represent task sequences using the network data structure available to us in GMSolid. We attempted to isolate common functions, but we felt free to add robot-dependent functions when it seemed reasonable. It is our plan to attach to the robot model a table specifying which of the functions are legal for that robot type. This is a generalization of an earlier plan to allow the user to specify which hardware options had been purchased for the robot being programmed, thus affecting some of the functions normally allowed for that robot type.

Our internal representation of the robot task sequence is in the form of data structures rather than text. One could consider our data structure to be the parsed form of a textual language; a syntax could be added to the language if desired, but we had no inclination to invent yet another robot programming language. In the remainder of this paper, when we speak of the RoboTeach language, we mean this network data structure.

Most of the effort of programming robots in the past has been devoted to the geometric aspects of the program. However, it is clear that future applications will become increasingly more demanding in their requirements for interactions with their environment, their need for complex decision making, and so on. There is a growing trend to include in robot programming languages some facilities that have long been available in more general programming languages: a variety of data types, input/output capabilities, modular program construction, structured programming logic functions, and others. This paper will not attempt to document the entire RoboTeach language, but, rather, will describe several aspects of the language which are important to off-line programming. The remainder of the language looks like any reasonably modern programming language.

Language Specifications—The current RoboTeach motion specification includes specification of two coordinate systems, a trajectory type, and a speed. One of the coordinate systems is the destination location; the robot tool's positioning coordinate system is made to coincide with this location as a result of the move command. The second coordinate system is used, along with the trajectory type, in determining the trajectory. For instance, a robot moving with a straight line trajectory may move some point in the arm other than the tool's positioning coordinate system in a straight line.

References pp. 177-180

This trajectory specification is adequate for point-to-point applications such as spot welding and material handling. However, for continuous path applications such as spray painting, it will be necessary to provide additional forms for motion definitions. One such form might be the points along the curve implicitly defined by the intersection of two surfaces, with the orientation of the robot tool specified in relation to surface normals for the surfaces. Such a trajectory specification would also include information on velocity or acceleration. It will also be necessary to permit RoboTeach to acquire the robot trajectory from a user-defined (probably application-specific) source in some cases.

A location used in a motion specification may be one of three types: stationary, moving, or relative. Moving locations follow a predefined trajectory which is a function of time. Stationary locations may be moved explicitly during the program simulation, but do not move as a function of time. Relative locations are defined in a fixed relation to a base location, which may itself be any of the three types.

Locations may be modified during the course of simulating the robot program. For instance, the VAL language has a function which changes the value of a location to be the current position of the robot's tool. In this sense, there are both location constants and location variables in RoboTeach.

Work is still underway in the design of the program generation and simulation subsystems of RoboTeach. For that reason, the design of the RoboTeach language is not complete. This section has described the overall approach to the language and some of the decisions made in its design. In the following sections we discuss our plans for program generation and simulation.

GENERATION OF ROBOT TASK SEQUENCES

Most of the research issues in the program generation system are related to human factors issues. One of the first issues to be resolved is how dependent the system will be on the specific robot. This, in turn, depends on who will be using the system. If the plant floor robot programmers will use RoboTeach as a tool, then the user interface for program generation should probably be similar to the user interface for programming the physical robot, that is, with simulation of teach pendants, and so on. However, if central office personnel who must deal with a wide range of robots will be the primary users, then the program generation user interface should be quite uniform for all robots.

Application Independence—One issue which was discussed earlier is how application independent the system should be. As explained above, we have decided to make the initial RoboTeach system application independent, even at the expense of asking the user to do more of the intermediate level programming than would be required for an application-specific system.

Geometric or Textual Programming—Another issue involves the difference between the geometric and the logical features of the robot task sequence. It is fairly clear how to allow the user to specify the geometric portions of the robot task by pointing at the locations (or curves or other trajectories) on the graphics screen. It is less clear how to specify the logic of the program, the use of sensor input, the handling of asynchronous interrupts, and so forth, using a graphics system.

One approach would be to allow the user to write a textual program to specify these nongeometric features and then use the graphics system for adding the geometric features to the program. This is similar to the approach taken by VAL and other languages today: the logic of the program is prepared textually with the locations specified by name; then the named locations are defined when the program is first executed on the robot. However, at the time the textual logic is being written, no error checks for interference or reachability can be made. In addition, we hope to have process engineers who are not expert computer programmers using RoboTeach. For these reasons, we would like to take advantage of the presence of a sophisticated graphics system to provide an alternative to a textual programming language.

Simulation Level—Another issue to be resolved in this portion of RoboTeach is how much of the simulation subsystem to incorporate. The user will likely want to see the robot in position at each requested location, so checks for tool orientation and clearance can be made as the program is being generated. It is less clear whether to simulate trajectories between specified locations, determine cycle times, and perform operations (such as grasping a part) as the program is being generated.

Editing Issues—The program generation subsystem of RoboTeach includes both the initial program creation and also subsequent program editing. The editing portion raises other interesting issues about determining where in the program the editing is desired. Must the user simulate the program up to the point where editing is to be done? Could the user select a location and indicate that editing is to be done in the portion of the program which operates on that location?

Not all the issues discussed in this section have as yet been resolved for RoboTeach, so no definitive answers can be given for them.

SIMULATION

When completed, the simulation system will operate on several robots, their associated task sequences, and the initial geometric model of the environment. It will modify the geometric model to reflect concurrent execution of the various robot programs, report cycle times, and perform a certain amount of automatic verification. Our remarks are quite speculative; the simulation system is currently the least well defined portion of RoboTeach. In the discussion below, we focus first on simulation and then consider verification.

High-Level Simulator—We propose to study and design independently (insofar as possible) two simulation subsystems. The high-level, or process indepen-

References pp. 177-180

dent, simulator is largely unaware of the particular processes it simulates and is thus extensible to components of a manufacturing cell other than traditional robots (N/C machines, sensors, conveyors, and so forth). The high-level simulator assumes a particular model of concurrent computation, possibly based on message passing, and emulates the execution of a number of processes on a serial computer. It will provide break-point, trace, and restart capabilities and will also manage a mechanism for interprocess communication. (The high-level simulator is not a sophisticated multirobot controller. Such a controller would be modeled as another kind of low-level process.)

Low-Level Simulator—The low-level, or process, simulators are responsible for executing programs understandable to the process and for modeling the effects of the process on the geometric environment. In the initial system, a process corresponds to a robot controller, and the primary effect produced is manipulator motion. Initially, we plan to use very simple process models corresponding to the "rules of thumb" currently employed by process engineers to estimate velocity and acceleration profiles. These rules of thumb have two main properties. First, they are deterministic: the motion of the manipulator is known precisely, and operations have deterministic results. Second, they are grossly simplified: dynamical effects are ignored. More accurate simulations should be possible, if enough is known about the particular controller, through the use of dynamical mechanism analysis techniques. Nondeterminism can be built into the process simulator by producing somewhat random changes to the geometric environment. Thus, instances of missing and improperly positioned parts, and other anomalies, can be modeled. (The nature of the nondeterminism is not currently represented in the world model itself.)

Unresolved Issues—Difficult issues are raised by verification, error handling, and transitions between program generation and simulation. Each of these is nearly manageable when there is a single low-level process, but they become quite complex when multiple communicating processes are simulated. It will be increasingly rare to find robots which operate independently of other machinery in the workcell. Some of the interactions between objects in the workcell (*e.g.,* signal lines connecting robots) will involve communications between the objects, while others will be purely timed interactions.

Some execution errors and constraint violations, such as joint position, velocity, and acceleration limits, obviously may be detected by the process simulators and reported to the high-level simulator. Errors such as collisions, races, and deadlocks raise two interesting issues. First, how should such errors be detected (*i.e.,* by what algorithm), and second, which part of the system is responsible for detecting the error (*e.g.,* the process simulator, the high-level simulator, or some other verification process that communicates with the individual processes)?

Algorithms for static interference testing between solids are known and can easily be extended to assemblies of solids and mechanisms, but the algorithms are generally slow. Dynamic interference based on three- and four-dimensional swept volumes has been studied by [de Pennington *et al.* 1983] and [Esterling and Van Rosendale 1983], among others. Recent techniques based on recursive subdivision may lead to efficient and robust algorithms for this class of problems [Sarraga and Waters 1984]. In the event that portions of the geometric environment are modeled as wire frame objects, similar operations can be performed on solids and lines.

Because the process simulators cannot actually execute concurrently, it is difficult to imagine how they would perform dynamic interference tests. Instead, they will have to communicate their actions to the high-level simulator for further processing. The details have not yet been worked out. Detection of races and deadlocks is also unresolved.

One of the major goals of the RoboTeach project is to provide a smooth transition between program simulation and modification. The simulation system must accommodate certain interruptable states (*e.g.,* break points set by the user, error conditions, and so forth) at which the user can stop simulating and begin modifying programs.

PROGRAM TRANSLATION

The final subsystem of RoboTeach to be discussed here is program translation. The task sequence must be translated from its internal representation to a robot-specific program. There is also considerable desire among potential users of off-line robot programming systems to be able to reverse this translation process and transform existing robot programs into task sequences which can be simulated and edited.

As mentioned earlier, there is currently work underway to try to define a standard robot function set and a format for standard programs which is at a level analogous to the CLDATA format for N/C machines. The ICAM project has defined another potential standard with MCL [Wood and Fugelso 1983]. However, until some such standard comes into widespread use, it will be necessary to implement a postprocessor to produce the robot specific program from the task sequence representation for each new robot type added to RoboTeach.

Another area where standardization will have a beneficial effect on off-line programming systems is in communications with robots, thus easing the problem of down-loading the final robot program into the robot on the plant floor or up-loading an existing program into the off-line system.

The feasibility study mentioned earlier produced VAL programs which were executed on the PUMA 600 robot. We have also implemented part of the translator for the Cincinnati Milacron T^3 robot. However, the translation process is only peripherally related to the solid modeling research issues which are our primary interest and that process will not be discussed further here.

References pp. 177-180

RELATED RESEARCH DIRECTIONS

We have now described the various components of the RoboTeach system and have discussed some of the research issues which they engender. RoboTeach will also provide an excellent test-bed for a number of related research issues, described in this section.

The current emphasis of RoboTeach is on robot-level programming. However, there are many aspects of RoboTeach which would be directly useful in a task-level programming system. For instance, RoboTeach contains information required for the world modeling needed in a task-level system: geometric and physical descriptions of much of the task environment, kinematic descriptions of the robot and mechanism linkages, and such robot characteristics as joint limits and kinematic parameters. In addition to research in trajectory planning and in application-specific analysis, additions to RoboTeach which would be necessary for comprehensive task-level programming include tolerances of parts and their positions in the environment, automatic determination of new kinematic limitations imposed by the geometry of nearby parts, and analysis of closed-loop mechanisms.

Related to the automatic generation of robot programs is the more global issue of determining which tasks should be assigned to each robot in an integrated manufacturing cell. This form of process planning would benefit from the ability of RoboTeach to determine potential collisions, compute cycle times, and so forth. (Recently, related work has been done in this area [Udupa 1977, Brooks 1982, Lozano-Pérez 1983].)

Since the simulation subsystem of RoboTeach is designed to allow the addition of new robot controller simulators readily, RoboTeach would provide an excellent test-bed for new control algorithms.

CONCLUSIONS

We shall close with a few remarks regarding the importance of solid modeling in manufacturing applications. Our primary rationale for basing RoboTeach on GMSolid was to relieve the application of the need to understand how geometric objects are represented and manipulated. We have learned much from our experiences to date.

GMSolid provides a reasonably convenient procedural interface to its object manipulation and display procedures; this interface will be used extensively by the workcell layout and simulation subsystem. The only geometric calculations performed by RoboTeach are robot inverse kinematics. As mentioned earlier, there are some geometric capabilities missing from GMSolid that will eventually be needed by RoboTeach (and other applications). Some of these are reasonably well defined and are widely recognized as important research topics, for example, efficient dynamic collision detection and minimum distance calculation. Others, such as the capability to represent and manipulate uncertainty and nondeterminism in the world model, are less well defined. Current research in tolerancing and the symbolic manipulation of geometric constraints may be relevant to such problems. We believe that advanced applications will provide a focus for continued research in solid modeling.

To gather input for GMSolid's manipulation procedures, RoboTeach is required to understand at least some of GMSolid's representational conventions. This is not a serious problem for us because the use of a particular network database and other features of the General Motors Corporate Graphics System (CGS) is encouraged to promote the integration of the various CAD/CAM systems within General Motors. The result, however, is that RoboTeach (and other applications that are integrated within CGS) cannot easily be modified for use with other solid modeling or graphics systems. Efforts to standardize solely the representations of geometric or graphic objects will not alleviate this problem; standardized interfaces to procedures for object creation, editing, manipulation, and display are also required, although it is probably premature to seek such standards today.

The vast majority of our efforts to date on RoboTeach have not been directed towards geometric modeling but towards robot programming and simulation. Some advocates of solid modeling have fostered the misconception that manufacturing automation will emerge, naturally and simply, once powerful geometric modeling capabilities are in hand. We now believe that applications like off-line programming will require significant research and development efforts, some of which are related only peripherally to solid modeling. Solid modeling will play an important role in advanced manufacturing applications, but much work remains in order to fully exploit this potential.

ACKNOWLEDGMENTS

We would like to express our thanks to the many other people who have been involved in certain aspects of this research effort. Joe Jenei initially introduced us to the problems of programming robots on-line; he has also provided many insights into the requirements for an off-line robot programming system. Ruth and Tony Zarger were instrumental in the work on the feasibility study described in this report. Sandy Altucher, Dan Filip, Pierre McDougall, and Peggy Norris all provided valuable assistance in the implementation of the Robo-Teach system. Russ DaCosta willingly served as a guinea pig in the initial test of the workcell layout subsystem. We owe a special debt to John Boyse, who provided invaluable guidance in the early stages of this project.

REFERENCES

[Bonner and Shin 1982]
Susan Bonner and Kang G. Shin, "A Comparative Study of Robot Languages," *Computer*, Vol. 15, No. 12, December 1982, pp. 82–96.

[Boyse and Gilchrist 1982]
John W. Boyse and Jack E. Gilchrist, "GMSolid: Interactive Modeling for Design and Analysis of Solids," *IEEE Computer Graphics and Applications*, Vol. 2, No. 2, March 1982, pp. 27–40.

[Brooks 1982]
Rodney A. Brooks, "Symbolic Error Analysis and Robot Planning," *The International Journal of Robotics Research*, Vol. 1, No. 4, Winter 1982, pp. 29–68.

[CAM-I 1983]
CAM-I Robotics Software Project, PR-82-ASPP-01.1, Computer Aided Manufacturing International, Arlington, Texas, 1983.

[de Pennington *et al.* 1983]
Alan de Pennington, M. Susan Bloor, and Mazin Balila, "Geometric Modeling: A Contribution Towards Intelligent Robots," *Proceedings of the 13th International Symposium on Industrial Robots*, Chicago, Illinois, April 1983, pp. 7/35–7/54.

[Derby 1982]
Stephen Derby, "Computer Graphics Simulation of Robot Arms: Using the GRASP Program," *Proceedings MIT Conference on CAD/CAM Technology for Manufacturing Engineering*, Cambridge, Masssachusetts, March 1982, pp. 192–200.

[Dillmann 1983]
Ruediger Dillmann, "A Graphical Emulation System for Robot Design and Program Testing," *Proceedings of the 13th International Symposium on Industrial Robots*, Chicago, Illinois, April 1983, pp. 7/1–7/15.

[D'Souza *et al.* 1983]
Chris D'Souza, Detlef Zuhlke, and Ch. Blume, "Aspects to Achieve Standardized Programming Interfaces for Industrial Robots," *Proceedings of the 13th International Symposium on Industrial Robots*, Chicago, Illinois, April 1983, pp. 7/110–7/121.

[Esterling and Van Rosendale 1983]
D. M. Esterling and J. Van Rosendale, "An Intersection Algorithm for Moving Parts," *Computer Aided Geometric Modeling Symposium* (NASA Conference Publication 2272), NASA Langley Research Center, Virginia, April 1983.

[Evans 1976]
David H. Evans, "Computer Programs for the Quadrature Approximation for Statistical Tolerancing," *Journal of Quality Technology*, Vol. 8, No. 2, April 1976, pp. 108–114.

[Gruver *et al.* 1983]
William A. Gruver, Barry I. Soroka, John J. Craig, and Timothy L. Turner, "Evaluation of Commercially Available Robot Programming Languages," *Proceedings of the 13th International Symposium on Industrial Robots*, Chicago, Illinois, April 1983, pp. 12/58–12/68.

[Gugel 1974]
H. W. Gugel, "Monte Carlo Simulation with Interactive Graphics," Research Publication GMR-1531, General Motors Research Laboratories, Warren, Michigan, October 1974.

[Guthrie *et al.* 1982]
D. E. Guthrie, J. W. Boyse, L. C. Chastain, J. Jenei, M. S. Pickett, and P. R. Smith, "General Requirements for a Corporate Off-Line Robot Programming Facility," General Motors Corporation, Warren, Michigan, October 1982.

[Kretch 1982]
Stuart J. Kretch, "CAD/CAM for Robotics," *Proceedings of the Robots VI Conference,* Detroit, Michigan, March 1982.

[Lozano-Pérez 1982]
Tomás Lozano-Pérez, "Robot Programming," A. I. Memo 698, Artificial Intelligence Laboratory, Massachusetts Institute of Technology, Cambridge, Massachusetts, December 1982.

[Lozano-Pérez 1983]
Tomás Lozano-Pérez, "Spatial Planning: A Configuration Space Approach," *IEEE Transactions on Computers,* Vol. C-32, No. 2, February 1983, pp. 108–120.

[Meyer 1981]
Jeanine Meyer, "An Emulation System for Programmable Sensory Robots," *IBM Journal of Research and Development,* Vol. 25, No. 6, November 1981, pp. 955–962.

[Paul 1982]
Richard P. Paul, *Robot Manipulators: Mathematics, Programming, and Control,* The M.I.T. Press, Cambridge, Massachusetts, 1982.

[Pickett and Zarger 1983]
Mary S. Pickett and Ruth M. Zarger, "Off-Line Robot Programming in GMSolid: A Feasibility Study," Research Publication GMR-4484, General Motors Research Laboratories, Warren, Michigan, September 1983.

[Requicha 1984]
A. A. G. Requicha, "Representations of Tolerances in Solid Modeling: Issues and Alternative Approaches," *Solid Modeling by Computers: From Theory to Applications.* Mary S. Pickett and John W. Boyse, eds., Plenum Press, New York, New York, 1984.

[Sarraga and Waters 1984]
Ramon F. Sarraga and William C. Waters, "Free-Form Surfaces in GMSolid: Goals and Issues," *Solid Modeling by Computers: From Theory to Applications,* Mary S. Pickett and John W. Boyse, eds., Plenum Press, New York, New York, 1984.

[Sjolund and Donath 1983]
Paul Sjolund and Max Donath, "Robot Task Planning: Programming Using Interactive Computer Graphics," *Proceedings of the 13th International Symposium on Industrial Robots,* Chicago, Illinois, April 1983, pp. 7/122–7/135.

[Soroka 1980]
Barry I. Soroka, "Debugging Robot Programs with a Simulator," *CADCAM-8 Conference Proceedings,* Anaheim, California, November 1980.

[Soroka 1982]
Barry I. Soroka, "A Program for Computer-Aided Robot Design," *Proceedings of the ASME Second International Computer Engineering Conference,* San Diego, California, August 1982.

[Soroka 1983]
Barry I. Soroka, "What Can't Robot Laguages Do?" *Proceedings of the 13th Internaional Symposium on Industrial Robots,* Chicago, Illinois, April 1983, pp. 12/1–12/8.

[Tilove 1983]
Robert B. Tilove, "Extending Solid Modeling Systems for Mechanism Design and Kinematic Simulation," *IEEE Computer Graphics and Applications,* Vol. 3, No. 3, May/June 1983, pp. 9–19.

[Tsai and Morgan 1984]
Lung-Wen Tsai and Alexander P. Morgan, "Solving the Indirect-Position Problems for General 6-Revolute-Joint Manipulators by Continuation Methods," Research Publication GMR-4631, General Motors Research Laboratories, Warren, Michigan, February 1984.

[Udupa 1977]
Shriram M. Udupa, "Collision Detection and Avoidance in Computer Controlled Manipulators," *Proceedings of the 5th International Joint Conference on Artificial Intelligence*, Cambridge, Massachusetts, August 1977, pp. 737–748.

[Warn 1975]
David R. Warn, "VDAM — A Virtual Data Access Manager for Computer Aided Design," Research Publication GMR-1899, General Motors Research Laboratories, Warren, Michigan, September 1975.

[Wesley and Markowsky 1984]
Michael A. Wesley and George Markowsky, "Generation of Solid Models from Two-Dimensional and Three-Dimensional Data," *Solid Modeling by Computers: From Theory to Applications,* Mary S. Pickett and John W. Boyse, eds., Plenum Press, New York, New York, 1984.

[Wood and Fugelso 1983]
Brian O. Wood and Mark A. Fugelso, "MCL: The Manufacturing Control Language," *Proceedings of the 13th International Symposium on Industrial Robots,* Chicago, Illinois, April 1983, pp. 12/84-12/96.

DISCUSSION

James Korein *(University of Pennsylvania)*

I assume that since you're trying to get a fairly general solution to the inverse kinematics problem, you're going to be using a numerical solution, while most of your robots will be using analytic solutions because they need speed. The solutions to these problems aren't unique. Your iterative method will converge to a particular solution, while the solution chosen by the robot program may be arbitrary among the available solutions. Do you have any idea of how to deal with that problem?

Pickett

Since Tsai and Morgan are here, I'll let them comment on that.

Lung-Wen Tsai *(General Motors Research Laboratories)*

The question is really this: For a given robot and a given desired position, there may be more than one way the robot can reach that position. For a general robot there are sixteen configurations. Our program can always find all configurations, so that would allow the user to pick out the best one.

Pickett

There is also the whole issue of what you do when there are ambiguities. For instance, if the robot arm is reaching straight up so that several of the axes are aligned, there are an infinite number of solutions. I don't think that that's been dealt with very well in the closed form solutions.

M. S. Pickett

Tsai

In that case our program will find all the discrete solutions and one point on the curve containing the infinite set of solutions.

John Hinds *(General Electric)*

Is there some kind of minimal energy principle you can apply? Once you started on a path you could, like humans, take the course of least energy.

Pickett

The solution for the Puma does something like that. If joint angle five is zero, the axes for joints four and six are aligned and there are an infinite number of solutions; they leave joint four at whatever was its last position and only move joint six. So there are some heuristic ways of solving this problem. I don't know that anyone has ever really addressed it analytically very well.

Tomás Lozano-Pérez *(Massachusetts Institute of Technology)*

One solution to the problem is simply to specify everything in joint angles to the robot. Since you're writing the program off-line, you can compute the joint angles or whatever you choose and then specify the joint angles to the robot. That's the simple solution.

Pickett

Once our system has determined the joint angles for each possible kinematic configuration, the user can select the desired configuration. If the robot will accept joint angles in its program, the joint angles will be output by RoboTeach.

Lozano-Pérez

My question has to do with tolerances. For spot welding, I don't know what the tolerance requirements are; but I do know that if you want to get into assembly the tolerance requirements are going to be fairly tight, and any variations in the kinematics in the real robot and the position of the parts relative to what you have in your model might make the whole operation infeasible. Have you thought about this problem?

Pickett

Yes, we've started to think about it. We don't have any answers, but we recognize that it's a very important area to look at.

Robert Johnson (R.H. Johnson & Associates)

Do you plan to add vision or vision simulation to the system?

Pickett

We haven't looked in too much depth yet at what we are going to do about sensors, but that's one of the next research areas for the system.

Pat Ambler (University of Edinburgh)

Do you have any comments to make on the difficulties of pointing to a graphics image to indicate points in three-dimensional space?

Pickett

We have not found that to be a problem because we have a very rich set of tools for building these coordinate systems. All the GMSolid data is available in double precision, which is far more accurate than any of the robot motion is going to be anyway, so you can get the initial points quite accurately. Then, for instance, you can request ten points evenly spaced between two points. We have many capabilities for getting surface normals, aligning a vector with another point, or aligning a vector with another vector. The engineer uses that set of tools to build up the work point and orientation and then simply pokes at the coordinate system with his light pen. So we don't have any of the problems with trying to select a point in several different views and then correlating these to determine which point you're really talking about.

Ambler

How would you indicate the surface for which you're interested in getting the normal?

Pickett

We use a ray casting technique. The engineer pokes with the light pen at the surface. Then if there are several surfaces that have been intersected by the ray, we display each in turn and ask if it's the one he wanted.

Norman Badler *(University of Pennsylvania)*

When the user has constructed a motion interactively, is there a way of saving that information for retrieval and modification later? If so, is that amenable for off-line input, in other words, for batch or programming language input to the simulation?

Pickett

Today we're not saving the trajectories but we're experimenting with what the data structure should look like. Storing these trajectories will be straightforward.

The second part of the question, which is, I think, the more interesting, is whether there is going to be some way of inputting that from an off-line mechanism.

In the overview slide of RoboTeach, the arrows between the robot and the system were two-directional. We would like to be able to take existing robot programs and bring them back into the system, because we do a lot of work where there are minor changes each year as the model changes. We're also talking to our users right now and debating internally as to whether we should wrap some syntax around this internal data structure that we have and invent yet another robot programming language. We're fighting against that, although we may end up having to do it because there really are some difficult issues with how you specify the logic of a program. If you're a programmer, it's easy to write down an IF-THEN-ELSE statement; it's difficult to see how to do that graphically.

Christopher Brown *(University of Rochester)*

Do you have provisions in the system now for specifying compliant motion or perhaps automatically deriving it when necessary?

Pickett

We do not have that yet. The task specification and simulation has just been developed over the last couple of months.

John Woodwark *(University of Bath)*

You mentioned that when you have more than one object moving in a scene, you might want to use four-dimensional B-splines. This sounds awfully sophisticated and also time consuming. Suppose you have the scene itself (we'll call that A) and two objects (called B and C). What is the problem of comparing A and B, then A and C, and finally B and C as separate operations?

Can you not leave one of the moving objects stationary and then compare the second moving object with the first moving object in addition to the stationary scene?

Pickett

The problem is that the second object might have gotten out of the way of the first object by the time the first object got to where the second one started.

Michael Wesley *(IBM)*

I think what John is suggesting is to consider the motion of one object relative to another, rather than looking at absolute motion.

Pickett

We haven't investigated that; it might turn out to work well. However, given the complexity of robot arms, it would be difficult to determine what that relative motion is when you've got several six-degree-of-freedom manipulators.

SESSION III
GENERAL SURFACES
IN SOLID MODELERS

Session Chairman
JOHN K. HINDS

General Electric Company
Schenectady, New York

FREE-FORM SURFACES IN GMSOLID: GOALS AND ISSUES

RAMON F. SARRAGA

General Motors Research Laboratories
Warren, Michigan

WILLIAM C. WATERS

General Motors Advanced Product and Manufacturing Engineering Staff
Warren, Michigan

ABSTRACT

The GMSolid system for modeling solids is being enhanced by the addition of free-form surfaces represented as B-splines. The major reason for this enhancement is that a wide variety of automotive parts cannot be modeled satisfactorily using existing GMSolid methods based on quadric surfaces. Free-form surfaces, which can be conformed to twisting, nonquadric surface regions, are required for efficient and accurate modeling. Representing free-form surfaces as B-splines provides a convenient mathematical foundation for many of the computational geometry algorithms needed in a solid modeler.

This paper presents an overview of parts in the automotive industry for which free-form surfaces are either necessary or greatly desirable, as well as a description of the methods currently employed within GMSolid to construct B-spline surfaces and to render them using both vector and shaded displays. It concludes with a brief discussion of the issues involved and the approach being followed when the Boolean operations of solid modeling are applied to solids enclosed by free-form surfaces.

INTRODUCTION

In the late 1960s and early 1970s General Motors was one of the pioneers in the application of computer graphics to automotive design. This effort produced a software system for surface design and wire frame modeling that is now embedded in GM's Corporate Graphics System (CGS). The mathematics for surface design is based on spline-blended surface interpolation [Gordon 1969] through a network of curves supplied by the user of the system (*e.g.*, from a clay model of a car body).

In the late 1970s, GMSolid, a software system for modeling solids, was designed [Boyse 1979, Boyse and Gilchrist 1982, Morgan and Sarraga 1982, Roth 1982, Sarraga 1983, Morgan 1983]. This solid modeler utilizes the principles of the University of Rochester's PADL system [Voelcker and Requicha 1977, Requicha and Voelcker 1982]. Like the surface design system, GMSolid is embedded in CGS but its surface representations are currently restricted to planes and some quadric surfaces (*i.e.*, cylinders, cones, and spheres) which are represented implicitly rather than parametrically.

Restricting surfaces to quadrics simplifies many of the surface manipulation algorithms that underlie the operations of a solid modeler, for example, the surface-surface intersections used to build a boundary file after a Boolean operation on solids, and the line-surface intersections performed for mass-property calculations. Moreover, a wide variety of mechanical parts can be modeled effectively using only quadrics. The constructive solid geometry tree [Voelcker and Requicha 1977, Requicha and Voelcker 1982] provides a useful means of representing multifaceted solids of this type.

Nevertheless, experience with GMSolid at General Motors has established that there are a significant number of automotive parts (and tools used to make automotive parts) that possess substantial surface regions that cannot be modeled satisfactorily with quadric surfaces. In essence, a single quadric surface cannot be conformed to such a region, while an approximation based on multiple quadric subregions is unfeasible because of the large number of subregions needed to achieve the modeling accuracy required for applications of the model. These parts include some cast and forged parts, duct work, pipes, housings, blades, dies, cores of car manifolds, and certain auto parts that are modeled in detail (such as particular regions of the interiors of combustion chambers).

Parts of this type can be modeled conveniently using free-form surfaces. However, the spline-blended interpolants of the surface design system are inconvenient for this purpose because of their globality. By contrast, a surface representation based on B-splines is locally modifiable [Gordon and Riesenfeld 1974] and can be conveniently manipulated by means of subdivision algorithms [Böhm 1980, Cohen *et al.* 1980, Böhm 1981]. (In fact, subdivision can also be applied to Bézier triangles, which are not degenerate tensor-product patches [Goldman 1983, Jensen 1984].) Thus, the current version of GMSolid represents free-form surfaces as B-splines, which can be regular (constructed in three-dimensional Euclidean space) or rational (constructed in projective space).

In spite of their advantages, B-splines are not as convenient as quadrics for operations such as surface-surface and line-surface intersections. For this reason, the version of GMSolid that is currently in development contains some limitations on the use of Boolean operations for free-form solids.

The next section of this paper describes in some detail the kind of automotive parts that require free-form surface modeling. Following that, the facilities being implemented within GMSolid are explained; these include a user interface based on lofting design techniques and a simple, preliminary method to display free-form solids together with quadric solids in the same scene. Then problems of performing Boolean operations on free-form solids are noted. Finally, GMSolid's approach, approximation through repatching, is presented.

NEED FOR FREE-FORM SURFACES

Parts requiring free-form surfaces in their design tend to fall into two categories. On the one hand, one finds parts whose functions require shapes that are essentially nonquadric. This category includes fan housings, engine manifolds, engine ports, cams, gears, and the like. On the other hand, there is a second and larger group of parts whose functions do not require nonquadric shapes, but which are designed with major nonquadric features because of important structural or manufacturing considerations. Some of these considerations are:

- To increase a part's structural strength,
- To satisfy space and packaging constraints,
- To facilitate casting or forging,
- To reduce weight, or
- To complete designs using fillets of varying radii.

In addition, experience with GMSolid has shown that users do not use a solid modeler to design a part if the resulting design will be modified further by hand because of major nonquadric features on the part. The user's attitude usually depends on whether the nonquadric features are major or minor, but often the distinction between major and minor features becomes blurred.

For some cases, GMSolid has facilities to approximate nonquadric features with quadric surfaces, but modeling of these features would be quicker, easier, and more accurate with free-form surfaces. For example, GMSolid has been used to model engine combustion chambers. These models are used as input to engine analysis programs that predict the engine's fuel economy and exhaust emissions (see [Sarraga 1982] and references therein). Although these approximate quadric models have proved useful, they are not adequate for some major applications that can be made of geometric models for combustion chambers. More realistic models are needed, which include nonquadric geometric details required by the function of the chambers. A combustion chamber must provide room for the base of the spark plug, the intake and exhaust valves, and their seals. The valves must be as large as possible for free engine breathing, and they must be able to open without interfering with anything else in the chamber. Therefore, even if the initial design is nominally quadric, the chambers become nonquadric as the design is refined and optimized. As engines are reduced in

References pp. 202-204

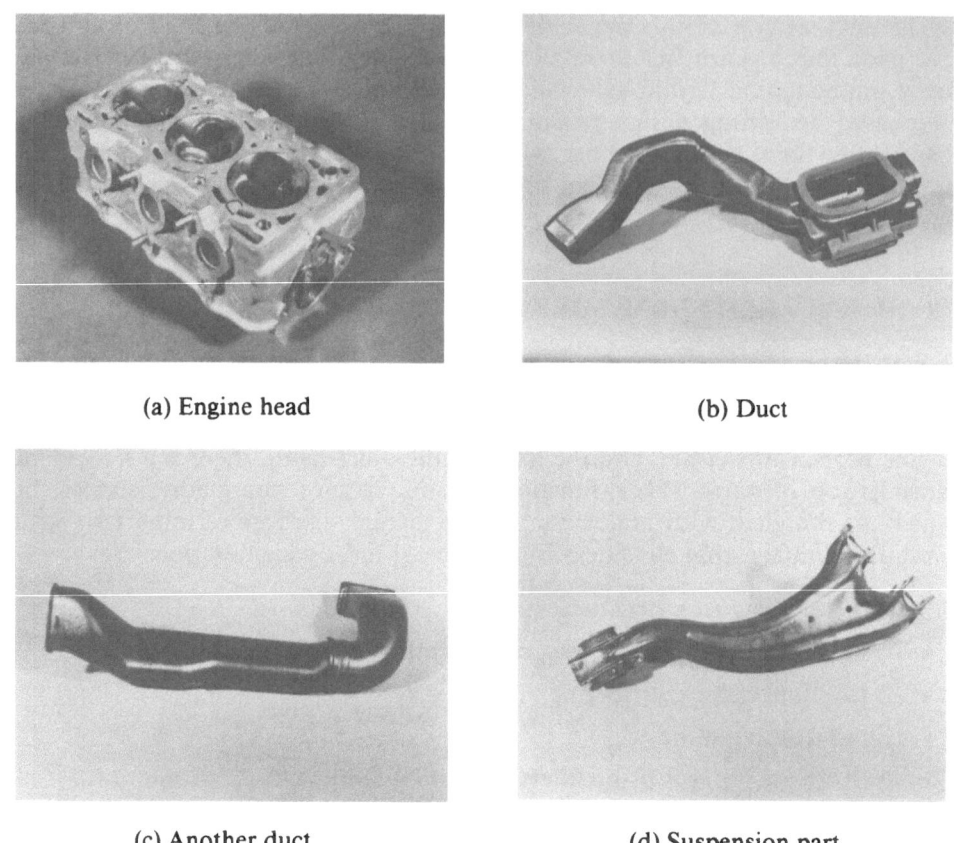

(a) Engine head   (b) Duct

(c) Another duct   (d) Suspension part

Figure 1. *Parts requiring free-form modeling.*

size, the problem becomes increasingly acute. An example is shown in Figure 1(a). These combustion chambers could be accurately modeled with free-form surfaces.

Air conditioning and heater ducts, as shown in Figures 1(b) and 1(c), are simple nonquadric parts. The ducts are shaped as they are in order to maximize their cross-sectional area while fitting them into the restricted space behind the dashboard and instrument panel. Free-form models of the ducts would be very useful for interference checking.

The suspension part shown in Figure 1(d) is an example of a part for which structural analysis plays a prominent design role. Using free-form surfaces, such parts could be modeled quite accurately with GMSolid, and finite element meshes (at least surface meshes) could be easily generated from those models in order to provide input for analysis programs.

(e) Oil pan   (f) Fan housing

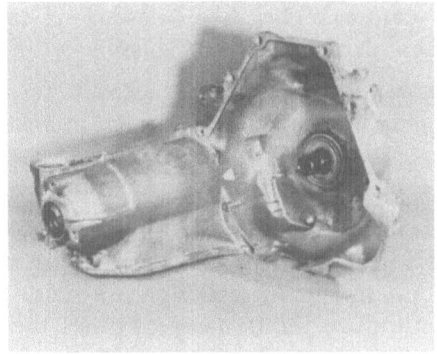

(g) Transaxle housing

Figure 1. Parts requiring free-form modeling.—continued

Engine or transmission oil pans (Figure 1(e)) are examples of relatively simple parts that contain nonquadric surfaces. For such simple parts, the die that is used to stamp the parts could be modeled by GMSolid and could be machined semiautomatically by utilizing the solid model to drive N/C programs based on parametric representations of the solid's surface.

Other types of parts that cannot be designed feasibly, or conveniently, using only quadrics are housings, including fan housings (Figure 1(f)), transaxle housings (Figure 1(g)), gas turbine housings, and air cleaner housings; engine blocks; and engine heads, including the portion outside the combustion chamber, as illustrated by Figure 1(a).

Finally, GMSolid will be quite useful for modeling the molds and cores that are used to manufacture castings. Once the molds and cores are accurately modeled, N/C machining programs will be able to create the patterns for casting the actual parts. Engine manifolds illustrate the need for free-form surfaces to model cores, because engine efficiency depends on the nonquadric shape of the manifold's air passages. The convergence or divergence of the cross-sectional area of these air passages must be accurately controlled even while the basic shape changes from a square to a circle and winds its way between fasteners and cooling water passages. Engine intake and exhaust ports present many of the same problems as manifolds.

USER INTERFACE FOR HANDLING FREE-FORM SOLIDS

The main goal of GMSolid's user interface for free-form surfaces is to provide the user with a convenient tool for exploiting the sculptured design capabilities of free-form surfaces. With this tool, the user is able to design complex primitive solids, that is, solids that are not the result of Boolean operations but possess complex surface features. The user interface is tailored to the current hardware and software environment of GMSolid.

Currently, GMSolid displays solids interactively on an IBM 3250 vector graphics console. This graphics device includes an attached light pen for selecting items from the screen. Items that can be selected are either alternatives in command menus or drawing features programmed to be selectable.

The command menus for handling free-form solids are being implemented as consistently as possible with the existing menus for quadrics. Modeling aids for quadrics that are relevant to free-form design are made available within free-form menus so as to minimize the number of times the light pen is required. These modeling aids include multiple views, multiple windows, picture enlargement and reduction, coordinate vector displays, and the like. The general goal is to maximize user convenience and minimize the need for training users.

Free-form design in GMSolid is currently based on the well-known technique of lofting [Faux and Pratt 1979]. In brief, the user creates a set of planes, draws cross-sectional spline outlines on the planes, and connects outlines from different planes to each other by means of longitudinal spline curves that blend the outlines into a tensor-product surface.

In GMSolid, the final surface must represent the enveloping surface of a proper solid. The lofting planes can be at any angle to each other, but the intersection line of any two planes may not cross a design curve drawn on either of them. The system includes facilities to create, delete, reorder, display, move, and perform other such operations on the lofting planes.

On the lofting planes, multiple cross-sectional outlines may be used to design features such as parallel protrusions (*e.g.*, fork prongs) or holes in a solid. However, the lofting menus are currently restricted (for convenience only) to disallow more than double nesting of the cross-sectional outlines. Thus, for example, a circularly symmetric bowl with a prong in the middle cannot be modeled in the current version of the system by using lofting planes perpendicular to the bowl's axis of symmetry, because three nested outlines are required on any lofting plane that cuts both the prong and the (finitely thick) shell of the bowl. The lofting menus also provide facilities for indicating the exact location of special geometric features such as the tips of prongs, where prongs start to fork, where holes terminate, and the like.

At this time, GMSolid already draws pictures of free-form surfaces on the IBM 3250; however, the lofting interface is still in development. The final version is expected to include:

- Creation of triangular patches that are not degenerate tensor-product patches [Farin 1982],

- Facilities to partially undo the construction and re-interpolate to create a modified surface,

- Tweaking of the final surface by moving its control points,

- Automatic offsetting of a surface to create a (possibly rescaled) copy, and

- Automatically performing all or some of the lofting construction steps using digitized data input.

DISPLAYS OF FREE-FORM SURFACES

GMSolid typically generates a new display after every major user operation, for example, after every Boolean operation. Both edges and profile curves are generated automatically for displayed solids. The system also accepts user commands to remove or to dash automatically all hidden lines in a display. Figure 2 shows a typical screen picture of a quadric solid with hidden lines removed. (Three views are displayed simultaneously.)

Hidden-line removal is accomplished by a simple ray tracing procedure, with the following basic steps:

- Approximate each edge (both real and profile) with a series of line intervals,

- Cast a ray back to the observer's eye point from each endpoint of an interval and determine whether the ray is stopped by some object,

- When one endpoint of an interval is invisible while the other is visible, use binary search to approximate the point at which the line becomes hidden.

Clearly, this method can miss some hidden lines when, for example, the interval between two sampled endpoints passes behind a corner of some object. Nevertheless, the method works fairly quickly and yet allows flaws (which are hardly noticeable) in only a small fraction of the pictures generated.

For free-form surfaces, a preliminary method has been implemented that is a simple extension of the approach used for quadrics. The user can specify contours to be displayed in addition to sharp edges and profile curves. Hidden-line

References pp. 202-204

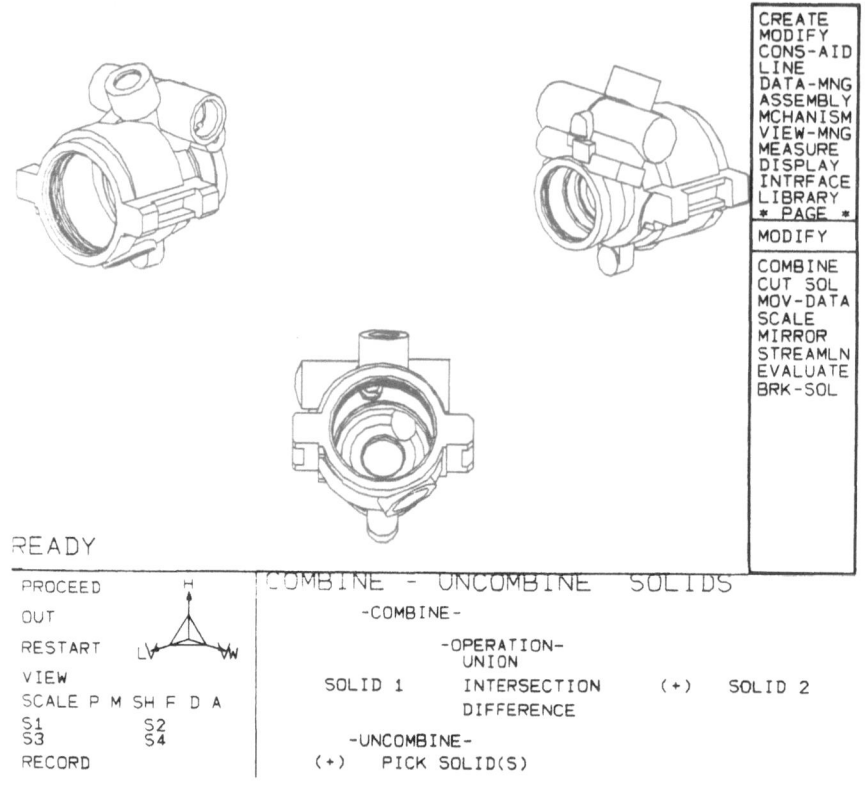

Figure 2. *Typical GMSolid screen display.*

removal is accomplished by approximating free-form surfaces with triangular planar facets and checking whether rays intersect the facets.

When the normals of two adjacent facets point in a different sense, one towards and one away from the observer, the common border of the triangles is used as a line segment of a profile curve. Unfortunately, in this approximation a profile curve that in reality is merely curved may form a jagged loop in some section of the curve. However, these loops can be made minute without a great sacrifice of speed; moreover, hidden-line removal also removes the looping segments. A second disadvantage of this approximation is that curving profiles often fork with minute dead-end branches that in reality are not features of the modeled surface at all. However, the dead-end branches can be made too small to be bothersome on the IBM 3250 without unduly sacrificing speed.

Despite such problems, a major advantage of this display method is its generality: it can be used to render free-form surfaces of any type, for example, regular or rational B-splines and the spline-blended surfaces of CGS. Moreover, since the same basic display method is employed for free-form surfaces and for

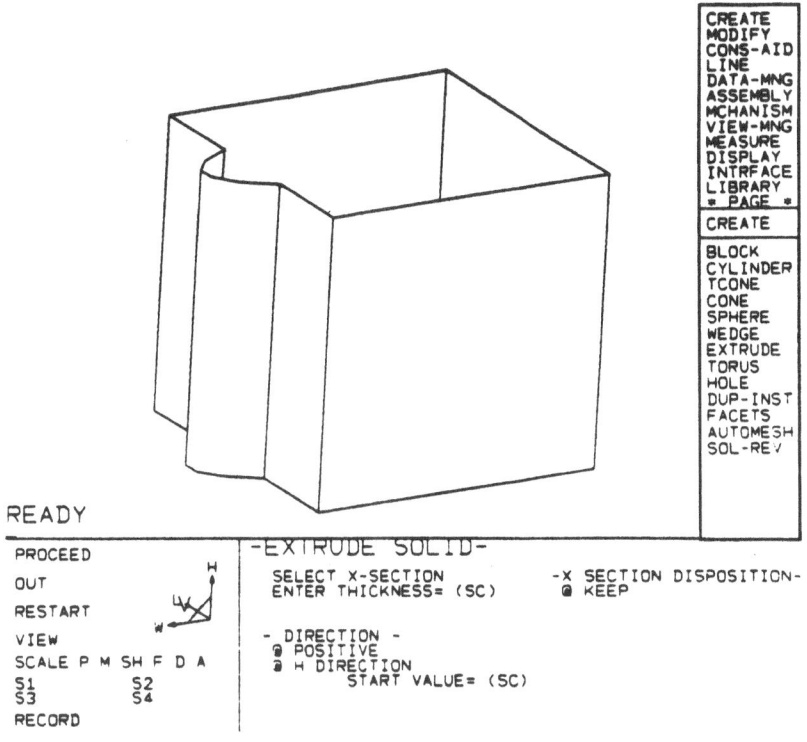

Figure 3. *Extruded planar outline.*

quadrics, both types of surfaces can easily be displayed together in the same scene.

Figures 3 and 4 show free-form surfaces rendered with hidden lines removed or dashed by this method. Figure 3 represents a free-form surface obtained by extruding a planar outline consisting of a rectangle with a jutting spline arc. The entire surface has been modeled using regular cubic B-splines. Multiple knots were used to obtain the sharp edges. Figure 4 shows three-sixteenths of a torus modeled exactly using three rational parabolic B-spline patches.

The triangular facets of the display approximation can also be used as input for GM's AUTOCOLOR system [Warn 1983], which generates color raster displays from polygonal data. Figures 5 and 6 show color shaded displays of the models in Figures 3 and 4. Figure 7 shows in color a duct that was modeled using the lofting facility.

PROBLEMS OF BOOLEAN OPERATIONS ON FREE-FORM SOLIDS

When performing a Boolean operation, GMSolid currently builds a boundary representation (also called a *boundary file*) that contains data for each edge at

References pp. 202-204

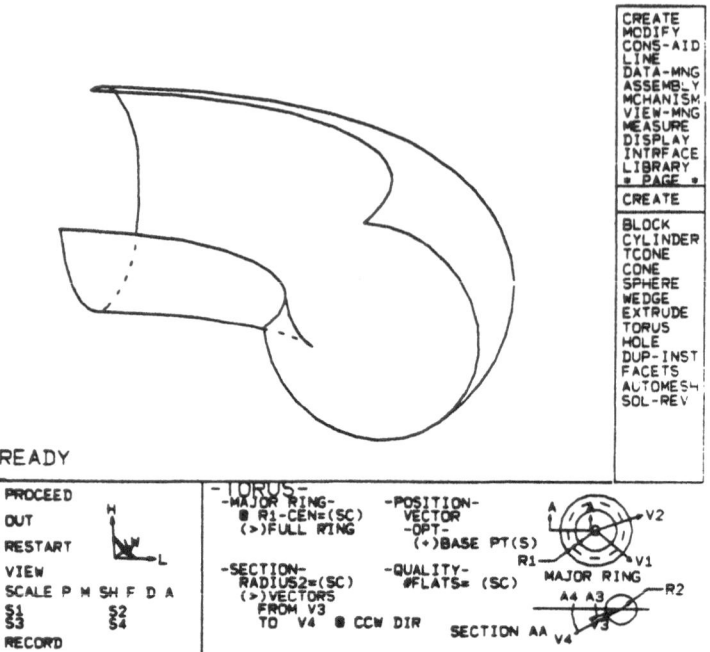

Figure 4. *Three-sixteenths of a torus.*

which two faces meet on the constructed solid. For quadrics, the edges are classified according to whether they are segments of planar or nonplanar intersection curves. In either case, an edge segment is represented parametrically with respect to some coordinate system that is fixed either on a plane or on some ruled quadric containing the intersection curve. The completed boundary file records data such as the starting and ending parameter values for edges, ensuring that singular points (*e.g.*, a point on a nonplanar edge at which the normals of the two adjoining faces are colinear) do not lie in the interior of an edge segment [Sarraga 1983]. In brief, all edges are furnished with a well-defined neighborhood model [Tilove 1980].

This scheme for representing boundaries is satisfactory for quadrics because quadrics are relatively simple surfaces. Thus, a subsequent operation on the constructed solid, which, for example, might need to calculate sample points along an edge, will easily obtain the needed data from the stored boundary information.

By contrast, free-form surfaces present a much greater challenge, first, because obtaining the type of data currently stored for quadrics is decidedly more difficult, and, second, because this data alone is insufficient to guarantee that subsequent operations can be carried out successfully.

As an example, consider the case in which two free-form surfaces coincide, or nearly coincide, throughout two-dimensional regions of their parameter spaces.

Figure 5. Shaded display of an extruded planar outline
(see color plates following p. 158).

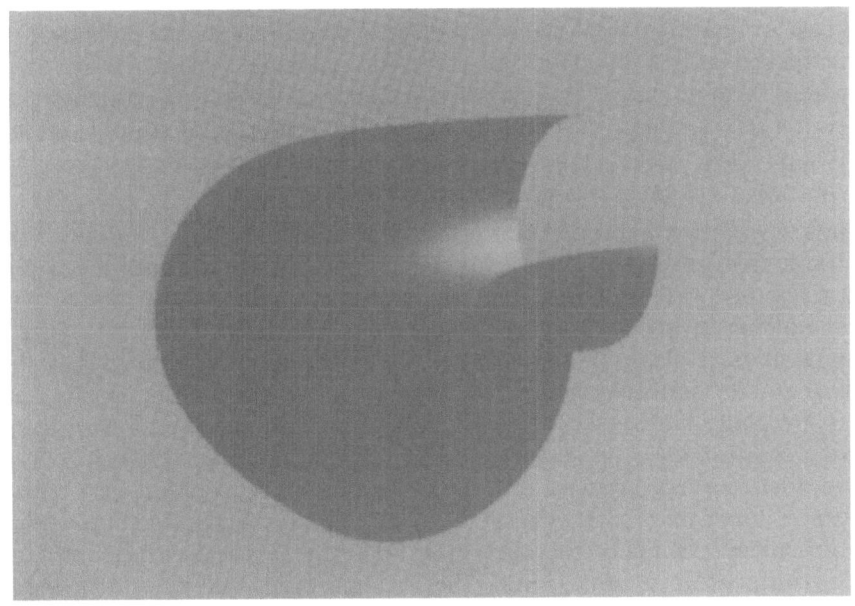

Figure 6. Shaded display of three-sixteenths of a torus
(see color plates following p. 158).

References pp. 202-204

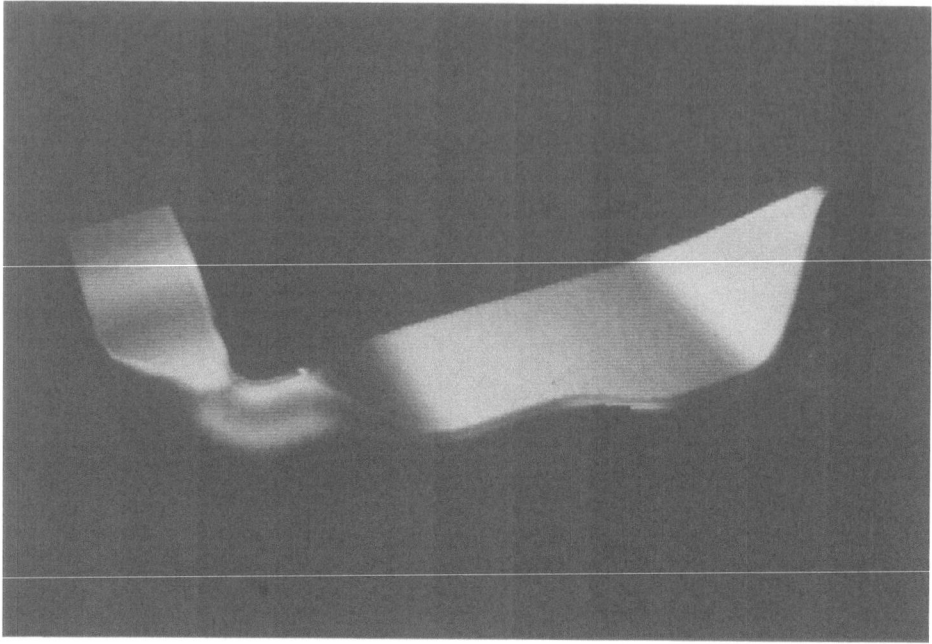

Figure 7. *A duct modeled with the lofting facility (see color plates following p. 158).*

In the case of quadrics, this type of problem is simplified by the facts that if two (irreducible) quadrics coincide in a two-dimensional region, they coincide everywhere in their range, and that if two quadrics are nearly coincident, their intersection curve, albeit numerically painful to compute, is simply one of the few cases into which quadric intersection curves can be classified.

On the other hand, a free-form surface can have derivative discontinuities and thus may have a proper subregion that coincides with another surface. Even if one treats each two-dimensional span between discontinuities as a separate surface, one will find that regions of near coincidence can contain many branches of the intersection curve, as depicted from two views in Figure 8. A full mathematical classification of such instances requires a study of the algebraic geometry pertinent to the implicit surfaces whose parametrically defined patches are being intersected. (For a bicubic, the implicit equation in terms of Cartesian coordinates is of degree at least 18 [Sederberg *et al.* 1983].) In essence, ensuring that in every intersection case every branch is recorded in a boundary structure is infeasible; moreover, it is most probably a useless effort because near coincidence is likely to mean just an unintended interference between modeled surfaces or an intentional "gluing" operation that should produce no cavities or crevices.

The approach being implemented for GMSolid in cases of near coincidence is to identify such regions using recursive subdivision techniques and to query the

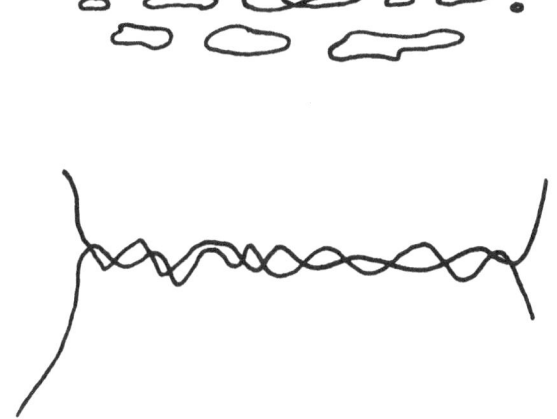

Figure 8. Bumpy surfaces (bottom) can produce a disconnected curve (top).

user interactively for the proper disposition of the Boolean operation in such regions.

Another problem pertaining to free-form surfaces is the difficulty in computing a suitably large, ordered set of precise points on the intersection curve of two such surfaces. For quadrics, this problem is resolved quite well by the boundary representation. To find points along an edge, one simply marches along the edge by incrementing its parameter. If the edge is planar, a simple equation yields the desired point in a coordinate system fixed on the plane. If the edge is nonplanar, one easily finds the generator of the ruled quadric that corresponds to the parameter and intersects this line with a different quadric that contains the edge.

A corresponding approach for free-form surfaces is to march along the edge by solving an ordinary differential equation (ODE) that characterizes the edge. However, ODE solvers are significantly less reliable than the simple methods sketched above for planar and nonplanar quadric intersection curves. For example, the ODE solver may fail in a neighborhood of a singular point, or it may jump to another branch of the curve if two branches come close to each other in some region. To remedy such problems, the boundary file might contain numerical data, for instance, a recommended step size for the ODE solver to use in certain subintervals of an edge. Nevertheless, this solution only pushes the problem back from the ODE solver to the process of building the boundary representation.

In summary, given the potential complexity of free-form surfaces, it is unreasonable to expect boundary files (which are based on implicit intersection curves) to be as reliable for these surfaces as they are for quadrics. And boundary files for quadrics have hardly proved to be paragons of reliability!

References pp. 202-204

APPROXIMATING THE RESULTS OF BOOLEAN OPERATIONS

Since free-form surfaces are clearly needed, the current version of GMSolid has opted for a compromise approach to Boolean operations involving free-form surfaces. The following discussion describes the basic philosophy of this approach and outlines the mathematical steps in general.

As a starting point, consider the intersection of two free-form surface patches as a result of some Boolean operation. An ordered set of approximate sample points can be obtained on the intersection curve by a combination of methods, including subdivision. This process also identifies at least the most prominent branches of the curve. The points on each branch can be used to define an approximate curve for that branch. The approximate curve in turn can be used, by segments, as a boundary curve for new patches that approximate those regions of the original patches that remain as faces of the constructed solid. Proceeding systematically in this manner, one obtains a boundary representation consisting solely of patches with their boundary curves. An edge becomes simply a patch-boundary curve along which the adjoining patches are not C^1 continuous. In the following discussion, this approximation scheme is called the *repatching* method.

Figure 9 illustrates the basic scheme of the repatching method for a rather simple configuration of intersecting patches. Patches A and B belong to different solids that are being combined through a Boolean operation. These patches intersect along curve x, which is approximated by curve y. New patches C and D are constructed which have curve y as their common boundary, and which ap-

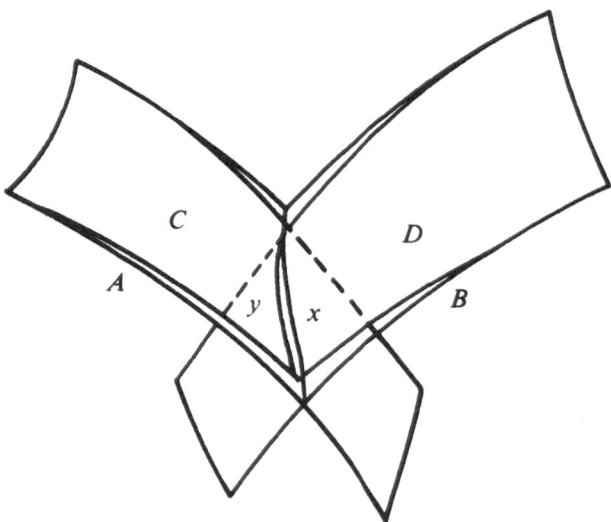

Figure 9. *Simple case of repatching.*

proximate the portions of A and B that remain as face regions of the new solid formed by the Boolean operation. Along y, the nontangential component of a directional derivative defined on the surface is discontinuous.

Repatching has several distinct disadvantages for modeling. An obvious one is that the boundary representation defines a solid that is only an approximation of the solid denoted by the Boolean operations. In particular, performing the Boolean operations in a different order results in a different approximate solid. Moreover, consider a patch that is intersected many times by other patches during the exact execution of a sequence of Boolean operations. Each Boolean operation in the sequence gives rise to a new set of approximate subpatches. If each set is constructed as an approximation of the previous set, and not of the original patch, the final constructed solid could be quite different from the intended one in the region that is repatched many times.

Let us postpone a discussion of these disadvantages, however, to consider the advantages of the approximation scheme. Clearly, following an edge becomes trivial, for every edge lies on an isoparametric curve. More generally, the approximate solid is consistently defined. For example, if some branch of the intersection curve is missed during boundary evaluation, the branch is, so to speak, redefined out of the new solid. There is no chance that a subsequent operation on the constructed solid will discover the missing branch and either fail as a result or further compromise the consistency of the database.

Another advantage of repatching is that it produces an explicit parameterization of every face, that is, every face is a collection of patches, and within each patch every value of the parameter domain maps to a point on the face. This fact simplifies many applications of solid modeling, such as interference checking, surface intersection, and finite element mesh generation.

Repatching does require a *tour de force* of the surface-definition database using function interpolation and approximation methods. However, computers are sufficiently fast and the mathematics is sufficiently well developed to handle the problem, at least if the Boolean operations to be performed do not affect too many faces of the solids to be combined. In essence, this approach does not appear to be a practical substitute for the standard method of constructing solids based on quadric surfaces. But this approach should work well for the parts requiring free-form modeling we discussed earlier, which can be constructed mostly from a lofting interface and completed without too many or too far-reaching Boolean operations.

If the Boolean operations are thus restricted in practice, then the modeling disadvantages of repatching that were mentioned earlier can be lessened to a great degree. In addition, the user can resort to special aids such as:

- Tweaking the approximate solid where needed,
- Keeping a copy of original patches or solids to improve the accuracy of the approximate solid throughout a wider region than can be tweaked conveniently, and

References pp. 202-204

- Keeping special auxiliary surface models of surface features that are to be approximated with particular accuracy, for example, a blend or fillet of some type.

The auxiliary models could be defined very accurately, using for example, non-polynomial surfaces, because the models are not manipulated as solids, that is, there is no need for interference checking, surface-surface intersections, and the like.

Repatching is essentially a compromise between the mathematical complexity of free-form surfaces and the requirements of solid modeling, particularly the requirement that the results of a Boolean operation should be independent of the order of the operands. Future advances in the mathematics of free-form surfaces may render such a compromise unnecessary.

SUMMARY

Experience with GMSolid has shown that a significant number of parts related to automobile manufacturing can be modeled neither feasibly nor conveniently without free-form surfaces. Thus, a joint program by General Motors Research Laboratories and Advanced Product and Manufacturing Engineering Staff is underway to incorporate free-form surfaces into GMSolid. B-splines, both regular and rational, have been selected to represent free-form surfaces because of their mathematical properties, which facilitate the extension of GMSolid operations to free-form surfaces.

Nevertheless, no type of free-form surface that is sufficiently general and flexible can compete with quadrics in numerical reliability and ease of implementation. Therefore, the current version of GMSolid will approximate solids modeled through Boolean operations when free-form surfaces are involved. The approximation consists of repatching those surfaces that are found to intersect as a result of a Boolean operation.

GMSolid is currently displaying free-form solids jointly with quadric solids. A powerful user interface based on lofting techniques is being implemented to construct complex free-form solids with a minimum of Boolean operations.

ACKNOWLEDGEMENT

We gratefully acknowledge the assistance of Mr. M. Lucius, Dr. R. Shantaram, and Mr. R. A. Tischler of Sirco Enterprises for programming many of the subroutines that create and manipulate free-form surfaces.

REFERENCES

[Böhm 1980]
   Wolfgang Böhm, "Inserting New Knots into B-Spline Curves," *Computer Aided Design*, Vol. 12, No. 4, July 1980, pp. 199–201.

[Böhm 1981]
Wolfgang Böhm, "Generating the Bézier Points of B-Spline Curves and Surfaces," *Computer Aided Design*, Vol. 13, No. 6, November 1981, pp. 365–366.

[Boyse 1979]
J. W. Boyse, "Data Structure for a Solid Modeler," Research Publication GMR-2933, Computer Science Department, General Motors Research Laboratories, Warren, Michigan, March 1979.

[Boyse and Gilchrist 1982]
J. W. Boyse and J. E. Gilchrist. "GMSolid: Interactive Modeling for Design and Analysis of Solids," *IEEE Computer Graphics and Applications*, Vol. 2, No. 2, March 1982, pp. 27–40.

[Cohen *et al.* 1980]
E. Cohen, T. Lyche, and R. Riesenfeld, "Discrete B-Splines and Subdivision Techniques in Computer-Aided Geometric Design and Computer Graphics," *Computer Graphics and Image Processing.* Vol. 14, 1980, pp. 87–111.

[Farin 1982]
Gerald Farin, "Designing C^1 Surfaces Consisting of Triangular Cubic Patches," *Computer Aided Design*, Vol. 14, No. 5, September 1982, pp. 253–256.

[Faux and Pratt 1979]
I. D. Faux and M. J. Pratt, *Computational Geometry for Design and Manufacture*, John Wiley and Sons. New York, New York, 1979.

[Goldman 1983]
R. N. Goldman, "Subdivision Algorithms for Bézier Triangles," *Computer Aided Design*, Vol. 15, No. 3, May 1983, pp. 159–166.

[Gordon 1969]
W. J. Gordon, "Distributive Lattices and the Approximation of Multivariate Functions," *Approximation with Special Emphasis on Spline Functions*, Academic Press, New York, New York, 1969, pp. 223–277.

[Gordon and Riesenfeld 1974]
W. J. Gordon and R. F. Riesenfeld, "B-Spline Curves and Surfaces," *Computer Aided Geometric Design*, R. E. Barnhill and R. F. Riesenfeld, eds., Academic Press, New York, New York, 1974, pp. 95–126.

[Jensen 1984]
T. Jensen, "Generalizing the Representation of Surfaces," Ph.D. Dissertation, Department of Mathematics, University of Utah, Salt Lake City, Utah, 1984.

[Morgan 1983]
A. P. Morgan, "A Method for Computing All Solutions to Systems of Polynomial Equations," *ACM Transactions on Mathematical Software*, Vol. 9, No. 1, March 1983, pp. 1–17.

[Morgan and Sarraga 1982]
A. P. Morgan and R. F. Sarraga, "A Method for Computing Three Surface Intersection Points in GMSolid," Research Publication GMR-3964, General Motors Research Laboratories, Warren, Michigan, 1982.

[Requicha and Voelcker 1982]
A. A. G. Requicha and H. B. Voelcker, "Solid Modeling: A Historical Summary and Contemporary Assessment," *IEEE Computer Graphics and Applications*, Vol. 2, No. 2, March 1982, pp. 9–24.

[Roth 1982]
S. D. Roth, "Ray Casting for Modeling Solids," *Computer Graphics and Image Processing*, Vol. 18, 1982, pp. 109–144.

[Sarraga 1982]
R. F. Sarraga, "Computation of Surface Areas in GMSolid," *IEEE Computer Graphics and Applications*, Vol. 2, No. 7, September 1982, pp. 65–70.

[Sarraga 1983]
R. F. Sarraga, "Algebraic Methods for Intersections of Quadric Surfaces in GMSolid," *Computer Vision, Graphics, and Image Processing*, Vol. 22, No. 2, May 1983, pp. 222–238.

[Sederberg *et al.* 1983]
T. W. Sederberg, D. C. Anderson, and R. N. Goldman, "Implicit Representation of Parametric Curves and Surfaces," accepted for publication in *Computer Graphics, Vision, and Image Processing*; see also T. W. Sederberg, "Implicit and Parametric Curves and Surfaces for Computer Aided Design," Ph.D. Dissertation. Purdue University, Lafayette, Indiana, 1983.

[Tilove 1980]
R. B. Tilove, "Set Membership Classification: A Unified Approach to Geometric Intersection Problems," *IEEE Transactions on Computers*, Vol. C-29, No. 10, October 1980, pp. 874–883.

[Voelcker and Requicha 1977]
H. B. Voelcker and A. A. G. Requicha, "Geometric Modeling of Mechanical Parts and Processes." *Computer*, Vol. 10, No. 12, December 1977, pp. 48–57.

[Warn 1983]
D. R. Warn, "Lighting Controls for Synthetic Images," Research Publication GMR-4219, Computer Science Department, General Motors Research Laboratories, Warren, Michigan, 1983.

DISCUSSION

Martin Newell *(CADLINK)*

As you pointed out, the parameter space is rectangular. What happens if you get strange topologies in the subdivided patch (for example, a hole in the middle of a patch)? How do you then represent the remaining patch as a rectangular region?

Hinds

The question is, how can you guarantee fitting when the intersections are so weird? Can you really fit patches well in the difficult cases? The thing we're fitting with is basically rectangular and the shapes that are being generated are highly nonrectangular.

Sarraga

Well, it's quite clear that I didn't go into those details in the talk. In the case that you're suggesting, the system would have to divide the original patch first, so that we would not have the situation in which the hole is completely surrounded by one single patch. The resulting patches would have to be subdivided until we get a collection of patches around the curve. One can do this subdivision so that some subpatches exactly coincide with the one that was there originally. But then in a region along the intersection curve one would have to refit in some fashion; the hope is that one would be able to have good control over that refitting. This is not yet implemented. An algorithm is needed to do this repatching and the subdivision of patches in a systematic fashion.

R. F. Sarraga

James Korein *(University of Pennsylvania)*

How do you store the intersection curve between patches in such a way that it's useful for regeneration of the new approximating patch?

Sarraga

Again, I have not looked into that problem in a thorough way. It would be possible, for example, to keep the original surfaces around; then one would go back to redo the process that was originally done in order to create the intersection. That is the first method that we have considered as a possibility. But we have not, for example, designed data structures that would accomplish this or determined exactly how this could be done.

Burkard Wördenweber *(University of Cambridge)*

I'd like to know what you are going to use the intersection routines for. Do you intend to provide a general intersection routine that can be used for things other than set operations?

Sarraga

Could you give an example?

Wördenweber

Well, for example, a mesh generator might want to divide along point positions on a patch where it intersects with a certain line you give it. There are a number of other applications I can think of that would require more knowledge about the geometry.

Sarraga

There may be situations in which it would be necessary to deal with an implicit intersection. For example, an application that we have dealt with in the past is the combustion chamber. For this, one wants to track the flame front of the burned gases from a spark plug during the milliseconds that it takes to fill the combustion chamber. One would like graphs, with respect to time, of the volume enclosed by this flame front, the surface area of the flame front, and the wetted part of the chamber (that part of the chamber inside the flame front).

To get those intersection curves from a special algorithm is probably a lot better than repatching. You'd simply deal with the intersection curve and apply the algorithms to it. In cases like that there would be a need to work with the implicit intersection curves. Is that the kind of application that you have in mind?

Wördenweber

Not particularly. Perhaps I can rephrase it. What applications are you actually using in GMSolid with the B-spline?

Sarraga

One type of application that we have in mind is interference checking, starting with static interference checking. The interference checking would be done in a well-known way using B-spline subdivision and a polyhedral approximation to the surface. Then check polyhedra versus polyhedra to detect interference. This type of algorithm is simplified if each patch is always a face.

Waters

Other applications that will be using B-splines are numerical control, die design and other applications in the construction of automotive parts with nonquadric areas.

W. C. Waters

Sarraga

I don't really believe that Boolean operations will be performed very many times in a given part, especially not many times in the same region of a part. Consider the parts Bill showed. The regions of the part that require free-form surfaces are distant from the regions that require quadrics. There are some exceptions to that, like the holes inside the combustion chamber. In that case, a user might not achieve the desired precision with repatching and would have to define those holes very painstakingly using lofting in that region. But there are many parts—the oil pan, for example—where it is not productive for a user to spend a lot of computational and debugging time in an effort to model an oil pan with high precision.

Ronald Goldman *(Control Data Corporation)*

When you define a new patch to approximate the old patch and go through the intersection curve, is there a possibility of introducing new intersections that weren't there before? What would you do about that?

Sarraga

The program would have to check the new repatched solid for self-intersection after it was completely generated. It would ignore the intersection of a new patch with an old patch until the entire repatching was completed because it would be possible for that new intersection to be in a region that was going to be repatched anyway.

Goldman

I'm wondering if there could be some interference in the region that you are approximating.

Sarraga

Yes, there could be. If the interferences still exist after so many iterations, query the user; that would be the procedure. This approach is not supposed to be a cure-all for these problems. It is a way to make sure that we're going to get a consistent boundary representation for the new solid so that various applications can use it confidently.

Michael Wesley *(IBM)*

Can you give some idea of the cost of introducing free-form surfaces into your modeling system—perhaps both the number of extra codes that have to be written and the change in execution times.

Waters

On the software side I would estimate 25 percent of what we have currently for quadric surfaces. Concerning execution time, for complex parts, it looks as if it will be faster than what we've been doing with quadrics; for simple parts, probably slower. We also need fewer data to describe complicated undulations on the surface.

Sarraga

The lofting technique allows us to create parts that would be very complex modeled as quadrics, and we can work with them much faster in the computer than we could if they were modeled as quadrics. That's from the point of view of computer efficiency. The space required is actually less because the boundary representation which we currently use for quadrics takes a lot of space. If the part is sufficiently complex there is a definite saving in using free-form surfaces. Concerning the development of the codes, the lofting menu is very simple to develop. The graphics part is pretty much the same for both.

I really do not expect that Boolean operations are going to take a tremendous amount of software either. But I do think that the software has to be designed very carefully and there may be hidden problems. For instance, I keep saying "let's query the user," but querying the user is not going to be simple. We will have to have proper graphic aids, and so on, in order to have a good interface and there I really can't give you an estimate of the complexity.

Hinds

OC6.*

Sarraga

No, no. If we start getting too many OC6's then Bill and I will be out of a job.

Hinds

We're near the end of the time for Ray and Bill. I would like to put in my two bits.

The boundary file is a very significant operation in solid modeling, but it is not the only operation. You can do lots of things on the original primitives; don't ignore that fact. That would be my advice. Obviously some complications are encountered out in the boundary file; you may reach situations that are very difficult and you could end up consuming lots of your time on those. On the other hand, you might be able to get results if you just change your approach on how to solve the problem. Forget about the boundary file sometimes, go back to the original primitives, establish the operations. We have some participants in the audience, such as those from SynthaVision, that have done quite well for a long time prior to generating the boundary file.

Waters

Our combustion chamber analysis program does not use the boundary file.

Hinds

I feel there's an excessive emphasis on the boundary file problem. There are other things that can be done in solid models.

---

*OC6 is a system code of IBM's MVS operating system, indicating a terminal execution error.

DESIGN METHODS OF FREE-FORM SURFACES AND THEIR INTEGRATION INTO THE SOLID MODELING PACKAGE GEOMAP-III

FUMIHIKO KIMURA

University of Tokyo
Tokyo, Japan

ABSTRACT

Two powerful methods are shown for the construction of complex solid shapes with free-form surfaces: local modification operations for constructing rough shapes and their smoothing, and complete set operations among curved objects. For actually realizing these methods, it is necessary to develop a basic theory for treating problems which cannot be solved thoroughly by the conventional theories, such as smooth connection of surface patches under various restrictive conditions, and generation of irregular (nonrectangular) surface patches. Some theoretical results are described which are based on the control point approach of Bézier and which are useful for these problems. The two methods are integrated into our comprehensive solid modeling package GEO-MAP-III which is soon to be operational and which will serve as a basis for sophisticated shape design and integrated CAD/CAM systems.

INTRODUCTION

Research and development work for various computer applications in engineering are now being performed more and more actively in every field of industry. CAD/CAM technology will surely become very important as a key technology for the achievement of higher productivity and survival of individual companies. In these situations, the importance of integrating and rationalizing the whole production process from initial conceptual design to final manufacturing control is well understood.

For integration of CAD/CAM, modeling capability for products to be designed and manufactured plays an essential role. All the product information

References pp. 232-234

which is utilized in production processes should be organized and represented as product models within a computer. In conventional manual practice, we use the so-called engineering drawings for this purpose. Human designers use various kinds of engineering drawings as tools for thinking, object description and information transfer. These drawings are somewhat dependent on types of products, and thus have different forms and meanings. They depict different information, such as overall structure, functions, assembly, parts, and production information. Product models are required to represent the same kind of information as these engineering drawings do.

In mechanical engineering, it is obvious that shape information is extremely important for product description. Much work has already been done with geometric modeling for the representation of shape information. There has also been much research in the powerful concept of solid modeling [IEEE 1982], and many solid modeling systems exist which can be used as a basis for product modeling.

Actually, solid modeling capabilities have not yet been utilized fully in practical design and manufacturing. Several technical problems, such as dimensioning and tolerancing, user interface, and speed and robustness of processing, still remain. The treatment of solid objects with free-form surfaces is one of the major problems. Conventionally, free-form surface design has been discussed in applications involving design of high-quality surfaces of an aesthetic nature. Furthermore, several sophisticated systems for surface design have been used in daily production. Nevertheless, a strong desire arises to totally integrate the whole production process, that is, to integrate the surface design capability with the solid modeling functions in order to achieve more advanced applications. In addition, even if we restrict our attention to the treatment of rather conventional machine parts, it sometimes becomes necessary to process a variety of complex surfaces which arise as a result of rounding and filleting operations.

The main objective of this paper is to describe a basic theory and methods for combining solid modeling and free-form surface design functions which are conventionally treated as different disciplines.

In the following two sections, we quickly survey our approach to solid modeling and surface design. Later in this paper we introduce two methods for integration of free-form surface design into solid modeling: local modification operations and set operations.

THE GEOMAP-III SOLID MODELING PACKAGE

We started our study of geometric modeling in the late 1960s [Hosaka *et al.* 1974]. Since then, we have developed two solid modeling packages for various purposes. GEOMAP-I [Hosaka and Kimura 1977], our first comprehensive solid modeling package, which is very compact and efficient and equipped with powerful input/output facilities, is used in many places. GEOMAP-II [Kimura *et al.* 1982], furnished with database facilities, is used as a basic component of an integrated CAD/CAM system. Through our experience in using GEOMAP-I and GEOMAP-II, we found some shortcomings in the existing packages for effective integration of solid modeling functions in CAD/CAM processes. To cope with these shortcomings, we are now developing a new solid modeling package, GEOMAP-III [Kimura *et al.* 1983a].

Three requirements of a solid modeling system were considered in developing GEOMAP-III.

- The system should provide a basis for the integration of CAD/CAM processes. For this purpose, it ought to allow easy extension or modification of various types of models to be treated. The definition of models should be clear so that the models can be shared and used by various application programs. It ought to be possible to add various nongeometric data to the geometric models or associate such data with them. Therefore models should be defined and managed by special data management routines.

- The system should provide various methods for model synthesis. In conventional manual practices, there are many methods for shape design.

- The system ought to include free-form shape synthesis capability. There is a strong desire to be able to handle free-form shapes in CAD/CAM systems for mechanical products.

Based on these requirements, we determined the structure of GEOMAP-III, as shown in Figure 1. Some of its important features are:

- It incorporates a specially designed data structure management system (DSMS), and all the model data are managed by it. The system accepts the definitions of models described by a simple data description language and associated model manipulation functions. The basic data structure which can be represented by this system is a general network structure. It has some special features, for instance, to represent variable length arrays for storing geometric data.

- By use of DSMS, arbitrary data can be added to the elements of geometric models. Alternatively, such data can be stored in the newly defined data records, and new relations can be established between the records and geometric models. For instance, it is possible to define complex machine assemblies or various functional structures which express the functions of the object to be designed. But GEOMAP-III does not take care of the meaning of these additional data. It only stores and manipulates them formally. Their meanings must be processed by separate processors especially prepared for those purposes.

- For the shape design, in addition to basic set operations, many special operations which conform to usual manual design methods are provided. These shape modification operations are especially useful for generating and modifying free-form shapes and fillets, and for corner rounding. We are now developing a handwriting drawing input method which corresponds to

References pp. 232-234

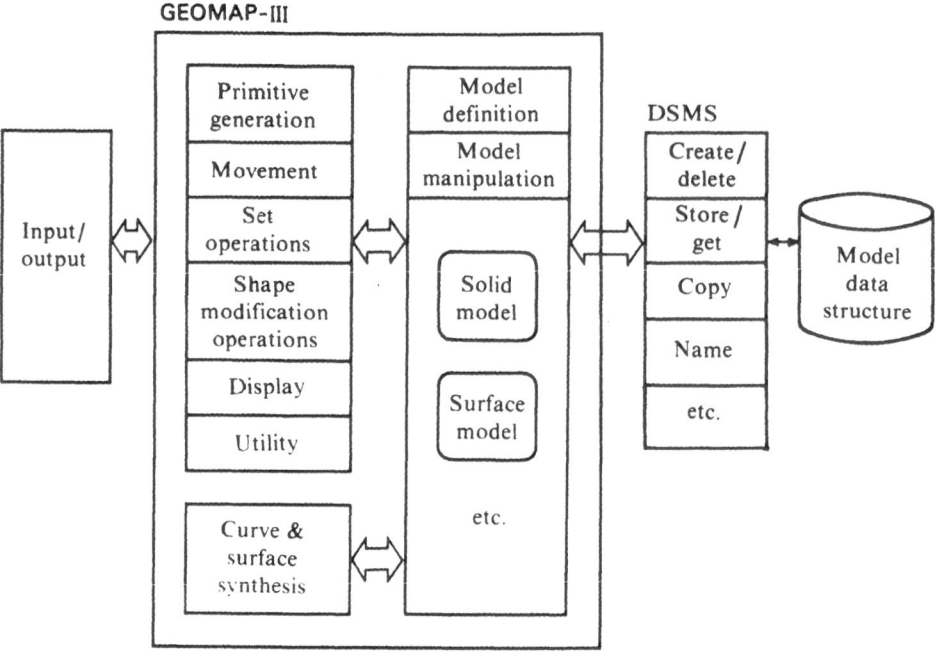

Figure 1. Structure of the solid modeling package GEOMAP-III.

these operations. It is expected that this method will give a very good man-machine interface for shape design.

• A powerful free-form curve and surface synthesis module has been developed. This module is independent of GEOMAP-III and can be used with the GEOMAP-III model data. Surface expressions are basically of the Bézier type, but many new features and extensions have been added, and various synthesis methods, described in the next section, have been implemented. Some of the examples which are synthesized by GEOMAP-III are shown in Figure 2 and Figure 3.

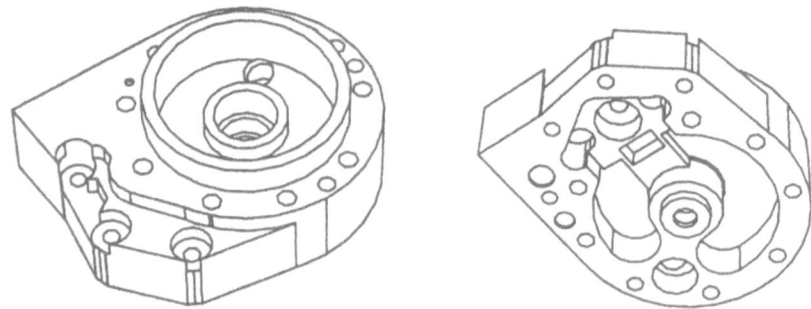

Figure 2. Examples of solid construction.

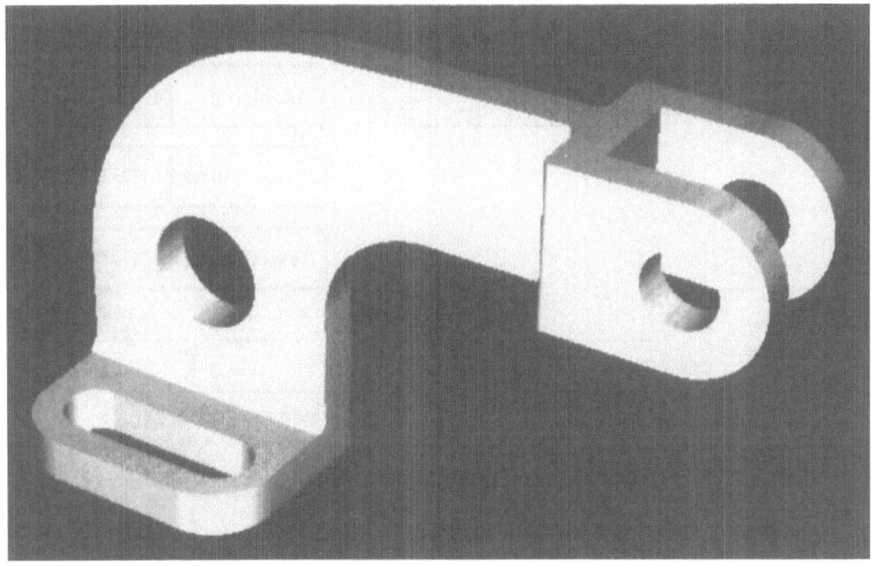

(a) Bracket (see color plates following p. 158).

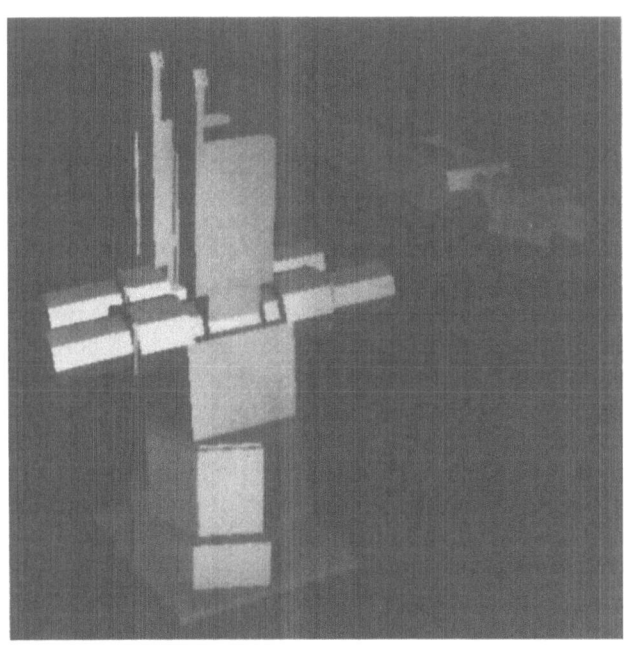

(b) Robot (see color plates following p. 158).

Figure 3. *Examples of shaded output display.*

References pp. 232-234

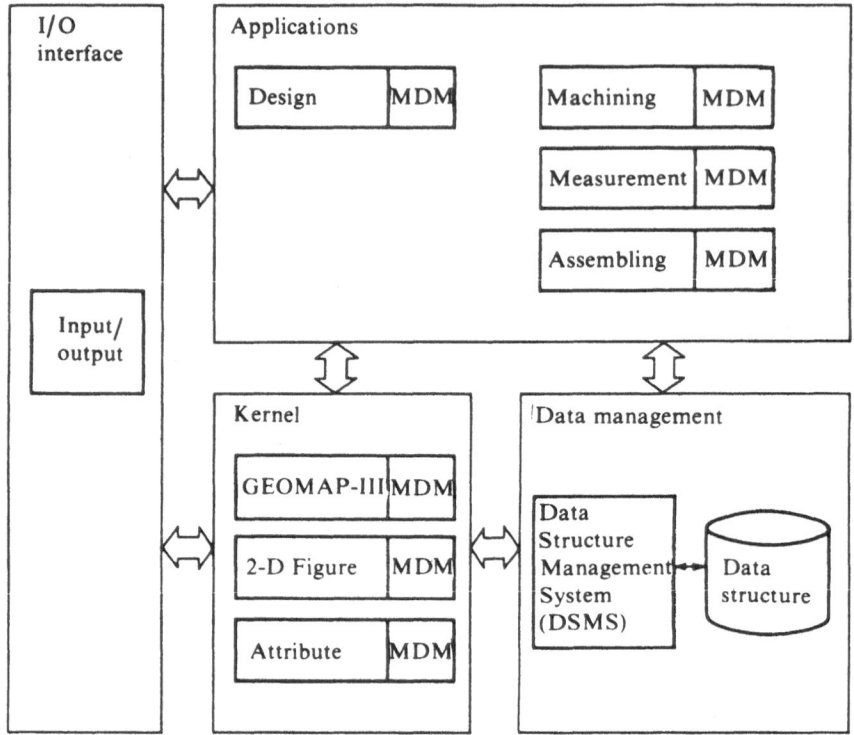

MDM: model definition and manipulation

Figure 4. Conceptual structure of an integrated CAD/CAM system.

For the application of GEOMAP-III to integrate CAD and CAM, we can consider the conceptual framework shown in Figure 4. It consists of four major subsystems: applications, kernel, data management, and input/output interface. The applications subsystem includes various programs for design and manufacturing activities. Pertinent models corresponding to each activity are associated with each program. The models are defined based on the predefined models in the kernel subsystem and are manipulated by the data structure management system (DSMS). Because different products require different design and manufacturing methods, not all the necessary programs and models can be prepared beforehand. Rather it is desirable that the appropriate programs and models can be easily augmented when required. For this purpose, various basic programs and models useful for treating machine products are prepared in the kernel subsystem. Solid modeling functions (GEOMAP-III) are included in this subsystem. They are used as fundamental components for building various applications programs.

Based on this general structure, we tried several typical applications of solid modeling functions to CAD/CAM. They include N/C machining [Kawabe *et al.*

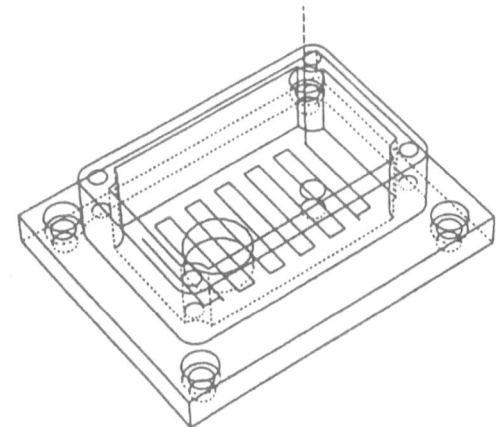

(a) Generation of machining information

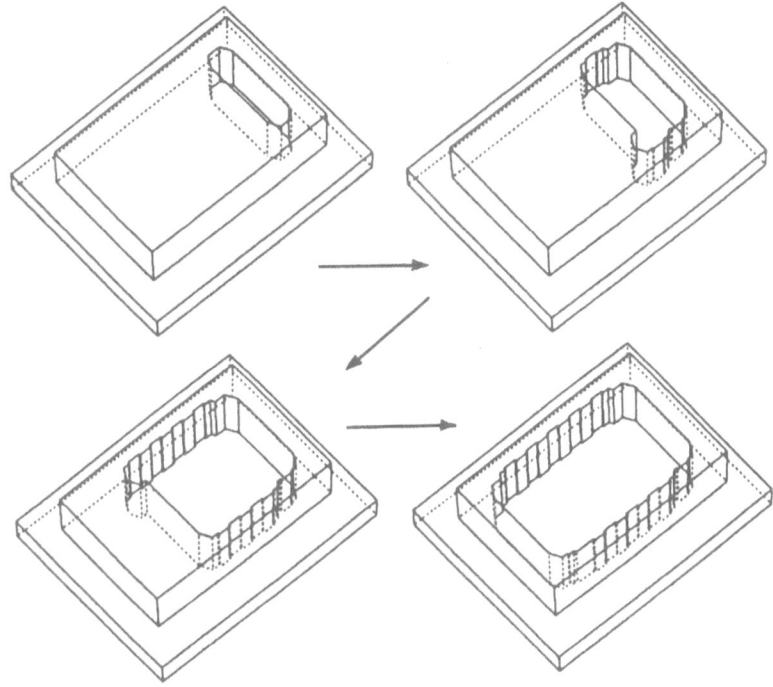

(b) Simulation of machining

Figure 5. *Generation of machining information and simulation of machining based on part models.*

1980a, Kawabe *et al.* 1983], N/C measuring [Kawabe *et al.* 1980b], and robot manipulations [Sata *et al.* 1981]. A simple example of N/C machining is shown in Figure 5.

References pp. 232-234

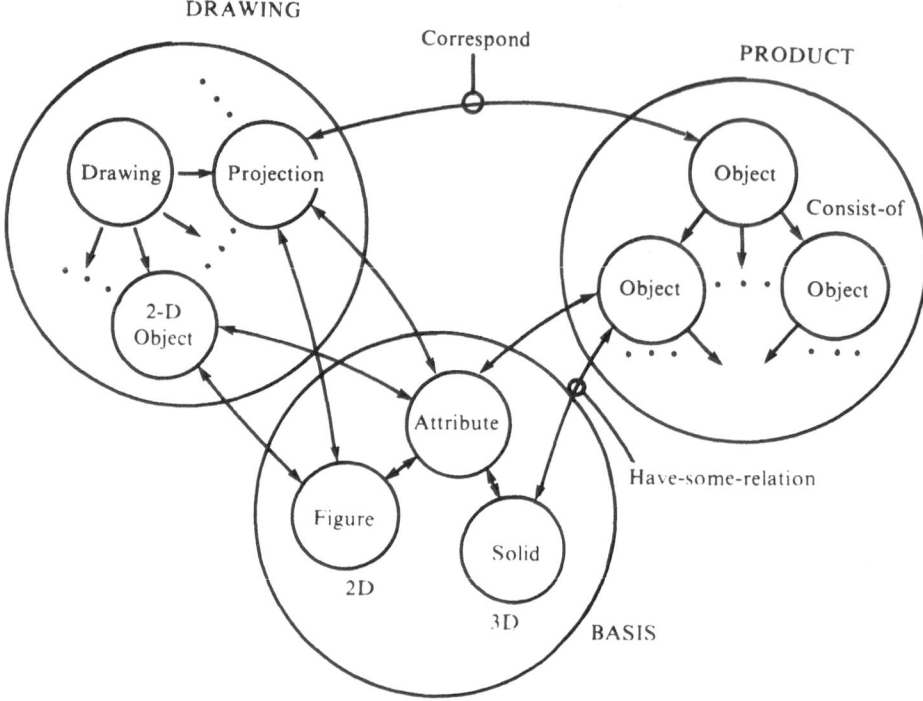

Figure 6. *Conceptual structure of a product model.*

For actually realizing the above applications of CAD/CAM, we need a comprehensive modeling framework for machine products on top of the geometric modeling framework. We do not want to go into details about this topic here, but we show the typical structure of a model for machine products in Figure 6 [Kimura *et al.* 1983b].

Internal representation of a solid is shown schematically in Figure 7. This is a rather conventional boundary-based representation of solids. Surface geometry can include plane, quadric and free-form surfaces. But currently there are some restrictions about set operations among them.

FREE-FORM SURFACE DESIGN

Design methods for free-form surface shapes are, generally speaking, very complicated as compared to the methods for solid object construction with simple surfaces. The methods are rather different from one product to another and are dependent on human designers' expertise. It is hard to make clear the whole design process from the standpoint of computer processing. However, we can roughly divide the process into three stages.

- *Stage 1.* Based on initial sketches, renderings, or drawings made by designers, pertinent geometric data are extracted, and space-curve network models

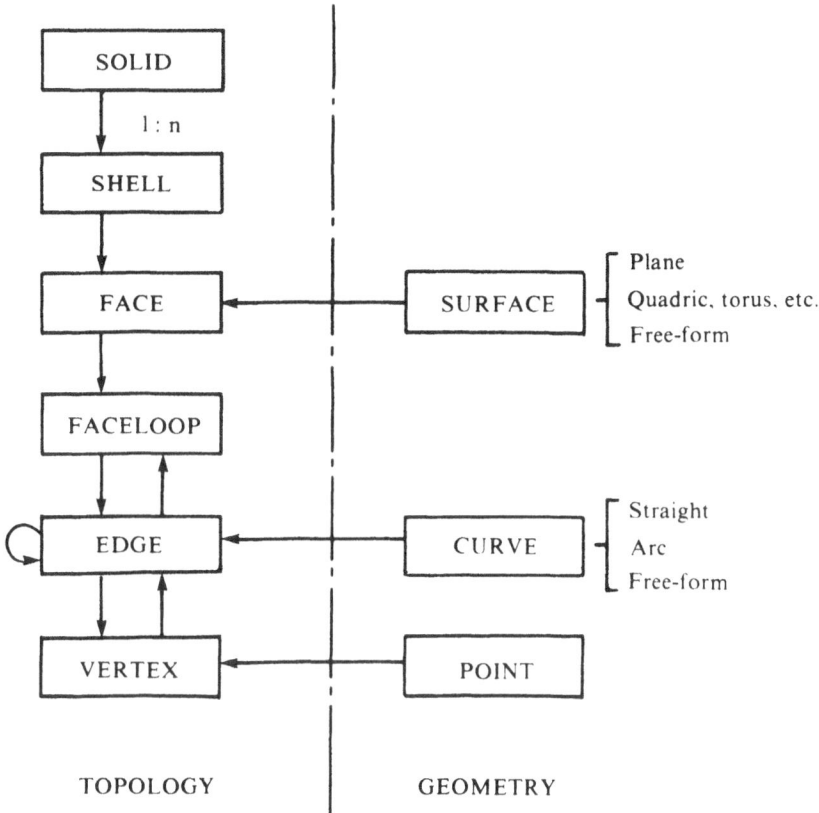

Figure 7. *Internal representaton of a solid in GEOMAP-III.*

are created, which adequately exhibit the designers' intentions for the surface shapes to be designed. Generated curve models are displayed and evaluated and modified by designers. Therefore, space-curve generation is a highly interactive process.

- **Stage 2.** Surface patches are generated to cover the space-curve network with the specified constraints. Resulting surfaces are evaluated by displaying them or by making real three-dimensional models. This surface generation process should be made as automatic as possible, because it is fairly difficult for designers to control surface shapes directly. Instead, it is far easier to control space-curve networks.

- **Stage 3.** In order to generate further subtle features of shapes, various operations, such as intersection and filleting, are performed.

In our geometric modeling systems, Stage 1 and Stage 2 are realized as the curve and surface synthesis module as shown in Figure 8. This is embedded in

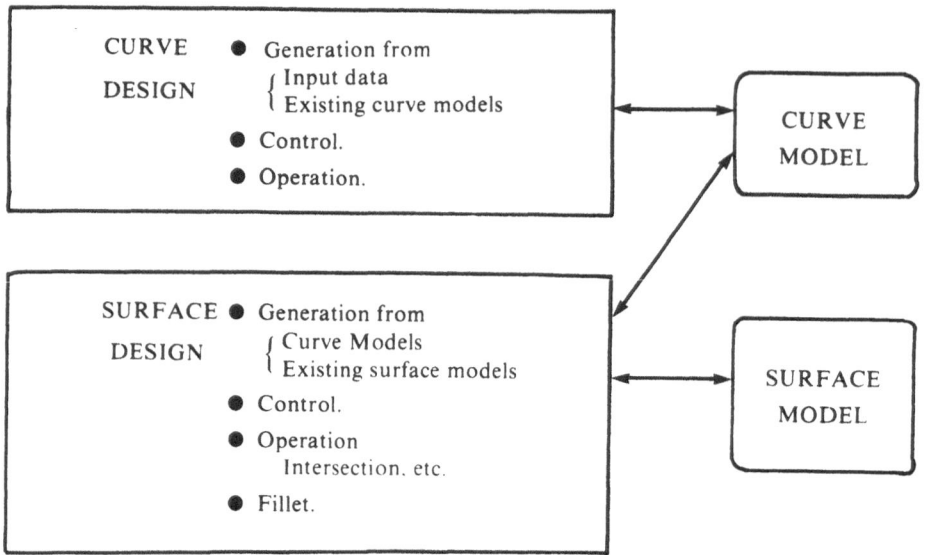

Figure 8. *The curve and surface synthesis module.*

the solid modeling package shown earlier in Figure 1. Stage 3 of the process is realized, in our package, as set operations and local modification operations among solids which include the specified surfaces. In addition some simple operations can be performed within the curve and surface synthesis module.

The space-curve generation of Stage 1 is not treated fully here, but a new approach to this problem is described later in the paper. The method is not necessarily applicable to all cases of curve generation, but it is quite useful for a certain kind of shapes. As compared to the curve generation, the surface generation is a very difficult problem from the theoretical viewpoint. As space-curve networks are created by designers' strong desires to express their images about shapes, they do not necessarily form a regular mesh network but frequently are arbitrarily connected complex networks as shown in Figure 9. These networks correspond to a designer's various specifications of shapes, such as section lines, characteristic lines, roundings, fillets, and so forth. The case (a) in Figure 9 is easy to handle. But in cases (b) and (c), it is rather difficult to generate surface patches over the given networks.

There already exists much research on these topics [Forrest 1978, Barnhill and Riesenfeld 1974, Faux and Pratt 1979, Barnhill and Böhm 1983]. However, at present, there seems to exist no adequate theory or method to handle these cases. Therefore, based on the control point approach of Bézier [Bézier 1972] and Riesenfeld [Riesenfeld 1973], we have developed a new formulation of free-form curves and surfaces [Hosaka and Kimura 1978, 1980, 1981, 1982, Chiyokura and Kimura 1983], and we have proposed several methods for these cases. For example, the degree of a surface patch expression is raised or a region surrounded by the given network is divided to make some buffering regions.

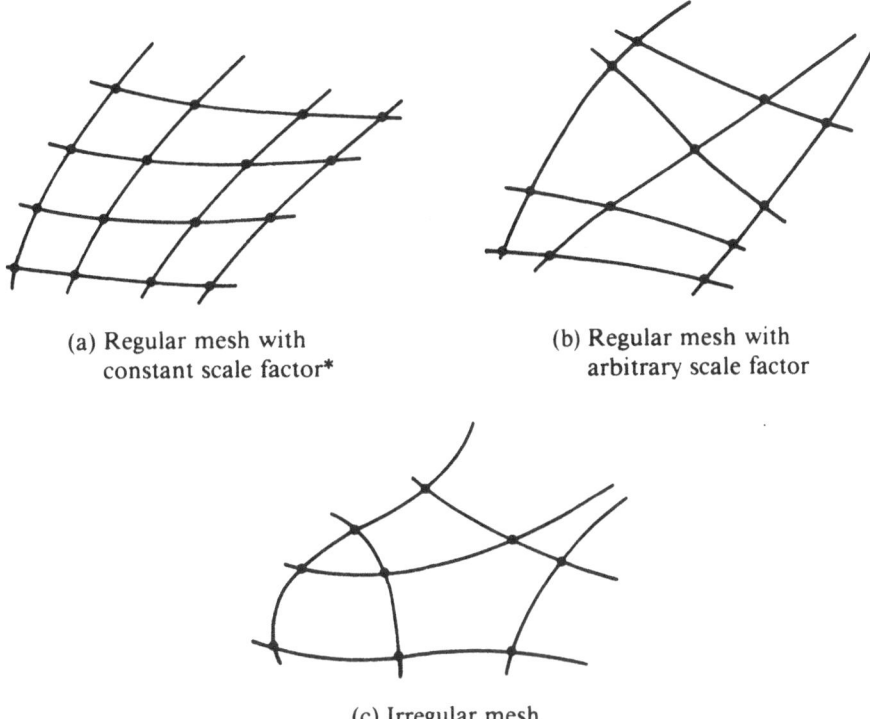

(a) Regular mesh with
constant scale factor*

(b) Regular mesh with
arbitrary scale factor

(c) Irregular mesh

Figure 9. *Curve models that characterize surface models.*
(*For scale factors, refer to Figure 11 and Figure 12.)

Some of the proposed methods are practical to use. But sometimes they are cumbersome and are not easy to use. So it is necessary to formulate more straightforward and powerful methods. They are described after we provide some definitions.

Basic Expressions and Connection of Surface Patches—Before discussing the difficult cases (b) and (c) of Figure 9, we first review the basic surface expressions.

As a basic expression for a curve segment, we adopt the Bézier curve, as shown in Figure 10(a). We express the Bézier curve $R(t)$ of order $n+1$ or degree n with control points $P_0, \ldots, P_n$ in the generating form:

$$R(t) = (1-t+tE)^n P_0 \quad t \in [0,1] \tag{1}$$

where t is a parameter and E is a shifting operator for subscripts of P_i's, that is,

$$EP_i = P_{i+1} \tag{2}$$

Similarly we express the Bézier surface patch $S(u,v)$ of degree $m \times n$, shown in Figure 10(b), in the following form:

$$S(u,v) = (1-u+uE)^m (1-v+vF)^n P_{00} \quad u, v \in [0,1] \tag{3}$$

References pp. 232-234

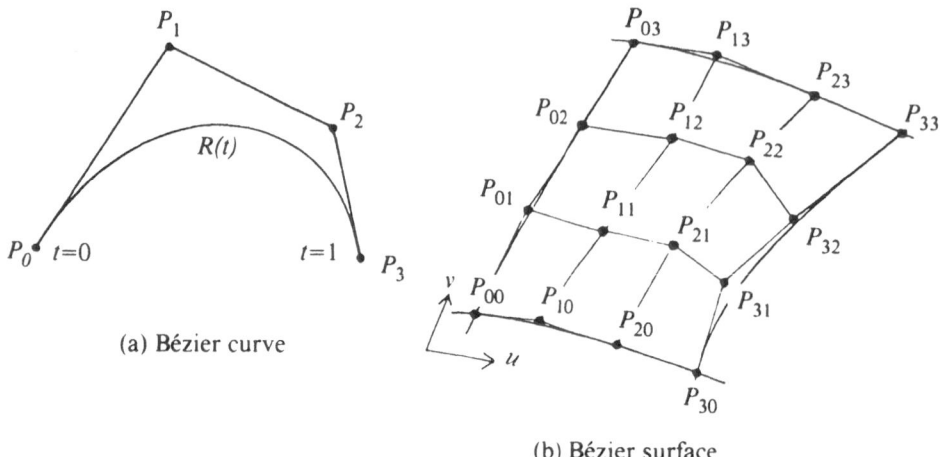

(a) Bézier curve

(b) Bézier surface

Figure 10. *Control points for Bézier curve and surface.*

where u and v are parameters and E and F are shifting operators for subscripts of P_{ij}'s. That is

$$EP_{ij} = P_{i+1,j} \qquad FP_{ij} = P_{i,j+1} \tag{4}$$

The derivation of these expressions, their equivalence to the original Bézier formulation, and their various geometric properties are fully explained elsewhere [Hosaka and Kimura 1978, 1980].

We assume here that boundary curves for surface patches are expressed as connections of the Bézier curves of degree 3. Also surface patches surrounded by boundary curves are assumed to be expressed as (possibly a combination of) Bézier surface patches of degree 3×3. For the case of the regular mesh network, boundary curves are usually composed of Bézier curve segments of degree 3 connected smoothly up to curvature as shown in Figure 11. The smooth curve can be easily calculated from the given connecting points if scale factors k_i's are given [Hosaka and Kimura 1981].

There are two cases for surface patch interpolation over the regular mesh network as shown earlier in Figure 9, and detailed in Figure 12. In the case of a regular mesh network with constant scale factors, all k values in the u-direction are set equal. Similarly, all k values in the v-direction are set equal. Then the bicubic Bézier surface patches can cover the regions made by the regular mesh boundaries and can connect to each other with slope continuity along the boundaries. If the ratios of span lengths between cross points of boundary curves in the v-direction and in the u-direction are not largely different along the u-direction and the v-direction respectively as shown in Figure 12(a), the scale factors can be made equal. But if the ratios are extremely different as shown in Figure 12(b), we cannot obtain good boundary-curve shapes if we set the values of the scale factors equal. Therefore, in such cases, at each boundary

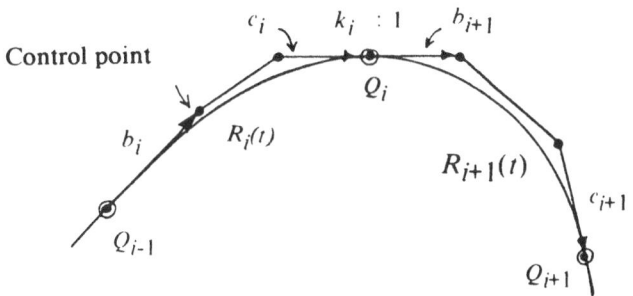

Q_i : Connecting points.

k_i : Scale factor of curve segments $R_i(t)$ and $R_{i+1}(t)$ and is normally set to $\dfrac{Q_i Q_{i-1}}{Q_{i+1} Q_i}$

b_i, c_i : Determined so as to satisfy the relation $c_i = k_i \bullet b_{i+1}$

Figure 11. *Connection of Bézier curves.*

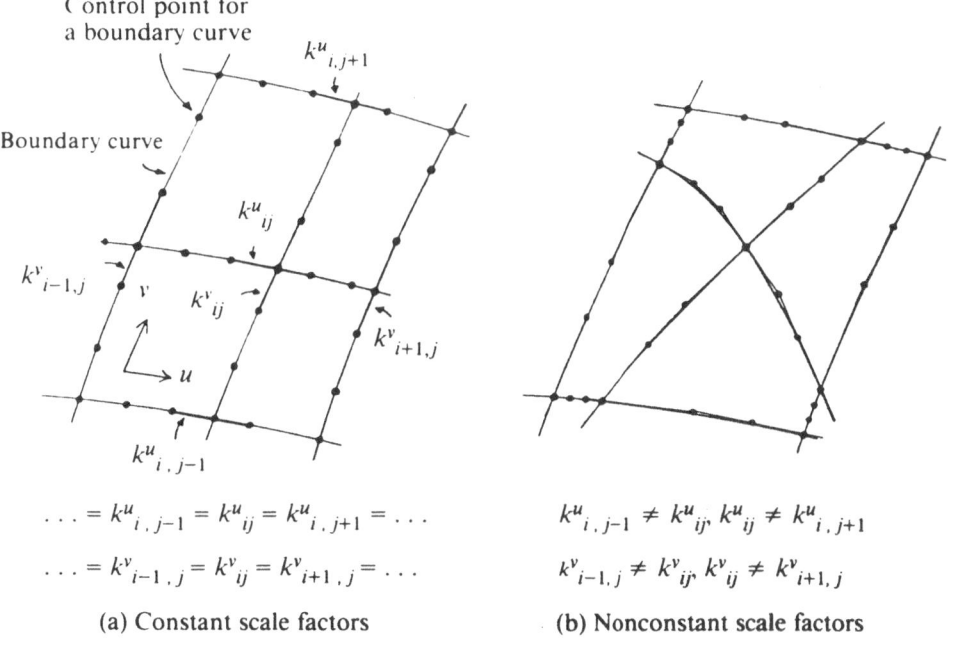

$\cdots = k^u_{i,j-1} = k^u_{ij} = k^u_{i,j+1} = \cdots$ $k^u_{i,j-1} \neq k^u_{ij}, \; k^u_{ij} \neq k^u_{i,j+1}$

$\cdots = k^v_{i-1,j} = k^v_{ij} = k^v_{i+1,j} = \cdots$ $k^v_{i-1,j} \neq k^v_{ij}, \; k^v_{ij} \neq k^v_{i+1,j}$

(a) Constant scale factors   (b) Nonconstant scale factors

Figure 12. *Connection of Bézier surfaces.*

curve we must select appropriate scale factors. Then we cannot connect the bicubic Bézier patches smoothly along the boundaries.

New Surface Expression—This section describes a new surface patch expression which copes with the difficult surface patch connection. The bicubic surface patch $S(u,v)$, can interpolate four boundary curves and normal derivatives

References pp. 232-234

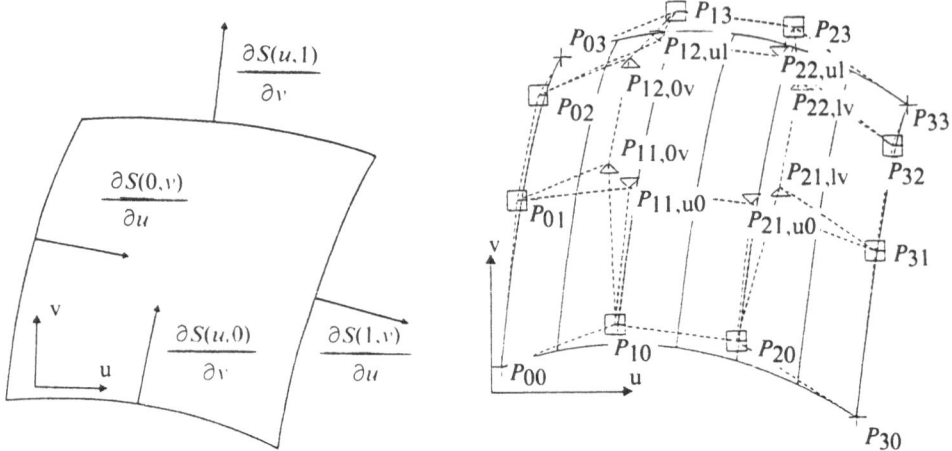

Figure 13. *Normal derivatives of a surface patch.*   **Figure 14.** *Control points for a generalized Bézier surface patch.*

along boundary curves, as shown in Figure 13. However, these normal derivatives cannot be specified independently. They satisfy the following equation at the four corners of a patch.

$$\partial^2 S(u,v)/\partial u \partial v = \partial^2 S(u,v)/\partial v \partial u \tag{5}$$

When various surfaces are interpolated by this patch, this compatibility condition becomes a severe constraint. Therefore, we modify a bicubic Bézier patch to devise a new expression. As shown in Figure 14, this new patch $S(u,v)$ is defined by twenty control points; the equations are as follows:

$$S(u,v) = (1-u+uE)^3(1-v+vF)^3 P_{00}(u,v) \quad u,v \in [0,1] \tag{6}$$

$$P_{11}(u,v) = \frac{uP_{11,u0} + vP_{11,0v}}{v + u}$$

$$P_{12}(u,v) = \frac{uP_{12,u1} + (1-v)P_{12,0v}}{(1-v) + u}$$

$$P_{21}(u,v) = \frac{(1-u) P_{21,u0} + vP_{21,1v}}{v + (1-u)}$$

$$P_{22}(u,v) = \frac{(1-u)P_{22,u1} + (1-v)P_{22,1v}}{(1-v) + (1-u)}$$

These equations mean that the position of a point on this patch is represented as an addition of sixteen points to which various weights are given. Point P_{11} moves on a straight line segment between two control points $P_{11,u0}$ and $P_{11,0v}$ according to parameters u and v. Similarly, points P_{12}, P_{21} and P_{22}

move on straight line segments between two corresponding control points. Twelve other points which define boundary curves are fixed points. Like a Bézier patch, this patch has the convex hull property, that is, an arbitrary point on the patch exists in the convex hull defined by all control points. This property is advantageous for rough intersection checks.

Now we consider the smooth connection of surface patches to represent free-form surface shapes. We discuss here the case where only the surface normal direction should be made continuous across the boundary curves. If we also require the continuity of curvature, the problem becomes far more complex.

By using the expression (6), we can treat the connection problem without considering the compatibility condition. This means that we can consider the surface patch connection side by side, for instance $u = 0$ or $u = 1$, etc., without considering the other sides. Along a particular boundary, surface connection is established by the following steps:

- Estimate the tangent plane normal along the boundary curve. (This estimation should ·be done solely by using the information about the boundary curve data.)
- Determine the control points associated with the boundary curve.

These steps are repeated along all boundary curves with respect to all surface patches.

Based on the above considerations, we can solve the connection problem of case (b) of Figure 12. Even if the boundary curves are not continuous in slope at their intersection points, pertinent surface patches are generated by the above methods [Chiyokura and Kimura 1983]. If we take the more general weighting functions for determining P_{ij} in the expression (6), then we can achieve the more general surface patch connection.

Next, we consider the treatment of case (c) of Figure 9, that is, surface patch connection for an irregular mesh. By using the same approach adopted in case (b), the normal derivatives across the boundary curves are determined. Then internal curves satisfying these derivatives are generated and faces are subdivided into several rectangular faces, as shown in Figure 15. Then surface patches are generated over these rectangular faces. These procedures are done automatically. Methods using subdivision have already been proposed. But, if conventional bicubic patches are used in these methods, the connections of patches on the internal curves and the boundary curves are difficult. Our method can avoid this difficulty.

In some cases, the subdivision of an irregular patch is rather cumbersome, and the generated surface patches are hard to control to realize good shapes that designers want to make. To cope with this problem, we consider a further generalization of the expression (6). We treat here the case of expressions of degree 3. As shown in Figure 16, inner control points are allocated corresponding to respective patch corners. That is, an n-sided patch has n inner control points. But actually each inner control point consists of two control points which are

References pp. 232-234

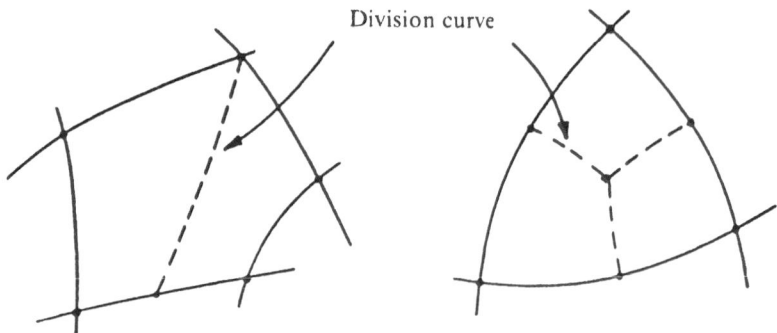

Division curve

Figure 15. *Irregular-shaped surface patches*

combined in a manner similar to the expression (6). We denote the inner control points as ② in Figure 16. Then, by using the $3n$ boundary control points and the n inner control points, we can derive a surface expression which covers the n-sided patch. The most important fact is that the n-sided patch expressed by this new method can be viewed as a rectangular patch if seen outside along the respective curve boundaries. This means that, when these irregular patches are smoothly connected, we can employ the same method as the one used for rectangular surface patch connection. This expression is quite complex, and the details will be reported elsewhere.

SOLID DESIGN BY LOCAL MODIFICATION OPERATIONS

In this section, we consider a method for solid shape design with free-form surfaces based on local modification operations. The method consists of two steps:

- Generation of space-curve networks with the use of local modification operations.

- Generation of surface patches which cover the generated space-curve networks.

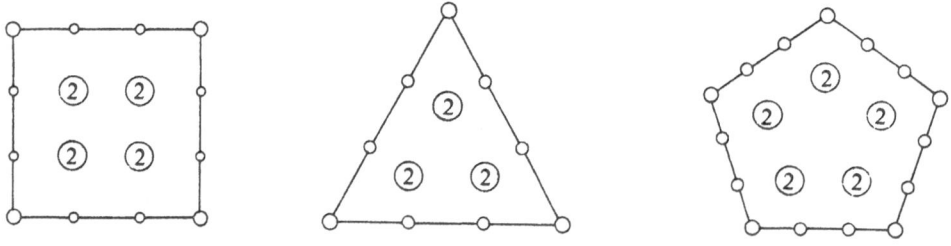

Figure 16. *Arrangements of control points for generalized surface patches.*

The second step has already been described in the previous section. Therefore, we concentrate on the first step in the following discussions. Conventionally space-curve generation has been treated as discussed earlier in Stage 1 of the section on free-form surface design [Higashi *et al.* 1983]. The method described in this section is rather different and can be seen as a complementary approach to the conventional one.

First, a polyhedral model which serves as a basis for free-form shape design is generated by local modification operations. Using local modifications, geometrical and topological information representing the shape of a solid can be changed locally by producing, deleting and moving local elements of a solid such as faces, edges and vertices. Next, a curve model for a free-form shape is generated from this polyhedral model. Finally, surface equations interpolating over the curve model are generated. The construction of the shapes by using local modifications can readily be understood by a designer in many cases. From an implementer's point of view, local modifications and our surface interpolation method are easy and their execution does not require much time.

The local modification operations have already been developed and used by many systems (for instance [Braid *et al.* 1980] or [Mäntylä and Sulonen 1982]). While these operations have been used in order to construct polyhedra and solids with simple curved surfaces, we devised a rounding modification as one of the local modifications to round off edges and corners of solids locally. We use local modifications to construct complex free-form shapes.

Some methods for rounding off corners and edges of polyhedra have been proposed [Catmull and Clark 1978, Doo 1978]. But their method seems to have some difficulties with, for example, local control of generated shapes. To solve these problems, we devised a new method employing local modification operations called *lift, make, kill* and *move* [Chiyokura and Kimura 1983]; their functions are illustrated in Figure 17. *Lift* is an operation to add a solid generated by sweeping local elements in the original solid. *Make* and *kill* change the topology of solids and are often used as preparations for lifting and rounding modifications. *Move* is an operation to translate local elements. It is difficult to change shapes by moving if the condition that solids must be polyhedra is imposed. But, for our purpose, it is useful to employ the moving operation even though it means losing the face planarity condition. Some examples of shape construction using these operations are shown in Figures 18 and 19.

Once these local modification operations are carried out to change topology, the *round* modification is performed as shown in Figure 20. Edges to be rounded off are selected, and new edges are created across the selected edges. The newly created edges determine the sectional shape of the rounded edges. Topological consistency is checked, unnecessary edges and vertices are deleted, and required relations among geometrical elements are established. An example of rounding modification is shown in Figure 21, which includes a rather complex combination of surface patches.

References pp. 232-234

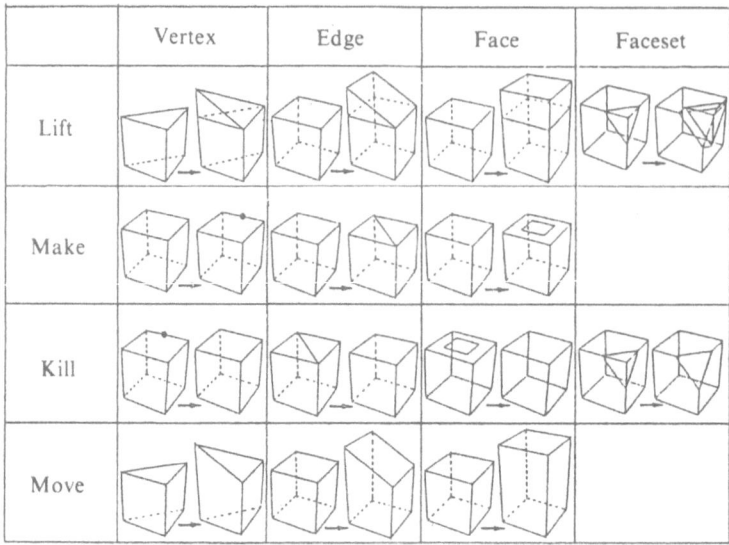

Figure 17. *Local modification operations.*

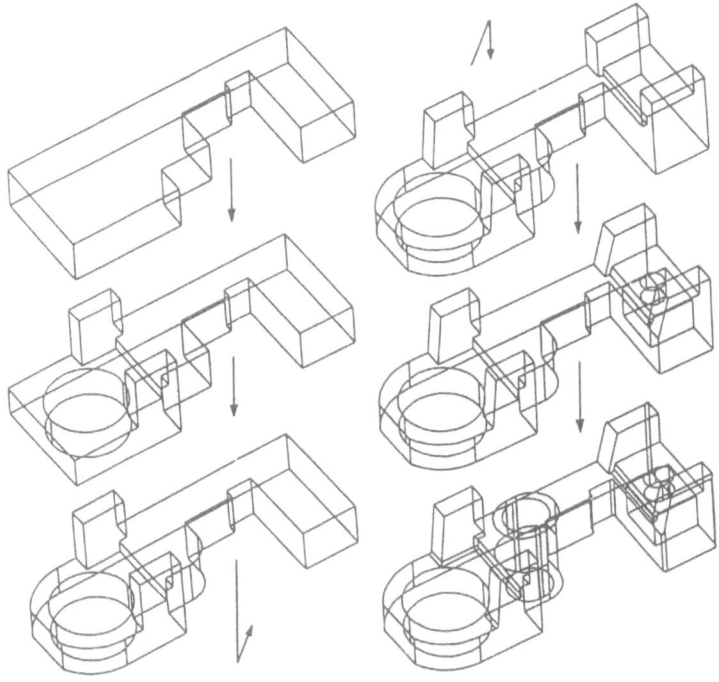

Figure 18. *Process of shape construction by use of local modification operations.*

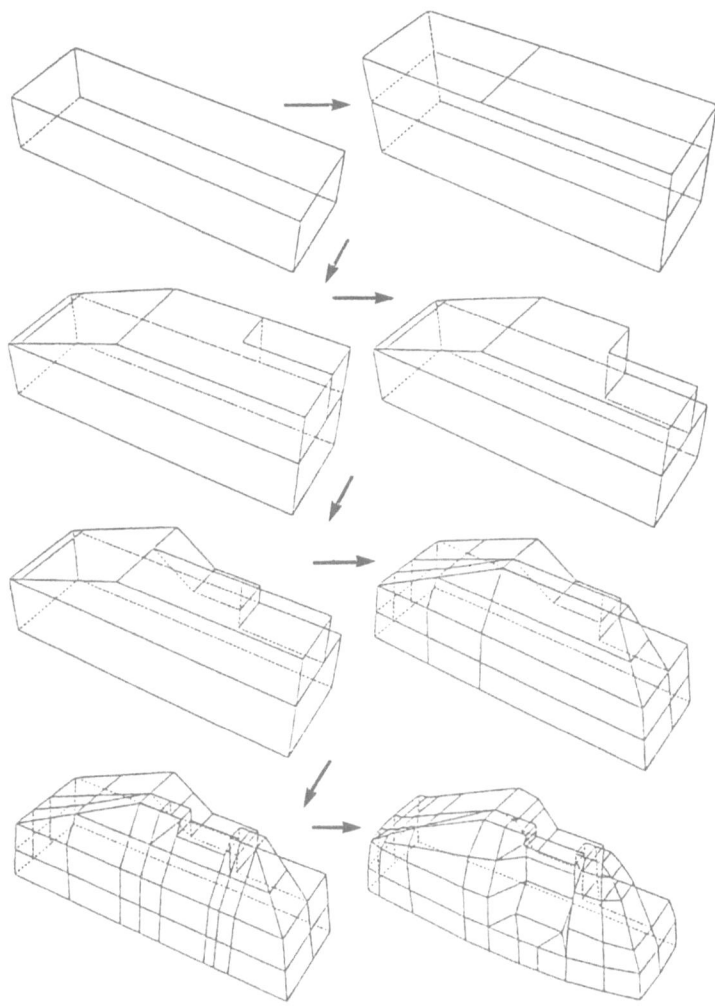

Figure 19. *Process of shape construction by use of local modification operations.*

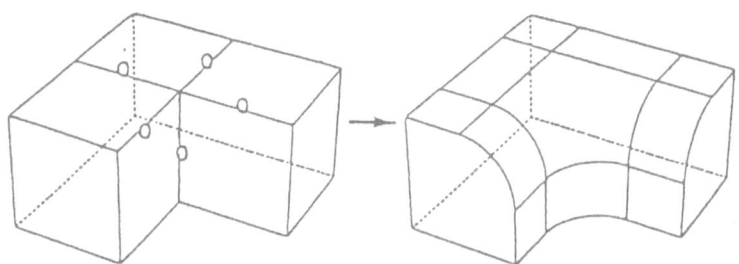

Figure 20. *Rounding modification.*

References pp. 232-234

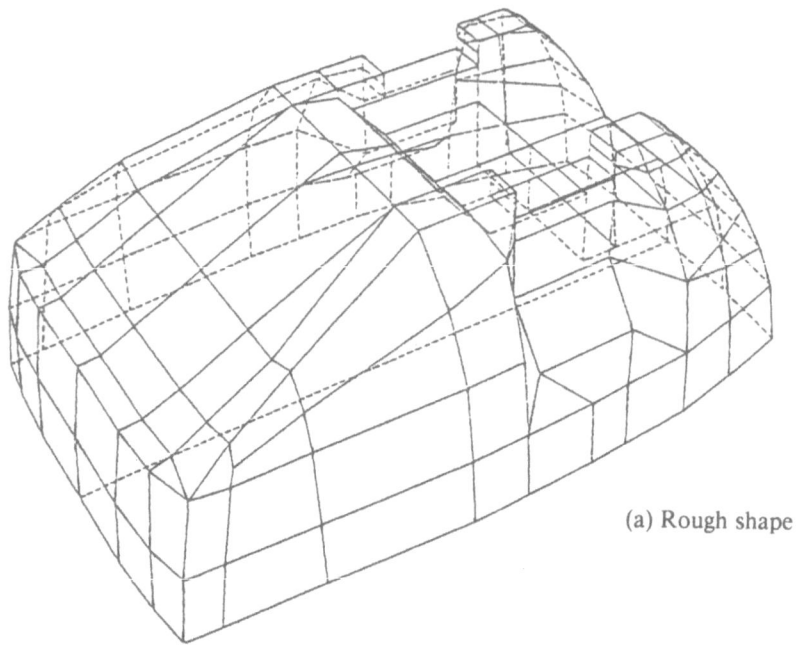

(a) Rough shape

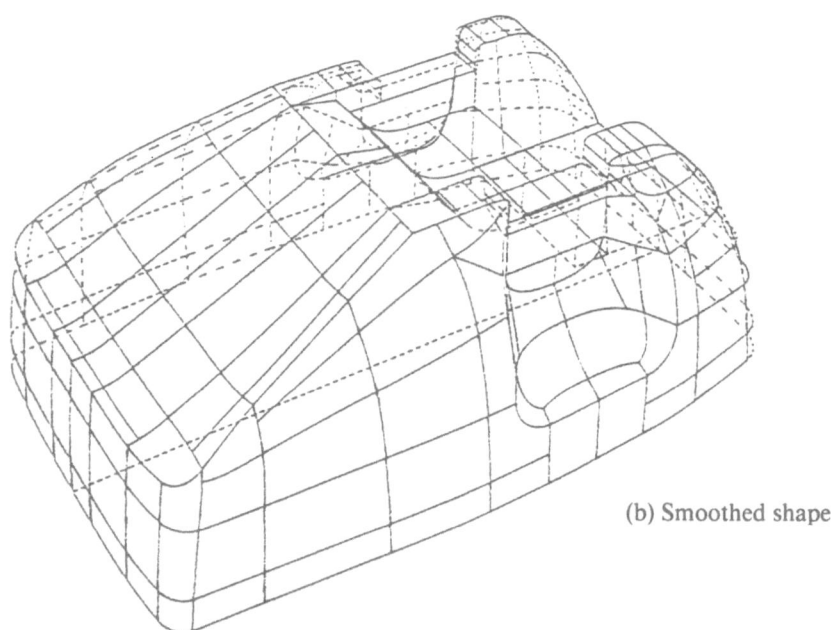

(b) Smoothed shape

Figure 21. An example of rounding modification.

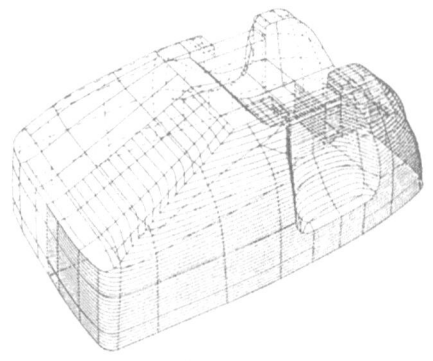

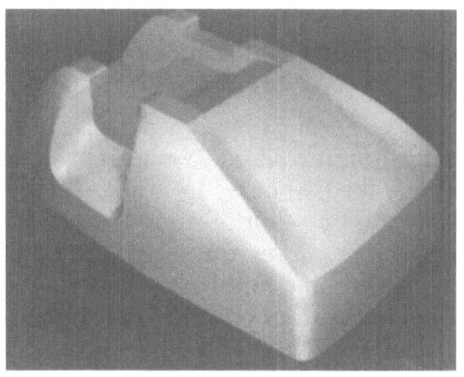

(a) Perspective display with
contour lines

(b) Shaded display (see color
plates following p. 158).

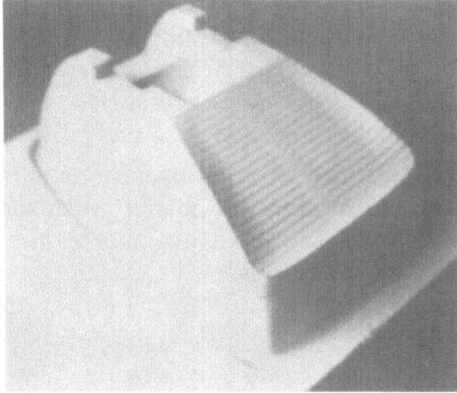

(c) Real three-dimensional
cut-out model (see color
plates following p. 158).

Figure 22. *Various outputs of a generated solid model.*

After the generation of space-curve networks by the above method, pertinent surface patches are generated by using the method described earlier in this paper. An example is shown in Figure 22.

SOLID DESIGN BY SET OPERATIONS

General algorithms for set operations among solids have become rather well known in recent years, and many modelers realize set operations among solids with planar and quadric surfaces. But, if we want to extend the functions of set operations to solids with free-form surfaces, it becomes a problem to compute intersections between free-form surfaces exactly and efficiently. Theoretically

References pp. 232-234

rigorous algorithms are well known for computing the intersections between plane, quadric and some special surfaces [Sarraga 1983, Goldman 1983]. For free-form surfaces, such a powerful algorithm has not yet been found.

Our surface expression has a good convex hull property with respect to the control points. Also we can use the subdivision algorithm which is similar to the one for B-splines. By using these properties, we can fairly well establish the stable computation of intersection curves between free-form surfaces. Resulting intersection curves are approximated by free-form curves in order to make their treatment in the following processing easier. But all the necessary information is stored in the data structure of the solid, so it is possible to recalculate the curves as required.

CONCLUSION

In this paper, we have summarized our activities on solid modeling and explained two methods for construction of solids with free-form surfaces. The important basic problem is how to generate a complex free-form surface over a complex space-curve network. We show a new surface expression which is powerful for smooth surface patch connection.

Solid generation with local modification operations is rather well established and can be applied to practical problems, possibly with some minor difficulties. But there remain many obstacles to the use of set operations in practice, particularly in their efficiency and robustness.

REFERENCES

[Bézier 1972]
P. E. Bézier, *Numerical Control—Mathematics and Applications*, John Wiley and Sons, London, England, 1972.

[Barnhill and Böhm 1983]
R. E. Barnhill and W. Böhm, eds., *Surfaces in Computer Aided Geometric Design*, North-Holland Publishing Company, Amsterdam, Netherlands, 1983.

[Barnhill and Riesenfeld 1974]
R. E. Barnhill and R. F. Riesenfeld, eds., *Computer Aided Geometric Design*, Academic Press, New York, New York, 1974.

[Braid *et al.* 1980]
I. C. Braid, R. C. Hillyard, and I. A. Stroud, "Stepwise Construction of Polyhedra in Geometric Modeling," *Mathematical Methods in Computer Graphics and Design*, Academic Press, London, England, 1980, pp. 123–141.

[Catmull and Clark 1978]
E. Catmull and J. Clark, "Recursively Generated B-Spline Surfaces on Arbitrary Topological Meshes," *Computer Aided Design*, Vol. 10, No. 6, November 1978, pp. 350–355.

[Chiyokura and Kimura 1983]
H. Chiyokura and F. Kimura, "Design of Solids with Free-Form Surfaces," *ACM Computer Graphics*, Vol. 17, No. 3 (SIGGRAPH '83 Conference Proceedings, Detroit, Michigan, July 25–29, 1983) pp. 289–298.

[Doo 1978]
D. Doo, "Subdivision Algorithm for Smoothing Down Irregular Shaped Polyhedrons," *IEEE Proceedings of the International Conference on Interactive Techniques in Computer Aided Design*, Bologna, Italy, September 21–23, 1978, pp. 157–165.

[Faux and Pratt 1979]
I. D. Faux and M. J. Pratt, *Computational Geometry for Design and Manufacture*, Ellis Horwood Limited, London, England, 1979.

[Forrest 1978]
A. R. Forrest, "A Unified Approach to Geometric Modeling," *ACM Computer Graphics*, Vol. 12, No. 3 (SIGGRAPH '78 Conference Proceedings, Atlanta, Georgia, August 23–25, 1978) pp. 264–269.

[Goldman 1983]
R. N. Goldman, "Quadrics of Revolution," *IEEE Computer Graphics and Applications*, Vol. 3, No. 2, March/April 1983, pp. 68–76.

[Higashi *et al.* 1983]
M. Higashi, I. Kohzen, and J. Nagasaka, "An Interactive CAD System for Construction of Shapes with High-Quality Surfaces," *Proceedings of CAPE '83*, Amsterdam, Netherlands, April 25–28, 1983, pp. 371–389.

[Hosaka and Kimura 1977]
M. Hosaka and F. Kimura, "An Interactive Geometrical Design System with Handwriting Input," *Proceedings of the 1977 IFIP Congress*, Toronto, Canada, August 1977, pp. 167–172.

[Hosaka and Kimura 1978]
M. Hosaka and F. Kimura, "Synthesis Methods of Curves and Surfaces in Interactive CAD," *IEEE Proceedings of the International Conference on Interactive Techniques in Computer Aided Design*, Bologna, Italy, September 21–23, 1978, pp. 151–156.

[Hosaka and Kimura 1980]
M. Hosaka and F. Kimura, "A Theory and Methods for Three Dimensional Free-Form Shape Construction," *Journal of Information Processing*, Vol. 3, No. 3, Information Processing Society of Japan, 1980, pp. 140–151.

[Hosaka and Kimura 1981]
M. Hosaka and F. Kimura, "Interactive Input Methods for Free-Form Shape Design," *Man-Machine Communication in CAD/CAM*, North-Holland Publishing Company, Amsterdam, Netherlands, 1981, pp. 103–118.

[Hosaka and Kimura 1982]
M. Hosaka and F. Kimura, "Methods of Surface Synthesis in GEOMAP-III," *Proceedings of MICAD '82*, Paris, France, 1982, p. 268–280.

[Hosaka *et al.* 1974]
M. Hosaka, F. Kimura and N. Kakishita, "A Unified Method for Processing Polyhedra," *Proceedings of the 1974 IFIP Congress*, Stockholm, Sweden, August 1974, pp. 768–772.

[IEEE 1982]
IEEE Special Issue on Solid Modeling, *IEEE Computer Graphics and Applications*, Vol. 2, No. 2, March 1982.

[Kawabe *et al.* 1980a]
S. Kawabe, F. Kimura, and T. Sata, "Generation of NC Commands for Sculptured Surface Machining for 3-Coordinate Measuring Data," *Annals of the CIRP*, Vol. 29, No. 1, 1980, pp. 369–372.

[Kawabe *et al.* 1980b]
S. Kawabe, F. Kimura, and T. Sata, "Automatic Generation of NC Commands for a 3-Coordinate Measuring Machine," *Proceedings of ICPE*, Tokyo, Japan, 1980, pp. 941–946.

[Kawabe *et al.* 1983]
S. Kawabe, S. Shimura, M. Miyashita, F. Kimura, and T. Sata, "Programming for Machining Based on Workpiece Models in Computers," *Annals of the CIRP*, Vol. 32, No. 1, 1983, pp. 351–355.

[Kimura *et al.* 1982]
F. Kimura, Y. Yamaguchi, Y. Sasaki, K. Kido, and M. Hosaka, "Construction and Uses of an Engineering Data Base in Design and Manufacturing Environments," *File Structures and Data Bases for CAD*, North-Holland Publishing Company, Amsterdam, Netherlands, 1982, pp. 95–116.

[Kimura *et al.* 1983a]
F. Kimura, T. Sata, and M. Hosaka, "Integration of Design and Manufacturing Activities based on Object Modeling," *Advances in CAD/CAM* (PROLAMAT '82), North-Holland Publishing Company, Amsterdam, Netherlands, 1983, pp. 375–385.

[Kimura *et al.* 1983b]
F. Kimura, S. Kawabe, T. Sata, and M. Hosaka, "A Study on Product Modeling for Integration of CAD/CAM," *Integration of CAD/CAM*, North-Holland Publishing Company, Amsterdam, Netherlands, 1983, pp. 227–251.

[Mäntylä and Sulonen 1982]
M. Mäntylä and R. Sulonen, "GWB: A Solid Modeler with Euler Operators," *IEEE Computer Graphics and Applications*, Vol. 2, No. 7, September 1982, pp. 17–31.

[Riesenfeld 1973]
R. F. Riesenfeld, "Application of B-Spline Approximations to Geometric Problems of Computer Aided Design," Ph.D. Dissertation, Syracuse University, Syracuse, New York, May 1973.

[Sarraga 1983]
R. F. Sarraga, "Algebraic Methods for Intersection of Quadric Surfaces in GMSolid," *Computer Vision, Graphics, and Image Processing*, Vol. 22, No. 2, May 1983, pp. 222–238.

[Sata *et al.* 1981]
T. Sata, F. Kimura, and A. Amano, "Robot Simulation System as a Task Programming Tool," *Proceedings of ISIR*, Tokyo, Japan, 1981, pp. 595–602.

DISCUSSION

Herbert Steinberg *(MAGI)*

Could you describe the process you use in rendering those pictures?

Kimura

We use a very crude, very simple ray-tracing method. It's very simple but it takes a long time.

F. Kimura

Sam Geisberg *(Applicon)*

Do you feel that any kind of natural language that specifies the blending operations or any other operations can be used so the engineer can build your surfaces without having to know these complicated mathematical expressions?

Hinds

I think the heart of Sam's question is what kind of interface do you provide to a user so that he can express these rounding functions and blending functions without the technical knowledge of coefficients.

Kimura

A system might furnish this, but as I explained, our surface synthesis process is two steps. In the first step, the designer designs curved wire frame models and then the computer automatically fills out the wire frame models. So the user need not care about complex surface expressions. Yet one task that the designer must do is make a good wire frame model. In order to make a good wire frame model, they have available good tools. They first make a rather rough model by using the conventional solid modeling facilities and then specify the edges. "Yes, I want to round off this corner." It's very simple.

Does that answer your question?

Geisberg

More or less. You said the user has to create good wire frame models; it seems that they should be good with respect to your surfacing technique or your rounding technique. What does "good" mean?

Kimura

The method for rounding is be applicable to some specific task, for making some specific curved object. Our major objective is to model this kind of rather functional object. In order to model a more complex surface like the shape of a car body or aircraft, we need another kind of technology or the conventional technologies to make some characteristic splines, to make some higher order splines, to make surfaces, and to control the derivatives. Our methods are rather well suited to designing the functional models that were addressed in the presentation by General Motors.

Graham Jared *(University of Cambridge)*

In your examples you showed how you could section objects with a free-form surface. Is there any limitation on the surfaces of the solid model that you can section with the free-form surface; can you section other free-form surfaces, quadric surfaces, toroids, and so forth?

Hinds

The question is to what degree you can do solid kinds of operations with these free-form surfaces. You put these things in by wire frame; but once they're in and you have defined a solid, what kind of operations can you do on that solid and what difficulties do you have?

Kimura

On free-form surfaces we have many kinds of limitations, of course. Basically we can perform a general set operation among the objects which include a free-form curved surface; but there are many difficult problems which were also mentioned in the General Motors presentation, and we have no idea how to avoid those kind of problems. Our basic idea is to keep logical descriptions as far as possible. For example, if we know that the surface is a cylindrical surface or that a surface is a ruled surface, then, from that kind of information, we can check for some singularity or difficult portions and then begin the actual numerical computations using subdivision methods and the convex hull properties of the Bézier-type surface. Difficulties arise under some singularity conditions and we can't treat all of those problems. So we have many problems with set operations on free-form surface objects.

INTRODUCING SCULPTURED SURFACES INTO A GEOMETRIC MODELER

ALYN P. ROCKWOOD

Shape Data, Ltd.
Cambridge, England

ABSTRACT

The frequent need in CAD/CAM for handling sculptured surfaces represents manifold problems which require solutions. There are, for example, many differences between the inputs for creating precision aircraft parts and those for the simple blending of two adjacent surfaces. The possible solutions vary greatly as well. The requirements and solutions for such problems are reviewed in the context of implementing sculptured surfaces in a solid geometric modeler.

Particular attention is given to the user interface. Its purpose is to relieve the user of the tedious details which are often unwarranted by the desired surface, but which exist in current systems because of the form of the surface representation. Algorithms for such an interface, namely, "rolling ball," Chaiken chamfering and surfaces of equipotentiality are compared. The next undertaking is to reduce the given surface to explicit patches and ensure good integration into the existing structure of the modeler.

INTRODUCTION

An appropriate interface between a designer and the underlying mathematics of a design system was aptly expressed by Gordon and Riesenfeld:

> In order to be successful, a system must have appeal to the designer—it must be simple, intuitive and easy to use. Ideally, an interactive design system makes no mathematical demands on the user other than those to which he has been formerly accustomed through drafting and design experience [Gordon and Riesenfeld 1974].

References pp. 252-253

In practise this ideal is often compromised for a wide variety of reasons. This paper focuses on two of them in particular. These have become apparent through the research effort at Shape Data to introduce sculptured surfaces into the ROMULUS geometric modeler.

The first pertains to the internal needs of the modeler. Whatever the surface formulation in a modeler is, it must generally allow for a surface topology and orientation, modes of rendering, sectioning and set operations of union, intersection, subtraction, etc. Although these are essential to the modeler, it often occurs that they unduly influence the type of mathematics used. It is a case of the tail wagging the dog.

The second factor is simply the lack of richer mathematical forms than those currently available. What makes this more than just a blanket statement is its relation to the modeling requirements just noted. One could first consider whether a mathematical form produces a surface with all the desired input and shape characteristics and then worry about whether it can be made to fulfill the other modeling requirements.

THE SURFACE INTERFACE

Early design systems used limited surface types such as piecewise planar or lofted surfaces. Later the quadric surfaces and surfaces of revolution were added. Coons introduced the concept of polynomial patches [Coons 1967], a concept which has been greatly enlarged by those who followed.

In any geometric modeling system there exists a trade-off between the diversity of the primitive surfaces employed and the complexity of the geometrical computations, but all of the surfaces mentioned so far have some common traits which make them useful primitives. They are all explicitly defined surfaces which can be sectioned. They can be rendered visually. They all submit to some topological scheme (edges, oriented faces, Euler equations, etc.) The latter is important for performing Boolean operations while retaining a sense of *in* and *out* on the surface. Collectively speaking, these will be referred to as *primitive traits*, and any surface possessing such traits will be referred to as a *primitive*.

Now consider a broader family of surfaces which is not restricted by primitive traits. In fact, there is only one significant restriction—it must be possible to reduce the surfaces to primitives or to approximate them by primitives.

This subtlety is illustrated later in the paper by surveying several examples of recent research, but first consider how this can affect the structure of the modeling software. One possible structure is diagrammed in Figure 1. The main part of the geometric modeler is below the dashed line. This part handles the primitives with all the standard functions. Here one can envisage the designed object neatly stitched together from parts of spheres, planes, cones, cylinders, B-spline patches and other primitives. It can be visualized, be sectioned or be the basis for milling tapes and volume or stress calculations.

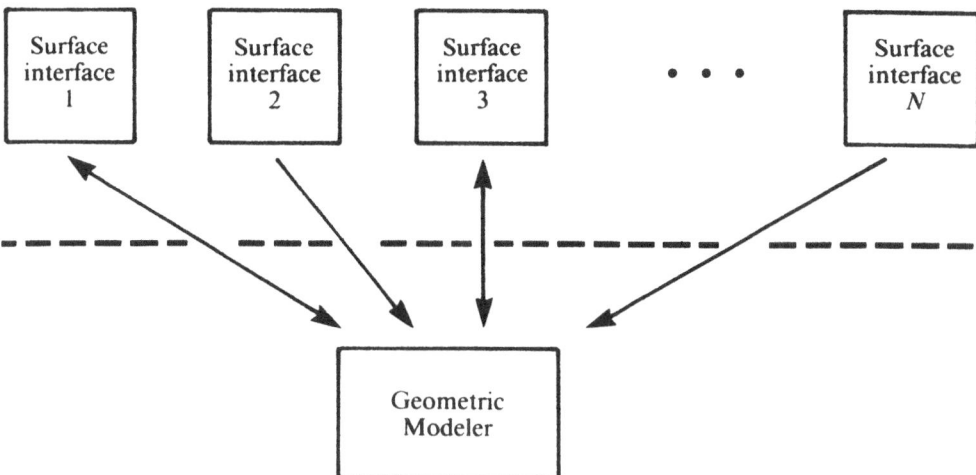

Figure 1. *Structure of the modeling software.*

The boxes above the dashed line represent separate interface routines. The surface mathematics in these boxes is totally unencumbered, except by the reducibility criterion which is represented by the down arrow. The emphasis above the line is on richness of surface types and ease of use.

Some of the arrows point in both directions. This indicates that some interface routines may use existing (primitive) objects. A generalized fillet routine, which smooths off sharp corners of an already existing object, would be a good example of this.

A further implication of the bidirectional arrows is that of recursion. Thus one could fillet an object by some general method, reduce the fillet to primitives and then fillet again, overlapping the new fillet with the old one along a different yet adjoining boundary (Figure 2). As another example, imagine designing a cup handle by a ducting method, reducing it to a patched surface and then using the fillet routine to blend the handle into the cylindrical part of the cup.

To better understand the nature of the interface routines which are seen as candidates for the upper boxes, it is helpful to do some preliminary classification of surface types.

SURFACE TYPES

Veenman suggests three broad categories for classifying doubly curved surfaces and notes that there are many possibilities for overlap within the categories. He defines them functionally; that is, they are based on the applications in which they are generally used [Veenman 1982]. These are:

- *Design surfaces*, which are precisely determined shapes requiring very exacting input for the entire surface,

References pp. 252-253

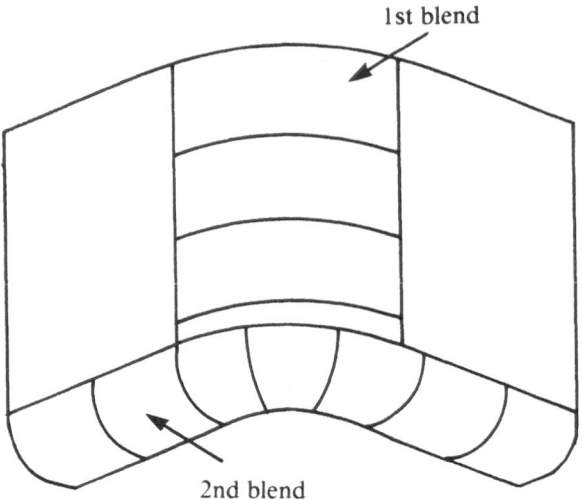

Figure 2. Blend on blend.

- *Fairings*, which are defined broadly in terms of general flow and overall shape, although some boundary conditions may need precise definition, and

- *Blends and fillets*, which join adjacent faces smoothly, but without stringent requirements with respect to exact shape.

Design surfaces are found extensively in the aircraft industry in such areas as turbine or airfoil design. Ship hulls and propellers are other examples of their use. The software to deal with design surfaces tends to be sophisticated and highly specialized. Suspension arms, manifolds and ducts are examples where faired surfaces are often useful. An exhaust manifold, for example, may have cross-sectional area constraints and yet be loosely defined with respect to its surface. Blends and fillets arise frequently in castings and forgings, where sharp corners are incompatible with production processes. They are also common in pipe junctions for enhancing fluid flow and strength. In these cases a minimum of input, such as the blend radius, is all that is needed or desired.

PARAMETRIC PATCHES

Many of the current systems for design with sculptured surfaces are based on parametric patches. In UNISURF, Bézier demonstrated a highly successful interface with which a user could manipulate his surface by defining and moving certain control points on a polyhedral control mesh [Bézier 1974]. Riesenfeld generalized this to B-spline patches [Riesenfeld 1973]. Many cross-sectional routines were also developed based on patches (for example [Gossling 1976]). There are, of course, many other nonpatch methods, but the patch methods, particularly the bicubic patches, enjoy considerable success because of their generality.

There are some shortcomings, however. In most existing patch-based systems the user has to be aware of the individual patch boundaries and manipulation of the surface is accomplished by an adjustment to the boundaries. The boundaries do not always correspond to the pertinent characteristics of the surface. This can mean an overspecification of the problem. In the case of simple fillets about a pipe junction, one finds the control mesh interface requiring far more input than warranted. The blending radius is basically the only information that is needed. One conceptual way of solving this is to roll a ball among the surfaces to be blended and let it sweep out the desired fillet. This is a nice, simple example of an interface above the dashed line which is easily reduced to primitives, that is, patches. When several pipes extrude from the same point, however, this procedure can be inadequate.

Parametric patches are essentially distortions of the unit square. This imposes a rectangular topology on the resulting surfaces. This is another problem with patches, since in practise there are many objects which are difficult to represent with a strictly rectangular topology. Forrest has illustrated several very simple ones [Forrest 1974]. A large amount of research has centered on developing nonrectangular patches for this reason [Barnhill 1977].

The following are examples of higher-level surface forms which obviate these and many other ticklish design problems. They use a wide variety of mathematical forms, but all are reducible to primitives.

SCULPTURING

It is natural when designing an object with sculptured surfaces to first think of it roughly in terms of its primitives and then to blend away corners and smooth out creases. It is, appropriately enough, akin to the way in which a sculptor works, first blocking out the major forms and then adding refinements. It also suggests one model for how an interface should work and which surface forms to investigate, at least in the case of blends, fillets and fairings.

One form which is almost inevitably suggested in this context is that of the minimum energy surface. Capturing the "soap film" effect between adjacent primitives is a seductive thought. It is unfortunately quite difficult to achieve from an algorithmic point of view.

Another way to achieve similar results is by successive chamfering. Chaiken introduced a method for creating curves by repeatedly cutting the corners off a polygonal path [Chaiken 1974]. When the lengths of the sides are reduced below the resolution of the display device, a smooth curve is apparent. It can be shown that in the limit the resulting curve is the quadratic B-spline based on the original polygonal path. This method has been generalized to three-dimensional polyhedra [Doo and Sabin 1978]. A test program, REMUS, was imple-

References pp. 252-253

mented at Shape Data to investigate its possibilities. Veenman gives a complete description of this [Veenman 1982].

When using this program one notices that the first chamfer can produce anomalous areas, that is, facets which are not four-sided (Figures 3(a) and 3(b)). Thereafter (Figure 3(c)) the chamfering produces only four-sided facets, but the anomalous areas remain, though reduced in size. If four of the four-sided facets meet at a vertex, then a quadratic B-spline patch can be defined there as suggested by Figure 3(d). The vertices of the patch are the centerpoints of the facets. The surface patch can immediately be put into the surface data structure of the model. If infinite chamfering on the four original facets were undertaken, then the same patch would result.

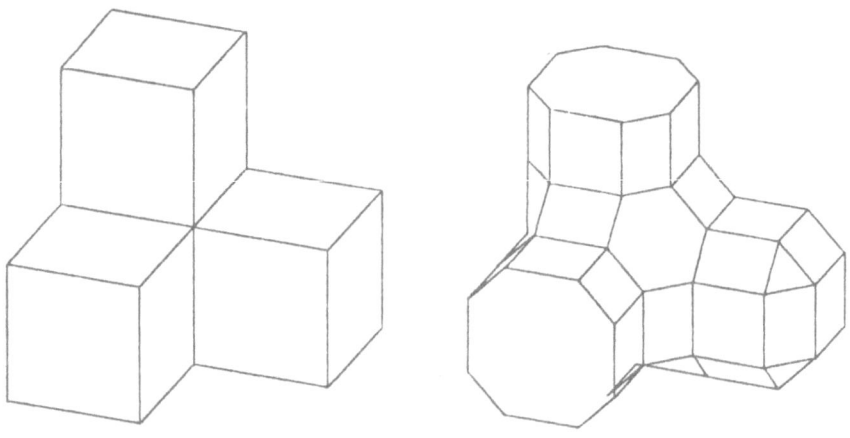

(a) Original object represented by primitives   (b) Result of first chamfer

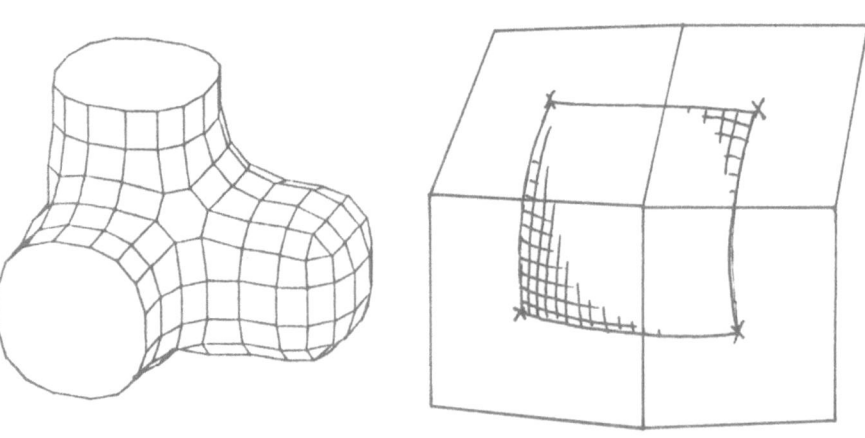

(c) Result of second chamfer   (d) From chamfer to patch

Figure 3. *Chamfering to refine a solid.*

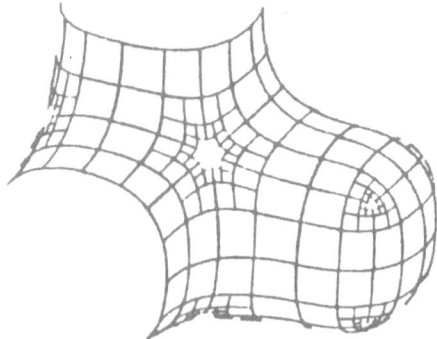

Figure 4. *Anomalous regions squeezed out.*

Unresolved regions still remain about the anomalous areas. Successive applications of the algorithm diminish these areas in size, however. They are subdivided into smaller and smaller four-sided facets which are then turned into surface patches. Ultimately the unwanted regions are squeezed out, their area being smaller than the tolerance of the model (Figure 4). Figures 5(a) and 5(b) show, respectively, the faceted and the patched version of a connecting arm. Figure 6 is an example of an automobile part after chamfering.

Recursive chamfering is best for designing shapes which are entirely fair, that is, shapes which only need to be somewhere near the defining polyhedral mesh. It does these shapes easily with only a few terse inputs. If the shape needs closer definition, however, then the routine becomes more cumbersome. It is very difficult to adapt the shape to an exact cross-section or to fit part of it to some predefined shape. This naturally limits the blends as well, since many blends smooth between precisely defined surfaces.

Recursive chamfering uses only planar faces as primitives so that any portion which must have exact reproduction is required to be piecewise flat. The temptation exists to devise a chamfering scheme which works on a wider range of primitives. There may be some merit in thinking about a way to apply Doo-Sabin recursion to something like a torus-cylinder intersection.

Another way to achieve similar results is embodied in the technique described next.

CONFORMAL SURFACES

In the design methodology which favors B-spline surface patches one can define specific points to be interpolated by the surface. Then an inversion process gives the control mesh for the desired interpolating surface. Finer adjustments to the design can then be made by manipulating the control mesh. A generalization of this would suggest interpolating not just to points but to pieces of primitives. Then primitives could be manipulated to do the fine tuning. It would also

References pp. 252-253

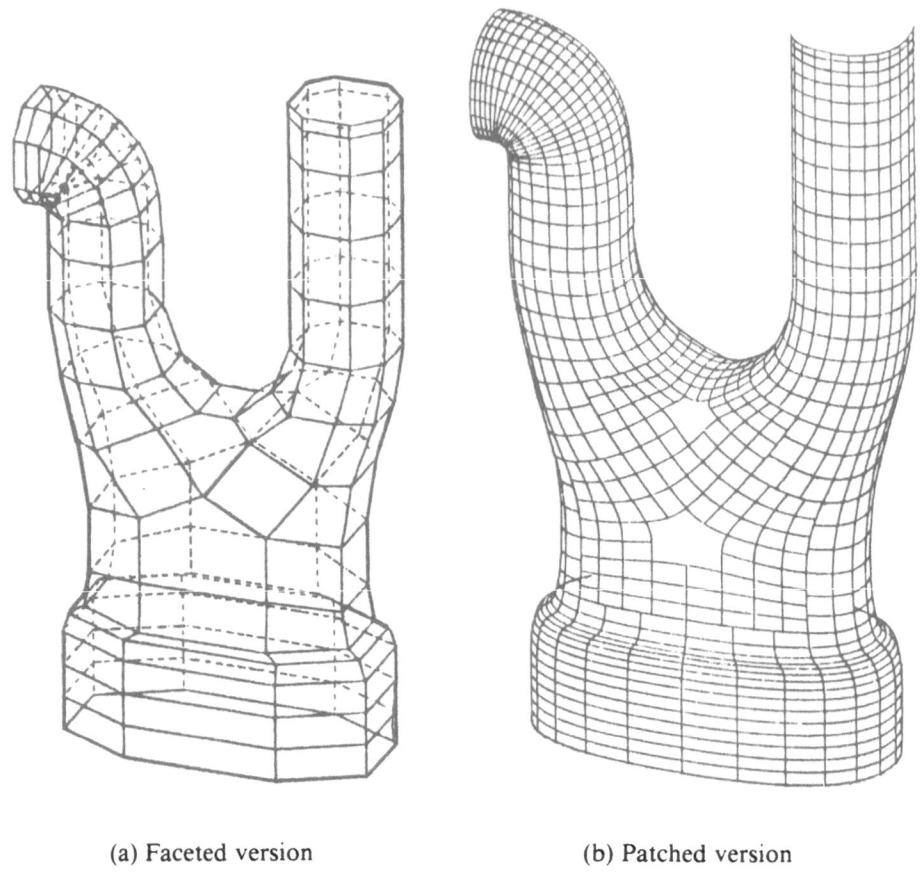

(a) Faceted version   (b) Patched version

Figure 5. *A connecting arm, faceted and patched.*

be desirable to have some handles for controlling the interpolating surface. In essence it simulates the way in which patternmakers work, that is, with modelling clay and their thumbs. They interpolate smoothly between primitives with the clay.

Recent work at Shape Data with conformal surface maps has shown some promise in achieving the effect of the "patternmaker's thumb." They are referred to as conformal because of the resemblance to similarly named mappings in complex analysis or hydraulics (see, for example, [Wylie 1975]). The smooth natural curves that result from the Schwarz-Christoffel transformation or other conformal maps provide the paradigm for blending out corners.

The idea is extended to planar surfaces in three dimensions. Any plane may be deformed to a variety of shapes by locally smooth coordinate transformations [Barr 1983]. Any blend between the planes is deformed by the same transformation in a natural way. That means, for instance, that any continuity of

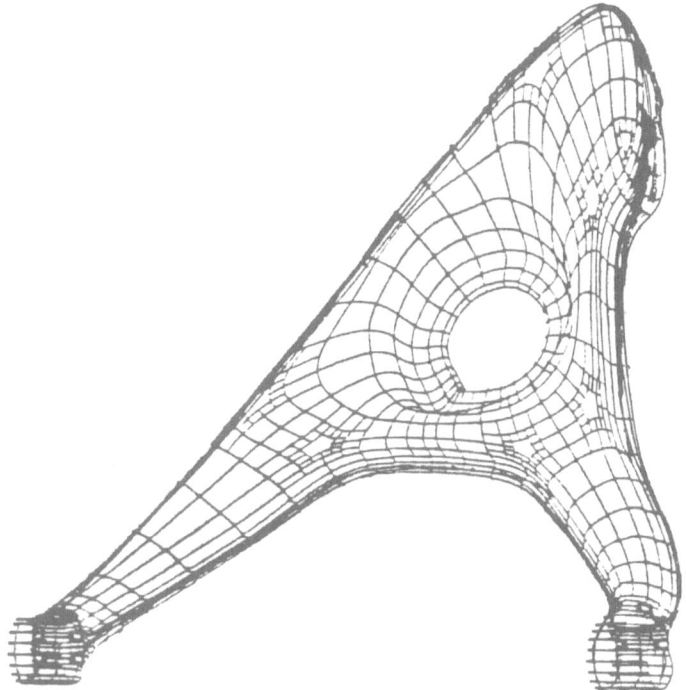

Figure 6. *Automobile part after chamfering.*

derivatives defined by the planar blends is maintained by the transformation. The set of primitives which can be blended by this method is therefore expanded to include any object which can be made by locally deforming the plane. At present this has been done for several ROMULUS primitives including cones, spheres, tori and cylinders. It could theoretically include many other shapes such as the quadrics.

Performing one blend on top of another is simply a matter of composing coordinate transformations. The computational load for such compositions does increase as n^2, where n is the level of recursion. Accuracy of such blended blends is not a problem since the surfaces can be formulated implicitly so that "finding" the surface is a matter of a good convergence routine and the number of iterations. There are no round-off errors based on level of recursion. This may not be true for other surface types, however.

One of the attractions of this approach is its economy of input. Between any two primitive surfaces there are only two necessary inputs. The first is the *range*, which defines the extent or size of the blend. The second is called the *thumbweight* and is a qualitative control on the overall shape of the blend. If the value of the thumbweight is large, then the blend is close to the underlying primitives, and hence its name. There is an optional input called the *asymmetry factor*, which can be used to scale the blend with respect to one primitive or the other.

References pp. 252-253

Both thumbweight and range are mixing parameters which are defined before the deformation. They mix the smooth conformal function to the underlying planes. Range mixes it so that the blend will have finite support; that is, the conformal map is exactly the plane beyond the given range. Thumbweight is an exponent to the mixing function. The higher the degree, the closer the weighted average of conformal map and planes will lie to the primitives.

Figure 7 shows blends which are intentionally simple so that the effects of these inputs can be demonstrated. The primitives for this figure are two cones, which are united so that their apexes are embedded within each other. Figure 7(a) shows the blend superimposed on the primitives. The thumbweight is 1. This results in a blend with a circular cross section. Figure 7(b) has the thumbweight equal to 2, which gives it a cross section of a superellipse. Figures 7(c) and 7(d) show the results of defining different factors of asymmetry; they have elliptical cross sections.

In corners and other places where several surfaces come together the blend is also natural and smooth. It is quite significant that such areas blend automatically. Figure 8(a) is made of two cones and two cylinders. It is completely blended in Figure 8(b) by assigning a blend range and thumbweight. Unfortu-

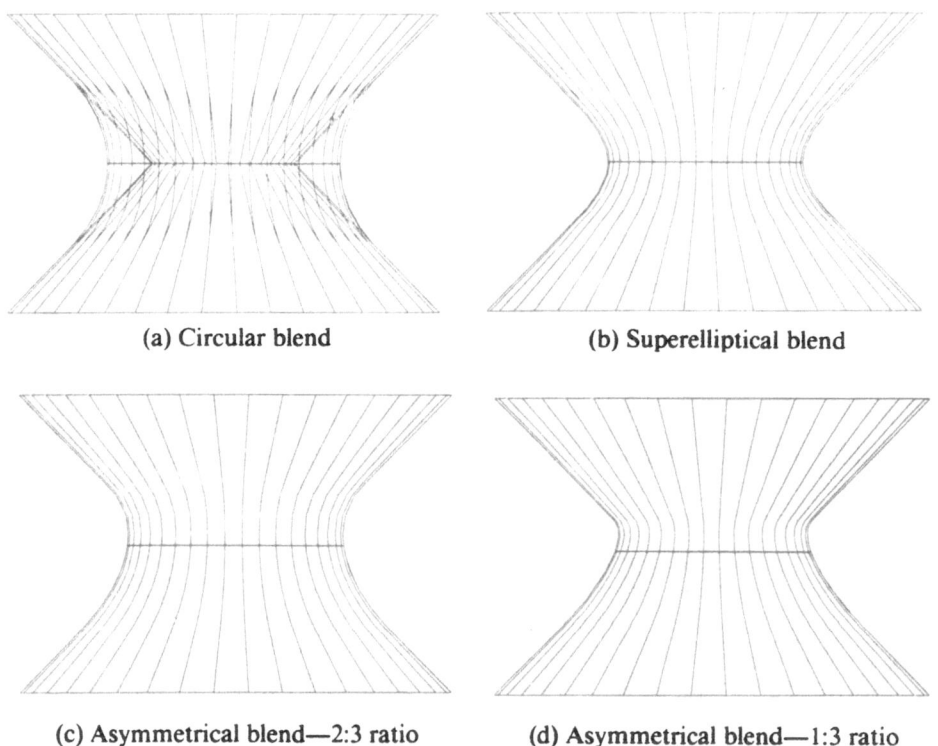

(a) Circular blend   (b) Superelliptical blend

(c) Asymmetrical blend—2:3 ratio   (d) Asymmetrical blend—1:3 ratio

Figure 7. Blends superimposed on two cones.

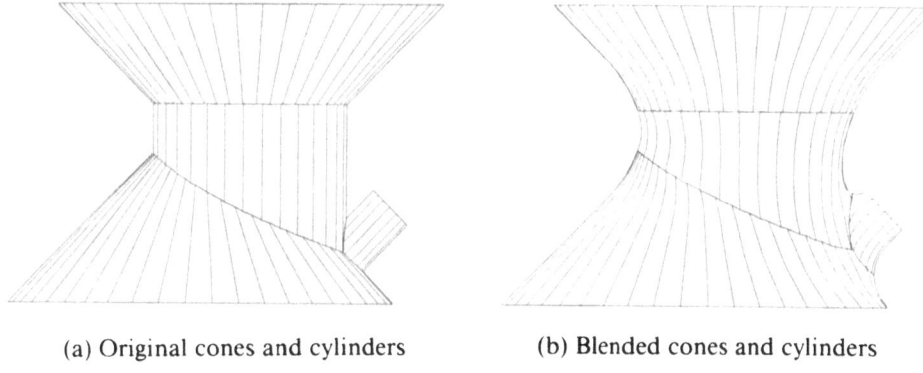

(a) Original cones and cylinders   (b) Blended cones and cylinders

Figure 8. *Blending three primitives.*

nately, the present rendering technique can project the underlying display lines onto the blend in a visually spurious manner. In spite of some purely visual distortions in this figure, it is easy to see how the blends flow together even where more than two primitives are involved in the calculations. One place to note this is on the left profile where two blends have merged together and overlap each other, and a second place to note this is on the right where the small cylinder protrudes from the large cylinder and cone. Here one sees how three adjacent primitives merge. Figures 9(a) and 9(b) offer another good example of this.

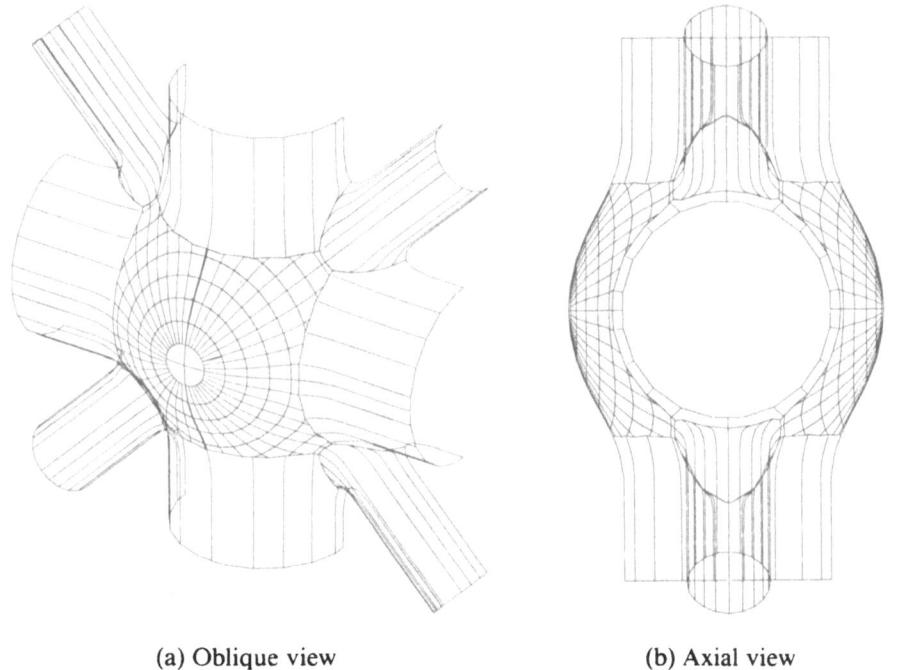

(a) Oblique view   (b) Axial view

Figure 9. *Blended sphere and cylinders.*

References pp. 252-253

They offer two views of an object made of several cylinders extruding from a sphere and then blended. Some areas of the blend are computed from four primitives, and yet the entire object was blended by assigning only two pieces of information to it—thumbweight and range.

The distinction between blend and fairing becomes blurred when one uses overlapping blends. Figures 10(a) and 10(b) are two views of a shampoo bottle. By adjusting the underlying primitives and the blending parameters it is quite possible to come up with what is essentially an aesthetic design.

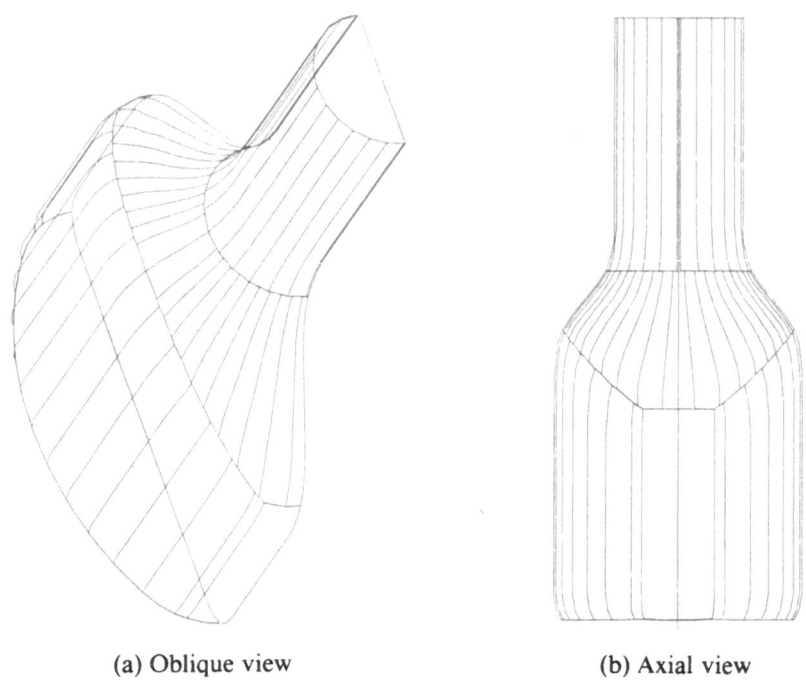

(a) Oblique view   (b) Axial view

Figure 10. *Shampoo bottle.*

The conformal mapping technique is most powerful in designing blends, fillets and tightly faired surfaces. In this sense it makes a nice complement to the chamfering technique. It is more challenging to reduce conformal mappings to B-spline surfaces than it is to reduce chamfers; however, the resulting patches tend to be more optimally sized, thus reducing the total number needed to represent the surface. Figures 11(a) and 11(b) show the B-spline surface *tapes*, that is, the blended region between primitives.

DUCTING

The two previous surface forms were based on the sculpturing metaphor. A different tack is to consider the design in two dimensions first and then sweep it

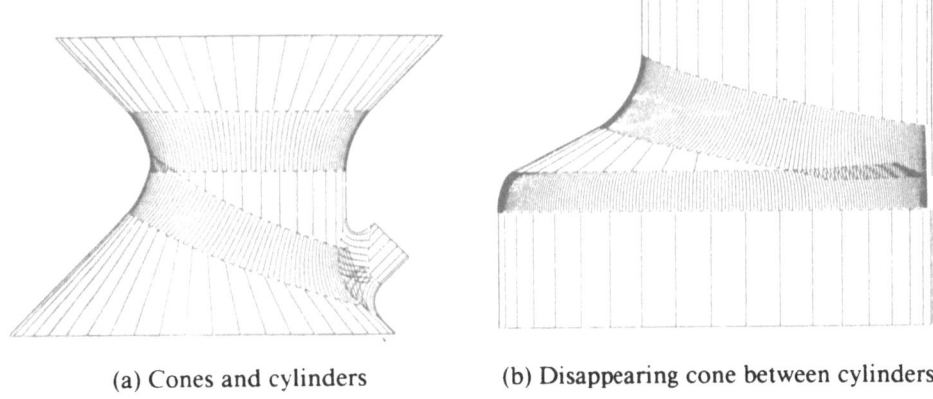

(a) Cones and cylinders   (b) Disappearing cone between cylinders

Figure 11. B-spline surface tapes.

into the third dimension. There are many such cross-sectional design methods (for example [Faux and Pratt 1979]) which would be candidates for the user interface. Since one can define rather precise cross sections with these methods, the resulting surfaces reside somewhere between the design and the faired surface categories. This makes them attractive as complements to the sculpturing methods.

In particular, some thought has gone into ducted surfaces. The elements of design in a ductlike object include a definition of a spine, the cross-sectional rib definitions and a way to blend between the ribs along the spine. To define the shape of the ribs a curve form similar to the one described by Rockwood and Jensen has been employed. This has a Bézier-like control polygon as seen in Figures 12 and 13, but with continuous derivatives of higher orders [Rockwood and Jensen 1981].

A second, more important attribute of this method is the natural parameterization that it can induce from one curve to a different one. This allows blending to be done along the spine. The final surface is strictly a one-dimensional mix between the successive ribs, not a collection of quadrilateral patches. In Figure 13 the top side of the first rectangular rib blends into a hooklike cross section in the next rib without affecting the other three sides. They map smoothly into three identical sections of the second rib without changing any continuity order at any point of the surface.

The user interaction needed to achieve this is straightforward. It requires only that the user indicate which segments of the control polygons are to correspond. It also retains an orientation and implied topology which is very useful for reducing the surface to primitives which then hang together in the modeler.

Another very important property of these ducts is that the method produces a smooth way of locally transforming from lines to curves. By integrating over cross sections of the duct, we define a mapping which allows one to apply the

References pp. 252-253

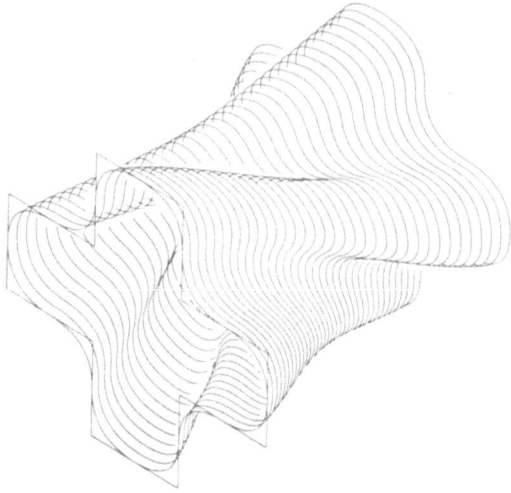

Figure 12. *Ducted object with defining polygon.*

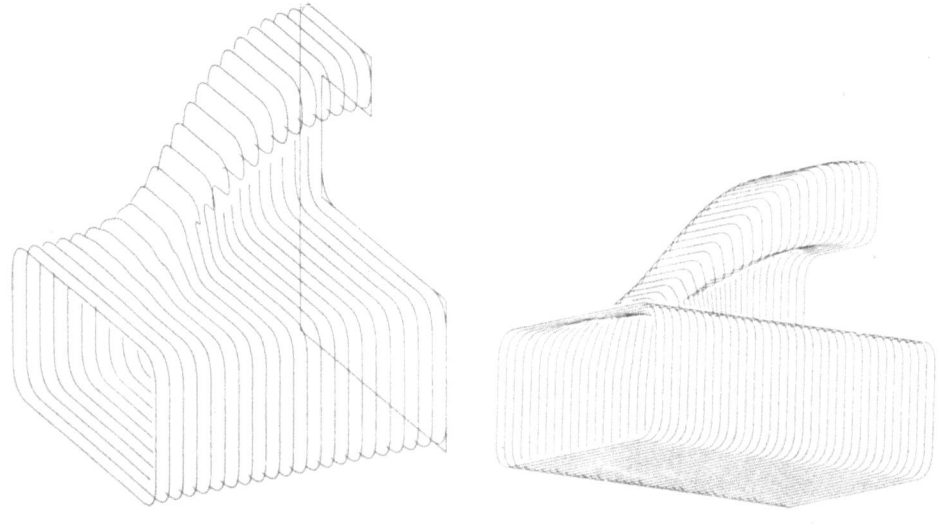

(a) Ribs with a defining control polygon   (b) Ribs with local refinements

Figure 13. *An example of ducting.*

conformal blending approach to the duct. This is the interaction between the two surface types. The ductlike objects can be used as primitives to the conformal blending method.

CONCLUSION

Consider one final design task. A turbine blade is precisely designed by cross-sectional methods. It is then filleted into its root. The root is designed princi-

Figure 14. *Turbine blade.*

pally from planar surfaces which need to have sharp edges knocked off. There are some channels which have been bored through the root and in some places extra metal must be added to strengthen the root where the channels have weakened it. One can envisage repeated applications of different surface interfaces for the different parts of the problem—a ducting program for the blade which may be quite different from the one for the channels, a fairing program for adding the extra metal, and a blending program for the fillets.

This is indicative of the ultimate methodology for complex designs, that is, access to a good library of surface interfaces and a powerful modeler for piecing the resulting surfaces together in a topologically coherent manner.

In this scheme the modeler is more than just a design system for the primitives. It defines the topology of the entire object and serves as the crucial link between the interface and primitive surfaces.

There is some research to do before this goal is achieved. There will always be newer and better surface interfaces to investigate. The present ones need more refining and understanding, which means user feedback. There are still points to be considered in the reduction of higher surfaces to primitive surfaces. The interaction of different surface types is not always as simple as given in the last two examples. Accuracy and optimization are other considerations. There is a pressing need in all this for a good general intersection routine. This is no surprize to anyone dealing with sculptured surfaces, but it is accentuated by the broader category of surfaces which this paper suggests.

References pp. 252-253

The results of the programming thus far at Shape Data have shown that these surface types are computationally reasonable (two to three minutes on a VAX 11/780 for the ducts and conformal blends) and that they have a natural appearance. REMUS surfaces have been milled. The others have only been drawn.

ACKNOWLEDGEMENTS

I am indebted for their observations and comments to my colleagues at Shape Data, especially P. Veenman, who has worked closely with me on this project.

REFERENCES

[Barnhill 1977]
   Robert E. Barnhill, "Representation and Approximation of Surfaces," *Mathematical Software*, J. R. Rice, ed., Academic Press, New York, New York, 1977, pp. 67–120.

[Barr 1983]
   Alan H. Barr, "Global and Local Deformations of Solid Primitives," *State-of-the-Art Image Synthesis Tutorial*, SIGGRAPH '83, Detroit, Michigan, July 25–29, 1983.

[Bézier 1974]
   P. Bézier, "Mathematical and Practical Possibilities of UNISURF," *Computer Aided Geometric Design*, R. E. Barnhill and R. F. Riesenfeld, eds., Academic Press, New York, New York, 1974, pp. 127–152.

[Coons 1967]
   Steven A. Coons, "Surfaces for Computer Aided Design of Space Forms," Report MAC-TR-41, Project MAC, Massachusetts Institute of Technology, Cambridge, Massachusetts, June 1967.

[Chaiken 1974]
   G. M. Chaiken, "An Algorithm for High-Speed Curve Generation," *Computer Graphics and Image Processing*, Vol. 3, 1974, pp. 346–349.

[Doo and Sabin 1978]
   D. V. H. Doo and Malcolm Sabin, "Behaviour of Recursive Division Surfaces near Extraordinary Points," *Computer Aided Design*, Vol. 10, No. 6, November 1978, pp. 356–360.

[Faux and Pratt 1979]
   I. D. Faux and M. J. Pratt, *Computational Geometry for Design and Manufacture*, Ellis Horwood Limited, Chichester, England, 1979.

[Forrest 1974]
   A. R. Forrest, "Computational Geometry — Achievements and Problems," *Computer Aided Design*, R. E. Barnhill and R. F. Riesenfeld, eds., Academic Press, New York, New York, 1974, pp. 17–44.

[Gordon and Riesenfeld 1974]
   William J. Gordon and Richard F. Riesenfeld, "B-Spline Curves and Surfaces," *Computer Aided Design*, R. E. Barnhill and R. F. Riesenfeld, eds., Academic Press, New York, New York, 1974, pp. 95–126.

[Gossling 1976]
    T. H. Gossling, "The DUCT System of Design for Practical Objects," *Proceedings of the World Congress on the Theory of Machines and Mechanisms*, Milan, Italy, 1976.

[Riesenfeld 1973]
    Richard F. Riesenfeld, "Applications of B-Spline Approximation to Geometric Problems of Computer Aided Design," Computer Science Department Report UTEC-CSc-73-126, University of Utah, Salt Lake City, Utah, 1973.

[Rockwood and Jensen 1981]
    Alyn P. Rockwood and Thomas W. Jensen, "Two Aspects of Domain Designing: C Curve Rendering and Blended Map Projections," *ACM Computer Graphics*, Vol. 15, No. 3 (SIGGRAPH/81 Conference Proceedings, Dallas, Texas, August 3-7, 1981) pp. 233–237.

[Veenman 1982]
    Peter Veenman, "The Design of Sculptured Surfaces using Recursive Subdivision Techniques," *Proceedings of the Conference on CAD/CAM Technology in Mechanical Engineering*, Massachusetts Institute of Technology, Cambridge, Massachusetts, March 24-26, 1982, pp. 54–63.

[Wylie 1975]
    C. Ray Wylie, *Advanced Engineering Mathematics*, McGraw-Hill, New York, New York, 1975.

DISCUSSION

John Woodwark *(University of Bath)*

We deal normally in ball type blends. Can you guarantee a circular blend, let's say, in the appropriate situation. In other words, where a toroidal blend is achievable, can you make a blending function achieve it?

Rockwood

If you're working with planar primitives I can, and also in some other cases. If you are blending a cylindrical primitive through a right corner, I can guarantee a circular blend. If you then replace the plane with a cylinder, it is a cylindrical deformation of that circular blend.

If you have the cylinder this way on a plane, I can give you a circular blend. It's just a little more difficult when they're not right angles; I have to do some trigonometric calculations to give you that piece of a circle. I can guarantee you an ellipse at any rate, but circular blends require some trigonometry.

A. P. Rockwood

Ramon Sarraga *(General Motors Research Laboratories)*

How do you provide for intersections of the blended surfaces with each other?

Rockwood

Good question. The original idea was simply to reduce it to B-spline patches and then do what General Motors is doing, but right now the research is centered on writing an intersection routine. We want to generate an intersection between two implicit surfaces, which is what these basically are. There are some advantages to these surfaces; they have certain curvature characteristics that you can depend upon and so you can perform a subdivision based on these curvature characteristics. This is similar to the Lane-Reisenfeld algorithm for convex hulls. That's what we're looking at; it is not finished yet and I might say that, as with everybody else, the difficulty is getting a good intersection routine. We are working on a good rendering routine as well. We have done some shaded renderings.

Fumihiko Kimura *(University of Tokyo)*

Do the tapes coincide where the blends overlap?

Rockwood

Yes, they do. Visually the parameter lines don't always appear to coincide but, if you were to mill it, they would.

Robert de Monts *(Dassault Systems)*

If they overlay exactly, does that mean it's a spherical portion of your fillets? Since your fillets are generated using two different generating planes for your filleted curves, then they shouldn't overlay exactly unless it is a sphere.

Rockwood

What happens is you get, if I can use the terminology, a sort of splining of ellipses in a cross-section. Where there are just two planes affecting it, you get an ellipse; where there's an area where three are affecting it, you get a different ellipse which however is continuous with other ellipses at the knot points. So you get a series of elliptical cross sections going across them. Of course, if you replace that plane with some other object you get the proper deformation of that elliptical "spline." I use the term ellipses to mean superellipses as well. Superellipses result from higher thumbweights.

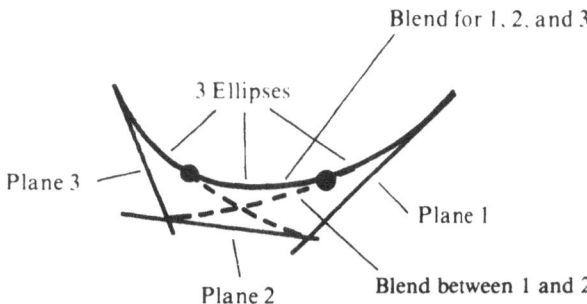

Hinds

I'd like to point out something here. This area of blends is one of the most exotic areas of geometric modeling right now. But when we position a cutter on several surfaces, that's what you're asking the poor manufacturing guy to do: position not just a ball, but arbitrary toroidal shapes, and the problem is being solved somehow. Some aspects of N/C are really close to the blending problem.

Herbert Voelcker *(University of Rochester)*

When you blend, do you blend curves or do you blend aggregates of surfaces?

Rockwood

I blend surfaces.

Voelcker

When you have curves of intersection between surfaces which lie within blends, such as blends interacting, is there an order to those blends?

Rockwood

You can order it. I'll hang out some dirty laundry here for you. On this blend for instance, notice the area where you have essentially a cylinder sitting in between the other blends; this area blends naturally and blends all at once. Along the run of this blend we can change the range or change one of the parameters so it gets thinner. Now, this is a problem area for me; if you do that and then you intersect it with something else, I won't guarantee you a nice, fair blend. You may get a little dimple in it because you're changing the domain of my function. If you don't, if you leave those unchanged so that (with respect to the face) it's well defined, then I can guarantee you a convex blend where the parameters are convex, variation diminishing, and that sort of thing. But if you're messing around with the domain variables, you have to look at the blend carefully. I'm not saying you'll always get a dimple in fact, you should look carefully at that bottle we designed. It was designed around this problem. Does that answer your question?

Changing blend radius

Problem area

Voelcker

Yes, I think so. I believe what you're saying is that if the user were to impose an ordering on blending (such as "the small pipe is first blended") and then you decide later that he wishes to blend the other things—

Rockwood

Yes, okay. If I were to blend first between the cylinder and the cone and then blend between the small cylinder and what remained, that would be the same blend as if I reversed the operation. I could do the small blend and then the big blend; regardless of the order, I would come out with the same sort of thing. We are looking into localizing these operations, which is more of a data structure problem but, yes, you get the same blend. It has to do with the fact that I only refer to the faces, and I compute the blend in the area where all three faces affect it. It's just a summation of their effects.

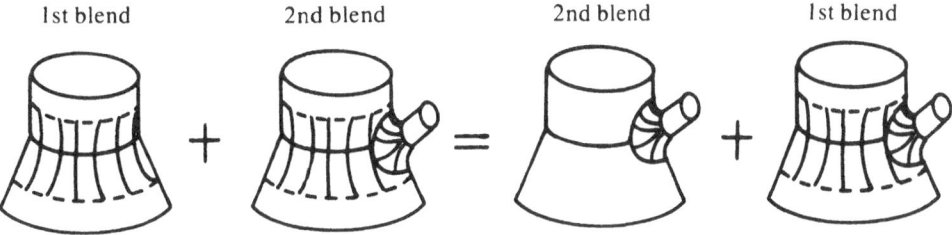

Voelcker

If I restrict the range very tightly on a blend, I could simply be blending two surfaces with a blended surface.

Rockwood

If you've defined a very strict range on one seam and a very broad range on a second seam, what you've in essence done on the bottom face is define two ranges. What do you get when they mix? We've played around with mixing functions and that's the point I was talking about earlier; that's where you might get a dimple. If you are mixing two ranges on the same face, you have a problem. If, however, you were to define one range on one face here and a very tight one here on a different face, that's automatic then. And it doesn't matter about the order that you pick.

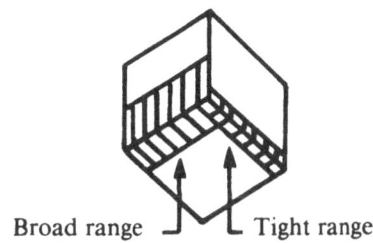

Broad range ⌐ ⌐ Tight range

Voelcker

In the world of ROMULUS, do these blends define new faces of the objects, new boundary representations?

Rockwood

You might notice in the pictures I displayed there were little seam lines which indeed represented the original topology of the ROMULUS object. These simply map onto the blend if I care to use it. That's actually a decision for somebody else at Shape Data to make but, yes, we can define the topology which is inherited from the original unblended object. That's how I foresee it.

Michel Melkanoff *(University of California–Los Angeles)*

What happens if one tape laps over itself or over another tape where it blends with the other and then has to blend with it at some other place?

Rockwood

It's no problem geometrically. Overlapping tapes are always in agreement geometrically. The problem you have is more a topological problem. If I want to localize that blend, how do I separate it from another area where the tape is run. I may just want to work in one area without affecting another. That's why I say the problem is more topological than geometrical. Does that answer your question?

Melkanoff

Thank you, it does.

PRECISE IMPLEMENTATION OF CAD PRIMITIVES USING RATIONAL PARAMETERIZATIONS OF STANDARD SURFACES

S. OCKEN and JACOB T. SCHWARTZ

New York University
New York, New York

M. SHARIR

Tel-Aviv University
Tel-Aviv, Israel

ABSTRACT

We discuss the problem of computing the intersection curve of two algebraic surfaces, each of which possesses rational parameterization. The special case where the two surfaces are quadric is analyzed in detail, using a general decomposition theorem which guarantees the existence of a simultaneous canonical reduction of two quadratic forms in Euclidean n-space. In homogeneous 4-space this yields a classification and simple parameterization of all possible intersections between two quadric surfaces. Using these results, we treat the problem of analyzing the structure of solid bodies defined by Boolean combinations of half-spaces bounded by arbitrary quadric surfaces. The analysis given leads to fast versions of some of the procedures required for geometric modeling systems which admit general quadric surfaces into their vocabulary of basic shapes.

INTRODUCTION

In developing a geometric design system, one must focus on a class of surfaces whose Boolean combinations can be handled with considerably greater efficiency than can algebraic surfaces in general. The following definition specifies a class of surfaces which is advantageous (but not necessarily sufficiently advantageous) in this regard.

References pp. 268-269

Definition: A surface S is said to be *rational* if

- S is defined by a polynomial equation $P(x,y,z) = 0$ having rational (or at least real algebraic) coefficients, and

- There exists a parameterization $x = X(u,v)$, $y = Y(u,v)$, $z = Z(u,v)$ of the surface S by functions X,Y,Z which are quotients of polynomials in u,v having rational (or at least real algebraic) coefficients. (We suppose this parameterization to be defined for u,v in some domain D which is itself defined in a simple way by polynomial inequalities in u,v, and we also suppose that except on a few equally simple curves and points this parameterization is 1–1.)

The advantage of working with such surfaces is that their intersections can be determined with relative efficiency, since if $P_1 = 0$ is the polynomial equation for one such surface S_1 and X_2, Y_2, Z_2 give the parametric representation for another surface S_2, then the intersection $S_1 * S_2$ is represented by the set of pairs satisfying the simple equation $P_1(X_2(u,v), Y_2(u,v), Z_2(u,v)) = 0$. Although a related algebraic condition can be written even if the surfaces S_1 and S_2 are not rational in the sense defined above, resultants would have to be used to derive this condition, substantially degrading the efficiency of the calculation required to deal with $S_1 * S_2$.

The class of real rational surfaces is extensive. Examples are as follows. Any surface of the form $z = P(x,y)$, where P is a polynomial or a quotient of polynomials, is evidently rational. This includes the paraboloid and the hyperboloid of one sheet. The sphere $x^2+y^2+z^2 =1$ is rational, since it has the (stereographic) parameterization

$$(x,y,z) = (\frac{1-u^2-v^2}{1+u^2+v^2}, \frac{2u}{1+u^2+v^2}, \frac{2y}{1+u^2+v^2}).$$

Similarly, the cone $z^2-x^2-y^2 = 0$ is rational, since it has the parameterization

$$(x,y,z) = v(\frac{1-u^2}{1+u^2}, \frac{2u}{1+u^2}, 1).$$

INTERSECTION OF QUADRIC SURFACES: ALGEBRAIC ANALYSIS OF THE *N*-DIMENSIONAL CASE

It is easy to see from the above remarks that all real quadric surfaces are rational. Indeed, if we proceed projectively, writing the polynomial equations for all our surfaces as homogeneous polynomial equations in four variables, then the equation for any quadric can be written as $La \cdot a = 0$, where L is a 4×4 symmetric matrix, and where a is a 4-vector (x,y,z,w). We can diagonalize L, which corresponds to carrying out an appropriate projective transformation of our surface, and normalize the transformed L so that each of its diagonal entries is either ± 1 or 0. Then this normalized L can be brought to a form in which it has at least as many positive as negative entries, and in which the diagonal entries of L are arranged so that the zero entries precede the positive ones which in turn precede the negative entries. Moreover, we can assume that L contains one negative and at least two positive diagonal entries, for otherwise it would represent a point, a line, a plane, or a pair of planes, all of whose intersections with another quadric surface may be easily computed.

Proceeding in this way, the transformed L will have one of the following forms:

- L has three positive and one negative entry, in which case it represents the sphere $x^2+y^2+z^2-w^2 = 0$; or

- L has two positive and two negative entries, in which case it represents the single-sheeted hyperboloid $x^2+y^2-z^2-w^2 = 0$; or

- L has two positive, one negative and one zero entry, in which case it represents the cylinder $y^2+z^2-w^2 = 0$, or, equivalently, the cone.

Let Λ and Σ be two quadric surfaces, represented respectively by the 4×4 matrices L, S in the manner described above. Applying the same projective transformation to both surfaces, we may assume that L has one of the three canonical forms listed above and that S is still symmetric. Thus L represents either a sphere, a single-sheeted hyperboloid, or a cylinder, and we are left with the problem of finding the intersection curve of such a surface with a second arbitrary quadric surface. This problem was studied by J. Levin [Levin 1976], who gave a fairly systematic account of these intersections. However, the situation is simpler when viewed projectively than when only affine simplifications are used, and a projective analysis leads to a simple classification of all intersection curves of quadric surfaces. For this, we transform the homogeneous 4-space projectively so as to bring both quadratic forms (Lx,x) and (Sx,x) to simple form from which the intersection curves can easily be obtained. More specifically, it is possible to decompose homogeneous 4-space into a direct sum of canonical subspaces $Y_1 + Y_2 + ... + Y_k$, mutually orthogonal relative to both forms (Lx,x) and (Sx,x), in which these two forms have standard forms. This can in fact be done not only in 4-space but also for two symmetric forms acting in any number of dimensions. Specifically, if L is nonsingular we can introduce a basis for each of these spaces in which the quadratic forms $F(y) = (Ly,y)$ and $G(y) = (Sy,y)$ have one of the following representations (real eigenvalue case):

$$F(y) = \pm\ (2y_0y_{n-1}+ ... + 2y_my_{n-m-1}) \qquad m = (n-2)/2 \text{ if } n \text{ is even;}$$

$$F(y) = \pm\ (2y_0y_{n-1} + ... + 2y_{m-1}y_{n-m} + y_my_m) \qquad m = (n-1)/2 \text{ if } n \text{ is odd.}$$

$$G(y) = \pm\ (2y_0y_{n-2} + ... + 2y_my_{n-m-2}) + \lambda F(y) \qquad m = (n-3)/2 \text{ if } n \text{ is odd;}$$

$$G(y) = \pm\ (2y_0y_{n-2} + ... + 2y_{m-1}y_{n-m-1} + y_my_m) + \lambda F(y)$$
$$m = (n-2)/2 \text{ if } n \text{ is even.}$$

where λ is some real quantity.

References pp. 268-269

It is clear that if n is even, the signature of F is $(n/2,n/2)$, while if n is odd, the signature of F is either $((n-1)/2, (n+1)/2)$ or $((n+1)/2, (n-1)/2)$. The differing signatures distinguish the two cases in which n is odd, but, even if n is even, the "+" and the "−" cases are easily seen to be nonisomorphic. It is convenient to introduce symbolic designations for these various cases; we will use the symbols $[\lambda,m,m+1]$ and $[\lambda,m+1,m]$ to designate the two cases in which n is odd, and $[\lambda,m,m,+]$, $[\lambda,m,m,-]$ to designate the two cases in which n is even.

Corresponding complex cases are also possible and lead to the following forms:

$$F(y,z) = 2y_0 y_{n-1} + \ldots + 2y_m y_{n-m-1} - 2z_0 z_{n-1} - \ldots - 2z_m z_{n-m-1}$$
$$m = (n-2)/2, \text{ if } n \text{ is even};$$

$$F(y,z) = 2y_0 y_{n-1} + \ldots + 2y_{m-1} y_{n-m} + y_m y_m - 2z_0 z_{n-1} - \ldots - 2z_{m-1} z_{n-m} - z_m z_m$$
$$m = (n-1)/2, \text{ if } n \text{ is odd}.$$

Moreover, in this same basis (Su,u) has the representation

$$G(y,z) = 2y_0 y_{n-2} + \ldots + 2y_m y_{n-m-2} - 2z_0 z_{n-2} - \ldots - 2z_m z_{n-m-2}$$
$$+ a_1 F(y,z) + 2a_2(y_0 z_{n-1} + \ldots + y_{n-1} z_0)$$
$$m = (n-3)/2, \text{ if } n \text{ is odd};$$

$$G(y,z) = 2y_0 y_{n-2} + \ldots + 2y_{m-1} y_{n-m-2} + y_m y_m - 2z_0 z_{n-2} - \ldots - 2z_{m-1} z_{n-m-2} - z_m z_m$$
$$+ a_1 F(y,z) + 2a_2(y_0 z_{n-1} + \ldots + y_{n-1} z_0)$$
$$m = (n-2)/2, \text{ if } n \text{ is even}.$$

Here a_1 and a_2 are the real and imaginary parts of a complex quantity λ. These pairs of quadratic forms are defined uniquely by the complex number λ and by the dimension n, and we can therefore designate them by (λ,n,n), λ complex.

The following theorem, which should be compared to the corresponding result for the complex case [Hodge and Pedoe 1952], summarizes the preceding analysis.

Theorem 1: Let L and S be a pair of symmetric matrices acting in a real vector space X, and suppose that L is nonsingular. Then X can be decomposed as a direct sum of canonical subspaces Y which are simultaneously orthogonal to each other in the two bilinear forms (Lx,y) and (Sx,y). A descriptor characterizing the representation in a standard basis for Y of each of these two forms is associated with each such Y. The following table shows the dimension of the space Y and the signature of the form (Lx,v) on Y for every possible descriptor:

Descriptor	Dimension of Y	Signature of (Lx,y) on Y
$[\lambda,m,m+1]$, λ real	$2m+1$	$(m,m+1)$
$[\lambda,m+1,m]$, λ real	$2m+1$	$(m+1,m)$
$[\lambda,m,m,+]$, λ real	$2m$	(m,m)
$[\lambda,m,m,-]$, λ real	$2m$	(m,m)
$[\lambda,m,m]$, λ complex	$2m$	(m,m)

The representations which the forms (Lx,y) and (Sx,y) take on in standard bases for spaces having these descriptors are detailed in the preceding paragraphs.

The situation in which L is singular can be handled in similar fashion. Here X can be decomposed into subspaces, mutually orthogonal with respect to both L and S, in each of which the quadratic forms $F = Lv \bullet v$ and $G = Sv \bullet v$ have one of the four following representations:

Case $[2n,2n+1]$:
$$F(x) = 2x_2x_3 + \ldots + 2x_{2n}x_{2n+1} \qquad n>0$$
$$G(x) = 2x_1x_2 + \ldots + 2x_{2n-1}x_{2n} \pm x_{2n+1}^2$$

$$\text{(simplest case: } 0,x^2\text{).}$$

Case $[2n-2,2n]$:

$$F(x) = 2x_2x_3 + \ldots + 2x_{2n-2}x_{2n-1} \qquad n>1$$
$$G(x) = 2x_1x_2 + \ldots + 2x_{2n-1}x_{2n}$$

$$\text{(simplest case: } 0,2xy\text{).}$$

Case $[2n-1,2n]$:

$$F(x) = 2x_2x_3 + \ldots + 2x_{2n-2}x_{2n-1} \pm x_{2n}^2 \qquad n>1$$
$$G(x) = 2x_1x_2 + \ldots + 2x_{2n-1}x_{2n}$$

$$\text{(simplest case: } y^2,2xy\text{).}$$

Case $[2n,2n]$:

$$F(x) = 2x_2x_3 + \ldots + 2x_{2n}x_{2n+1} \qquad n>1$$
$$G(x) = 2x_1x_2 + \ldots + 2x_{2n-1}x_{2n}$$

$$\text{(simplest case: } 2xy,2yz\text{).}$$

References pp. 268-269

We can use the symbols $[2n,2n+1]$, $[2n-2,2n]$, $[2n-1,2n]$, $[2n,2n]$ respectively as designators for these linear spaces. The following table gives the dimensions and ranks of L and S.

Designator	Dimension	Rank of L	Rank of S
$[2n,2n+1]$	$2n+1, n>0$	$2n$	$2n+1$
$[2n-2,2n]$	$2n, n>1$	$2n-2$	$2n$
$[2n-1,2n]$	$2n, n>1$	$2n-1$	$2n$
$[2n,2n]$	$2n+1, n>1$	$2n$	$2n$

We will use the symbol $[0]$ to designate a one-dimensional space in which both the quadratic forms L and S are 0.

Note that S is nonsingular in all these spaces with the exception of the space $[2n,2n]$. Thus each of the spaces $[2n,2n+1]$, $[2n-2,2n]$, $[2n-1,2n]$ can be regarded as a kind of reverse of spaces (or sums of spaces) that we have already encountered, obtained by interchanging L and S. It is easily seen that in this sense $[2n+1,2n]$ is the reverse of either $[0,n,n+1]$ or $[0,n+1,n]$; that $[2n-2,2n]$ is the sum of two isomorphic spaces, each of which is the reverse of one of the spaces $[0,k,k+1]$, $[0,k+1,k]$, $[0,k,k,+]$, or $[0,k,k,-]$; and that $[2n-1,2n]$ is the reverse of either $[0,n,n,+]$ or $[0,n,n,-]$. The exceptional space $[2n,2n]$ is its own reverse.

In view of those facts, it is convenient to introduce the notation $[\lambda,m,m+1]^*, \ldots$ for the reverse of $[\lambda,m,m+1], \ldots$.

The following theorem extends Theorem 1 to cover the case in which L is singular.

Theorem 2: Let L and S be a pair of symmetric matrices acting in a real vector space X. Then X can be decomposed as a direct sum of canonical subspaces Y which are simultaneously orthogonal to each other in the two bilinear forms (Lx,y) and (Sx,y). A descriptor characterizing the representation in a standard basis for Y of each of these two forms is associated with each such Y. Each such descriptor, and its associated space and form, is either one of those appearing in Theorem 1, or one of the spaces described by $[0,m,m+1]^*$, $[0,m+1,m]^*$, $[0,m,m,+]^*$, or $[0, m,m,-]^*$, where D^* designates the result of taking the space and pair of canonical forms described by D and interchanging the two forms, or is the one-dimensional space with both forms zero, whose descriptor is $[0]$, or is an odd-dimensional space with descriptor $[n,n]$ and forms

$$x_1x_2+\ldots+x_{2n-1}x_{2n} \text{ and } x_2x_3+\ldots+x_{2n}x_{2n+1}.$$

APPLICATION TO COMPUTATION OF INTERSECTION CURVES

We can easily apply the preceding analysis of the general n-dimensional case to the four-dimensional case required for our geometric application. Suppose first that LS has a nonsimple real eigenvalue, λ, of dimension n.

Let λ and n be as in Theorem 1 and make $\lambda=0$ by subtracting λL from S. Note that n equals either 2, 3, or 4. If $n=2$, then Y has coordinates in which (Lu,u) and (Su,u) have the respective forms $\pm 2zw$ and $\pm z^2$. Thus if we pass to inhomogeneous coordinates for the whole of our original Euclidean 3-space by dividing by z, the equations $(Lu,u) = 0 = (Su,u)$ take on the form

$$Q_1(x,y) + 2w = 0 = Q_2(x,y) + 1$$

where Q_1 and Q_2 are quadratic forms in two variables. The second of these equations defines a quadratic plane curve to which we can easily give a rational parameterization, and then the first equation gives the w coordinate for the corresponding points on the intersection of Λ and Σ. Thus in this case the intersection curve of Λ and Σ has rational parameterization.

Next suppose that $n=3$. Then, on Y, the forms (Lu,u) and (Su,u) can be represented as $\pm(2yw + z^2)$ and $\pm 2yz$. Pass to inhomogeneous 3-space coordinates by dividing by z, so that $(Lu,u) = 0 = (Su,u)$ takes on the form

$$\pm x^2 + 2yw + 1 = 0 = ax^2 + 2y.$$

In this case the second of these equations can be used to eliminate y from the first, giving the equation of an elementary curve in the x,w plane, and then the second equation gives the y coordinate for the corresponding points on the intersection of Λ and Σ. Hence the intersection curve of Λ and Σ is simply $(x,-ax^2/2,(1 \pm x^2)/(ax^2))$.

Finally suppose that $n=4$. Then (Lu,u) and (Su,u) can be represented as $\pm(2xw + 2yz)$ and $\pm(2xz + y^2)$. Here we can pass to inhomogeneous coordinates by dividing by y, which gives the equation

$$xw + z = 0 = 2xz + 1$$

whose elementary parameterization is $(x,w,z) = (1/t, t^2/2, -t/2)$.

Many of the cases that can arise have this relatively elementary flavor. In other typical cases we can introduce a coordinate system which represents the intersection curve of the two quadric surfaces being examined as the intersection of the unit sphere or the single-sheeted hyperboloid $x^2+y^2-z^2=1$ with a vertical elliptic or hyperbolic cylinder (or with one or two planes) whose base quadratic curve Q lies in the x,y plane and has its center at the origin. Details are given in [Ocken *et al.* 1983].

BOOLEAN COMBINATIONS OF QUADRIC SURFACES

For a solid geometry system one will need to use the detailed information concerning quadric surface intersections developed in the preceding section to

References pp. 268-269

represent the geometry of an arbitrary Boolean combination B of volumes bounded by such surfaces. The solid B is formed by applying intersection, symmetric difference and union operators to halfspaces H_i, each defined by an equation of the form

$$P_i(x,y,z) > 0 \quad \text{or} \quad P_i(x,y,z) < 0$$

where each P_i is a quadratic polynomial. Let Σ_i be the quadric boundary surface defined by $P_i(x,y,z) = 0$. If necessary, we can apply infinitesimal translations to the surfaces Σ_i to ensure that they are in general position, that is, that any two such surfaces which meet will intersect transversally. Thus the boundary of the solid B is the union of closed subregions R_i of Σ_i, where R_i is the intersection of Σ_i with the boundary of B. In a geometric modeling system which admits general quadric surfaces to its vocabulary of basic shapes, we will have to determine the precise geometry of the region R_i for each quadric surface Σ_i.

To do this, we consider a fixed surface Σ and study the intersection curves C_i of Σ and Σ_i ($i>1$). This network of curves divides Σ into a collection of two-dimensional cells k_j, each of which is bounded by finitely many piecewise differentiable arcs a lying on various curves C_i, the arcs lying along C_i being separated by the intersection points of C_i with other curves C_j. The region $R = R_i$ we seek is a union of certain of the cells k_j. We shall show how to determine the geometry of the region R by dividing it into patches, each a union of one or more cells. Intuitively speaking, these patches are the connected subregions of R. More precisely, patches which meet only at isolated points will be considered to be distinct; that is, patches are defined as closures of the connected components of the interior of R. Thus distinct patches have disjoint interiors and either are disjoint or intersect at finitely many boundary points.

Algorithms for manipulating algebraic numbers, like those reviewed in [Schwartz and Sharir 1982], can be used to determine the ordering along a fixed parameterized intersection curve C_i of this curve's intersections with all other curves C_j.

The results sketched in the previous section show that each curve C_i can be parameterized by coordinate functions $x_i(u)$, $y_i(u)$, and $z_i(u)$, each of which is a rational combination of polynomials, or square roots of polynomials, in the real parameter u. This remains true even after we apply projective transformations to the parameterizations given in the last section in order to transform all of them into a common coordinate system. Let S and S_i be the matrices which represent the surfaces Σ and Σ_i respectively. Examination of the intersection paramaterizations listed above shows that except for the case in which the product SS_i has two pairs of complex eigenvalues, each such coordinate function either has the form

$$\frac{p(u) + d(u)^{1/2}}{1 + u^2}$$

where p and d are of degrees at most two and four respectively, or a similar form with denominator u^2, or is a rational fraction with denominator u and numerator at most quadratic, or is a rational fraction with denominator $1+u^2$ and numerator at most biquadratic, or is a simple quadratic polynomial. In the above formula, the polynomial d which appears under the radical is the same, up to a constant factor, for all three coordinate functions x, y, and z. The intersection points of C_i and some other curve C_j are the same as the intersections of C_i and the surface Σ_j, and may be determined by substituting the coordinate functions above into the defining polynomial $P_j(x,y,z) = 0$ of the surface Σ_j. This yields a polynomial equation $q_j(u) = 0$, of degree at most eight.

In the exceptional case that the product SS_i has two pairs of complex eigenvalues, one of the coordinate functions is of the form shown above, but with numerator multiplied by u. In this case, which can only occur when both quadratic forms have signature (2,2), substitution of the intersection parameterizations in the polynomial P_j may yield a polynomial of degree twelve. However, even in this case, a slight variation of approach will make it unnecessary to work with algebraic equations of degree higher than eight.

It follows that the intersection points of the fixed parameterized curve C_i and the various other curves C_j have coordinates $(x_i(t),y_i(t),z_i(t))$, where t is a real root of some q_j of degree at most eight. In order to determine the sequence of arcs into which the collection of all such intersection points divides the curve C_i, we can make use of algorithms which perform exact computations with algebraic numbers, that is, roots of arbitrary rational polynomials [Schwartz and Sharir 1982]. Given a polynomial q, these algorithms show how to find disjoint intervals on the real line, each having rational endpoints and containing precisely one root of q. By combining such root-isolating intervals corresponding to different polynomials q_j, one may determine the relative ordering of the collection of roots of all the polynomials q_j of our discussion. Thus we may assume that each intersection curve C_i has been divided into arcs a, each bounded by intersection points of C_i with other curves, and that the ordering of these arcs and points is known.

Standard topological methods can then be used to determine how the various cells into which the network of curves C_i divides the surface Σ combine to form surface patches on Σ. From this, the topology of the surface and volume of the body in which we are interested can be calculated [Ocken et al. 1983]. This geometric information can be used for various computations involving the boundary of R, for example, in connection with a drawing or surface area algorithm.

ACKNOWLEDGEMENT

Work on this paper has been supported by ONR Grants N00014–75–C–0571 and N00014–82–K–0381 and by a grant from the U.S.-Israeli Binational Science Foundation.

References pp. 268-269

REFERENCES

[Brown 1982]
C. M. Brown, "PADL-2: A Technical Summary," *IEEE Computer Graphics and Applications*, Vol. 2, No. 2, March 1982, pp. 69–84.

[Fisher *et al.* 1977]
W. B. Fisher, *et al.*, "The PADL-1.0/n Processor: Overview and System Documentation," PADL System Document-01, Production Automation Project, University of Rochester, Rochester, New York, 1977.

[Fisher, *et al.* 1978]
W. B. Fisher, *et al.*, "Part and Assembly Description Languages-II," Technical Memorandum 20b, Production Automation Project, University of Rochester, Rochester, New York, 1978.

[Hartquist *et al.* 1977]
E. E. Hartquist, *et al.*, "Representations in the PADL-1.0/n Processor: Boundary Representations and the BFILE/1 System," PADL System Document-10, Production Automation Project, University of Rochester, Rochester, New York, 1977.

[Hillyard 1982]
R. Hillyard, "The BUILD Group of Solid Modelers," *IEEE Computer Graphics and Applications*, Vol. 2, No. 2, March 1982, pp. 43–52.

[Hodge and Pedoe 1952]
W. V. D. Hodge and D. Pedoe, *Methods of Algebraic Geometry*, 3 vols., Cambridge University Press, Cambridge, England, 1952 (See especially Vol. II, Chap. XIII).

[Levin 1976]
J. Levin, "A Parametric Algorithm for Drawing Pictures of Solid Objects Composed of Quadric Surfaces," *Communications of the ACM*, Vol. 19, No. 10, October 1976, pp. 555–563.

[Ocken *et al.* 1983]
S. Ocken, J. T. Schwartz, and M. Sharir, " Precise Implementation of CAD Primitives using Rational Parametrizations of Standard Surfaces," Technical Report No. 67, Department of Computer Science, New York University, New York, New York, March 1983.

[Requicha 1977]
A. A. G. Requicha, "Part and Assembly Description Languages I: Dimensioning and Tolerancing," Technical Memorandum 19, Production Automation Project, University of Rochester, Rochester, New York, 1977.

[Requicha and Voelcker 1982]
A. A. G. Requicha and H. B. Voelcker, "Solid Modeling: A Historical Summary and Contemporary Assessment," *IEEE Computer Graphics and Applications*, Vol. 2, No. 2, March 1982, pp. 9–24.

[Schwartz and Sharir 1982]
J. T. Schwartz and M. Sharir, "On the 'Piano-Movers' Problem–II: General Techniques for Computing Topological Properties of Real Algebraic Manifolds," Computer Science Technical Report No. 41, Courant Institute of Mathematical Sciences, New York University, New York, New York, February 1982.

[Tarski 1951]
A. Tarski, *A Decision Method for Elementary Algebra and Geometry*, Second Edition, Revised, University of California Press, Berkeley, California, 1951.

[Tilove 1977]
R. B. Tilove, "Representations in the PADL-1.0/n Processor: Simple Geometric Entities," PADL System Document-02, Production Automation Project, University of Rochester, Rochester, New York, 1977.

[Wesley 1980]
M. A. Wesley, "Construction and Use of Geometric Models," *Computer Aided Design*, J. Encarnacao, ed., Lecture Notes in Computer Science No. 89, Springer-Verlag, New York, New York, 1980, pp. 79–136.

DISCUSSION

Brian Barsky *(University of California–Berkeley)*

The degree of the explicit forms sounds very much like the work of Tom Sederberg. I'm wondering if, from a mathematical standpoint, there is a general theory that we're unaware of and that we should be looking at?

Schwartz

You can always get crude results by the classical general resultant theorem simply by eliminating variables. There are two forms of that: step-wise elimination and the use of the so-called Cayley resultant or eliminant, which is a less well-known technique but which offers some promise of better control over the degree. Beyond that, it's a matter of looking for algebraic tricks in particular cases. I wouldn't know any general theory.

J. T. Schwartz

Barsky

I wonder also if it would be unfair to call on Ron Goldman. Can you comment on whether that's similar or not?

Ronald Goldman *(Control Data Corporation)*

Yes, it is Cayley's resultant.

Barskey

So it is coming straight from this mathematical theory?

Goldman

Yes.

Aristides Requicha *(University of Rochester)*

Are you planning to do exact algebraic computation?

Schwartz

The trouble with exact algebraic calculations is that the precise calculation with algebraic numbers is very expensive. Work is needed to improve the efficiency of these methods. What one probably needs to do is make approximate calculations in some sort of significance system as long as they are known to be safe, and only to resort to precise semisymbolic calculations in those (hopefully rare) cases which just can't be discriminated using numerical calculations alone.

Donald Peterson *(Sandia Laboratories)*

How sensitive is your topological analysis to the situation in which two curves intersect the given curve at the same point?

Schwartz

The algebraic techniques are capable of handling that. In the sense of my last remarks, that is presumably a case whose existence you'd become aware of by the fact that you were getting an irresolvable ambiguity from the numerical calculations; at that point you would resort to a symbolic calculation.

Ramon Sarraga *(General Motors Research Laboratories)*

One of the basic issues here is to find at least one sample point on each of the real branches of the intersection curve because, of course, the intersection curve in general can be complex and really of no interest in CAD. At one time Alex Morgan and I looked into this problem and saw that it was related to Hilbert's sixteenth problem. We looked that up in AMS proceedings on Hilbert's problems and we found there was nothing on Hilbert's sixteenth problem published —no progress in the last several years. Would you care to comment on what we could expect for, say, spline surfaces?

Schwartz

General algebraic techniques (if you can stand the cost of the computation) will in principle identify all curve branches no matter how small, and are capable of giving you a point on each. These techniques are classical, but the key problem is to find ways of reducing their cost to something tolerable.

Requicha

These techniques are like the composition of algebraic sets and that sort of thing?

Schwartz

Yes, in general. Of course, that's the most prohibitively expensive form and the question is how much it can be reduced.

Alexander Morgan *(General Motors Research Laboratories)*

The method that you're outlining involves dividing things up into cases. You commented that it's numerical and that you are anticipating structuring the method in such a way that you're adding to numerical subtleties, that you go to some sort of symbolic decision as to which direction to go. Could you say more about that?

Schwartz

The rudimentary form of the problem is basically this. Suppose I give you a polynomial equation of degree 300, and I ask "Is the 27th largest real root of this equation positive or negative?" This question has a definite binary answer, but a numerical technique can fail if the answer is close to zero and if the polynomial has lots of (possibly multiple) roots near zero. However, semisymbolic techniques for working with algebraic numbers will answer that question decisively in every case. I don't want to enter into details here, but the techniques that I'm talking about are essentially extensions of the semisymbolic approach.

Morgan

So, am I understanding you to say that ordinarily numerical computation is sufficient, but you'll have in your logic the ability to switch to something more sophisticated?

Schwartz

That's right, where there's a numerical ambiguity.

Hinds

Ray, you're on safe ground with enough time and resources and computer power.

Herbert Steinberg *(MAGI)*

Could you describe precisely what is the polynomial equation of 20th degree discussed earlier?

Schwartz

I certainly can describe where it comes from algebraically. If you simply write out the three equations:
$$x = F_1 (u,v)$$
$$y = F_2 (u,v)$$
$$z = F_3 (u,v)$$
you then can simply eliminate u and v from those three equations.

Steinberg

It's not clear what problem you are trying to define.

Schwartz

You want to get a polynomial equation that is satisfied by a quadratic spline patch.

Steinberg

The reason I'm puzzled is that a straight line intersecting such a patch gives an equation of 8th degree.

Schwartz

I take three such surfaces which intersect at a vertex and I ask if that vertex is inside or outside something else. I need a systematic approach or I just cannot answer that question accurately.

Steinberg

Well, I don't see why that has to be 20th degree.

Schwartz

If you do the elimination, you sort out the three algebraic equations of degree four in the variables u and v, and you then eliminate those two variables and the degree just goes up very quickly. We should work it out over a piece of paper.

Steinberg

Well, I've worked it out and I'm coming out with 8th degree equations.

SESSION IV
SOLID MODELING AND
ARTIFICIAL INTELLIGENCE

Session Chairman
A. PAT AMBLER

University of Edinburgh
Edinburgh, Scotland

SOLID MODELING, ASPECT GRAPHS, AND ROBOT VISION

GLEN M. CASTORE

National Bureau of Standards
Washington, D.C.

ABSTRACT

At the National Bureau of Standards, a method is being developed for transferring sufficient information directly from the solid modeling system to the robot vision system to enable the robot to recognize a part. The information is encoded in the form of a graph, called an aspect graph, together with functions associated to each vertex of the graph. Aspect graphs were developed by J. J. Koenderink of the State University of Utrecht in the Netherlands, as part of an attempt to understand how shape information is represented by the human vision system.

Currently the method is being developed for parts designed on the PADL-2 system. In particular, it does not yet handle contoured surfaces. Extensions to deal with contoured surfaces appear to be feasible and are mentioned briefly.

INTRODUCTION

In an automated manufacturing facility a tremendous amount of data must be generated to provide machines with sufficient information to produce parts. This data may be in the form of programs for various pieces of equipment, part descriptions for vision or tactile image processing systems, or information on equipment characteristics. An impediment to the efficient utilization of automated manufacturing techniques is the reliance upon hand or semiautomated coding to produce this data. Robots are programmed using on-line teaching methods; information is passed to a vision system by typing a description of the part or by displaying the part in several orientations. These are comparatively slow, labor-intensive procedures and can cause the overall system to be fairly inefficient.

References pp. 287-288

In the Automated Manufacturing Research Facility at the National Bureau of Standards we are attempting to understand and deal with some of these issues [Simpson *et al.* 1982]. The Machine Vision Group, directed by Dr. Ernest Kent, is developing a method for transferring geometric information about a part directly from a solid modeler, such as PADL-2, to a robot vision system. The technique is based upon encoding geometric information in structures called aspect graphs. The aspect graph, together with pointers to certain metric information, then becomes part of a world model which is referenced by the vision system. The aspect graphs are produced automatically from the boundary file within the solid modeler.

The notion of an aspect graph stems from work done by J. J. Koenderink and A. J. van Doorn of the Rijksuniversitat at Utrecht [Koenderink and van Doorn 1979]. They developed this concept as part of a theory on how the human vision system encodes information. At NBS the major effort has been toward developing algorithms for generating aspect graphs from boundary file descriptions of objects, and then incorporating the aspect graphs into the world model for the robot control system.

WHAT ARE ASPECT GRAPHS?

For purposes of illustration most of the discussion will be restricted to faceted objects such as polyhedra. An *aspect* of an object, in this case, is the set of all faces which are visible from some viewpoint. Some aspects of a wedge are shown in Figure 1. Since there is no viewpoint from which both the top and the bottom are visible, there is no aspect labeled (D,E).

Associated with each aspect is a vertex in the aspect graph. Two vertices are connected by an edge if there is a continuous motion of the observer from the viewpoints for one aspect into the viewpoints for the other, without passing through any intermediate aspects. The aspect graph for the wedge, and the viewpoints corresponding to some aspects, are shown in Figure 2. Since there is no continuous motion which can take the viewer who sees only the top to a position from which only the bottom can be seen, without passing through intermediate views, there is no edge connecting the vertices D and E associated with the top and bottom aspects.

The region of space from which a particular aspect is visible is called a *cell*. Two vertices are joined by an edge if and only if the corresponding cells have a

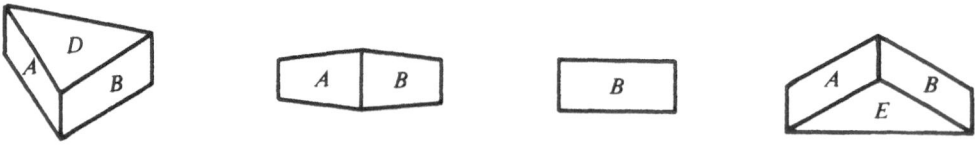

Figure 1. Some aspects of a wedge.

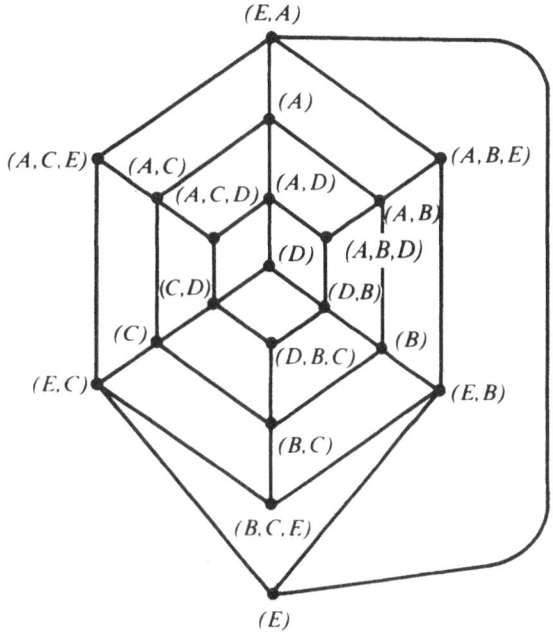

(a) Aspect graph

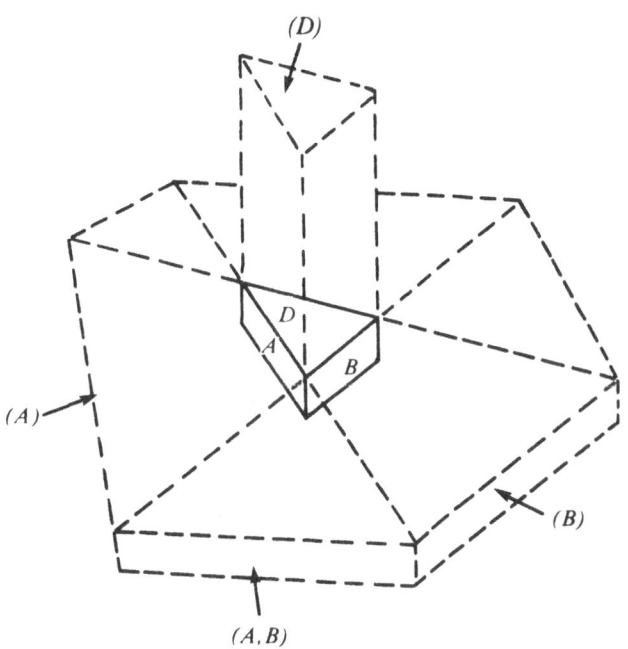

(b) Parcellation of space

Figure 2. *An aspect graph and parcellation of space for a wedge.*

two-dimensional segment of a face in common. Every object partitions the surrounding space into such cells. The complete partition is called a *parcellation of space* by Koenderink. The aspect graph records the combinatorial structure of this parcellation. Figure 2(b) displays a portion of the parcellation associated with a wedge. For instance, (A, B) is the cell from which only the faces A and B are visible. Figure 3 shows some cells for a slightly more complicated object. A structure very similar to an aspect graph is utilized by Goad to develop a hidden surface elimination technique [Goad 1982].

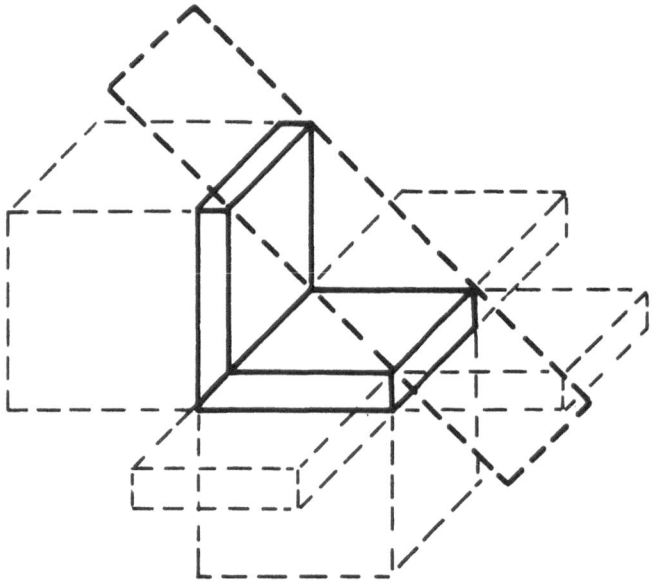

Figure 3. *Cells of a parcellation for an L-shaped solid.*

A solid is not unambiguously characterized by its aspect graph. For example, the three parallelepipeds in Figure 4 have identical graphs. The aspect graph contains information about the affine structure of these polygons, but very little information about their metric structure. In general, if there is an affine transformation taking one object to another, they will have isomorphic aspect graphs. The crucial feature of affine transformations, in this context, is that they preserve parallelism.

METRIC INFORMATION

Since, as the examples in Figure 4 indicate, most metric information is lost in the construction of the aspect graph, a function describing metric properties of each aspect is attached to the corresponding vertex in the graph. Before explain-

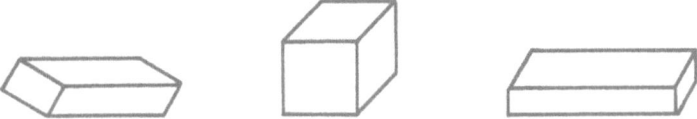

Figure 4. Objects for which aspect graphs are ambiguous.

ing the workings of this function, a few comments will be made about the meaning of *object range* and *orientation* in the NBS vision system. The range and orientation of a part are the principal arguments of the metric function.

Figure 5 shows the relationships among the camera, light sources, and object. The camera and light sources are mounted on the end of the robot arm. Range and orientation of a part are calculated in a coordinate system fixed with respect to the robot gripper. The six degrees of freedom that establish position and orientation of a rigid body in this coordinate system are determined using two frames of video data taken sequentially from the same camera position [Albus *et al.* 1982].

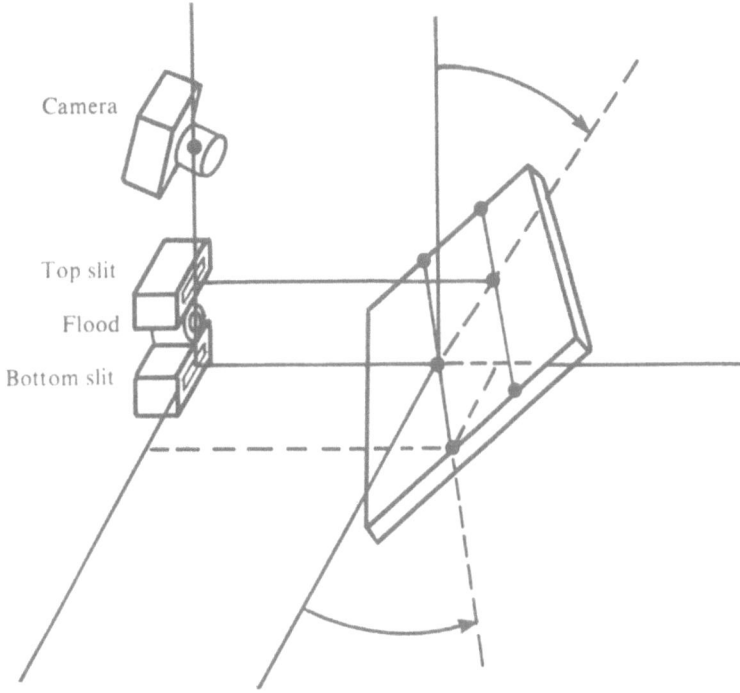

Figure 5. NBS six-degree-of-freedom vision system.

References pp. 287-288

The first frame, produced by two parallel planes of light, yields sufficient information to compute range, pitch and yaw for a planar or cylindrical surface. *Range* is the distance from the origin of the gripper coordinate system to the nearest point on the piece illuminated by the planes of light. The second frame, produced by the point source, can be analyzed to obtain the elevation, azimuth, and roll of the surface, again with respect to the gripper coordinate system. This information is provided about 30 times per second.

The function referred to above uses parallel projection to map the given aspect onto a plane perpendicular to the line of sight, as shown in Figure 6. A second algorithm, which depends upon object range, camera focal length, and characteristics of the pixel array, transforms this projection into an expected image in pixel dimensions. Details of these algorithms will be presented in a forthcoming paper.

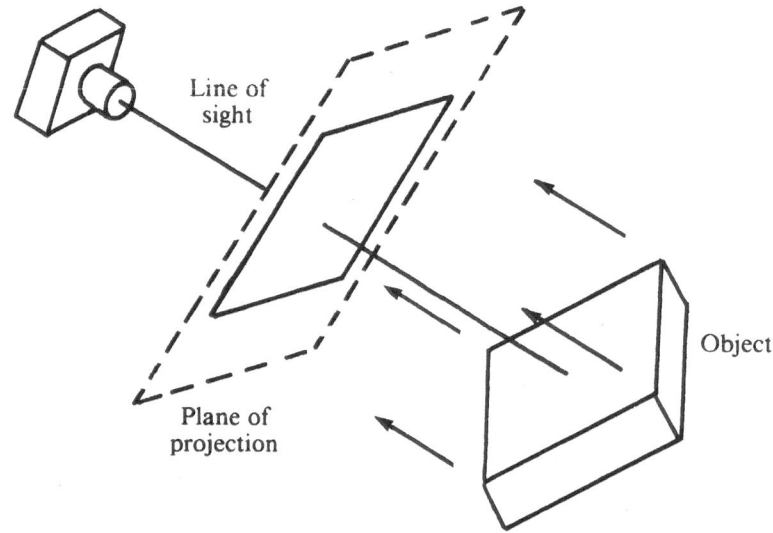

Figure 6. *Parallel projection of an aspect.*

CONSTRUCTION OF ASPECT GRAPHS

The algorithms used to generate the aspect graphs have as input a boundary file representation of the object. It is necessary to have some representation from which the normal vectors can be computed. The first step is to build a face-edge graph from the boundary file. This graph has a vertex for each face of the object, and two vertices are joined by an edge if the corresponding faces have an edge in common. Associated with each vertex is the normal vector N of the corresponding face. If the part contains a cylindrical face A, then $N(A)$ will be a vector-valued function.

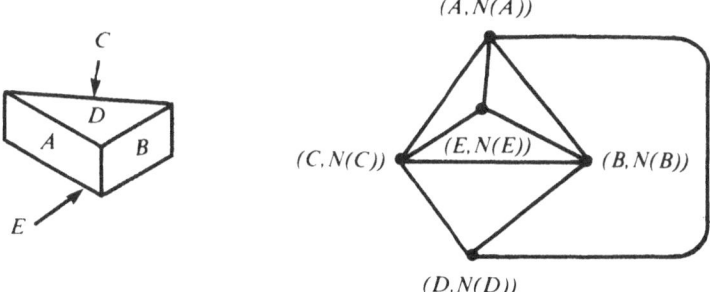

Figure 7. *Face-edge graph for a wedge.*

The algorithm for producing the aspect graph is outlined here for the case of convex, 2.5-*D* prismatic solids (Figure 8). The first step is to pick, at random, a side face of the solid and find all aspects which contain that face. If $F(i)$ is the face chosen, then there is an aspect labeled

$$(F(i-k), \ldots, F(i), \ldots, F(i+n))$$

if and only if

$$b(1) + \ldots + b(n) < 180° - (a(1) + \ldots + a(k)).$$

When equality is achieved it means that the face $F(i+n)$ is parallel to the face $F(i-k)$, so there can be no aspect containing both of these faces. Because the solid is convex, aspects can contain only consecutive faces. Consequently, when

$$b(1) + \ldots + b(n) \geqslant 180° - (a(1) + \ldots + a(k))$$

the algorithm moves on to search for all aspects containing $F(i+1)$. The angles $a(i)$ and $b(j)$ are calculated from the normal vectors. Aspects containing the top and bottom faces are generated using rules referring to the face-edge graph. Two vertices are joined by an edge if the corresponding aspects differ only by one face.

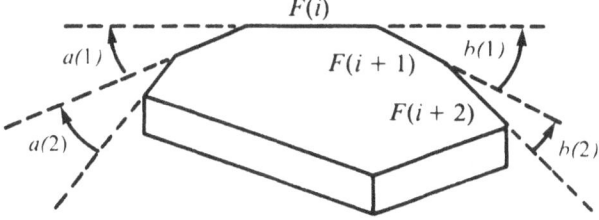

Figure 8. *Generating the aspect graph for a 2.5-D solid.*

References pp. 287-288

When the solid is concave, the algorithm first generates the aspect graph of the convex hull. Concavity is detected, through the normal vectors, as folds in a modified Gauss map (Figure 9). The convex hull is then deformed to recover the original object. The aspect graph of the convex hull undergoes a corresponding transformation to become the graph of the original concave solid. Figure 10 shows this process for a wedge being transformed into an L-shaped object.

As the deformation of a face takes place, an *auxiliary plane* is formed across the tips of the concavity which gives rise to new cells in the parcellation. In the aspect graph of the wedge, the change that takes place is that every vertex labeled with the name of the deformed face may split into two vertices, each of which will correspond to a new cell. Whether this vertex splitting actually takes place depends on geometric relationships among the faces.

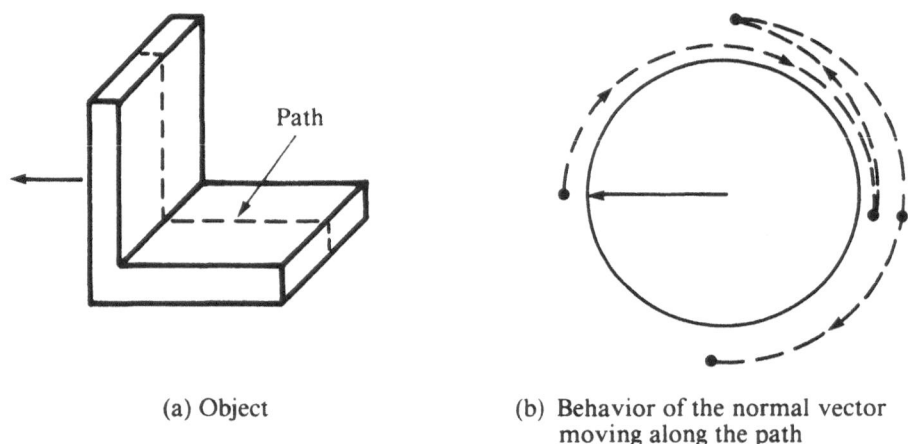

(a) Object   (b) Behavior of the normal vector
                                        moving along the path

Figure 9. Detecting concavity.

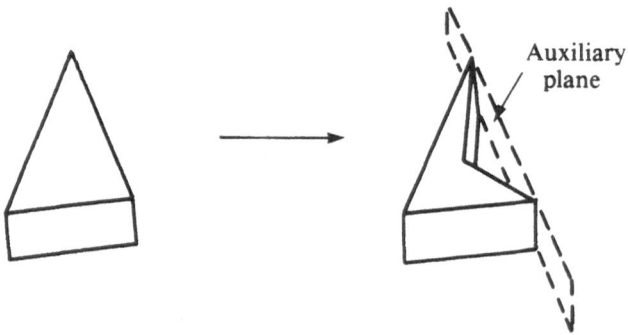

Figure 10. Deformation of a wedge.

These techniques for generating aspect graphs can be extended to objects which have cylindrical faces or which contain holes. Figure 11 shows the aspect graph of a cylinder. Faces are defined, effectively, in terms of the Gauss map. The Gauss map associates with each point on a surface the unit surface normal translated to the origin. Hence the image of the Gauss map is on the unit sphere. In the simple world of solids with cylindrical and planar faces, planar faces are points and cylindrical faces are lines in the Gaussian image (Figure 12).

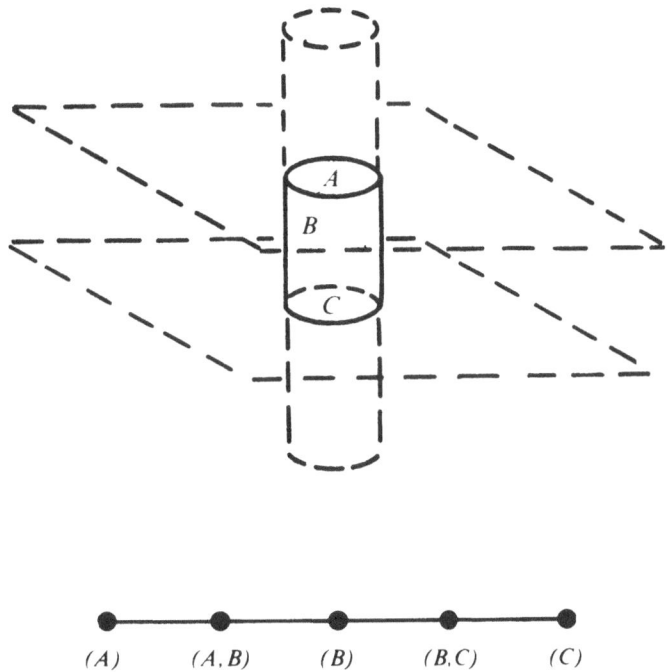

(A)   *(A,B)*   *(B)*   *(B,C)*   *(C)*

Figure 11. *Cylinder and its aspect graph.*

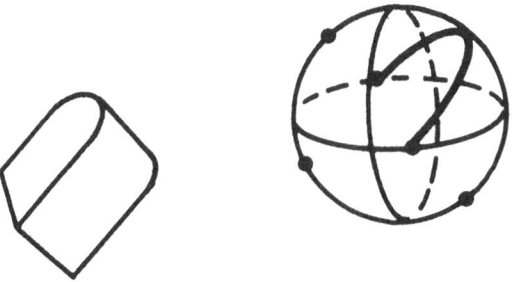

Figure 12. *A solid and its Gaussian image.*

References pp. 287-288

The Gauss map is useful when developing aspect graphs for these fairly simple objects and is essential for dealing with contoured surfaces. In the design of a solid modeler, one very nice feature would be a set of subroutines allowing easy access to this information.

Holes are handled by treating the top, the bottom, and the inside surface as three separate faces. The cell generated by a hole has a conical shape (Figure 13). As the camera crosses into the top of the cone, the bottom of the hole becomes visible.

At present, aspect graphs can be generated automatically for a fairly wide class of objects. These include 2.5-D prismatic solids, 2.5-D solids with some cylindrical faces and holes, and 3-D convex polyhedra.

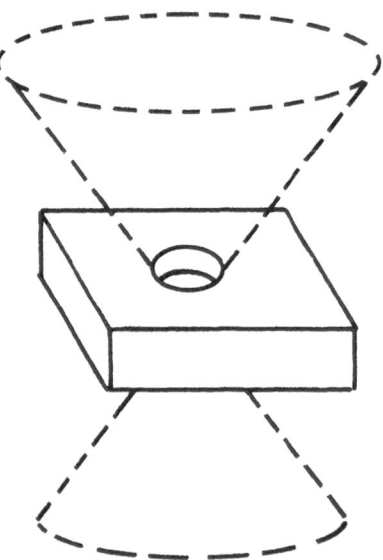

Figure 13. *Cell generated by a hole.*

FURTHER RESEARCH

There are a number of issues concerning aspect graphs which are not well understood. To be used effectively over a range of machine vision applications, further work will need to be done in these areas. Several of the research areas are listed here.

Efficient Algorithms—Efficient algorithms for the computation of aspect graphs and methods for calculating the graphs of nonconvex 3-D prismatic objects must be developed.

Graph Theory—Graph theoretic properties of aspect graphs for 2.5-D objects have been useful in developing computational techniques. How the complexity or symmetry of the object is reflected in the structure of the graph must be determined.

Search Strategies—If the aspect seen by the vision system is not the one expected, it becomes necessary to identify the part. Whether the aspect graph can be used to generate efficient search strategies and which motion is likely to yield the most information are questions needing to be answered.

Contoured Surfaces—Most of Koenderink's work is on developing aspect graphs for contoured surfaces. This involves studying singularities of the Gauss map of a surface. Effective ways of doing this using a solid modeler need to be devised.

On a larger scale there is the question of how this approach to encoding geometric information for machine vision can be usefully blended with other work in this area. Aspect graphs, as applied at NBS, are used to generate expectations for the vision system. These are of the form: "If the orientation is B relative to part A, then the camera should see this configuration of faces." The data from the vision system is matched against these expectations.

It should be possible to generate more detailed expectations using a solid model. Koenderink's work suggests that the singular points of the Gauss map are significant for visual recognition of contoured surfaces. Horn has developed techniques for extracting surface information from image intensities [Horn 1977, Ikeuchi and Horn 1981]. This suggests using special purpose hardware to quickly calculate anticipated image intensities, as a pixel array, in neighborhoods of singular points. This computed pixel array can then be compared with the actual data.

REFERENCES

[Albus *et al.* 1982]
J. Albus, E. Kent, M. Nashman, P. Mansbach, L. Palombo, and M. Shneier, "Six-Dimensional Vision System," *Robot Vision*, Proceedings of the SPIE, Vol. 336, 1982, pp. 142–153.

[Goad 1982]
C. Goad, "Special Purpose Automatic Programming for Hidden Surface Elimination," *ACM Computer Graphics*, Vol. 16, No. 3 (SIGGRAPH '82 Conference Proceedings, Boston, Massachusetts, July 26-30, 1982) pp. 167–178.

[Horn 1977]
B. K. P. Horn, "Understanding Image Intensities," *Artificial Intelligence*, Vol. 8, 1977, pp. 201–231.

[Ikeuchi and Horn 1981]
K. Ikeuchi and B. K. P. Horn, "Numerical Shape from Shading and Occluding Boundaries," *Artificial Intelligence*, Vol. 17, 1981, pp. 141–184.

[Koenderink and van Doorn 1979]
J. J. Koenderink and A. J. van Doorn, "The Internal Representation of Solid Shape with Respect to Vision," *Biological Cybernetics*, Vol. 32, 1979, pp. 211–216.

[Simpson *et al.* 1982]
J. A. Simpson, R. J. Hocken, and J. S. Albus, "The Automated Manufacturing Research Facility of the National Bureau of Standards," *Journal of Manufacturing Research*, Vol. 1, No. 1, 1982, pp. 17–31.

DISCUSSION

Norman Badler *(University of Pennsylvania)*

Aspect graphs are a very old idea, cast in an unstable framework. Underwood and Coats* did some very seminal work in simulating multiple views of polyhedra; they built a graph structure very much like an aspect graph except they based it on projected invariance which they knew they could measure unequivocally from the image.

You made a statement in the definition of an aspect graph that a transition from one face to three faces is illegal. I see no reason why it is illegal. You simply move the camera along the bisector of the angle between the faces.

Castore

The point is that if you are getting vision information at a rate of about thirty frames per second then the camera takes up some space whereas the bisector is a line. At some point as you move from one to the other, it is almost certain that you will see two faces.

G. M. Castore

---

*S. A. Underwood and C. L. Coates, "Visual Learning from Multiple Views," IEEE Transactions on Computers, *Vol. C-24, 1975, pp. 651–661.*

Badler

But that is not a theoretical consideration. That is simply a decision that you have made: you are not going to allow some sort of degenerate positions to occur. If you want to make that part of your definition, then I will accept it; but I do not think that there is a physical reason to do it.

Castore

It is physically important in that it is unlikely that the vision system will be looking at one face of a cube, and then, after moving a very small distance, be looking at three faces, without seeing two faces as an intermediate configuration. If we find this somewhat arbitrary definition to be causing problems, we will change it.

T. C. Woo *(University of Michigan)*

Consider the analogy between constructing an aspect graph and rolling an n-sided die on a flat table. You can roll from a face to an edge (which allows you to see two faces), but you can also roll across a vertex, in which case you make a transition to three faces.

Castore

The issue here is how a vision system works. The chances that it is going to hit upon a singular point are very small.

Christopher Brown *(University of Rochester)*

I would like to know more about auxiliary planes. Consider an L bracket with some structure inside it, for example, a slot. Do you make an aspect graph for something with that level of detail?

Castore

The auxiliary planes are not strictly the convex hull. When we have a very complex object, we do not use that level of detail so we omit it.

Woo

When you construct an aspect graph, do you use parallel projection or perspective projection?

Castore

I use parallel projection.

John Woodwark *(University of Bath)*

Even if you are using parallel projection, you can get a change in an aspect graph as the distance from the camera to the object changes.

Castore

Consider a hex nut seen from the side. You will have two aspect graphs: one for close to the hex nut, one for farther away. Inside the region bounded by extending the two neighboring faces on either side of a particular face, you will see only the one face; outside the region, you will see three faces.

Woodwark

Suppose that you have an object that has two faces at an angle. If you are near that angle, then you will be able to see both faces; but beyond a certain point, you will not be able to see both faces and therefore it seems that the aspect graph must change.

Castore

The aspect graph depends on the part geometry only. In practice the camera is usually fairly close to the part (from 2 inches to 36 inches), so we sometimes throw away unneeded levels of detail in the graph.

Woodwark

The closer you are to the part, the more perspective projection is involved.

Castore

I do not see that there is a problem.

Robert Haar *(General Motors Research Laboratories)*

You are using the output of the boundary file from PADL. What information from a different kind of modeler might be more useful? What information would you like to have that you do not have?

Castore

We need easy access to information about normal vectors and the rate of change of normal vectors. From these we can calculate the faces used to build the aspect graph. With PADL, we have to massage the boundary file data because the face boundaries do not always coincide with edges.

For example, the "face"

of the object

(which is built from a block and a cylinder) has, with PADL, the boundary file representation:

Thus, it indicates an edge where the vision system will detect no edge. We also need nongeometric information, such a surface reflectance, attached to the model.

Haar

In describing the technique for forming the aspect graphs for polyhedral objects, you talked about using the planar surfaces and you said you have a working program to do the same thing for a cylindrical surface. How do you do that?

Castore

For convex objects, cylindrical faces are treated very much as planar faces. The curved faces are extended in space, thus creating the boundaries for cells of the parcellation. An example is a cylinder:

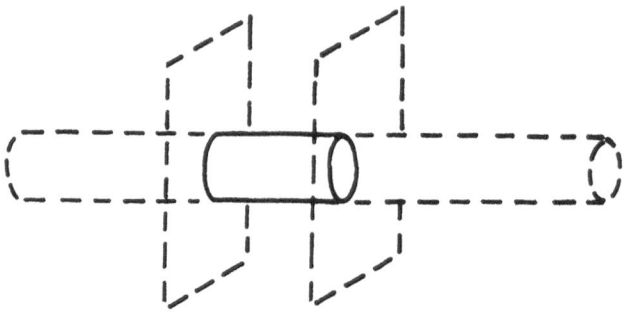

For holes, which are curved faces, we have special rules.

AN APPROACH TO AUTOMATIC ROBOT PROGRAMMING

TOMÁS LOZANO-PÉREZ and RODNEY A. BROOKS

Massachusetts Institute of Technology
Cambridge, Massachusetts

ABSTRACT

In this paper we propose an architecture for a new task-level system, which we call ATLAS (Automatic Task Level Assembly Synthesizer). Task-level programming attempts to simplify the robot programming process by requiring that the user specify only goals for the physical relationships among objects, rather than the motions of the robot needed to achieve those goals. A task-level specification is meant to be completely robot independent; no positions or paths that depend on the robot geometry or kinematics are specified by the user. We have two goals for this paper. The first is to present a more unified treatment of some individual pieces of task planning research whose relationships have not previously been described. The second is to provide a new framework for further research in task planning. We stress, however, that ATLAS as a whole has not been implemented and therefore, the description here indicates primarily a direction for future research.

INTRODUCTION

One of the earliest and most elusive goals of robotics has been the ability to program manipulators at the level of task operations rather than at the level of individual motions. What at first appeared to be a relatively simple problem was soon discovered to have unsuspected depths. As a result, several proposals to develop such task-level robot programming have not culminated in a working system. Nevertheless attempts to implement the proposals have led to crisper problem statements and better algorithms. Above all, they have pro-

References pp. 324-327

vided a useful framework for research. Over the past six or seven years, partly in response to difficulties encountered in implementing these systems, significant advances have been made in the theory and practice of task-level robot programming. As a result of these recent developments, the earlier proposals no longer afford an adequate framework for research.

In this paper we propose an architecture for a new task-level system, which we call ATLAS (Automatic Task Level Assembly Synthesizer). In contrast to earlier proposals, much of the theoretical underpinning of ATLAS exists and many of the components have been implemented and tested as stand-alone systems. Although these components are not, by any means, in final form, we believe they provide a solid enough basis to justify a new effort at integration. We have two goals for this paper. The first is to present a more unified treatment of some individual pieces of research in task planning, whose relationships have not previously been described. The second is to provide a new framework for further research in task-planning. We stress, however, that ATLAS as a whole has not been implemented and, therefore, the description here indicates primarily a direction for future research.

This paper will first discuss what is involved in task-level programming. Next it will present an overview of the total ATLAS system. Finally, it will examine in greater detail approaches to the key task planning modules of ATLAS.

Levels of Robot Programming—Most robots are programmed by manually moving them through a sequence of desired positions, recording the internal joint coordinates corresponding to each position, and recording any operations, such as closing the gripper or activating a welding gun, at those positions. The resulting program is a sequence of vectors of joint coordinates plus activation signals for external equipment. These programs are executed by moving the robot through the specified sequence of joint coordinates and issuing the indicated signals. This method of robot programming is known as teaching by showing, or *guiding*.

Guiding is simple to use and to implement but is subject to some important limitations, particularly in the use of sensors. The programmer, during guiding, specifies a single execution sequence for the robot; there are no loops, conditionals, or computations. In some applications, such as spot welding, painting, and simple materials handling, this is enough. In many other applications, however, such as mechanical assembly and inspection, one needs to specify the desired action of the robot in response to sensory input, data retrieval, or computation. In these cases, robot programming requires the capabilities of a general-purpose computer programming language.

Traditional computer programming languages have been extended with commands to access sensors and to specify robot motions. We refer to these as *robot-level* languages. The key advantage of robot-level languages is that data from external sensors, such as vision and force, may be used to modify the robot's motions. Sensing enables robots to cope with greater uncertainty in the position of external objects, thereby increasing their range of application. The key drawback of robot-level programming languages, relative to guiding, is the requirement that the robot programmer be expert in computer programming and in the design of sensor-based motion strategies.

Task-level programming attempts to simplify the robot programming process by requiring that the user specify only goals for the physical relationships among objects, rather than the motions of the robot needed to achieve those goals. A task-level specification is meant to be completely robot-independent; no positions or paths that depend on the robot geometry or kinematics are specified by the user. Task-level programming systems require complete geometric models of the environment and of the robot as input; for this reason, they are also referred to as *world modeling systems.*

Basic Problems in Task Planning—In task-level programming, the *task planner* must convert a user's specification of a task into a robot-level program to carry out the task. We assume that the input description of the task completely specifies the sequence of assembly.* The main role of the task planner is to plan the robot-specific motion and sensing commands necessary to achieve the task.

Consider the very simple block stacking task shown in Figure 1; the task can be specified as follows (where the notation $X.i$ means face i of object X):

PLACE A SUCH THAT (A.4 AGAINST TABLE) AND
                       (A.1 AGAINST F.1) AND (A.2 AGAINST F.2)

PLACE B SUCH THAT (B.4 AGAINST A.3) AND
                       (A.1 COPLANAR B.1) AND (A.2 COPLANAR B.2)

In the absence of any positioning errors in the manipulator or in our knowledge of the position of parts, this task could be accomplished with the following relatively simple program:

OPEN-FINGERS TO <width of A + epsilon>

MOVE TO <location of grasp on A> VIA <path-1>

CLOSE-FINGERS TO <width of A − epsilon>

MOVE TO <location at F> VIA <path-2>

OPEN-FINGERS TO <width of B + epsilon>

MOVE TO <location of grasp on B> VIA <path-3>

CLOSE-FINGERS TO <width of B − epsilon>

MOVE TO <location on A> VIA <path-4>

OPEN-FINGERS TO <width of B + epsilon>

Alternatively, another program called an assembly planner *produces such a description from the user's description.*

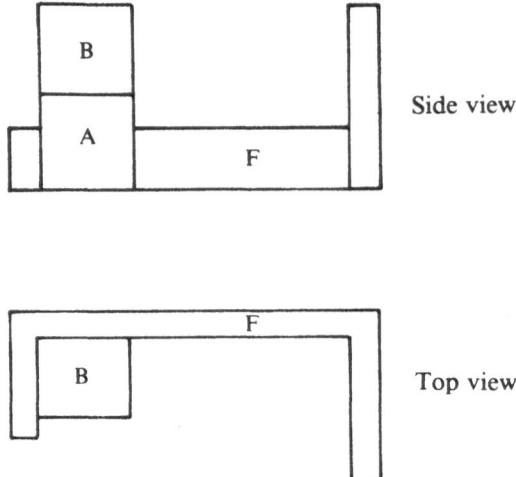

Side view

Top view

Figure 1. Example of a block stacking task.

Generating this program requires the task planner to choose positions for objects initially in the workspace, determine how new objects will be fed into the workspace, pick grasp points on parts, and find paths that avoid collisions. These problems are not the only ones that face a task planner. In practice, the simple program would fail to achieve the desired goals because of the presence of errors in the robot control system and in the system's knowledge of the location of the parts. The use of sensing can, in many cases, overcome these problems, but this requires that the task planner decide what sensing is useful and how to combine it with the appropriate motions. In fact, dealing with uncertainty permeates all of task planning.

In summary, a realistic task planner must solve the following problems in converting a task-level specification to a robot-level specification:

Parts feeding—The planner must choose how each of the parts required for the assembly is to be introduced into the workspace so as to maximize speed and reliability in acquiring the parts. In the example shown in Figure 1, the type of feeder for A and B must be determined.

Layout—The planner must choose where in the workspace each operation is to take place so as to minimize sensing and positioning error as well as reduce the time for the complete assembly. In the example, the location of F and of the feeders for A and B must be chosen.

Fixturing—The planner must choose any jigs and fixtures required to hold the parts to the required accuracy under the forces generated by assembly motions. In the example, F serves the function of a fixture; no further fixturing is needed.

Fine motion—The planner must choose a strategy of sensing and motion that guarantees that parts mating operations can be achieved reliably in the face of errors in control and sensing. In the example, strategies must be chosen that guarantee that A reaches the corner of F and that B is aligned with A.

Grasping—The planner must choose how to grasp each part so the grasp is stable and so as to avoid collisions while grasping or while placing the part at its destination. In the example, the planner must ensure that the grasp points on A and B are stable, that they enable the assembly operations to take place, and that the grasping motions do not introduce too much error in position.

Gross motion—The planner must choose efficient collision-free paths for the manipulator and the parts it carries. In the example, the path taking A from the feeder to near F and taking B from the feeder to above A are chosen so as to avoid collisions of the manipulator with F and with the feeder (even in the presence of position control errors).

One possible program for the example task (taking into account the likelihood of errors) has the following structure:

OPEN-FINGERS TO <width-1>

MOVE TO <location of grasp on A> VIA <path-1>

CLOSE-FINGERS TO <width-2>

MOVE TO <approach location near F> VIA <path-2>

COMPLIANT-MOVE ALONG <direction-1> UNTIL <contact with F.1 and F.2>

COMPLIANT-MOVE ALONG <direction-2> UNTIL <contact with TABLE>

OPEN-FINGERS TO <width-3>

VISION-LOCATE B NEAR <expected location of B>

OPEN-FINGERS TO <width-4>

MOVE TO <location of grasp on B> VIA <path-3>

CLOSE-FINGERS TO <width-5>

VISION-LOCATE B NEAR <expected location of B in fingers>

MOVE TO <approach location near A> VIA <path-4>

COMPLIANT-MOVE ALONG <direction-3> UNTIL <contact with A.3>

Note that, because of the presence of positioning errors and uncertainty, a very simple task-level description leads to a fairly complex robot-level program. In fact, the program above is not adequate for the task because it does not provide for the likelihood that some operations will fail due to unexpected events. No program ever handles *all* possible eventualities, but the addition of sensing significantly increases the reliability of the operations, usually at some expense

References pp. 324-327

of speed. This example points out the difficulty of robot-level programming and the potential value of task-level robot programming.

Many of the decisions that had to be made in synthesizing the example program above are not obvious from a first glance at the program. These complex decisions manifest themselves only in the numeric values of positions, for example, the positions of feeders, grasp points, the width of finger openings, directions of compliant motions, and the paths for positioning motions. The basic program structure itself, (for example, the need for the compliant motions and the vision sensing operations) is based on numerical estimates of errors in sensing and control, which in turn are based on the results of previous decisions. These decisions are tightly interrelated and propagate across what, on the surface, appear to be independent operations. For example, the choice of grasp points affects the assembly operations, the need for sensing, and the choice of paths. This interdependence is discussed more fully in the section that follows.

Hierarchical Decomposition and Robot Programming—Decomposition into independent subproblems, especially hierarchical decomposition, is one of the most common and powerful of conceptual tools for problem solving. It is no surprise that it forms the foundation of almost all programming methodologies. Structured programming, for example, is essentially an endorsement of hierarchical decomposition in programs. More recent developments in programming languages, such as data encapsulation, apply this approach for data structures. Of course, even the simplest programming tasks are not completely decomposable; side effects, such as modification of databases, propagate dependencies across operations. The driving force behind most programming methodologies is to minimize these dependencies.

It is natural to attempt to apply methodologies based on hierarchical decomposition to robot programming and control. The fundamental character of robot operations limits the scope of such decomposition, however. The key difficulties are error and geometry, both of which are nonlocal. The choice of grasp point on a part, for example, determines what motions of the hand are required to position the part. The choice of grasp point, in turn, is determined by subsequent assembly operations; for example, we do not want a finger on a surface that is to be against another surface. Nor do we want the axis between the fingers to be perpendicular to large applied forces since only friction is holding the object along that direction. Similarly, the existence of a path to a destination might depend on how the part is held in the hand. Finally, each operation makes certain assumptions about accuracy in locations and shape which affect subsequent operations. These dependencies conspire to make robot operations appear monolithic; one often concludes that everything must be decided before anything at all is decided.

The use of sensing and compliance increases the class of situations in which particular operations will succeed and thereby reduces interdependence among operations. As an extreme, each operation can sense the complete current environment and decide independently which method is adequate to perform its task. This is extremely wasteful even assuming that the sensing is free; it will require frequent regrasping, for example. In general, the low-level decisions made in carrying out each task-level step (layout, grasping, paths, and sensing) influence the decisions that need to be made for steps before and after this one [Brooks 1982, Taylor 1976]. Because of this, ATLAS involves a two-level approach to task planning based upon propagation of constraints on physical quantities.

The ATLAS approach to robot program synthesis starts by expanding the task-level description into a *skeleton program*. This skeleton program makes reference to quantities provided in the input, quantities that must be chosen by the system, and error quantities on which only bounds are available. Symbolic algebraic constraints are used to make explicit the interactions among the quantities across program steps. The goal of the system is to make few arbitrary decisions, but, instead, to exploit the mutual constraints among steps to force decisions. Each planning module restricts the values of variables in the skeleton plan in addition to determining the actual operations needed to achieve a step in the program. The planner propagates the restrictions on variables across operations: forwards, from constraints on input quantities to constraints on output quantities, and backwards, from constraints on output quantities to constraints on input quantities [Brooks 1982].

Modeling Requirements—Task-level planners require a complete world model and a complete task specification.

The world model—The legal motions of an object are constrained by the presence of other objects in the environment, and the form of the constraints depends in detail on the shapes of the objects. Therefore, a task planner needs complete geometric descriptions of objects. There are additional constraints on motion imposed by the kinematic structure of the robot itself. If the robot is turning a crank or opening a valve, then the kinematics of the crank and the valve impose additional restrictions on the robot's motion. The kinematic models provide the task planner with the information required to plan manipulator motions that are consistent with external constraints. Note that as a result of the robot's operation, new linkages may be created and old linkages destroyed, and the task planner must be apprised of the changes.

In planning robot operations, many of the physical characteristics of objects play important roles. The mass and inertia of parts, for example, determine how fast they can be moved or how much force can be applied to them before they fall over. Similarly, the coefficient of friction between a peg and a hole affects the jamming conditions during insertion. Likewise the physical constants of the robot links are used in the dynamics computation and in the control of the robot.

The geometrical, kinematical, and physical descriptions of a robot are insufficient to completely characterize its feasible operations. One important additional aspect of a robot system is its sensing capabilities: touch, force, and vision sensing. For task planning purposes, vision enables obtaining the configuration of an object to some specified accuracy at execution time; force sensing allows the use of compliant motions; touch information could serve in both capacities. In addition to sensing, there are many individual characteristics of manipulators that must be described: velocity and acceleration bounds, positioning accuracy of each of the joints, and workspace bounds are examples.

The task model—A model state is given by the configurations of all the objects in the environment at a given moment; tasks are actually defined by sequences of states of the world model or transformations of the states. The level of detail in the sequence needed to fully specify a task depends on the capabilities of the task planner.

The configurations of objects needed to specify a model state can be provided explicitly, for example, as offsets and Euler angles for rigid bodies and as joint parameters for linkages; but this type of specification is cumbersome and error prone. Three alternative methods for specifying configurations have been developed:

- Use of a light pen to position CAD models of the objects at the desired configurations,
- Use of the robot itself to specify robot configurations and to locate features of the objects [Grossman and Taylor 1978], and
- Use of symbolic spatial relationships among object features to constrain the configurations of objects, for example, <face-1> AGAINST <face-2> [Popplestone *et al.* 1978].

One advantage of using symbolic spatial relationships is that the configurations they denote are not limited to the accuracy of a light pen or of a manipulator. Another advantage of this method is that families of configurations such as those on a surface or along an edge can be expressed. The relationships, furthermore, are easy to interpret by a human and therefore easy to specify and modify. The principal disadvantage of using symbolic spatial relationships is that they do not specify configurations directly; they must be converted into numbers or equations before they can be used.

Model states are simply sets of configurations. If task specifications were simply sequences of models then, given a method such as symbolic spatial relationships for specifying configurations, we should be able to specify tasks. This approach has several important limitations, however. One is that a set of configurations may overspecify a state, for example, a round pin in a round hole. This problem can be solved by treating the symbolic spatial relationships themselves as specifying the state, since these relationships can express families of configurations. A more fundamental limitation is that geometric and kinematic models of an operation's final state are not always a complete specification of the desired operation. One example of this is the need to specify how hard to tighten a bolt during an assembly. In general, a complete description of a task may need to include parameters of the operations used to reach one task state from another.

The alternative to task specification by a sequence of model states is specification by a sequence of operations. Thus, instead of building a model of an object in its desired configuration, we can describe the operation by which it can be achieved. The description should still be object oriented, not robot oriented; for example, the target torque for tightening a bolt should be specified relative to the bolt and not the manipulator. Most operations also include a goal statement involving spatial relationships between objects. The spatial relationships given in the goal specification not only describe configurations but also indicate the physical relationships between objects that should be achieved by the operation. Specifying that two surfaces are *against* each other, for example, should produce a compliant motion that moves until the contact is actually detected, not a motion to the configuration where contact is supposed to occur. For these reasons, existing proposals for task-level programming languages have adopted an operation-centered approach to task specification [Lieberman and Wesley 1977, Lozano-Pérez 1976]. ATLAS also assumes this form of input.

Previous Work—A number of task-level language systems have been proposed, but no complete system has been implemented. In this section we briefly review these proposals.

Research at Stanford—The Stanford Hand-Eye system [Feldman et al. 1971] was the first of the task-level system proposals. A subset of this proposal called Move-Instance was implemented [Paul 1972]. This program chose stable grasping positions on polyhedra and planned a motion to approach and move the object. The planning did not involve obstacle avoidance (except for the table surface) or the planning of sensory operations.

The initial definition of AL [Finkel et al. 1974] called for the ability to specify models in AL and to allow specification of operations in terms of these models. This has been the subject of some research [Binford 1979, Taylor 1976], but the results have not been incorporated into the existing AL system. Some additional work within the context of Stanford's Acronym system [Brooks 1981] has dealt with planning grasp positions [Binford 1979], but AL has been viewed as the target language rather than the user language.

Taylor discusses an approach to the synthesis of sensor-based AL programs from task-level specifications [Taylor 1976]. Taylor's method relies on representing prototypical motion strategies for particular tasks as parameterized robot programs, known as *procedure skeletons*. A skeleton has all the motions, error tests, and computations needed to carry out a task, but many of the parameters needed to specify motions and tests remain to be specified. The applicability of a particular skeleton to a task depends on the presence of certain features in the model and the values of parameters such as clearances and uncertainties. Choices among alternative strategies for a single operation are made by first computing the values of a set of parameters specific to the task, such as

References pp. 324-327

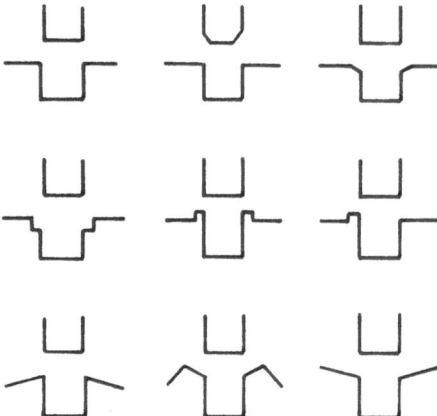

Figure 2. *Similar peg-in-hole tasks which require different strategies.*

the magnitude of uncertainty region for the peg in peg-in-hole insertion, and then using these parameters to choose the best (for example, fastest) strategy. Having chosen a strategy, the planner computes the additional parameters needed to specify the strategy motions, such as grasp positions and approach positions. A program is produced by inserting these parameters into the procedure skeleton that implements the chosen strategy.

Taylor's work on making planning decisions by manipulating constraints on positions that explicitly model error was significantly extended by Brooks [Brooks 1982]. The principal extension was the use of these symbolic constraints not only forwards to get error bounds but backwards to restrict the choices on plan variables and to introduce appropriate sensing into the program. This approach underlies much of ATLAS and is described in detail later.

The approach to strategy synthesis based on procedure skeletons assumes that task geometry for common subtasks is predictable and can be divided into a manageable number of classes, each requiring a different skeleton. This assumption is needed because the sequence of motions in the skeleton will only be consistent with a particular class of geometries. The assumption does not seem to be true in general. In particular, the presence of additional surfaces in tasks may generate unexpected contacts, leading to failures. This approach is in contrast to an approach which derives the strategy directly from consideration of the task description [Lozano-Pérez et al. 1984]. In the ATLAS design, both types of approaches play a role.

The LAMA system—The LAMA system was designed at MIT [Lozano-Pérez 1976, Lozano-Pérez and Winston 1977] as a task-level language, but was only partially implemented. LAMA formulated the relationship of task specification, obstacle avoidance, grasping, skeleton-based strategy synthesis, and error detection within one system. More recent work at MIT has explored issues in task planning in more detail outside the context of any particular system [Brooks

1982, 1983a, 1983b, Brooks and Lozano-Pérez 1983, Lozano-Pérez 1981, 1983, Lozano-Pérez *et al.* 1984, and Mason 1981, 1982].

The AUTOPASS system—AUTOPASS, developed at IBM [Lieberman and Wesley 1977], defined the syntax and semantics of a task-level language and an approach to its implementation. A subset of the most general operation, the PLACE statement, was implemented. The major part of the implementation effort focused on a method for planning collision-free paths for Cartesian robots among polyhedral obstacles [Lozano-Pérez and Wesley 1979].

The RAPT system—RAPT [Popplestone *et al.* 1978] is an implemented system for transforming symbolic specifications of geometric goals, together with a program which specifies the directions of the motions but not their length, into a sequence of end-effector positions. RAPT's emphasis has been primarily on task specification; it has not dealt yet with obstacle avoidance, automatic grasping or sensory operations.

LM-GEO and ROBEX systems—Some robot-level language systems have proposed extensions to allow some task-level specifications. LM-GEO is an implemented extension to LM [Latombe and Mazer 1981] which incorporates symbolic specifications of destinations. The specification of ROBEX [Weck and Zuhlke 1981] includes the ability to automatically plan collision-free motions and to generate programs that use sensory information available during execution. A full-blown ROBEX, including these capabilities, has not been implemented.

OVERVIEW OF THE ATLAS SYSTEM

The geometry of the world determines how ATLAS refines a given sequence of object motions into a detailed plan of action, including sensing steps, to be carried out by a manipulator.

Because of the complex interactions between the plan's steps, ATLAS must refine each step with as little commitment as possible to decisions within that refinement until the effects of decisions made in refining other of the plan's steps are known. One approach might be to generate all the constraints that each step implies for other steps and ultimately pick a set of motions and sense operations satisfying all those constraints. However, because of the number of possibilities in refining a single step and the interdependencies between steps, we cannot in general obtain a complete set of constraints without making some decisions within individual steps. Hence the plan will fail if these decisions are incorrect. The planner therefore needs to employ a backtracking mechanism where decisions can be made and later undone in case of failure.

The ATLAS approach is first to model all plan steps at a broad level (as instantiated plan skeletons) and generate all constraints which the steps imply for every one of their possible refinements. The effects of the constraints are propagated throughout the complete plan. Then each step is refined into further de-

References pp. 324-327

tail. Again constraints are propagated and, in case of failure, dependency-directed backtracking occurs.

The order in which steps are refined depends on the type of operation they describe and their sensitivity to decisions made elsewhere in the plan. For example, gross motion planning is done last, as it is almost completely insensitive to any fine motion strategies or sensing operations planned elsewhere. On rare occasions the choice of sensor location or jig layout for some force-directed motion strategy might block the workspace and make gross motion planning impossible. On the other hand, the position of a workpiece relative to a sensor can affect whether the sensor can make useful measurements on it. Thus sensing operations should be planned before the workspace is laid out, so that constraints from those operations can be taken into account.

Constraints as a Communication Mechanism—The key to the above is the ability to represent and manipulate geometric constraints, and to distinguish between that which is not yet decided in the planning process and that which cannot be known even at plan execution time due to manipulator error, sensor error and parts tolerances. Brooks devised a scheme which is used by ATLAS [Brooks 1982].

Constraints are represented by inequalities between explicit expressions over formal variables. These variables are of three types: *physical quantity variables, plan variables,* and *uncertainty variables.* There are two legal classes of expressions over these types: expressions which can include both plan and uncertainty variables, and expressions containing only physical quantities. The two classes of expressions can appear on opposite sides of an inequality or an equality. The semantics of the variables are as follows:

- *Physical quantity variables*—These represent actual physical quantities in the real world. They are used to label quantities in the geometric world model.

- *Plan variables*—These represent quantities whose values must be decided by the time of plan execution. Values for them are chosen as part of the planning process. Plan variables provide a mechanism for deferring decisions during planning, and constraints including plan variables provide a representation for reasoning about the implications of how those decisions will turn out. Often plan variables are used to represent nominal values for physical quantities.

- *Uncertainty variables*—These represent quantities whose values can never be known, even at plan execution time; usually they represent the difference between a physical quantity and the nominal value which will be chosen for it by the planner. Thus they represent uncertainties in the planner's and plan executor's knowledge of the state of the world. Although their values can never be known, bounds on their magnitudes can either be known *a priori* (*e.g.*, the manufacturing tolerance of a workpiece) or can be deduced by reasoning about the motions and sense operations leading up to the establishment of the appropriate physical quantity.

To illustrate these concepts consider the two-dimensional situation shown in Figure 3. The workpiece, a box, is to be placed somewhere on a table by a two link manipulator. Suppose the error, e in the x direction, made by the manipulator in trying to place the box with a planned x coordinate p_x is given by

$$-0.2+0.005 \times p_x \le e \le 0.2-0.005 \times p_x. \tag{1}$$

Further, suppose that the working range of the manipulator is such that commanded positions for the box must satisfy

$$5 \le p_x \le 20. \tag{2}$$

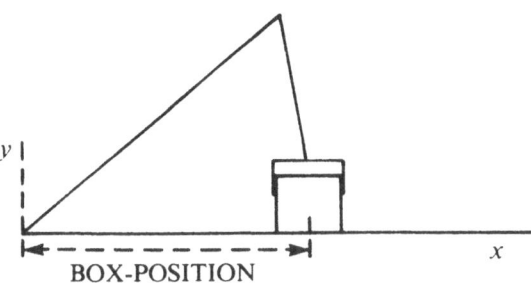

Figure 3. *Definition of BOX-POSITION*

We represent the constraints so placed on the physical situation by using three variables:

- BOX-POSITION: a physical quantity variable representing the actual physical value which will be achieved as the x coordinate of where the box will be placed.

- BOX-NOM: a plan variable representing the nominal value which will be chosen during planning and will be passed to the robot controller as the destination position commanded for the manipulator's motion while grasping the box.

- BOX-UNC: an uncertainty variable representing the error which will be made by the manipulator in placement of the box.

The above definitions imply

$$\text{BOX-POSITION} = \text{BOX-NOM} + \text{BOX-UNC}. \tag{3}$$

This provides a link from the geometric representation of the world, where BOX-POSITION is a parameter, to the constraint language which will be used in reasoning during the planning process.

References pp. 324-327

The facts about the manipulator mentioned above when applied to the physical action of moving the box to its destination give two constraints on the plan and uncertainty variables. The reach of the manipulator determines plausible planned locations for the box, that is,

$$5 \leq \text{BOX-NOM} \leq 20$$

and the manipulator accuracy determines bounds on the uncertainty in the physical location of the box as a function of the commanded position for it, yielding

$$-0.2 + 0.005 \times \text{BOX-NOM} \leq \text{BOX-UNC} \leq 0.2 - 0.005 \times \text{BOX-NOM}. \quad (4)$$

Given a suitable inference engine [Brooks 1981], we can now make deductions useful for the planning process. For instance, no matter which legal value is chosen for the nominal box position, the uncertainty about where it will actually be placed is no bigger than ± 0.175. Conversely, if during the planning process it becomes necessary to ensure that the position of the box is known to ± 0.15, then two possibilities are that the nominal position be constrained by

$$10 \leq \text{BOX-NOM}$$

or by introducing a sense operation immediately after placement of the box to see where it was placed. In the latter case the sensor must be chosen, and the nominal value of the box position may need to be constrained, so that the box will be within a region where the sensor error is bounded by ± 0.15.

Geometric models, equalities such as equation (3), and inequalities such as equation (4) thus combine to form representations of classes of physical situations. Each physical situation in a class corresponds to one or more points in the satisfying set of all the inequalities. Such points with different values for plan variables correspond to different refinements of a plan. Points with identical values for all plan variables, but different values for uncertainty variables correspond to different physical realizations of a single planned situation.

The Modules—The task planner consists of a *constraint propagator* and a *skeleton matcher* along with three planning modules; other modules might be added. The planning modules are a *fine motion planner*, a *grasp planner*, and a *gross motion planner*. The planner also has a library of *plan skeletons*.

Constraints are propagated between plan steps, providing the propagator with constraints on layout and enabling it to introduce sensing steps when necessary. Initially plan steps are modeled by instantiated plan skeletons, and are later refined into more detail by the planning modules. Constraint propagation continues as the plan is refined, propagating the interrelating constraints back and forth between plan steps.

Broadly speaking, each planning module is given a class of situations for which it must produce a detailed plan step. The planning module can

- Fail, with no reason given,

- Fail, giving a reason and perhaps incorporating a suggestion to change the given situation, or

- Succeed, producing a detailed plan and perhaps a further set of constraints which should be applied to the given situation in order to refine it further.

Furthermore, each planning module can act as a generator of success/restriction pairs. As it is reinvoked it generates another solution or, eventually, fails. The generators define the search space for the constraint-propagation-triggered backtracking. The restrictions associated with each solution give the backtracking dependency direction (see, for example [Stallman and Sussman 1977]).

Control Structure—The task-level plan specification consists of a series of changes in location for objects in the workspace. These can be deduced by comparing consecutive world descriptions. The task planner then proceeds with the following phases.

Phase 1. The executive turns each motion into a sequence consisting of

- Gross manipulator motion

- Grasp

- Gross manipulator motion

- Fine motion

- Ungrasp

Phase 2. Every one of these plan steps is then instantiated by a skeleton. This is done by the skeleton matcher. It is guaranteed to find a skeleton which matches. All gross manipulator motions are matched by the same skeleton, as are grasps and ungrasps. Some fine motions will be matched by specific skeletons (such as bolt-in-hole) and the remainder are matched by a catch-all skeleton for synthesized fine motion, called SFM below. Skeleton matching includes identification of different physical locations. Each location is associated with the plan step where it first gains physical meaning (for instance, the position of an object on a table first becomes real during the put-down fine motion of the manipulator).

Phase 3. A dependency analysis is carried out for locations; that is, it is determined which physical placements of objects depend on others. The analysis forms multiple fibers running through a linear arrangement of plan steps, sometimes skipping over one or more steps.

Phase 4. Precondition and propagation constraints, for example, equations (2) and (1), are propagated through the plan from one plan step to another. Sometimes the preconditions, called *applicability constraints* below, will not be guaranteed to be satisfied. In that case backing up may be necessary. The dependency graph is followed. Backing up can introduce sensing. Skeletons for synthesized fine motion cannot be backed through directly. It is possible, however, to make certain inferences concerning whether sensing will be necessary and the minimum bounds on the cost of sensing. These are used to direct the backtracking. Note that this phase does not guarantee a workable plan, even at this level of abstraction. It is essentially a branch and bound search and later it may turn out that some bounds were incorrect and more sensing will be necessary in non-SFM steps than is produced at this point. If a non-SFM fine motion skeleton causes failure, as discussed below, then the skeleton generator for that motion is reinvoked, a new skeleton is selected, and this phase is repeated.

Phase 5. We now have some constraints on many of the locations. With these we do a coarse layout, identifying large reasonable areas to place planned locations. For each SFM step the manipulator error is analyzed over these large areas, which may be partitioned into subsets having widely different error ball upper bounds. The partitions are ordered with the smallest error bound first, and a list of pairs of error balls and work areas is formed. These will be used to drive generators for syntheses of fine motion strategies. If all possible gross layouts have already been tried, then the planner fails.

Phase 6. For each SFM generator we look at its first error ball and work area but do not remove them from the generator list. If an actual fine motion synthesis has not yet been done for this step of the plan, we then do it. The result is a series of sets R from which the synthesized fine motion is guaranteed to succeed. The fine motion planner also generates a *guard volume* where the motion will happen. This volume is the subject of the layout phase, Phase 10. If an SFM generator is already exhausted, then we back up to Phase 5 for a new gross layout.

Phase 7. Using branch and bound on cost estimates, we propagate constraints through the plan with the old SFM skeletons replaced by actual fine motions. The smallest set R (of initial locations) is chosen for each fine motion which can be guaranteed to be reached (*i.e.*, the manipulator error ball fits inside it). If some fine motion causes plan failure, then it is removed from its generator and we back up to Phase 6 for a new synthesis.

Phase 8. For each object which must be grasped, we generate a list of possible grasp configurations ordered by criteria such as firmness of grip and accessibility of the grasp surfaces. A grasp depends on both the initial configuration of the object and its goal configuration. The interaction of the hand with the fine motion at the end of any gross motion of the object must also be considered. If we fail to find any grasp at all, some new terminal strategy must be necessary, so we back up to Phase 6 for a new fine motion synthesis. The actual positions of the grasp might depend on plan variables. Each grasp produces a guard volume which must be free of obstacles so that the hand can fit in a position necessary to achieve the grasp. Note that the guard volume, appropriately translated and perhaps reoriented, must be free both at pick up and at put down. The first grasp in the list of grasps is used in subsequent planning phases, although these later phases may back up to this phase for a new grasp.

Phase 9. Constraints are propagated through the plan, moving forward until some precondition constraints are not met, and then backing up to introduce sensing or otherwise constrain plan variables. This phase is essentially a repeat of Phase 4, except that we have more detailed instantiations of each plan step. Thus we can now back through fine motion steps and perhaps introduce sensing steps to achieve the preconditions necessary for the success of such steps. Failure during constraint propagation can only be due to a synthesized fine motion having excessively strong preconditions. In that case planning is backed up to Phase 6 for a new fine motion synthesis.

Phase 10. Actual physical locations for the initial location of every object and for the nominal locations to be used in all intermediate steps of the plan are now chosen. This is the detailed layout of the workspace. On failure due to clutter of some work area by numerous objects and tasks (such as may happen in an area where the manipulator is most accurate) we back up to Phase 5 for a new gross layout. The result is that new, more difficult, fine motion syntheses will have to be carried out which will succeed in areas with less accurate manipulator characteristics. On failure due to the impossibility of keeping a guard volume free for the hand, we return to Phase 8 for the next available grasp.

Phase 11. Collision-free motions for the manipulator must be planned in order to achieve each gross change in location of objects, and to move the manipulator from the release of one object to the acquisition of the next. If gross motion planning fails, then we back up to either Phase 5 (gross layout), Phase 8 (grasp analysis) or Phase 10 (detailed layout), depending on the reason for failure. If no path could be found for the payload due to reorientation difficulties, then we variously try tweaking detailed layout in Phase 10 (such as making wider corridors of free space at the failed path segments) or retry the grasp analysis at Phase 8 (such as selecting candidate grasps which place a different part of the object along the center of rotation of the last manipulator joint axis). If collisions with the upperarm or forearm were the main problem, then we back up to Phase 5 for a new gross layout of the workspace.

Skeletons—A plan skeleton models a step in a plan in terms of its inputs and outputs. The idea is that the details of the step can be treated as a black box by the rest of the plan, the rest being only affected by the input/output behavior of an individual plan step.

Skeletons can describe plan steps at different levels of detail. For instance there might be a skeleton for pick-up used early in the planning process. Later in the process the action might be modeled by a series of four finer plan steps each instantiated by a skeleton (*e.g.*, gross manipulator motion, fine manipulator motion, grasp and gross manipulator motion).

A skeleton is specified by a geometric description of objects and their state in a world and by two sets of constraints: a set of *applicability constraints* and a set of *propagation constraints*. The skeleton is instantiated by finding a match between the geometric description and the known world state. Both sets of constraints in the skeleton are expressed in variables which are instantiated by physical quantity variables as a byproduct of the geometric matching.

References pp. 324-327

Once instantiated, the feasibility of using such a plan step can be considered. If the applicability constraints are satisfied by a physical situation, then the plan step modeled by the skeleton is guaranteed to succeed. The propagation constraints put bounds on the possible physical situations which can be produced by the plan step given any initial situation satisfying the applicability constraints.

Consider, as an example, a skeleton to describe insertion of a peg into a hole. For simplicity we will assume a two-dimensional world and ignore the details of vertical motions even in that world. To match a physical situation and plan step there must be a bolt and a hole. The applicability constraint set consists of

$$\text{PEG-SHAFT-RADIUS} \leq \text{HOLE-RADIUS},$$

$$\text{PEG-TIP-RADIUS} - \text{HOLE-RADIUS}$$
$$\leq \text{HOLE-POSITION} - \text{PEG-POSITION}$$
$$\leq \text{HOLE-RADIUS} - \text{PEG-TIP-RADIUS},$$

and

$$nominal(\text{HOLE-POSITION}) = nominal(\text{PEG-POSITION}).$$

The propagation constraint set is simply:

$$\text{PEG-SHAFT-RADIUS} - \text{HOLE-RADIUS}$$
$$\leq \text{HOLE-POSITION} - \text{PEG-RESULT-POSITION}$$
$$\leq \text{HOLE-RADIUS} - \text{PEG-SHAFT-RADIUS}$$

and

$$nominal(\text{HOLE-POSITION}) = nominal(\text{PEG-RESULT-POSITION}).$$

The metafunction *nominal* refers to the planned value for a physical quantity.

Now consider the physical situation shown in Figure 4. The peg is labeled A and the hole is labeled B. In this example both the peg and hole have definite radii. After matching the skeleton to the physical situation, the constraint sets are instantiated as follows. The applicability constraints are:

$$0.2 \leq 0.25,$$

which is trivially true,

$$-0.20 \leq \text{B-POSITION} - \text{A-POSITION} \leq 0.20$$

and

$$nominal(\text{B-POSITION}) = nominal(\text{A-POSITION}),$$

while the propagation constraints are:

$$-0.05 \leq \text{B-POSITION} - \text{A-RESULT-POSITION} \leq 0.05$$

and

$$nominal(\text{B-POSITION}) = nominal(\text{A-RESULT-POSITION}).$$

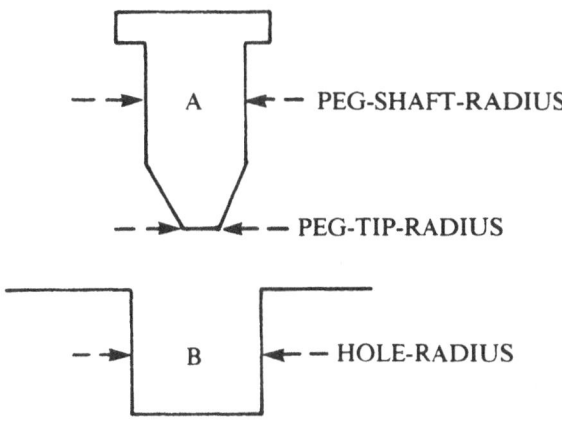

Figure 4. *Bolt-in-hole example.*

The physical quantities are expanded into plan and uncertainty components using

$$A\text{-POSITION} = B\text{-NOM} + A\text{-UNC}$$
$$B\text{-POSITION} = B\text{-NOM} + B\text{-UNC}$$
$$A\text{-RESULT-POSITION} = B\text{-NOM} + A\text{-RESULT-UNC}$$

where the equalities in the constraints are used to substitute equal values. The choice of using B-NOM as the nominal value for all three physical quantities is for readability only; internally it is more likely to be something like G0487. The constraint equalities have dictated that the peg should be nominally aligned with the hole before the insertion. This is manifested by the peg and hole being given the same nominal value in this step. The constraint propagator forces this to be true by, for instance, specifying the nominal end point of the previous gross motion that moves the peg to the vicinity of the hole.

Now the applicability constraints reduce to:

$$-0.20 \le B\text{-UNC} - A\text{-UNC} \le 0.20$$

and the propagation constraints to:

$$-0.05 \le B\text{-UNC} - A\text{-RESULT-UNC} \le 0.05.$$

The methods developed in [Brooks 1982] can be used to find ways of guaranteeing that the applicability constraints are met. For instance it may be necessary to sense the position of the hole before a previous plan step of moving the peg to a nominal position above the hole. This sensing would give a new, more accurate estimate of the location of the hole which in turn would give a new B-NOM value and a better bound on the possible values for B-UNC.

Given a range of values for B-UNC, the propagation constraint determines a range of values for A-RESULT-UNC, the uncertainty in peg position after insertion. Later steps in the plan may need to examine this range to see whether it meets their applicability constraints.

Skeletons for many other actions can be produced similarly. They need not be used only to model actions in detail. The constraint sets might be very underconstraining, allowing minimal requirements for a large class of actions to be simultaneously considered. Such skeletons must later be replaced by detailed plans produced by one of the specialist planning modules.

A plausible small library of skeletons includes:

- Gross motion
- Grasp
- Bolt in hole
- Ungrasp
- Dead reckon vertical align (*i.e.*, stack)
- Synthesized fine motion (a catch-all)

The Planner Modules in More Detail—The three planning modules are briefly described here in general form. Later in this paper we discuss these in greater detail and examine the published work that describes implementations of specializations of each of the module descriptions.

All modules have access to a current context world model, which has specifications via geometric descriptions and algebraic constraints of all the parts whose locations have been decided exactly or at least have been constrained to some set of possibilities.

Fine motion—The planner determines compliant motions which ensure that the parts will reach one of the final configurations if started from within the specified range of initial locations. Typically the planning process will also place additional constraints on the legal initial locations.

Input to the fine motion module is:

- Initial locations of parts
- Goal specification
- Assembly constraints
- Error bounds

Output from the fine motion module is:

- Compliant motion strategy
- Legal initial locations for each motion
- Guard volume

As inputs, the fine motion planner is given the sets of possible initial locations for the parts and a specification of the range of legal final configurations. It is also given bounds on the errors in measuring the manipulator's position and the forces acting on it, and bounds on the error in controlling the position and velocity of the manipulator. Lastly, it may be given constraints on the motions; such constraints might forbid hitting some surfaces or exceeding bounds on forces.

In general, achieving a goal will require several motions. For each of these a region of initial locations and corresponding motions will be computed. The planner returns each of these regions as well as the corresponding motions. These regions can serve as alternative goals for the gross motion planner.

The fine motion planner assumes it has a complete description of the environment. In ATLAS, however, fine motion planning is done before a final layout of the environment is available. The planner computes a *guard volume* where the introduction of another object would affect the planned strategy. These guard volumes are used in the final layout phase.

Grasping—The planner determines where the part should be grasped and the desired orientation of the hand relative to the surface. The planner also must determine a sequence of motions that guarantee that the desired grasp configuration is reached in the presence of errors in manipulator positioning and part location.

Input to the grasping module is:

- Pick-up location of part
- Put-down destination of part
- Grasp constraints
- Error bounds

Output from the grasping model is:

- Grasp configurations
- Grasp motions
- Guard volume

As inputs, the grasp planner is given the pick-up and put-down locations for the part to be grasped, possibly in terms of plan variables. It is also given bounds on the position error of the part at the pick-up location. As in fine motion planning, the planner may be given constraints on where the part should, or should not, be grasped.

The choice of where to place the fingers depends not only on the part, but also on the environment near the part at the initial and final locations. As with fine motion planning, the grasp planner specifies a guard volume in which the presence of objects would require replanning.

Gross motion—The planner produces a set of gross manipulator motions (perhaps parameterized in terms of plan variables) which guarantee motion of the hand or payload from any point in the initial set of configurations to some point in the final set.

References pp. 324-327

Input to the gross motion module is:

- Start locations
- Goal locations
- Trajectory constraints
- Error bounds

Output from the gross motion module is:

- Path (may be null)
- Restricted start locations
- Restricted goal locations

The gross motion planner determines collision-free motions for the manipulator as it moves to the general location of an object in order to grasp it and as it transfers an object within the workspace. The two classes of motions can be treated by a single algorithm—the volume occupied by the hand changes depending on what is grasped.

The planner is given initial and goal sets of configurations for the hand. It is given bounds (perhaps parameterized) on the location error of any payload relative to the hand, and on the position control error of the manipulator. Lastly it may be given constraints which must be met by the trajectory. These are of two types. They can limit the class of trajectories considered (*e.g.*, it might be demanded that the payload be reoriented only about a vertical axis) or they can provide a criterion for which trajectory from the considered class should be chosen (*e.g.*, minimization of trajectory length or of payload reorientation).

Figure 5 shows an example of gross motion control for moving a point in two dimensions (this might be the configuration space of some moving object with a more interesting shape). The task is to move the point from the point d_0 in set A to somewhere in set B. Three commands are generated: MOVE TO d_1, MOVE TO d_2 and MOVE TO d_3. Each is a command to lower level servo routines to move in a straight line to the desired point (using pure position control). Due to manipulator inaccuracies the true destinations of the motion commands will lie in the error balls D_1, D_2 and D_3 respectively.

Notice that D_3 is wholly contained in set B, so if it is reached the gross motion will have been successful.

Due to manipulator inaccuracies, straight line motions will not necessarily be achieved. The shaded regions in Figure 5 show all possible paths, demonstrating that whatever motion actually occurs is guaranteed to be collision free.

FINE MOTION SYNTHESIS

The problem of automatically synthesizing a fine motion from a geometric description has received little attention in the literature. Previous approaches

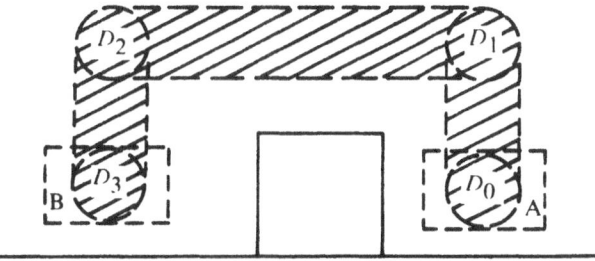

Figure 5. *Gross motion planning.*

were either based on skeletons [Taylor 1976, Lozano-Pérez 1976] or on learning strategies [Dufay and Latombe 1983]. In this section we outline an approach to automatic fine motion synthesis [Lozano-Pérez *et al.* 1984]. This approach is based on the notion of *configuration space* [Lozano-Pérez 1981, 1983, Brooks and Lozano-Pérez 1983]. (See the Appendix for a brief introduction.)

The fine motion planner constructs a sequence of motions which guarantee that some configuration from a specified range of goal configurations will be reached from anywhere within a computed range of start configurations. Each element in the motion sequence is a *guarded compliant motion* (in particular, a commanded velocity vector for a *generalized damper* [Whitney 1976]) and a termination predicate. The desired motion for a generalized damper is determined by the following relationship

$$f = B(v - v_0)$$

where f is the vector of forces acting on the moving object, v_0 is the commanded velocity vector, and v is the actual velocity vector. The effect of these compliant motions is to slide on the C-surfaces (see the Appendix) derived from the obstacles. When not in contact with a surface, the motion will be along the commanded vector (within some velocity uncertainty). The motion terminates when the associated predicate (a function of observed configuration, velocity, and elapsed time) evaluates to true.

Consider the simple task of moving the point p from its initial configuration to any one of the configurations in G (see Figure 6(b)). This is the C-space version of the two-dimensional peg-in-hole problem in Figure 6(a) when the axes of the peg and hole are constrained to be parallel. The basic step in the synthesis approach is to identify ranges of configurations from where p can reach G by a single motion. The directions of such motions can be represented as unit vectors, v_i. For each v_i, we can compute all those configurations, P_i, such that a motion along v_i from that configuration would reach some point of G. We call this range of configurations that can reach the goal by a single motion along a specified heading vector the *preimage* of the goal (for that vector). All we need do to guarantee that p reaches G from any point in any of the P_i is to use v_i as the commanded velocity vector for a damper.

References pp. 324-327

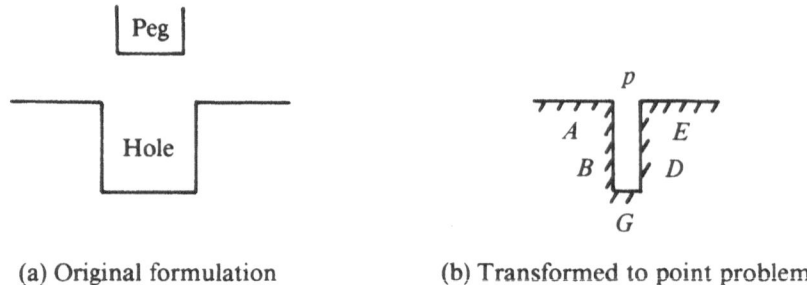

(a) Original formulation   (b) Transformed to point problem

Figure 6. Peg-in-hole problem.

The computation of preimages must take into account the possibility of the moving object sticking on a surface. In particular, assuming the motion is generated by a damper (with $B = b\mathrm{I}$), if the angle between the commanded velocity and the normal of a surface is less than the *friction angle* (the arctangent of the coefficient of friction) then the motion will *stick* on that surface.

If no preimage of G contains the peg's current configuration, then we can apply the same preimage computation recursively using each of the existing preimages as a possible goal. Each preimage of G, P_i, serves to define a new goal set. This process is repeated until some preimage contains some subset of the legal start configurations. From the chain of preimages we can construct a motion sequence.

One key problem in the synthesis method is discovering the sequence of command velocity vectors v_i. Our approach is to narrow in on feasible values of v_i by progressive refinement. We start with the complete range of possible v_i's and remove from that range any values that can possibly lead to failure (by sticking on a nongoal surface or by sliding away from the goal). At each step of the algorithm, we compute the preimage of the goal for the current *range* of v_i's. The preimage for a range of commanded velocities is the intersection of the preimages for each of the velocities. These are the configurations guaranteed to reach the goal for *all* the velocities in the range. If the preimage includes feasible starting configurations, then we have found a valid motion sequence, otherwise the current range of velocities must be narrowed further.

Figure 7 illustrates the method on a simple two-dimensional block-in-corner example. The directed graph shown there has nodes for each of the C-surfaces in the task and one node representing free C-space (C). There is a link from nodes m to n in the graph if some velocity in the current range may cause the robot to move from some point in m (which is not in n) to some point in n (which may be at the intersection of m and n) without going through points in any other node. We call this the *reachability graph* for that range of commanded velocities.

In the example, we start out with a range of commanded velocities including any velocity that will move p from nearby points onto the goal G (we diagram

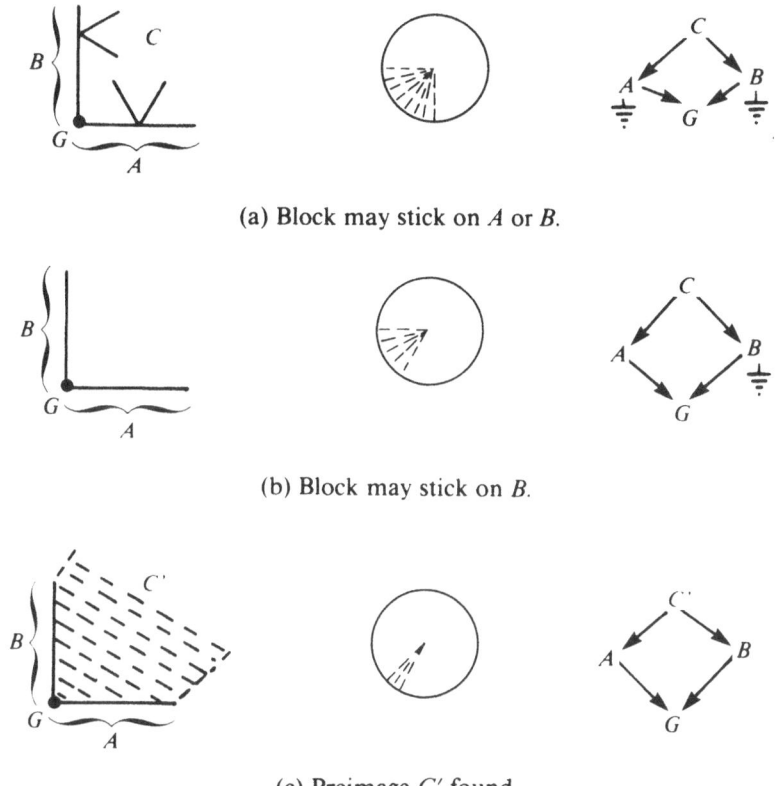

(a) Block may stick on A or B.

(b) Block may stick on B.

(c) Preimage C' found.

Figure 7. *Block-in-corner fine motion synthesis.*

ranges of commanded velocities as sectors of a circle). The reachability graph for this range of velocities is shown at the right in Figure 7(a). In these graphs, we have indicated those surfaces where the moving object may stick, using the electrical ground symbol. The potentially sticking surfaces are those whose friction cones overlap the current velocity range. At the left in Figure 7(a), two friction cones are shown for C-surfaces A and B. No preimage exists for the initial velocity range because of the possibility of sticking on either A or B. By removing velocities that may cause sticking on surface A or B from the current range of velocities, we obtain a velocity range for which a preimage (C') exists (Figure 7(c)). This preimage intersects the initial range of configurations, so a successful motion has been found.

The example above can be done with a single motion. We did not require recursive calls to the planner. In general, we have a choice of refining the range of directions or of using the current preimage as the goal for a recursive call to the same algorithm. This choice at each step defines the search space of motion sequences. Another important aspect of the approach is the synthesis of termination predicates for the motions [Lozano-Pérez *et al.* 1984].

References pp. 324-327

GRASPING

The problem of choosing a grasp point on an object has received significant attention in the literature [Paul 1972, Lozano-Pérez 1976, 1981, Wingham 1977, Brou 1980, Laugier 1981, Mason 1982, Laugier and Pertin 1983]. The approach to grasping described here is based on that described in [Lozano-Pérez 1981]; a more detailed treatment can be found there. This approach is also based on the notion of configuration space described in the Appendix.

The grasp planner chooses which object surfaces will be grasped and builds a description of the grasp configuration on those surfaces that satisfy the following constraints:

- The inside of the fingers are in contact with surfaces of P, the object to be grasped.
- There are no collisions between the manipulator hand and any nearby objects for any possible start configuration of P.
- There are no collisions between the manipulator hand and any nearby objects for any possible goal configuration of P.
- The grasp is stable, that is, can withstand forces generated during motion and assembly.

We assume that the manipulator hand is a parallel jaw. We further assume that the manipulator can be partitioned into an arm and a hand. The arm serves to place the wrist at any point in the workspace; the hand determines the final configuration of the gripper. This is a common kinematics configuration for manipulators and has a number of theoretical and practical advantages. The grasp planner determines candidate hand configurations; the gross motion planner must then pick some hand configuration that allows finding a collision-free path from the start to the goal.

The choice of grasp surfaces is done by ranking the surfaces on likelihood of finding a stable grasp and then choosing the highest ranked surface that leads to a feasible grasp configuration. A general treatment of stability in grasping is not yet available, although some promising approaches exist [Hanafusa and Asada 1977]. When the object to be grasped is small relative to the manipulator hand, two simple heuristics provide a fair chance of stable grasp (see also [Paul 1972, Brou 1980]). The heuristics are:

- Ensure at least a minimum contact area of the fingers with the grasp surfaces. The amount of overlap should depend on object properties such as weight and surface smoothness.
- The perpendicular projection of part P's center of mass should be near the contact area of the fingers and grasp surfaces.

The grasp planner computes feasible grasp configurations for the top-ranked candidate grasp surfaces. Note that, because the manipulator configuration will change while moving P from its start to its goal configuration, we represent the grasp configurations as the configuration of the hand relative to P. We can impose restrictions that reduce the dimensionality of the set of grasp configurations. One simple restriction, for parallel jaw hands, is to require that at least one of the surfaces grasped be planar (the other may be a planar surface, curved surface, edge, or vertex).

Let P_i be the planar face of P to be grasped, P_j be the other face (edge or vertex), and F_1 and F_2 be the inside faces of the manipulator's fingers. Under the restriction stated above, when P is grasped, either F_1 or F_2 is coplanar with P_i; without loss of generality, assume F_1 is coplanar with P_i. Under these conditions, the legal (x, y, z) positions of all points on the hand are restricted to be on some plane parallel to P_i. The hand may rotate about the normal to this plane. Let G be the set of configurations of the hand for which P_i and F_1 are coplanar. G is called the *grasp set* for P_i.

Not all the configurations in G are feasible grasp configurations, either because the fingers are not in contact with the grasp surfaces or because the corresponding manipulator configuration causes a collision (at the start or at the goal). The constraint that the fingers touch the grasp surfaces can be readily enforced by restricting the grasp set to be the intersection of those hand configurations for which F_1 overlaps P_i and those for which F_2 overlaps P_j. This intersection set can be computed explicitly in low-dimensional C-space [Lozano-Pérez 1981, 1983, Brooks and Lozano-Pérez 1983]. Similarly, those hand configurations, defined relative to P, that cause collisions with objects at the start or at the goal can be computed. The grasp set G can then be intersected with their complement to obtain the set of feasible grasp configurations.

Figure 8 shows an example of the feasible grasp computation: (a) the pick-up and put-down orientations of the hand, (b) C-space obstacles at pick-up (the shaded region is the accessible part of the grasp set), (c) C-space obstacles at put-down, (d) put-down obstacles that constrain the grasp set further.

If P is free to move during the grasping operation and its initial position is not known to high accuracy, then the grasp planner must take into consideration the possible motions during planning. This is quite difficult in general [Mason 1982].

GROSS MOTION

After a trickle of early work on collision-free gross motion planning, there has been a recent avalanche of new ideas and developments.

The earliest reasonably general algorithms for manipulators were for the Stanford arm (which has one sliding and five revolute joints). One was implemented [Udupa 1977] and the other partially implemented [Widdoes 1974]. Both relied on approximations for the payload, limited wrist action, and tesselation of joint space to describe forbidden and free regions of real space. The problem with tesselation schemes is that to get adequate motion control a multidimensional space must be finely tesselated.

References pp. 324-327

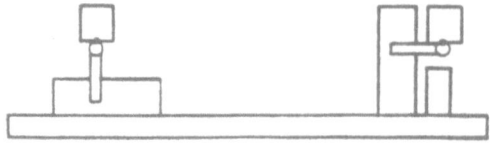

(a) Pick-up and put-down orientations

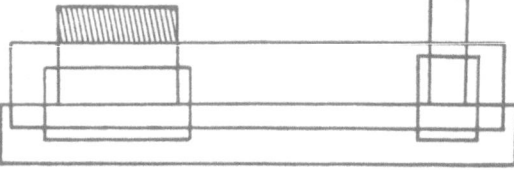

(b) C-space obstacles at pick-up

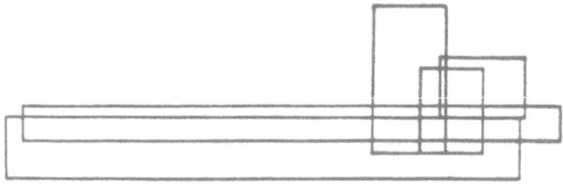

(c) C-space obstacles at put-down

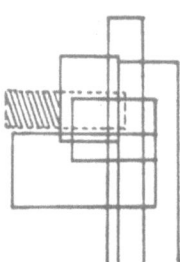

(d) Put-down obstacles that further constrain grasp set

Figure 8. *Grasp set computations.*

Lozano-Pérez presented an implemented algorithm for Cartesian manipulators. Cartesian manipulators have three sliding joints whose axes are orthogonal and thus can be used as the axes of space representation. Lozano-Pérez's algorithm used configuration space for the Cartesian portion of the manipulator (where the natural Euclidean axes of the configuration space correspond exactly to the joints of the manipulator) and subdivided ranges of angles for the hand, within each of which a bounding volume for the hand and payload is used [Lozano-Pérez 1981].

Schwartz and Sharir have shown that the problem is polynomial in the number of obstacle surfaces for a manipulator with a fixed number of joints. If n is the number of obstacle surfaces, the running time of their algorithm is $O(n^{64})$ for a six degree-of-freedom manipulator. It is, therefore, primarily of theoretical interest and not meant to be implemented [Schwartz and Sharir 1982].

Brooks and Lozano-Pérez have developed a practical and implemented algorithm for polygonal obstacle avoidance which produces paths which require arbitrarily difficult rotations up to a preset resolution [Brooks and Lozano-Pérez 1983].

Brooks developed a new representation for two-dimensional free space as overlapping freeways [Brooks 1983a]. This has led to the development and implementation of a gross motion algorithm for pick and place operations for a manipulator with revolute joints [Brooks 1983b]. The key idea is that free space should be explicitly represented in such terms that it is easy to determine the collision-free motion segments that can be made by the manipulator and its payload. Individual legal motion segments are linked to form a complete motion for the manipulator.

See Figure 9 for a diagram of the PUMA. Brooks' algorithm decomposes the problem by spending two degrees of freedom of the manipulator to partially decouple the payload and the upperarm of the manipulator. In the six degree of freedom PUMA, it keeps joint 4 fixed (there is no joint 4 for the five degree of freedom PUMA) and uses joint 5 to compensate for the payload orientation for the motions of the upper and forearms. Joint 6 is free to reorient the payload about its vertical axis, but such reorientation does not require motion of either the upper or the forearm—it is completely decoupled. This is only two-dimensional rotation. There is still coupling of translations of the payload and the motion of the upper links of the arm. A major new contribution of the algorithm is that motion of the components can at first be analyzed separately and then, later, constraints are propagated between the solutions to account for the remaining coupling.

The algorithm finds paths where the payload is moved in straight lines, either horizontal or vertical, and is only reoriented by rotations about the vertical axis of the world coordinate system. Thus only four degrees of freedom are considered for the PUMA.

The payload and the hand are merged geometrically, and the payload is considered to be a prism, with convex cross section. The payload can rotate about the vertical as joint 6 rotates.

Obstacles in the work space are of two types: those supported from below and those hanging from above. Both are prisms with convex cross sections. Nonconvex obstacles can be modeled by overlapping prisms. Prisms can be supported from below if they rest on the workspace table or on one another as long as they are fully supported. Thus no point in free space ever has a bottom supported obstacle above it. Such obstacle descriptions have been extracted from depth

References pp. 324-327

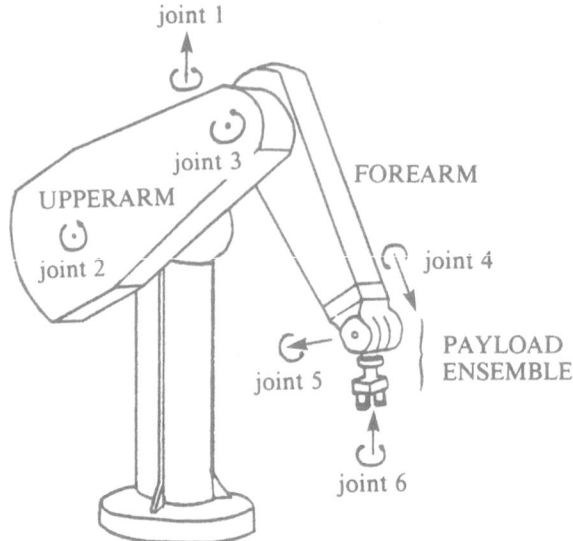

Figure 9. *Unimation PUMA manipulator.*

measurements from a stereo pair of overhead cameras. The algorithm has generated collision-free paths from that data.

Similar predefined obstacles may also hang from above, intruding into the workspace of the upperarm and forearm. Obstacles are precluded from a cylinder surrounding the manipulator base.

The class of motions allowed suffices for many assembly operations, and, with as yet unknown algorithms for reorienting the payload without major arm motion, the algorithm could provide gross motion planning for all but the most difficult realistic problems.

CONCLUSIONS

In this paper we have proposed an architecture for a new task-level system, which we call ATLAS (Automatic Task Level Assembly Synthesizer). Our goal has been to define a unified framework for existing and future research on task planning. We have summarized approaches to several of the key problems in task planning: fine motion synthesis, grasping, and gross motion planning. These areas are relatively mature. Some other areas such as automatic parts layout, feeding, and fixturing have received significantly less attention. We plan a prototype implementation of ATLAS in the next few years where the focus will be on the interaction between the modules described in this paper.

ACKNOWLEDGEMENTS

This report describes research done at the Artificial Intelligence Laboratory of the Massachusetts Institute of Technology. Support for the Laboratory's Artificial Intelligence research is provided in part by the Systems Development Foundation, in part by the Office of Naval Research under Office of Naval Research contract N00014-81-K-0494, and in part by the Advanced Research Projects Agency under Office of Naval Research contracts N00014-80-C-0505 and N00014-82-K-0334.

APPENDIX: CONFIGURATION SPACE

A *configuration* of an object is the set of parameters needed to completely specify the position of all points of the object. The configuration of a rigid two-dimensional object, for example, can be specified by two displacements and an angle, that of a rigid three-dimensional object by three displacements and three angles, and that of a robot arm by its joint angles. For concreteness, we will be dealing exclusively with Cartesian configurations, for example (x,y,θ) for objects in the plane, and not joint angle configurations. The space of all possible configurations for an object is known as the configuration space *(C-space)* of that object [Lozano-Pérez 1981, 1983]. An object A is represented as a point in its C-space; the coordinates of that point are the configuration parameters of A.

Stationary obstacles in the environment of a moving object A can be mapped into the configuration space of A. The resulting *C-space obstacles* are those configurations of A which would lead to collisions between A and the obstacles. Configurations on the surface of the C-space obstacle due to B are those where some surface of A is just touching a surface of B. If A and B are both three-dimensional polyhedra, the surfaces of the C-space obstacle for B arise from each of the feasible contacts between vertices, edges, and faces of A and B (see Figure 10) [Lozano-Pérez 1983]. Therefore, each face of a C-space obstacle represents a particular type of geometric constraint on A. A range of positions (and orientations) of A can be represented as a volume in the C-space of A and a motion of A is a curve in the C-space.

As an illustration of the use of C-space surfaces, consider the familiar two-dimensional peg-in-hole problem from Figure 6. We can construct a three-dimensional C-space of (x,y,θ) configurations of the peg. In this space, the hole defines an obstacle (see Figure 11(a)). Note that although the resulting surfaces are curved, for each value of θ the (x,y) cross section of the C-space surfaces is polygonal. The surfaces represent one-point contacts and the edges at the intersections of surfaces represent two-point contacts. Line-line contacts also give rise to edges at the intersections of one-point contact surfaces. Figure 11(b) shows cross sections for a peg and a chamfered hole.

The C-space representation can be extended to more general kinematic situations. In general, motion subject to geometric and kinematic constraints can be

References pp. 324-327

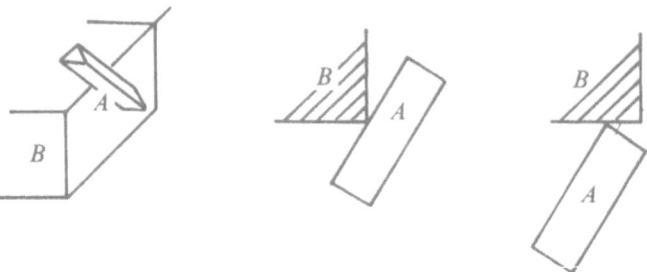

Figure 10. *Geometric conditions giving rise to C-surfaces.*

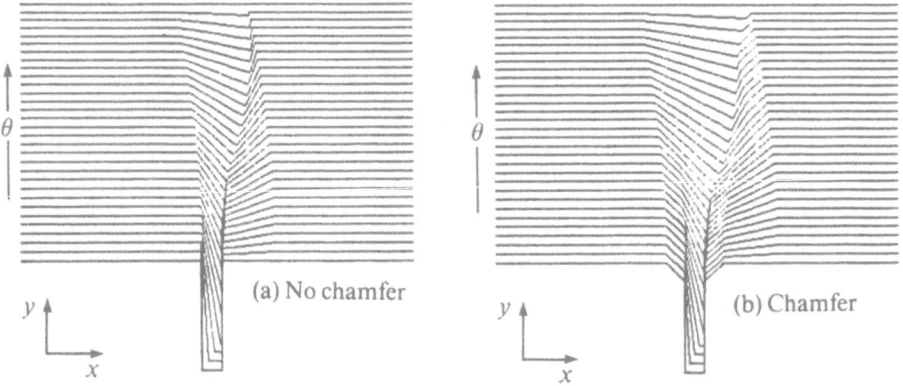

Figure 11. *Cross sections of peg-in-hole C-surfaces*

defined as collections of equalities and inequalities that must hold among the parameters that determine the configurations of the robot and the objects in the task. These inequalities represent C-surfaces [Mason 1981]. Take the constraint that a robot hand remain in contact with a crank handle as it rotates. The constraint relating the position of the hand, (x,y), to the position of the crank (a constant) and its current angle, α, is a curve (one-dimensional surface) in the configuration space of the task, that is the (x,y,α) space.

REFERENCES

[Binford 1979]
   T. O. Binford, "The AL Language for Intelligent Robots," IRIA Seminar on Languages and Methods of Programming Industrial Robots, Rocquencourt, France, June 1979.

[Brooks 1981]
   R. A. Brooks, "Symbolic Reasoning among 3-D Models and 2-D Images," *Artificial Intelligence*, Vol. 17, 1981, pp. 285–348.

[Brooks 1982]
R. A. Brooks, "Symbolic Error Analysis and Robot Planning," *The International Journal of Robotics Research*, Vol. 1, No. 4, Winter 1982, pp. 29–68.

[Brooks 1983a]
R. A. Brooks, "Solving the Find-Path Problem by Good Representation of Free Space," *IEEE Transactions on Systems, Man and Cybernetics*, Vol. SMC-13, No. 2, March/April 1983, pp. 190–197.

[Brooks 1983b]
R. A. Brooks, "Plannning Collision Free Motions for Pick and Place Operations," *Proceedings of the First International Symposium on Robotics Research*, Bretton Woods, New Hampshire, August 1983.

[Brooks and Lozano-Pérez 1983]
R. A. Brooks and T. Lozano-Pérez, "A Subdivision Algorithm in Configuration Space for Findpath with Rotation," *Proceedings of the Eighth International Joint Conference on Artificial Intelligence*, Karlsruhe, West Germany, August 8-12, 1983, pp. 799–806.

[Brou 1980]
P. Brou, "Implementation of High-Level Commands for Robots," M. S. Thesis, Department of Electrical Engineering and Computer Science, Massachusetts Institute of Technology, Cambridge, Massachusetts, December 1980.

[Dufay and Latombe 1983]
B. Dufay and J. C. Latombe, "An Approach to Automatic Robot Programming based on Inductive Learning," *Proceedings of the First International Symposium on Robotics Research*, Bretton Woods, New Hampshire, August 1983.

[Feldman et al. 1971]
J. Feldman et al., "The Stanford Hand-Eye Project," *Proceedings of the First International Conference on Artificial Intelligence*, London, England, September 1971.

[Finkel et al. 1974]
R. Finkel, R. Taylor, R. Bolles, R. Paul, and J. Feldman, "AL, a Programming System for Automation," Artificial Intelligence Laboratory Memo AIM-243 (also published as Computer Science Report STAN-CS-74-456), Stanford University, Stanford, California, November 1974.

[Grossman and Taylor 1978]
D. D. Grossman and R. H. Taylor, "Interactive Generation of Object Models with a Manipulator," *IEEE Transactions on Systems, Man and Cybernetics*, Vol. SMC-8, No. 9, September 1978, pp. 667–689.

[Hanafusa and Asada 1977]
H. Hanafusa and H. Asada, "A Robotic Hand with Elastic Fingers and Its Application to Assembly Process," *IFAC Symposium on Information and Control Problems in Manufacturing Technology*, Tokyo, Japan, 1977.

[Latombe and Mazer 1981]
J. C. Latombe and E. Mazer, "LM: A High-Level Programming Language for Controlling Assembly Robots," *Proceedings of the Eleventh International Symposium on Industrial Robots*, Tokyo, Japan, October 7-9, 1981, pp. 680–683.

[Laugier 1981]
C. Laugier, "A Program for Automatic Grasping of Objects with a Robot Arm," *Proceedings of the Eleventh International Symposium on Industrial Robots*, Tokyo, Japan, October 7-9, 1981, pp. 287–294.

[Laugier and Pertin 1983]
C. Laugier and J. Pertin, "Automatic Grasping: A Case Study in Accessibility Analysis," Laboratoire IMAG Report No. 342, Saint Martin d'Heres, France, January 1983.

[Lieberman and Wesley 1977]
L. I. Lieberman and M. A. Wesley, "AUTOPASS: An Automatic Programming System for Computer Controlled Mechanical Assembly," *IBM Journal of Research and Development*, Vol. 21, No. 4, July 1977, pp. 321-334.

[Lozano-Pérez 1976]
T. Lozano-Pérez, "The Design of a Mechanical Assembly System," Artificial Intelligence Laboratory Technical Report No. TR-397, Massachusetts Institute of Technology, Cambridge, Massachusetts, December 1976.

[Lozano-Pérez 1981]
T. Lozano-Pérez, "Automatic Planning of Manipulator Transfer Movements," *IEEE Transactions on Systems, Man and Cybernetics*, Vol. SMC-11, No. 10, October 1981, pp. 681-698.

[Lozano-Pérez 1983]
T. Lozano-Pérez, "Spatial Planning: A Configuration Space Approach," *IEEE Transactions on Computers*, Vol. C-32, No. 2, February 1983, pp. 108-120.

[Lozano-Pérez and Wesley 1979]
T. Lozano-Pérez and M. A. Wesley, "An Algorithm for Planning Collision-Free Paths among Polyhedral Obstacles," *Communications of the ACM*, Vol. 22, No. 10, October 1979, pp. 560-570.

[Lozano-Pérez and Winston 1977]
T. Lozano-Pérez and P. H. Winston, "LAMA: A Language for Automatic Mechanical Assembly," *Proceedings of the 5th International Joint Conference on Artificial Intelligence*, Cambridge, Massachusetts, August 1977, pp. 710-716.

[Lozano-Pérez et al. 1984]
T. Lozano-Pérez, M. T. Mason, and R. H. Taylor, "Automatic Synthesis of Fine-Motion Strategies for Robots," *International Journal of Robotics Research*, Vol. 3, No. 1, Spring 1984, pp. 3-24.

[Mason 1981]
M. T. Mason, "Compliance and Force Control for Computer Controlled Manipulators," *IEEE Transactions on Systems, Man and Cybernetics*, Vol. SMC-11, No. 6, June 1981, pp. 418-432.

[Mason 1982]
M. T. Mason, "Manipulator Grasping and Pushing Operations," Ph.D. Dissertation, Artificial Intelligence Laboratory, Massachusetts Institute of Technology, Cambridge, Massachusetts, 1982.

[Paul 1972]
R. P. Paul, "Modeling Trajectory Calculation, and Servoing of a Controlled Arm," Artificial Intelligence Laboratory Memo AIM 177, Stanford University, Stanford, California, November 1972.

[Popplestone et al. 1978]
R. J. Popplestone, A. P. Ambler, and I. Bellos, "RAPT, a Language for Describing Assemblies," *Industrial Robot*, Vol. 5, No. 3, September 1978, pp. 131-137.

[Schwartz and Sharir 1982]
J. R. Schwartz and M. Sharir, "On the 'Piano-Movers' Problem—II: General Techniques for Computing Topological Properties of Real Algebraic Manifolds," Computer

Science Technical Report No. 41, Courant Institute of Mathematical Sciences, New York University, New York, New York, February 1982.

[Stallman and Sussman 1977]
R. M. Stallman and G. J. Sussman, "Forward Reasoning and Dependency-Directed Backtracking in a System for Computer-Aided Circuit Analysis," *Artificial Intelligence*, Vol. 9, 1977, pp. 135–196.

[Taylor 1976]
R. H. Taylor, "The Synthesis of Manipulator Control Programs from Task-Level Specifications," Artificial Intelligence Laboratory Memo AIM-282, Stanford University, Stanford, California, July 1976.

[Udupa 1977]
S. M. Udupa, "Collision Detection and Avoidance in Computer Controlled Manipulators," *Proceedings of the 5th International Joint Conference on Artificial Intelligence*, Cambridge, Massachusetts, August 1977, pp. 737–748.

[Weck and Zuhlke 1981]
M. Weck and D. Zuhlke, "Fundamentals for the Development of a High-Level Programming Language for Numerically Controlled Industrial Robots," AUTOFACT West, Dearborn, Michigan, 1981.

[Whitney 1976]
D. E. Whitney, "Force Feedback Control of Manipulator Fine Motions," *ASME Transactions on Dynamic Systems, Measurement, and Control*, Vol. 99, Series G, June 1976, pp. 91–97.

[Widdoes 1974]
L. C. Widdoes, "Obstacle Avoidance, a Heuristic Collision Avoider for the Stanford Robot Arm," Unpublished Memo, Artificial Intelligence Laboratory, Stanford University, Stanford, California, 1974.

[Wingham 1977]
M. Wingham, "Planning How to Grasp Objects in a Cluttered Environment," M.Ph. Thesis, University of Edinburgh, Edinburgh, Scotland, 1977.

DISCUSSION

Robert de Monts *(Dassault Systems)*

Your work emphasizes programming languages for grasping and collision avoidance. Can you use graphics for robot planning to simulate programs for grasping or collision avoidance?

Lozano-Pérez

Yes, but our goal is to be able to automate the whole problem. Only when you try to integrate the whole problem and take it completely away from the human user does it become interesting. Consider a compiler. If it omitted some capability such as register optimization you would not use it. I think that automating the whole process is a useful goal. A uniform methodology based on configuration space is beginning to emerge for grasping, obstacle avoidance, and planning fine motions.

T. Lozano-Pérez

GARI:
AN EXPERT SYSTEM FOR PROCESS PLANNING

YANNICK DESCOTTE

Laboratoire de Marcoussis
Marcoussis, France

JEAN-CLAUDE LATOMBE

National Polytechnic Institute
Grenoble, France

ABSTRACT

We present a system, GARI, for planning the sequence of machining cuts of mechanical parts. It consists of an expert knowledge base made of manufacturing rules and a planner. Under specified conditions, each rule provides the system with weighted pieces of advice, which can be used by the planner to constrain the machining plan. The planner combines artificial intelligence techniques for nonlinear planning, for propagating constraints, and for processing contradictions. Parts to be machined are described as sets of interrelated features such as faces, bores, grooves, holes, notches. Each type of feature conveys an operational meaning with respect to the cutting process, which is exploited by the manufacturing rules.

INTRODUCTION

The goal of process planning in the metal cutting industry is to produce plans for machining parts, given their drawings. These plans should specify the cuts to be executed, their ordering, the machine tools to be used, the surfaces by which the part is to be clamped and located during each cut, and so forth. Such planning involves taking into account both technological and economical considerations. For instance:

- If a hole, H1, opens into another hole, H2, then it is recommended to machine H2 before H1 in order to avoid risks of damaging the drill.

References p. 344

- Executing several cuts on the same machine with the same fixing may be advantageous in order to reduce the time spent in setting up the work on the machine.

There is a great variety of such pieces of knowledge which are useful for process planning. Furthermore, they are not constraints but preferences among which compromises may be necessary. They also may differ from one company to another, because they often represent both the experience and the know-how of engineers.

Automatic process planning is regarded as an important problem of CAD/CAM. But because of both the variety and the empirical nature of the knowledge to be applied, it is a difficult one. Thus, although a number of systems have been developed [Weill 1979, Matsushima *et al.* 1982], none seems to be widely applicable. We have found that automatic process planning is an interesting application for artificial intelligence methods developed in the context of robot planning [Nilsson 1980] and expert systems [Barr and Feigenbaum 1982]. This led us to design a new type of process planning system, GARI, based on these grounds [Descotte 1981].

The main advantage of GARI over earlier process planning systems is that it makes use of a specialized incremental knowledge base which is independent from the planner. Therefore knowledge can be modified and extended to suit the needs of a particular company.

This paper is a description of the major components of GARI. It extends a previous paper [Descotte and Latombe 1981] in many respects. In addition it discusses possible extensions of the system.

OVERVIEW OF GARI

GARI is structured like an expert system: it consists of a specialized knowledge base and a planner.

The knowledge base is represented by production rules, called manufacturing rules. The left-hand side of a rule is a conjunctive set of conditions about the part to be manufactured, the available machines, and/or the machining plan. The right-hand side consists of pieces of advice representing technological and economical preferences. Each piece of advice is weighted according to its importance.

The planner first generates a loosely constrained initial machining plan from the input model of the part. This model describes the part in terms of features such as holes, grooves and faces. It *a priori* determines the set of potential cuts. Indeed, in the current implementation of GARI, each feature may require a maximum of two cuts, a roughing cut and a finishing cut. Then the planner proceeds by iteratively constraining the current solution. Each constraint—for instance, cut A is to be executed before cut B, cuts C and D are to be executed in the same phase (*i.e.*, on the same machine with the same fixing), cut E is to be executed on a grinding machine—is drawn from the currently available pieces of advice, that is, those pieces of advice which are provided by instances of rules the left-hand sides of which are currently satisfied.

At any moment, the current solution defines a set of machining plans. Indeed the successively applied constraints, combined with the initial plan, imply a partial ordering on the set of cuts and incompletely specify the characteristics of each cut. However, it may happen that some constraints are contradictory and so determine an empty set of plans.

A contradiction means that some pieces of advice are conflicting. This should not be a surprise because in most cases process planning requires compromises among antagonist preferences. Since the planner cannot satisfy conflicting pieces of advice simultaneously, it solves each contradiction by rejecting one piece of advice among those which have been used so far, and it resumes the iterative planning process. Later in the process, if it becomes useful, an earlier solution to a conflict can be reconsidered in order to reintroduce a piece of advice that has been previously rejected. The constraints are applied and the contradictions are solved so as to minimize the highest weight of those pieces of advice which are contradicted by the final solution. This solution usually does not determine a unique plan. Remaining choices are to be made at execution time.

PART DESCRIPTION

A part is described to GARI as a set of features of various types: trapped holes, countersunk holes, bores, grooves, notches, faces, etc. This description is made of three elements:

- Description of each feature. For example:
    (H (type countersunk-hole)
        (starting-from F1) (opening-into F3)
        (diameter 6) (countersink-diameter 12))

- Dimensions between features. For example:
    (distance H F2 19)
    (distance F1 F2 20 ± 50)
    (perpendicularity H F3 ± 50)
    (concentricity H1 H2 ± 100)
    (countersink-depth H F1 3 ± 80)

- General pieces of information. For example:
    (matter XC38)
    (quality 6.3)
    (tolerance ± 100)

Dimensions and tolerances are input as they appear on the drawing. General pieces of information apply to the whole part except where they are locally specified. For instance, the general piece of information (tolerance ± 100) will apply to the dimension (distance H F2 19), but not the dimension (distance F1 F2

References p. 344

20 ± 50). Some features, like grooves and notches, can be described in terms of faces. These faces are called the children of the upper-level features. The features which have no partners are called top-level features.

Figure 1 shows one view of a part that can be described to GARI. In the following description, xp denotes the positive x axis, etc.

- Description of each feature:
  (FXP (type face) (direction xp) (quality 3.2))
  (FXM (type face) (direction xm) (quality rough))
  (FYM (type face) (direction ym) (quality rough))
  (FYP (type face) (direction yp) (quality rough))
  (FZP (type face) (direction zp))
  (FZM (type face) (direction zm))
  (H1 (type countersunk-hole) (diameter 7)
      (countersink-diameter 11)
      (starting-from FZP) (opening-into P1))
  (H2 (type trapped-hole) (diameter 6)
      (starting-from FZM) (opening-into P3))
  (N1 (type notch) (quality 3.2) (width 20)
      (starting-from FXP) (opening-into FYM FYP)
      (children (P1 (type face) (direction zm))
              (P2 (type face) (direction xp))
              (P3 (type face) (direction zp))))
  (N2 (type notch) (width 2)
      (starting-from P2) (opening-into FYM FYP)
      (children (Q1 (type face) (direction zm))
              (Q2 (type face) (direction xp))
              (Q3 (type face) (direction zp))))

- Dimensions between features:
  (distance FXM FXP 38 ± 200)
  (distance P2 FXP 15 ± 1000)
  (distance Q2 P2 15 ± 1000)
  (distance (H1 H2) FXP 8.5 ± 300)
  (distance FYM FYP 38 ± 200)
  (distance (H1 H2) FYP 19 ± 100)
  (distance FZM FZP 38 ± 200)
  (countersink-depth FZP H1 6.5 ± 300)
  (distance P1 FZP 8 ± 100)
  (distance P3 Q3 1 ± 300)
  (concentricity H1 H2 ± 100)

- General pieces of information:
  (matter XC38)
  (quality 6.3)

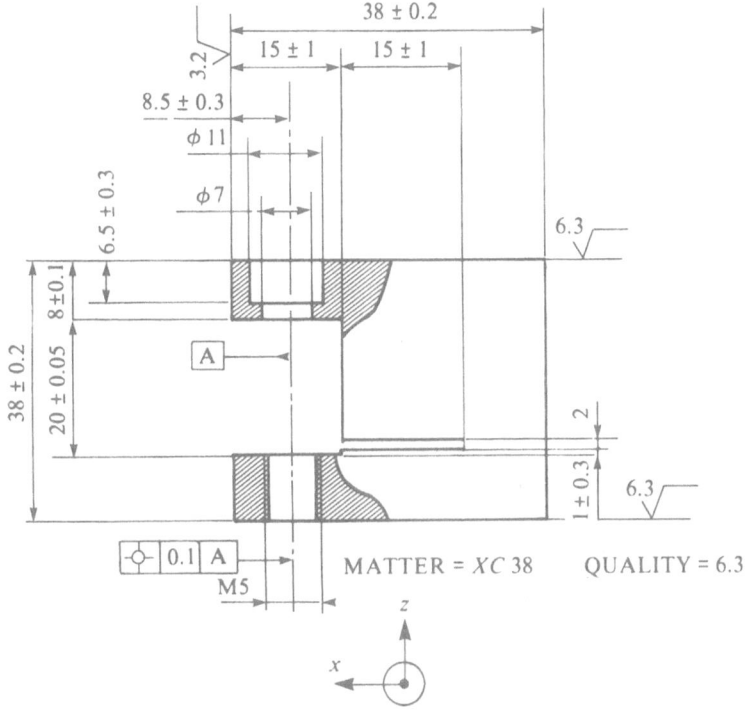

Figure 1. Plan view of a part which can be described to GARI.

The notion of features for describing mechanical parts is an important concept of GARI. Indeed the manufacturing rules make use of the semantic value, which is implicitly attached to each type of feature. Furthermore, features have a strong operational flavor, since the top-level ones *a priori* determine the set of potential cuts to be executed for manufacturing the part.

The same geometry may have several descriptions using different features. These descriptions may cause different manufacturing rules to become active and ultimately may result in different machining plans.

In addition, the description of some instances of features may include manufacturing data. For instance, in the example given above, the attributes "starting-from" and "opening-into" of H1 not only define the position of H1 with respect to other features, they also tell the system that the hole should be machined from FZP in the direction of P1. Therefore, the description of a part as a set of features conveys some expertise provided by the user.

MACHINE DESCRIPTION

Each available machine is described to GARI by a name and by properties which are regarded as important by the users. For instance, some properties

References p. 344

may be the type of the machine (milling machine, drilling machine), its precision, dimension attributes such as the distance between axes, and so forth. An example of machine description might be (CL1 (type chuck-lathe) (chuck-diameter 2000)).

MACHINING PLANS

Each top-level feature of the part to be manufactured requires a maximum of two cuts, a roughing cut and a finishing cut, if the surface quality of the feature is not to be rough. In a plan produced by GARI the cuts are ordered and grouped into operations and phases. An *operation* is a set of cuts to be executed simultaneously. A *phase* is a sequence of operations to be executed with the same fixing on the same machine. Therefore, a machining plan output by GARI is a sequence of phases. Each phase is detailed in terms of operations and cuts. Both the machine to be used and the face on which the part should rest are associated with each phase.

In general GARI produces multiple machining plans for a given part, as suggested earlier in the Overview. For example one plan generated by GARI for the part shown in Figure 1 would be:

- *Phase 1*   Machine: FU203   resting face: FXM
          Operation 1.1   roughing cut of FXP
          Operation 1.2   finishing cut of N1

- *Phase 2*   Machine: FU203   resting face: FXP
          Operation 2.1   finishing cut of FZP

- *Phase 3*   Machine: FU203   resting face: FZP
          Operation 3.1   finishing cut of FZM
          Operation 3.2   finishing cut of FXP
          Operation 3.3   finishing cut of N2

- *Phase 4*   Machine: GSP205   resting face: FZP
          Operation 4.1   finishing cut of H2

- *Phase 5*   Machine: GSP205   resting face: FZM
          Operation 5.1   finishing cut of H1

MANUFACTURING RULES

Each manufacturing rule is a production of the form:

$$\text{conditions} \Rightarrow \text{pieces of advice}$$

The conditions in the left-hand side (LHS) may bear on the part to be manufactured, the available machines, and/or the plan to be produced. The pieces of advice in the right-hand side (RHS) are weak constraints which apply to the manufacturing plan when the conditions in the LHS are satisfied. Each one is weighted by an integer between 1 and 10 representing the importance attached to its satisfaction (with 10 being the most important). Since process planning requires compromises, the plans that are output by GARI usually contradict several pieces of advice. The system makes use of their weights for making compromises among several conflicting pieces of advice.

Each manufacturing rule should be given the following declarative interpretation by the user,

> "If the conditions in the LHS are satisfied by the part, the machines, and a particular plan, then it is desirable that the pieces of advice in the RHS be satisfied by the plan."

On the other hand, each rule is given the following procedural interpretation by GARI:

> "When the conditions in the LHS are satisfied by the part, the machines, and the current solution (a set of plans), then the pieces of advice in the RHS are to be used to constrain the current solution."

The declarative interpretation does not depend on the method applied by GARI for generating a plan. The correspondence between the declarative interpretation and the procedural one is established by a property which is satisifed by any plan P output by GARI:

> "If the maximum weight of those pieces of advice which are contradicted by P is W, then there exists no plan P' such that the weight of each piece of advice contradicted by P' is lower than W."

In other words, this property says that the plans which are generated by using the procedural interpretation of the rules are the best according to the declarative interpretation.

Parameterization of the Rules—Rules can be parameterized by simple variables and set variables:

- A *simple variable* is prefixed by either & (indicating it represents a feature of the part) or $ (indicating it represents a cut).
- A *set variable* is prefixed by either && (indicating it represents a set of features), $$ (a set of cuts), or ** (a set of machines).

Variables in the RHS of a rule should also appear in the LHS so they can be instantiated. Simple variables are instantiated with values found in a pattern-matching operation on the conditions in the LHS of the rule.

Each set variable in a rule is given a value in the LHS by an expression such as:

$$(\&\&z \ \text{face} \ (\text{and} \ (// \ \&\&z \ \&x) \ ( ][\ \&\&z \ \&y)))$$

The first element, &&z, is the name of the set variable. The second element, face, is the name of a set (here the set of all the faces of the part). The third ele-

References p. 344

ment is a condition. The variable &&z evaluates to the subset of all the faces of the part which satisfy this condition. The name &&z is used in the condition to note any element of the set &&z. Thus every element in &&z must be parallel to both &x and &y, and its normal vector must have an opposite direction to the normal vector of &y.

An expression defining a set variable is also regarded as a condition which evaluates to true if the set variable evaluates to a nonempty set and to false if the variable evaluates to the empty set. The following examples illustrate rule parameterization:

- ($>$ (quality &x) 6.3) $\Rightarrow$ (9 (not roughing-cut &x))

  If the surface quality of a feature &x is higher (poorer) than 6.3, then it is advised (with weight 9) to avoid a roughing cut for &x.

- (geometrical-constraint-between &x &y)
  (not same-operation (finishing-cut &x) (finishing-cut &y))
  $\Rightarrow$ (4 (roughing-cut &x) (roughing-cut &y))

  If the finishing cuts of two features &x and &y, which are linked by an input geometrical constraint, are not in the same operation, then it is advised (with weight 4) to execute roughing cuts for both &x and &y.

- (is-a &x bore) (is-a &y bore) (coaxial &x &y)
  $\Rightarrow$ (6 (same-phase (finishing-cut &x) (finishing-cut &y))
      (machine (finishing-cut &x) lathe))

  If &x and &y are two bores linked by a coaxiality constraint, then it is advised (with weight 6) to execute their finishing cuts in the same phase on a lathe.

- (is-a &x hole) (is-a &y hole) (open-into &x &y)
  (not open-into &y &x)
  $\Rightarrow$ (9 (before (roughing-cut &y) (roughing-cut &x)))

  If a hole &x opens into a hole &y, and if &y does not open into &x, then it is advised (with weight 9) to execute the roughing cut of &y before the roughing cut of &x. In this rule, hole denotes a generic feature. It may be either a bore, a countersunk hole, or a tapped hole. GARI allows the use of other generic features to express manufacturing rules. For instance, a cubic is a notch, a groove, etc.

- ($<$ (quality &x) 3.2) ($>$ (extra-thickness &y) 3.0)
  (resting-on (roughing-cut &y) &x)
  $\Rightarrow$ (8 (before (roughing-cut &y) (finishing-cut &x)))

If the surface quality of a feature &x is to be lower than 3.2, and if the extra-thickness of a feature &y is greater than 3.0 mm, and if the part rests on &x during the roughing cut of &y, then it is advised (with weight 8) to execute the roughing cut of &y before the finishing cut of &x.

- (is-a $x finishing-cut) (machine $x grinding-machine)
  (not machine $y grinding-machine)
  $\Rightarrow$ (10 (before $y $x))

If a finishing cut $x is executed on a grinding machine, and if a cut $y is executed on another type of machine, then it is advised (with weight 10) to execute $y before $x.

- (is-a &x bore) ($<$ (quality &x) 6.0)
  (**y cylinder-grinding-machine ($<$ (quality **y) (quality &x)))
  $\Rightarrow$ (10 (machine (finishing-cut &x) **y))

If the surface quality of a bore &x is to be lower than 6.0, and if a cylinder grinding machine capable of providing this quality is available, then it is advised (with weight 10) to execute the finishing cut of &x on such a machine.

- (belongs-to &x (intersection face top))
  (&&y face (][&&y &x)) (&&z face ([[&&z &x))
  $\Rightarrow$ (10 (not resting-on &x &&z))
      (5 (resting-on &x &&y))
      (10 (machine &x (surface-grinding-machine turning-machine
          milling-machine cutting-center)))
      (5 (not machine &x turning-machine))

If &x is a face with no parent feature (*i.e.*, it is a top-level feature), and if &&y is the set of all the faces parallel to &x such that their normal vectors have an opposite direction to the normal vector of &x, and if &&z is the set of all the faces parallel to &x such that their normal vectors have the same direction as the normal vector of &x, then it is advised:

(with weight 10) not to execute cuts of &x while the part is
    resting on a face of &&z,

References p. 344

(with weight 5) to execute cuts of &x while the part is resting on a face of &&y,

(with weight 10) to execute cuts of &x with a surface grinding machine, a turning machine, a milling machine, or a cutting center.

(with weight 5) not to execute cuts of &x with a turning machine.

- (is-a &x face) (is-a &y face) ($<$ (tolerance distance &x &y) 20) $\Rightarrow$ (7 (same-phase (finishing-cut &x) (finishing-cut &y)))

If the tolerance on the distance between two faces is lower than 20μ, then it is advised (with weight 7) to execute the finishing cuts of these two faces in the same phase.

KNOWLEDGE ACTIVATION

States of the Knowledge—At any given moment in the process of generating a plan, the conditions in the left-hand side of a rule instance (*i.e.*, a rule in which constants have been substituted for variables) may either be satisfied (the rule instance is said to be *active*), be contradicted (the rule instance is said to be *inactive*), or be neither satisfied nor contradicted (the rule instance is said to be *pending*). A piece of advice provided by an active rule instance is either *applied* (it has already been used to constrain the current solution), *rejected* (it has been used to constrain the solution, but it has later been rejected because of a contradiction), or *available*.

Rule Activation—Knowledge activation consists of determining which rule instances are active at each moment. This is done by constructing an *activation tree* for each rule. The root of this tree is the rule. The nodes at depth i ($i \geq 1$) are all instances of the ith condition in the left-hand side of the rule. The construction of an activation tree is easy because we know the set (finite) of all the possible values of each simple variable, the type of which is determined by its prefix. The value of each set variable is computed according to the expression defining this value given earlier [Descotte 1981].

Each leaf of an activation tree uniquely corresponds to a rule instance. This rule instance is active if all the conditions on the path from the root of the tree to the leaf are satisfied. In order to determine the truth value of a condition, GARI runs a routine attached to the predicate of the condition. GARI makes use of several simplifications, which make knowledge activation more efficient. In particular:

- Since the truth value of a condition about either the part or the machines is known from the beginning, the corresponding node can be eliminated from the activation tree.

- GARI constructs the activation trees during the process of generating a plan. The successors of a node are produced only when the condition attached to that node is known to be satisfied. Therefore the successors of a contradicted condition are never produced.

PLAN GENERATION

Plan generation is an iterative process executing two steps:

- The current solution is constrained by applying a selected piece of advice,
- The constraint is propagated through the solution in order to detect a possible contradiction.

The input to each iteration is the current solution, that is, a set S of machining plans. The output is the updated solution, a subset of S. It is the empty set if a contradiction occurred. Between two iterations, if no contradiction has been detected, the module for activating pending rules is run; otherwise the contradiction is processed as explained later in this paper.

The input to the first iteration, that is, the initial solution, is a very loosely constrained set of plans. It can be regarded as a parallel plan, that is, a partial ordering, having as many branches as there are top-level features, the surface quality of which is not rough, in the model of the part. Each branch consists of two successive cuts, the roughing cut and the finishing cut, of the corresponding feature. Each cut forms a single operation, and each operation forms a single phase; however, merging operations and phases is allowed. In addition, the set of all the faces of the part, except those belonging to the corresponding feature, are attached to each phase as faces on which the part can rest for machining the feature; the set of all the machines is also attached to each phase. The process of generating a plan terminates at the end of the first step when the manufacturing rules do not permit GARI to constrain the current solution further.

Constraining the Solution—The constraint on the solution drawn from the selected piece of advice at each iteration of the plan generation process may be:

- Constrain a cut to be executed before another cut (*i.e.*, linearize the parallel plan),
- Merge two operations or two phases into one, or constrain two operations or two phases not to be merged together, or
- Restrict the set of faces (or the set of machines) attached to a phase to a subset.

Merging the two operations containing the roughing cut and the finishing cut of some feature F into the same operation means that there is no roughing cut of F. Inversely constraining these two operations not to be merged means there must be a roughing cut of F.

References p. 344

The algorithm for selecting the piece of advice is the following:

If there exists at least one available piece of advice,

then (1) apply a piece of advice among the available pieces of advice having the highest weight,

else **if** there exists a pending rule providing a piece of advice which is not satisifed by the current solution,

　　　　then (2) apply a new piece of advice constructed with the goal of making this rule inactive,

　　　　else (3) exit with the solution.

Step (2) of this algorithm deserves some comment. When there are no more available pieces of advice, there may still exist pending instances of rules. If this is the case, it means that some plans contained in the current solution contradict the conditions in the left-hand side of these rules instances, while some other plans satisfy them. If a pending rule instance R is active for a particular plan P contained in the solution, then the right-hand side of R may contain a piece of advice contradicted by P. In such a situation, GARI attempts to make the pending rule instance become inactive by constructing a new piece of advice with the purpose of contradicting the left-hand side conditions of the rule instance. This piece of advice is given a weight equal to 0.

Propagating the Constraint—Detecting contradictions usually requires complex deductions based on the semantics implicitly attached to such notions as operation, phase, machine, etc. The constraint propagation process is implemented as a pattern-directed inference system. Each new constraint on the solution fires a special-purpose routine attached to the type of the constraint. The facts that are deduced by this routine are considered as new constraints firing other routines. For instance, merging two operations into one implies the two phases to which these operations belong also be merged. This in turn requires attaching a set of machines to the resulting phase; this set is equal to the intersection of the sets of machines attached to the merged phases. A contradiction is detected whenever one of the following situations happens:

- Cut A is constrained to be executed before cut B, while B is constrained to be executed before A,
- Two operations or two phases are simultaneously constrained to be merged and not to be merged, or
- The set of machines or resting faces attached to a phase is empty.

CONTRADICTION PROCESSING

When a contradiction is detected, it is immediately processed. Basically the system rejects a previously applied piece of advice and updates the current solution accordingly before resuming plan generation. The implemented procedure is based on a few simple concepts. It consists of three main steps, which we present below. For this presentation let us assume that the contradiction to be processed is the first one which has been detected by the system.

Step 1. GARI rejects the piece of advice most recently applied among those which have the lowest weight. For example, if the following pieces of advice

$$A1 \quad A2 \quad A3 \quad A4 \quad A5 \quad A6$$

with the following weights

$$10 \quad 7 \quad 9 \quad 7 \quad 10 \quad 9$$

have been successively applied, when a contradiction is detected the system rejects $A4$.

Indeed, if it is the first contradiction, this piece of advice is necessarily responsible for the contradiction. Constraints on the solution are drawn from pieces of advice of decreasing weights. Thus, constraints drawn from $A4$ are necessary to the activation of those rules which provided $A5$ and $A6$. If that were not the case, those rules would have become active before the application of $A4$, so that $A5$ and $A6$ would have been used before $A4$.

Step 2. Rejecting a piece of advice must be accompanied by updating the current solution. Thus constraints derived when this piece of advice was applied must be removed. This usually leads to deactivating some rules. If these rules provide pieces of advice that were previously applied, the corresponding constraints must be removed in turn.

According to the reasoning justifying Step 1, the system is led to remove all the constraints produced after the application of the piece of advice which is now rejected. In the previous example, this consists of removing all the constraints derived from $A4$, $A5$ and $A6$.

Step 3. A contradiction is always due to a combination of conflicting pieces of advice. Thus, if a new contradiction occurs later, it may become useful to reintroduce a previously rejected piece of advice. However, in such a case, GARI must also solve the first contradiction in a different manner in order to avoid an infinite loop of successive contradictions.

For this purpose, the system proceeds as follows. Each time it rejects a piece of advice X, it generates the piece of advice $\sim X$ (not X) with the weight W equal to the lowest weight of those pieces of advice which were applied after X when the contradiction was discovered. This weight can be justified as follows: if we decided to maintain X in the same conditions as when it was applied (*i.e.*, without modifying the pieces of advice applied before X), then it would cost at least the rejection of a piece of advice having weight W for solving the contradiction. In the example illustrating Step 1, this leads to the system generating $\sim A4$ with weight 9 as a new available piece of advice. If the rejected piece of advice X is the one most recently applied, then $\sim X$ is generated with weight 10.

References p. 344

After the completion of Step 3, the process of generating a manufacturing plan is resumed.

When the contradiction is not the first one which has been detected by the system, there is no guarantee at Step 1 that the rejected piece of advice is relevant to the contradiction. However, it turns out that the simple choice made by GARI is a good heuristic, and the procedure sketched above proves to be an efficient one with respect to the problem at hand. The methods outlined for plan generation and contradiction processing guarantee that when a solution P is output by GARI, if the maximum weight of those pieces of advice which are contradicted by P is W, then there exists no solution P' such that the weight of each piece of advice contradicted by P' is lower than W [Descotte 1981].

IMPLEMENTATION

An implementation of GARI written in the MACLISP language operates on a HB-68 computer under the MULTICS system. It has been experimented with by machining engineers, who developed a knowledge base of approximately 50 rules, most of them providing multiple pieces of advice. The system has been run successfully on about 25 different parts of different levels of complexity, with a small set of machine tools (see [Descotte 81]).

The CPU time for generating a plan ranged between 30 seconds for simple parts to almost 12 minutes for reasonably complex ones. For the most difficult parts, the final solution was constrained by about 500 pieces of advice; it was obtained after processing approximately 150 contradictions. In fact, although the number of rules was rather small, several hundred instances of the rules became active for most parts.

At the current stage GARI is only a feasibility demonstration of the expert system approach to process planning. The successful experimentation with GARI makes us believe that a truly applicable system for process planning in the metal cutting industry is within reach. However, to achieve that goal, several extensions, some of which are discussed in the next section, are necessary.

FURTHER CONSIDERATIONS

About Part Modeling—First, the current implementation of GARI is not connected to a body modeler such as PADL-2, ROMULUS or GMSolid. When there is such a modeler, one can easily imagine the user specifying the features composing a part by showing them interactively on a graphical display of the part. It is also possible to think about some kind of automatic feature recognition procedure [Kyprianou 1980, Jared 1984]. However, because the notion of feature as it is used here is quite familiar to engineers, we believe that it should be directly embedded in the input language of the body modeler.

Second, there are several shortcomings to how parts are modeled in the current implementation of GARI. In particular:

- Parts must be *orthomorphic*, that is, axes and faces must be either parallel or perpendicular,

- The input part of the machining process is not explicitly described. The user can only associate the attribute "extra-thickness" to the features. The value of this attribute for a given feature defines how much material is to be cut away.

- The type of part description presented earlier in this paper is not appropriate for modeling turned parts.

Although extending the system in order to avoid these shortcomings is probably far from being easy, it would not modify the system operations in a fundamental way.

About Machine Description—Until now, very little effort has been dedicated to the machine description language of GARI. However, in order to get a practical system able to generate more detailed machining plans, we believe that a more comprehensive language is to be devised. In particular, such a language should permit the users to represent tools and fixtures and also to describe more of the geometry of the machines, so that the manufacturing rules can make use of this information.

About the Machining Plans—Properly speaking, GARI only generates the structure of a manufacturing plan. Indeed, most manufacturing plans used in industry are more detailed than those produced by GARI. The output of GARI could be postprocessed by local routines for detailing the way of executing each cut (tool to be used, speed of the machine, etc.) Such routines exist in many places, but none of them have been integrated into GARI yet. An expert system for producing detailed machining plans of holes [Matsushima *et al.* 1982] has been developed. This system is to be extended to other types of features.

Other existing specialized routines, for instance, for computing the execution times of input manufacturing plans, could be applied to the output of GARI in order to provide additional information to the users.

The current implementation of GARI handles only roughing and finishing cuts, but there is no fundamental limitation behind that. Extending the system to handle more types of cuts is not a theoretical problem, although the number of rules in the knowledge base is likely to increase.

About the Manufacturing Rules—Useful extensions of the current language for expressing manufacturing rules include constructs for stating left-hand side conditions about both the load and the physical distribution of the machines. The goal of such extensions is to make possible the use of GARI for on-line control of flexible shop floors.

Currently there is no facility for structuring the knowledge base of GARI. We believe that research on group technology should make possible structuring the

References p. 344

set of manufacturing rules so that a subset of them would be known to be useful to generate the plan for manufacturing a given part.

Facilities for editing and acquiring knowledge from human experts should also be implemented. To that purpose the planner should be completed by a module that explains its reasoning [Barr and Feigenbaum 1982].

ACKNOWLEDGEMENTS

The research for this paper was done at the IMAG Laboratory of the National Polytechnic Institute of Grenoble under contract and in collaboration with ADEPA (Agence Nationale pour le Développement de la Production Automatisée). Partial support has also been provided by the French National Project ARA (Automatique et Robotique Avancées). The group of Mr. Bourdet at ENSET developed the knowledge base of GARI.

REFERENCES

[Barr and Feigenbaum 1982]
A. Barr and E. A. Feigenbaum, *The Handbook of Artificial Intelligence*, Vol. 2, William Kaufmann Inc., Los Altos, California, 1982.

[Descotte 1981]
Y. Descotte, "Représentation et exploitation de connaissances <<expertes>> en génération de plans d'actions — Application à la conception automatique de gammes d'usinage," Thèse de 3 ème Cycle, INPG, Grenoble, France, December 1981 (in French).

[Descotte and Latombe 1981]
Y. Descotte and J. C. Latombe, "GARI: A Problem Solver that Plans How to Machine Mechanical Parts," *Proceedings of the 7th International Joint Conference on Artificial Intelligence*, Vancouver, British Columbia, Canada, August 24–28, 1981, pp. 766–772.

[Jared 1984]
G. E. M. Jared, "Shape Features in Geometric Modeling," *Solid Modeling by Computers: From Theory to Applications*, M. S. Pickett and J. W. Boyse, eds., Plenum Press, New York, New York, 1984.

[Kyprianou 1980]
L. K. Kyprianou, "Shape Classification in Computer-Aided Design," Ph.D. Dissertation, Computer Laboratory, University of Cambridge, Cambridge, England, July 1980.

[Matsushima *et al.* 1982]
K. Matsushima, N. Okada, and T. Sata, "The Integration of CAD and CAM by Application of Artificial Intelligence Techniques," *Annals of the CIRP*, Vol. 31, No. 1, 1982, pp. 329–332.

[Nilsson 1980]
N. J. Nilsson, *Principles of Artificial Intelligence*, Tioga Publishing Company, Palo Alto, California, 1980.

[Weill 1979]
R. Weill, "Etat d'avancement des systèmes automatiques d'établissement des gammes de fabrication," 2 èmes Journées Scientifiques et Techniques de la Production Automatisée, Nancy, France, 1979 (in French).

DISCUSSION

David Gossard *(Massachusetts Institute of Technology)*

This is a very powerful approach and it appears very promising. Can you tell me how many other researchers in the world are concentrating on the same area?

Latombe

There is work by Professor Sata in Japan about the TOM System that is similar in that it is also an expert system, but it concentrates on the generation of plans for one operation, such as cutting a hole. We try to generate the whole plan, but do not detail the cutting of the hole. There is also some work being done at Carnegie-Mellon, but I am not familiar with it. There is a lot of other work, but not using this approach.

Jean-Claude Latombe

Michel Melkanoff *(University of California–Los Angeles)*

Have you looked into the United Technologies project for producing plans? It sounds similar.

Latombe

Yes, I am aware of it. It is quite different.

Melkanoff

Your part feature is really a group technology code in a way, is it not?

Latombe

At the beginning of my talk I said that there was a distinction between the two approaches: variant and generative. In fact, this system shows that there is no real distinction because each rule classifies parts into categories. But this kind of system based on features is a very flexible classifier. You have tens or hundreds of rules and each rule classifies a little bit of the part in order to construct a plan. Thus you can move from the variant approach to the generative approach in a continuous way.

SYMPOSIUM SUMMARY

HERBERT B. VOELCKER

University of Rochester
Rochester, New York

MICHAEL A. WESLEY

IBM Thomas J. Watson Research Center
Yorktown Heights, New York

SUMMARY AND CONCLUSIONS

HERBERT B. VOELCKER

University of Rochester
Rochester, New York

MICHAEL A. WESLEY

IBM Thomas J. Watson Research Center
Yorktown Heights, New York

INTRODUCTION

Initial planning for a solid modeling symposium to be sponsored by the General Motors Research Laboratories was begun in mid-1980. However, the final decision about program topics was not made until early 1983. The change of emphasis in those few years, revealed by the contrasts between the earliest plans and the symposium as held, is interesting.

Not surprisingly, a few of the topics thought important in 1980, such as boundary evaluation, appeared less so in 1983 and were not covered. More interestingly, all of the topics covered in 1983 had been identified as important in 1980; however, it was not possible to find speakers for certain topics deemed important from the start, even though the list of potential speakers had grown significantly. (One such topic was theories or strategies for constructing and adaptively refining approximate representations of solids.) Finally, an element of evangelism evident in the 1980 program plan had vanished by 1983.

These changes reflect both a measure of maturation in the field and its continued fertility as a research area. In 1980, research in solid modeling was still concentrated in a few centers, almost no commercial systems were available, and most potential users were just beginning to ask, "What is solid modeling?" Today, research is more broadly based, one can choose from more than a dozen commercial systems, and one need no longer explain solid modeling. Solid modeling is widely acknowledged as central to increasingly automated design

References p. 357

and production systems, but it is also coming under criticism for failing to attain its potential, that is, for doing too little too slowly.

Thus we should ask: "What can solid modeling systems do *now*, who is using them and for what, and what new capabilities can we expect and on what schedule?" We shall return to the first two issues later. The symposium mainly addressed the third issue—new capabilities—as is appropriate for a research gathering.

Overall, this symposium has confirmed our belief that solid geometric modeling by computer is now an established and reputable field that is advancing and expanding rapidly. The field is advancing in that new formalisms, theories, and techniques are being developed. This puts older, perhaps more *ad hoc*, operations on a firmer foundation and also allows completely new operations. The field is expanding in that it is finding increasing acceptance in practice, and the domain of applicability is widening.

In convening this first major conference devoted exclusively to solid modeling, the organizers faced the problem of how best to cover this large field by structuring the two days of the conference into a relatively small number of invited papers, yet allowing substantial amounts of time for informal discussion. On the one hand, this approach allowed in-depth presentations on the chosen topics but, on the other, necessarily required that some important topics not be given space in the formal program. During the event, it was evident from the reactions of the attendees that the formal program did indeed provide the necessary stimulus for profitable discussion and that the opportunities for detailed technical exchange were well used.

The format we have chosen for this Summary and Conclusion has three parts: first, a discussion of the formal proceedings of the conference; second, an assessment of where the field of solid geometric modeling by computers is now; third, an estimation of the future directions solid geometric modeling will take.

CONFERENCE PROCEEDINGS

The subject of geometric modeling may be divided into three main areas:

- Theory,
- Applications,
- Systems.

Of these, the first and the second received approximately equal attention in the proceedings; however, little attention was given to the concept of systems for geometric modeling.

Theory of Geometric Modeling—The analytic aspects of the basic needs of boundary representation schemes—robustness and the ability to handle all cases—were addressed by Ocken, Schwartz and Sharir. Their paper on primitive surfaces and their intersections recognizes the need for a unifying approach to the analysis of surface intersections—in this case, planes, spheres, cylinders, and cones—so that simpler algorithms can handle all cases. An important achievement of their analysis that can be exploited by a unified implementation is an understanding of the numerical operations to be performed and the number of arithmetic steps involved.

Several papers recognised the possibility that important new areas may require changes to the way in which geometric modeling is performed. Requicha's paper on tolerancing presents the need for representation and analysis of tolerances and discusses how the needs of tolerancing, from functional and fabrication points of view, may interact with the primitive operations provided by the design modeling system. The paper on the specification of curved surfaces by Rockwood emphasised the desirability of separating the details of the methods of surface representation from the user, and of enabling the user to specify surfaces, or fairings, or fillets in a natural way without overconstraining the system's attempts to meet given needs.

Two papers discussed the need for, and the realisation of, free-form surfaces. Sarraga and Waters showed the requirements of an automobile manufacturer for free-form surfaces, how they are being embedded in an existing system (GMSolid), and their approach to approximations to simplify representation. Kimura, at the University of Tokyo, described his work on the integration of sculptured surfaces into a solid system and also his overall system design.

Jared described a grammar for feature description and the automatic identification of features in a model; this, too, shows the need to work between the modeling system interface and the interface used to describe application operations, in this case, features for fabrication steps. Wesley surveyed work on conversion of existing nonsolid databases to solid form and concluded that although no complete algorithm is known to exist, the basic tools do exist, and a highly automated (but interactive) conversion of some existing digital but nonsolid databases could be achieved soon.

Applications of Geometric Modeling—Although solid modeling has been shown to be a high productivity means for a designer to create a design, the real strength of solid modeling lies in applications that make use of the solid model database. The right application set can provide the link between CAD and CAM, and applications therefore have a very high payoff. The papers reflect the areas that are of high interest at the moment.

Analysis operations were represented by two papers on finite-element mesh generation. Shephard and Yerry from Rensselaer Polytechnic Institute described a mesh generation technique for an octree system. The approach allows variable density meshes and is claimed to be suitable for adaptive mesh generation. Wördenweber from the University of Cambridge described a partitioning scheme that works by nibbling away at a boundary representation.

An approach to generation of N/C code from solid models was described by Armstrong, Carey, and de Pennington from the University of Leeds. Their work

References p. 357

is based on decomposition into volume cells that partition the object into machinable subcomponents, allowing rapid investigation of the status of adjacent cells. The GARI system for model-based generation of overall process plans was described by Descotte and Latombe from the University of Grenoble.

Robotics, as the most visible automation technology today, was well represented. Some vision work (*i.e.*, sensor operations) was presented by Castore of the National Bureau of Standards. The General Motors off-line robot programming system RoboTeach, which is based on GMSolid, shows how a major company intends to program a very large number of robots in the near future. RoboTeach initially provides capabilities for workcell layout, to be followed by point-to-point robot motion specification and analysis for collision-free operation. Later work is expected to cover sensor-based operations and high-level (task domain) programming languages. Model-based robot programming in the presence of uncertainty was addressed by Lozano-Pérez and Brooks with their ATLAS system proposal. This system aims to bring together earlier work on gross motion planning with more recent developments in fine motion planning.

Systems for Geometric Modeling—As noted above, the content of the conference concentrated on the theory and applications of geometric modeling itself. However, as these capabilities mature it is important to recognize that these techniques must be embedded in systems. Systems have to be built, applications have to be developed, and other subsystems, for example, database management systems, have to be interfaced. These systems need modern software engineering techniques for effective implementation and we predict that system building will become recognized as an important topic in solid modeling.

CURRENT STATUS

Contemporary solid modelers can do only a few things automatically. Notably, they can do graphics (in profusion), calculation of mass properties (volume, moments of inertia, etc.), and static interference checking based on nominal, that is, untoleranced geometry. Typically they can do these things only for objects whose surface geometries are describable by polynomials of first or second degree [Requicha and Voelcker 1983]. Contemporary systems thus are "CADish" rather than "CAMish," but they cannot yet serve even all CAD needs because, for example, they cannot yet generate finite-element meshes automatically and hence cannot support automatic analysis using the finite-element method. But CAD enhancements and more diversified capabilities are coming along. Figure 1 shows a sampling of application areas and our subjective ordering as to when industrially useful versions will be available.

We know of no organisation that has wholly replaced earlier CAD/CAM technology with solid modeling, and indeed know of none wherein solid modeling is being used exclusively to design a wide range of products. In a few firms it has proved to be very effective for certain classes of design problems; IBM's use of GDP/GRIN for computer frame design and packaging provides a notable ex-

When available	Application	Symposium coverage
Soon		
	Closed loop kinematics and dynamics	no
	Automatic finite-element mesh generation	yes
	Simulation of N/C machining	yes
	Off-line robot programming	yes
	. .	
	Automatic verification of N/C and robot programs	yes
	Automatic generation of N/C tool path code	yes
	Automatic gross motion planning for robots	no
	Automatic process planning for machining	yes
	Optimisation of parametrically defined mechanical shapes	no
1990's and beyond	Automatic design of molds and rigging for casting and injection molding	yes
	Automatic fine motion planning for robots	yes
	Deformation process modeling and automated die design	no
	Automatic goal-directed robot planning	no
	. .	
	. .	
	Design for manufacturability	no
	. .	
	. .	
	Design automation	no

Figure 1. Applications of solid geometric modeling.

ample [Fitzgerald *et al.* 1981]. Most vendors and users seem to be taking the conservative approach of interfacing solid modelers to in-place wire frame systems. Programs to download wire frame systems from solid modelers usually are easy to write. The signal advantage of this marriage is that progress can be accommodated gracefully; as the capabilities of solid modeling grow, more applications can be supported automatically.

References p. 357

There are two main reasons why contemporary modelers support only a few applications automatically. The first is that many important applications, for example, process planning for machining and trajectory planning for automatic assembly, to name but two, are not understood well enough to permit mathematical models to be built and algorithms to be designed. The second reason is that solid modeling systems lack some important support facilities. To put it succinctly, we simply do not know how to write programs to do many desired applications and, even if we did, the internal facilities of contemporary modelers would not supply all of the necessary data and utility calculations.

FUTURE DIRECTIONS

In this section we try to address the issue of why, if solid geometric modeling by computer is really such an important and mature technology, we have been so cautious in our assessment of the current status of geometric modeling in industrial practice.

First of all, it must be recognized that this is a very rapidly moving field that is not yet close to its final maturity. In the two and one-half years between the initial planning of the symposium and its realisation, the field went from a relatively unknown research curiosity to a tool that is, as a matter of fact, in production use in several major companies. For such a rapidly developing technology, a symposium such as this captures a snapshot of the state of the field at the time of the proceedings. Although the majority of the papers reported results from research rather than industrial practice, the transfer to practice of much of the work presented can be expected to proceed very quickly, particularly in areas with high payoff.

Secondly, much of the reported work was prosecuted in a "can it be done at all" manner. Now that technical feasibility has been established, economic feasibility must be considered. Many algorithms use rather large amounts of computation and also have greedy data requirements. The coupling of a new generation of computationally efficient algorithms with rapidly falling computation costs means that this is not likely to remain a problem for long.

Finally, systems must be able to provide useful and usable function. The field has probably suffered from an emphasis on graphics to produce eye-catching pictures, rather than on the real user considerations of human requirements and application functions.

System Capability—A modeling system must be able to represent the class of objects needed by the user. Current experience is that planar systems are much simpler and faster than ones allowing curved surfaces. Many applications can be satisfied by a restricted class of surfaces, but others require smooth free-form surface capability. Users should be able to tailor systems to their needs and pay only for the function they want.

Another important capability that systems will need, both at the representational level and at the algorithmic level, is the ability to handle concepts relating to uncertainty. Existing systems basically attempt to handle exact information. The real world of manufacturing is, of course, inexact. In many cases in industrial practice, sensors are used to provide feedback—to detect tool wear, to establish the exact location of a part, and to control forces occurring in assembly. In this symposium two papers have dealt with this issue: one, by Requicha, deals with representation and analysis of tolerances; another, by Lozano-Pérez and Brooks, examines robot fine motion planning. This is a very important topic that will bring geometric modeling closer to the needs of industrial practice.

In order to become accepted in widespread practice, systems must work reliably and provide a natural and high-level interface without the user's having to be aware of internal restrictions that limit user actions. No system known to us is able to perform reliably under all possible inputs. Chance alignments, special geometric cases, and numerical problems can all be expected to bring a system to a halt, or at least a temporary hiccup. One hard-learned lesson of computer geometry is that implementing the simple cases of geometric problems is rather easy, but the ability to handle all possible cases may require an order of magnitude more work. Thus, existing systems have often fared badly in the opinions of real hands-on users. Again, the field has been hampered by the experiences of computer graphics. In graphics, an image may be generated to the resolution of the output device, and minor errors may go unnoticed by the user. In computer geometry, the output of one algorithm is generally the input to another; errors can therefore be expected to explode rapidly. The algorithm designer must aim for complete robustness under all data conditions.

Graphics has also conditioned users to expect very swift response from geometry systems, and this expectation is not easily met, at present, because solid modeling is more computationally intensive than are interactive graphics. However, as noted earlier, more efficient algorithms are being developed and computing costs are falling. A third factor—computers designed specifically for solid modeling—may prove decisive. Already one can buy "tiling engines," "polygon pushers," and graphic geometry engines that can display boundary representations very swiftly (and probably evaluate surface integrals swiftly as well). A more powerful and versatile family of true solid modeling engines looms, with "octree machines" imminent and curve/solid classification machines for use with CSG systems not far behind.

Completeness of Coverage—Although individual components of an integrated CAD/CAM system (for example, the solid modeler as a design tool) can be shown to be cost effective, much greater gains should be attainable if modeling systems can be made powerful enough to serve as master sources of part and product definitional data for all technical application programs. For example, in order to investigate the kinematic and dynamic properties of a mechanism from the design database, all the component parts of the mechanism must be avail-

References p. 357

able for solid modeling based analysis. If some parts do not occur in the database naturally (*e.g.*, through organisational choice, or because the modeling system cannot represent the parts' designs adequately), and must be entered especially for the analysis, the ease with which the analysis may be performed is decreased and the cost is increased. Similarly, automated application algorithms are needed to span design analysis (*e.g.*, finite-element analysis), fabrication (*e.g.*, numerically controlled machine tool programming), and assembly (*e.g.*, assembly robot programming). If the coverage of the parts and the algorithms is complete, then overall design for manufacture and design for automation can be performed, with feedback via the design database allowing designs to be modified rapidly and short lead times to be achieved.

Completeness of coverage implies also a product database where design and manufacturing data can reside and be shared. This too can be integrated with other components of the product process: orders, bills of materials, scheduling, and so on. This brings us back to the realm of system design with the need to integrate with solid modeling such other computer science technologies as graphics and database management. We would like to believe that systems can be implemented which meet the needs of companies of diverse size in diverse industries.

A consequence of the need for completeness of coverage is the need for very large models and aggregates of models. These are necessary for realistic analysis of the packaging of multicomponent products such as cars or airplanes. Scale* may be addressed in some cases by brute force, that is, by allowing larger and larger models and aggregates of models. At one extreme of the scale spectrum is the need to represent assemblies with tens or even hundreds of thousands of components, for example, in the design of an oil refinery. In this case selective reduction of detail is essential. At some points complete detail may be required, whereas at others gross simplifications may be adequate and essential to render the problem tractable. Automatic generation of levels of abstraction of models will clearly be needed.

Finally, there are inevitable trade-offs between completeness of coverage and availability for exploitation. If a potential user waits for an ultimate system, a system capable of handling the most complex parts and products, that user may miss at least a decade of profitable partial exploitation of solid modeling. Indeed, the trade-offs may be more subtle, because it is argued in some quarters that mechanical designers have entirely too much geometric freedom, and that modelers with restricted geometric domains (but very powerful application domains) should be used as a mechanism to bring mechanical design closer to the highly disciplined regimes of digital electronics. Scientific assessment of this view requires a much deeper understanding of design than we currently possess,

---

We thank Richard Newell, of Cambridge Interactive Systems, Ltd., for introducing and addressing the issue of scale in a short impromptu talk in the final session of the symposium.

but it would be interesting to see an adventurous company test it experimentally.

ACKNOWLEDGEMENTS

Our thanks, and the thanks of all the attendees, are given to the General Motors Corporation for organizing the symposium and holding it in such pleasant surroundings. At present it is still possible to get a large fraction of the workers in solid modeling by computer in one room; however, the field is expanding so rapidly that it may not be possible to do so again.

REFERENCES

[Fitzgerald et al. 1981]
W. Fitzgerald, F. Gracer, and R. Wolfe, "GRIN: Interactive Graphics for Modeling Solids," IBM Journal of Research and Development, Vol. 25, No. 4, July 1981, pp. 281–294.

[Requicha and Voelcker 1983]
A. A. G. Requicha and H. B. Voelcker, "Solid Modeling: Current Status and Research Directions," IEEE Computer Graphics and Applications, Vol. 3, No. 7, October 1983, pp. 25–37.

DISCUSSION

Christopher Brown *(University of Rochester)*

A problem we at Rochester have tagged as important—but that hasn't been mentioned here seriously—is modeling elastic, that is, nonrigid solids. That's certainly an important class of solids, and people seem to be looking the other way a lot about it. I just thought I'd throw out this tickler and hope somebody giggles.

Voelcker

Chris Brown is suggesting we address nonrigid solids. He could mean elastic in the Hooke's Law sense, or he could mean articulated in the mechanism sense, but I think he means limp or flexible, as in fabric.

Brown

Like the cables in the IBM cabling problem. The definition of such solids is a problem.

H. B. Voelcker

Tomás Lozano-Pérez *(Massachusetts Institute of Technology)*

I want to agree with Chris about the importance of this problem. Just a little story: When Mike Wesley and I were working at IBM on obstacle avoidance a number of years ago, we programmed a nice model of the IBM robot arm and had a great algorithm for moving it around. But when we actually got to try it, we noticed we had forgotten about the hydraulic lines, which stick out about a foot from the side of the robot. There the shape is changing all the time. We had to go back and redesign the models and spend another few months working on them.

Wesley

I think the point is that there's no direct ability to represent that class of objects. A number of people who wanted to use flexible objects somehow managed to think of a way around the problem using some form of rigid object in the path planning. As the RS-1 robot moves around, its cable configuration changes. We just put in dummy blocks to try somehow (moderately conservatively) to enclose the area that the cables covered without blocking up too much space.

A little bit of work has been done on power supply cables, where you have power supplies sliding out in a rack, and the cable system following them. That was simulated, essentially, in a rigid manner: for increments of motion you recomputed a new configuration for a cable and didn't worry too much about how it got between these increments.

Concerning the actual cabling application that I mentioned, by the time the problem gets to that level, one is not thinking about cables that are flexible. By the time you've got a hundred, or some substantial number, of wires all wrapped up together, the whole thing gets pretty rigid. But this is just ducking the issue, and yes, I agree that the ability to represent flexible objects is an important issue.

I've seen workers assembling a disk drive where the worker picks up the motor unit that comes with a cable and a connector on the end. The motor unit is placed down, and this cable is threaded through various holes. The idea of a robot being able to do that is one thing; the idea of being able to represent it in the modeling system and plan how the robot's going to do it is another thing. Nevertheless, a couple of weeks ago at Bretton Woods we did see a movie of a robot tying a knot in a piece of rope (which puts an end to the goal stated at one time of being able to get a robot to tie your shoelaces), but it wasn't clear how the program had been written.*

M. A. Wesley

Norman Badler *(University of Pennsylvania)*

In 1979 at the NSF workshop on 3-dimensional object representations, we reported a technique for modeling flexible objects. We used the technique to model a flexible Unimation Puma. In this case the method consisted of a flexed spline which was a B-spline patch; spheres were attached to the spline in a solid geometry configuration. As the fingers were moved, the control points of the patch at the edge were changed, which changed the palm shape that carried the spheres along and kept the shape coherent throughout the flexion. That was the only effort in modeling nonrigid objects as far as I know.

Michel Melkanoff *(University of Califoria–Los Angeles)*

It seems to me that we've been talking, correctly I think, about manufacturing applications, but there is a whole other world which is of great interest, and it might be worth just mentioning. We all knew about the games area, of course,

---

*H. Inoue, "Hand-Eye Coordination with Rope Handling," International Symposium on Robotics Research (Bretton Woods, New Hampshire, August 29–September 2, 1983) MIT Press, Cambridge, Massachusetts, 1984.

in which solid modeling actually has played the major role. I also feel that biology is a key area. We're talking, for example, to people in surgery about the possibility of setting up a solid model of the whole human body, including every muscle and bone in it, to teach anatomy. We think that we have a new possible avenue in art, that is, moving art, with objects that move in three dimensions.

Pat Ambler *(University of Edinburgh)*

I wanted to comment about Mike Wesley's remark on interference detection, which is limited to whether two objects are interfering or not. I certainly think that, as far as robotic application is concerned, it's not interference detection we are going to be concerned with, but questions like what's the minimum distance between two objects; similarly, we're going to be concerned with questions about what is the contact area between the two objects. So the issue isn't whether or not they're interfering; it's exactly *how* they are touching and *where* they are touching. I think these are questions that are going to be increasingly important.

Wesley

Actually this touches on something that I've been interested in recently, because we've been looking at simulating integrated circuit processes as three-dimensional transformations. Many of the problems that are on one's list of things to work on in mechanical design crop up in the integrated circuit area, but the ordering is very different. In the mechanical domain, tolerances are often quite small relative to nominal values. People have come a long way working on nominal values in the mechanical domain. In the integrated circuit domain, we find that the tolerances are half the line width and that, if you want to do anything very much, you've got to understand the significance of tolerances. Questions such as minimum distance and contact area also have very obvious electrical parallels, such as whether minimum distance goes to zero and you have a short circuit, and so on. Such questions we have to be able to answer. Another question involves minimum cross section, in order to know what the impedance of a part is going to be. So I think it's interesting that we've been looking in this other domain and are finding that we are reordering the sort of priorities of things that look as if they'd be worth working on, because this other domain has different parameters.

PARTICIPANTS

Agnew, William G.
GM Research Laboratories
Warren, Michigan

Aguiar, Ashok A.
Chevrolet Motor Division, GMC
Warren, Michigan

Allen, George A.
McDonnell Douglas Automation Company
Cypress, California

Ambler, A. Pat (Session Chairman)
University of Edinburgh
Edinburgh, Scotland

Anderson, Charles M.
University of Cambridge
Cambridge, England

Anderson, Lisle R.
GM Advanced Product and
Manufacturing Engineering Staff
Warren, Michigan

Arbab, Farhad
University of California
Los Angeles, California

Badler, Norman I.
University of Pennsylvania
Philadelphia, Pennsylvania

Bahk, Saeman
GM Research Laboratories
Warren, Michigan

Barsky, Brian A.
University of California
Berkeley, California

Basu, Asoke
Vauxhall Motors
Bedfordshire, England

Bennett, James A.
GM Research Laboratories
Warren, Michigan

Betts, John W.
Oldsmobile Division, GMC
Lansing, Michigan

Bliss, Frank W.
Ford Motor Company
Dearborn, Michigan

Borkin, Harold J.
The University of Michigan
Ann Arbor, Michigan

Boros, Victor B.
Bell Telephone Laboratories
Whippany, New Jersey

Boulet, J. A. M. (Speaker)
The Georgia Institute of Technology
Atlanta, Georgia

Boyse, John W. (Symposium Cochairman)
GM Research Laboratories
Warren, Michigan

Brauner, Kalman G.
Boeing Commercial Airplane Company
Seattle, Washington

Brown, Christopher M.
University of Rochester
Rochester, New York

Brown, David A.
GM Advanced Product and
Manufacturing Engineering Staff
Warren, Michigan

Brown, Russ A.
Evans and Sutherland Corporation
Salt Lake City, Utah

Brun, Jean-Marc
Matra Datavision
Les Ulis, France

Buzan, Lee R.
GM Research Laboratories
Warren, Michigan

Caplan, John D.
GM Research Laboratories
Warren, Michigan

Carey, Graham (Speaker)
The University of Leeds
Leeds, England

Castore, Glen M. (Speaker)
    National Bureau of Standards
    Washington, D.C.

Cavendish, James C.
    GM Research Laboratories
    Warren, Michigan

Chace, Milton A.
    The University of Michigan
    Ann Arbor, Michigan

Chern, Bernard
    National Science Foundation
    Washington, D.C.

Clark, Alan L.
    Ford Motor Company
    Dearborn, Michigan

Cole, Peter P.
    Computervision
    Bedford, Massachusetts

Cousineau, Dan K.
    Buick Motor Division, GMC
    Flint, Michigan

Craiglow, Charles R.
    Truck & Bus Group, GMC
    Pontiac, Michigan

Crawford, Richard
    Purdue University
    West Lafayette, Indiana

de Monts, Robert M.
    Dassault Systems
    Los Angeles, California

de Pennington, Alan (Session Chairman, Speaker)
    The University of Leeds
    Leeds, England

Dearing, Michael
    University of Wisconsin
    Madison, Wisconsin

Demasek, Frank W.
    GM Advanced Product and
        Manufacturing Engineering Staff
    Warren, Michigan

Derby, Stephen J.
    Rensselaer Polytechnic Institute
    Troy, New York

Dodd, George G.
    GM Research Laboratories
    Warren, Michigan

Eastman, Charles M.
    Formtek
    Pittsburgh, Pennsylvania

Eaton, Robert J.
    GM Advanced Product and
        Manufacturing Engineering Staff
    Warren, Michigan

Evans, Leonard
    GM Research Laboratories
    Warren, Michigan

Field, David A.
    GM Research Laboratories
    Warren, Michigan

Filip, Daniel J.
    GM Advanced Product and
        Manufacturing Engineering Staff
    Warren, Michigan

Forrest, A.R.
    University of East Anglia
    Norwich, England

Freeman, Herbert
    Rensselaer Polytechnic Institute
    Troy, New York

Frey, William H.
    GM Research Laboratories
    Warren, Michigan

Fridshal, Richard
    General Dynamics Corporation
    San Diego, California

Fritsche, B.
    ISYKON
    Bochum, West Germany

Frosch, Robert A.
    GM Research Laboratories
    Warren, Michigan

Garth, William
    GM Advanced Product and
        Manufacturing Engineering Staff
    Warren, Michigan

Geisberg, Sam P.
Applicon
Burlington, Massachusetts

Gilchrist, Jack E.
GM Advanced Product and
Manufacturing Engineering Staff
Warren, Michigan

Goldman, Ronald N.
Control Data Corporation
Arden Hills, Minnesota

Gordon, William J.
Drexel University
Philadelphia, Pennsylvania

Gossard, David C.
Massachusetts Institute of Technology
Cambridge, Massachusetts

Gray, Gary E.
GM Advanced Product and
Manufacturing Engineering Staff
Warren, Michigan

Gray, Richard A.
Chevrolet Motor Division, GMC
Warren, Michigan

Haar, Robert L.
GM Research Laboratories
Warren, Michigan

Hakala, Douglas
GM Advanced Product and
Manufacturing Engineering Staff
Warren, Michigan

Harkrader, Ron L.
Saginaw Steering Gear Division, GMC
Saginaw, Michigan

Henderson, Mark R.
Purdue University
West Lafayette, Indiana

Hinds, John K. (Session Chairman)
General Electric Company
Schenectady, New York

Holland, Steven W.
GM Research Laboratories
Warren, Michigan

Holzwarth, James C.
GM Research Laboratories
Warren, Michigan

Hopcroft, John E.
Cornell University
Ithaca, New York

Jared, Graham E. M. (Speaker)
University of Cambridge
Cambridge, England

Johnson, Robert H.
R. H. Johnson & Associates
Ann Arbor, Michigan

Johnston, Laird E.
GM Advanced Product and
Manufacturing Engineering Staff
Warren, Michigan

Joyce, John D.
GM Research Laboratories
Warren, Michigan

Joyce, M. A.
Pontiac Motor Division, GMC
Pontiac, Michigan

Kamal, Mounir M.
GM Research Laboratories
Warren, Michigan

Khan, Ray R.
Truck & Bus Group, GMC
Pontiac, Michigan

Kim, Chung-Whee
GM Advanced Product and
Manufacturing Engineering Staff
Warren, Michigan

Kimura, Fumihiko (Speaker)
University of Tokyo
Tokyo, Japan

Kirschner, Paul E.
United Technologies Research Center
East Hartford, Connecticut

Kjellberg, Torsten
The Royal Institute of Technology
Stockholm, Sweden

Klosterman, Albert L.
Structural Dynamics Research Corp.
Milford, Ohio

Korein, James U.
  The University of Pennsylvania
  Philadelphia, Pennsylvania

Korngold, Jacob C.
  GM Advanced Product and
    Manufacturing Engineering Staff
  Warren, Michigan

Kretch, Stuart J.
  McDonnell Douglas Automation Company
  St. Louis, Missouri

Krieger, Roger B.
  GM Research Laboratories
  Warren, Michigan

Krull, Fred N.
  GM Research Laboratories
  Warren, Michigan

Laning, J. H.
  The Charles Stark Draper Laboratory
  Cambridge, Massachusetts

Latombe, Jean-Claude (Speaker)
  I.M.A.G.
  Grenoble, France

Lozano-Pérez, Tomás (Speaker)
  Massachusetts Institute of Technology
  Cambridge, Massachusetts

Lucius, Michael E.
  Sirco Enterprises
  Troy, Michigan

Luckas, Richard C.
  Fisher Body Division, GMC
  Warren, Michigan

Lyles, James M.
  GM Advanced Product and
    Manufacturing Engineering Staff
  Warren, Michigan

Mahajan, Rakesh
  GM Advanced Product and
    Manufacturing Engineering Staff
  Warren, Michigan

Mair, Alex C.
  General Motors Corporation
  Detroit, Michigan

McDonald, Richard J.
  GM Research Laboratories
  Warren, Michigan

McDougall, Pierre A.
  Sirco Enterprises
  Troy, Michigan

Meagher, Donald J.
  Phoenix Data Systems
  Albany, New York

Melkanoff, Michel A. (Session Chairman)
  University of California
  Los Angeles, California

Morgan, Alexander P.
  GM Research Laboratories
  Warren, Michigan

Muench, Nils L.
  GM Research Laboratories
  Warren, Michigan

Myers, Ware
  IEEE Publications
  Los Alamitos, California

Nackman, Lee R.
  IBM Corporation
  Yorktown Heights, New York

Newell, Martin E.
  CADLINK
  Palo Alto, California

Newell, Richard G.
  Cambridge Interactive Systems
  Cambridge, England

Nicholas, Judy A.
  GM Advanced Product and
    Manufacturing Engineering Staff
  Warren, Michigan

Noffsinger, Gloria L.
  GM Advanced Product and
    Manufacturing Engineering Staff
  Warren, Michigan

Oh, K. P.
  GM Research Laboratories
  Warren, Michigan

Owen, Douglas C.
GM Advanced Product and
Manufacturing Engineering Staff
Warren, Michigan

Peck, Lawrence J.
GM Advanced Product and
Manufacturing Engineering Staff
Warren, Michigan

Pehlke, R. D.
The University of Michigan
Ann Arbor, Michigan

Peterson, Donald P.
Sandia Laboratories
Albuquerque, New Mexico

Pickett, Mary S. (Symposium Cochairman, Speaker)
GM Research Laboratories
Warren, Michigan

Pleck, Michael H.
University of Illinois
Urbana, Illinois

Racklyeft, David W.
GM Advanced Product and
Manufacturing Engineering Staff
Warren, Michigan

Reno, Thomas J.
GM Advanced Product and
Manufacturing Engineering Staff
Warren, Michigan

Requicha, Aristides A. G. (Speaker)
University of Rochester
Rochester, New York

Rockwood, Alyn P. (Speaker)
Shape Data
Cambridge, England

Roznowski, Frank J.
Oldsmobile Division, GMC
Lansing, Michigan

Russo, Jay E.
GM Research Laboratories
Warren, Michigan

Sanders, Barbara A.
GM Advanced Product and
Manufacturing Engineering Staff
Warren, Michigan

Sarraga, Ramon F. (Speaker)
GM Research Laboratories
Warren, Michigan

Scarchilli, David G.
GM Advanced Product and
Manufacturing Engineering Staff
Warren, Michigan

Schunck, Brian G.
GM Research Laboratories
Warren, Michigan

Schwartz, Jacob T. (Speaker)
New York University
New York, New York

Schwing, Richard C.
GM Research Laboratories
Warren, Michigan

Shah, Shreyas B.
GM Advanced Product and
Manufacturing Engineering Staff
Warren, Michigan

Shantaram, R.
University of Michigan
Flint, Michigan

Shapiro, Vadim (Speaker)
GM Research Laboratories
Warren, Michigan

Shephard, Mark S. (Speaker)
Rensselaer Polytechnic Institute
Troy, New York

Slade, Roy (Banquet Speaker)
Cranbrook Academy of Art
Bloomfield Hills, Michigan

Smith, Gerald S.
Truck & Bus Group, GMC
Pontiac, Michigan

Spewock, Nick A.
GM Advanced Product and
Manufacturing Engineering Staff
Warren, Michigan

Steinberg, Herbert A.
MAGI
Elmsford, New York

Szpara, Dennis A.
  Buick Motor Division, GMC
  Flint, Michigan

Tilove, Robert B. (Speaker)
  GM Research Laboratories
  Warren, Michigan

Tischler, Richard A.
  Sirco Enterprises
  Troy, Michigan

Tsai, Lung-Wen
  GM Research Laboratories
  Warren, Michigan

Tuesday, Charles S.
  GM Research Laboratories
  Warren, Michigan

Turner, James A.
  The University of Michigan
  Ann Arbor, Michigan

Uicker, John J.
  University of Wisconsin
  Madison, Wisconsin

Vickers, Donald L.
  Lawrence Livermore Laboratory
  Livermore, California

Voelcker, Herbert B. (Advisor, Speaker)
  University of Rochester
  Rochester, New York

Vogel, Carl
  Chevrolet Motor Division, GMC
  Warren, Michigan

Vossler, Donald L.
  McDonnell Douglas Automation Company
  Cypress, California

Wang, K. K.
  Cornell University
  Ithaca, New York

Waters, William C. (Speaker)
  GM Advanced Product and
    Manufacturing Engineering Staff
  Warren, Michigan

Werschler, Gary J.
  GM Advanced Product and
    Manufacturing Engineering Staff
  Warren, Michigan

Wesley, Michael A. (Advisor, Speaker)
  IBM Corporation
  Yorktown Heights, New York

Wilde, Douglas J.
  Stanford University
  Stanford, California

Wolfe, Robert N.
  IBM Corporation
  Yorktown Heights, New York

Woo, T. C.
  The University of Michigan
  Ann Arbor, Michigan

Woodwark, John R.
  University of Bath
  Bath, England

Wördenweber, Burkard (Speaker)
  University of Cambridge
  Cambridge, England

Wysner, Shirley W.
  GM Research Laboratories
  Warren, Michigan

Zarger, Ruth M.
  GM Advanced Product and
    Manufacturing Engineering Staff
  Warren, Michigan

AUTHOR AND CONTRIBUTOR INDEX

The page numbers for complete bibliographic
citations appear in italics.

Feldman, J., 301, *325*
Fenves, S. J., 72, *75*
Finkel, R., 301, *325*
Fisher, W. B., 107, *115, 268*
Fitzgerald, W. J., 10, *18,* 40-41, *46,* 353, *357*
Flinn, R. A., 107, *115*
Forrest, A. R., 83, *99,* 220, *233,* 241, *252*
Fugelso, M. A., 175, *180*

Gago, J., 56, *75*
Gallagher, R. H., 54, *75*
Geigenbaum, F. A., 330, 344, *344*
Geisberg, S., 21, 133, 235-236
Gilchrist, J. E., 53, *74,* 159, *178,* 188, *203*
Gill, J. I., 83, *99*
Goad, C., 280, *287*
Goldman, R. N., 188, 198, *203-204,* 207-208, 232, *233,* 270
Gopin, A. M., 10, *19*
Gordon, W. J., 188, *203,* 237, *252*
Gossard, D. C., 10, *19,* 21, 39, 45-46, *47,* 50, 135-136, 345
Gossling, T. H., 107, *115,* 240, *253*
Goto, E., 33, *47*
Gracer, F., 353, *357*
Grayer, A. R., 122, *132*
Greenberg, D. P., 54, *75*
Grossman, D. D., 25, *47,* 300, *325*
Gruver, W. A., 160, *178*
Gugel, H. W., 165, *178*
Guthrie, D. E., 161, *178*

Haar, R., 290-291
Haber, R. B., 54, *75*
Hanafusa, H., 318, *325*
Hansen, D. C., 55, *76*
Hartquist, E. E., 107, *115, 268*
Henrion, M., *46*
Higashi, M., 227, *233*
Hillyard, R. C., 10-11, *19,* 84, *99,* 227, *232, 268*
Hinds, J. K., 49, 156, 181, 204, 209, 235-236, 255, 272
Hocken, R. J., 278, *288*
Hodge, W. V. D., 262, *268*
Horn, B. K. P., 287, *287*
Hosaka, M., 212-213, 218, 220, 222, *233-234*

Huffman, D. A., 30, *47*
Humphrey, D. L., 56, *75*
Hunt, W. A., 140-141, *153*

Idesawa, M., 33, *47*
Ikeuchi, K., 287, *287*
Inoue, H., *359*

Jackins, C. L., 58, *75*
Jared, G. E. M., 133-137, 236, 342, *344*
Jenei, J., 161, *178*
Jensen, T. W., 188, *203,* 249, *253*
Johnson, R., 48-49, 182
Jones, J. C., 23, *47*

Kakishita, N., 212, *233*
Kanade, T., 30, *47*
Kawabe, S., 216-218, *234*
Kelly, D. W., 56, *75*
Kent, E., 280, *287*
Kido, K., 212, *234*
Kimura, F., 51, 212-213, 216-218, 220, 222, 225, 227, *233-234,* 235-236, 254
Kleiber, M., 72, *75*
Koenderink, J. J., 278, *287*
Kohzen, I., 227, *233*
Korein, J. U., 119, 135, 180, 205
Kotschi, R., 106, *115*
Kretch, S. J., 160-161, *179*
Kyprianou, L. K., 84, 97, *99,* 122-123, *132,* 342, *344*

Lafue, G., 33, *47*
Latombe, J. C., 303, 315, *325,* 330, *344,* 345-346
Laugier, C., 318, *325-326*
Law, K. H., 72, *75*
Levin, J., 261, *268*
Leyvraz, R., 86, *100*
Lieberman, L. I., 301, 303, *326*
Light, R. A., 10, *19,* 45, *47*
Lin, V. C., 10, *19*
Lozano-Pérez, T., 170, 176, *179,* 181-182, 301-302, 315, 317-321, 323, *325-326,* 328, 358
Lutoborski, A., 72, *75*
Lyche, T., 188, *203*

Mansbach, P., 280, *287*
Mäntylä, M., 227, *234*

SUBJECT INDEX

W